SAVING "OLD GLORY"

SAVING
"OLD GLORY"

The History of the American Flag Desecration Controversy

ROBERT JUSTIN GOLDSTEIN

Westview Press

Boulder • San Francisco • Oxford

Copyright © 1995 by Westview Press, Inc.

Published in 1995 in the United States of America by Westview Press, Inc., 5500 Central Avenue, Boulder, Colorado 80301-2877, and in the United Kingdom by Westview Press, 36 Lonsdale Road, Summertown, Oxford OX2 7EW

Library of Congress Cataloging-in-Publication Data
Goldstein, Robert Justin.
  Saving "Old Glory" : the history of the American flag desecration
  controversy / Robert Justin Goldstein.
    p.   cm.
  Includes bibliographical references and index.
  ISBN 0-8133-2325-8
  1. Flags—United States—Desecration.   I. Title.
CR113.G57 1995
929.9'2'0973–dc20   94-29362
                                                                       CIP

Printed and bound in the United States of America

The paper used in this publication meets the requirements
of the American National Standard for Permanence of Paper
for Printed Library Materials Z39.48-1984.

10   9   8   7   6   5   4   3   2   1

For Barbara,
whose dedication never flags

Contents

Preface

WRITING to a German friend who had expressed doubt about the importance of flags, Theodore Herzl (1860–1904), the Austrian Jew who is today regarded as the founder of modern Zionism, declared:

> You might ask mockingly: "A flag? What's that? A stick with a rag on it?" No sir, a flag is much more. With a flag you lead men, for a flag, men live and die. In fact, it is the only thing for which they are ready to die in masses, if you train them for it. Believe me, the politics of an entire people ... can be manipulated only through the imponderables that float in thin air.[1]

Certainly the importance of a flag for both political leaders and the general population of an entire nation was rarely demonstrated so clearly as in the United States in 1989–90, when a controversy over whether it should be legal to burn the American flag for the purpose of expressing political dissent became a dominant item on the political agenda for an entire year. During this period, the U.S. Supreme Court twice declared that such conduct was protected by the First Amendment to the Constitution, massive public majorities expressed disagreement with this point of view in opinion polls, and the president of the United States unsuccessfully urged the passage of a constitutional amendment to overrule the Court. The Congress of the United States, after literally thousands of pages of hearings and floor debate, rejected such an amendment in both 1989 and 1990. However, in 1989 Congress overwhelmingly passed a law that sought to overturn the Court's original 1989 decision. After the Court declared the new law unconstitutional in a second decision in 1990, the entire issue disappeared almost immediately, no doubt partly because few people actually ever witnessed a protest flag burning or were truly affected in their daily lives by such an almost purely symbolic issue. Moreover, public opinion by then appears to have turned away from what had in effect become a "summer re-rerun" to far more concrete issues, such as economic and budgetary problems and the crisis that developed after the Iraqi invasion of Kuwait in August, 1990.

This book primarily focuses upon developments related to the American flag desecration controversy prior to the 1989–90 furor. Although it originated as a study of the 1989–90 controversy, as I began to dig in to the historical background to that dispute, it became clear that the issue had deep, and largely unexplored, historical roots that cried out for excavation. There had been a similar controversy over symbolic flag protest during the Vietnam War—as I vaguely remembered from having lived through it. It also became clear—as neither I nor anyone else seemed to recall—that the American debate over flag desecration actually dated from the late nineteenth century.

It was during this time that the first laws outlawing flag "desecration" were passed and enforced (by states rather than the federal government) and when the first debate over the wisdom of such action developed—laws that (sometimes in revised form) later led to the numerous flag desecration prosecutions of the Vietnam War era and ultimately to the prosecution of Gregory Lee Johnson for a 1984 flag burning in Dallas that touched off the 1989–90 ruckus.

As I continued to dig deeper into the origins of the 1989–90 flag desecration controversy, I increasingly uncovered what struck me as a neglected treasure trove of largely—and often completely—previously ignored pamphlets, court decisions, legislative debates, and other materials from the pre–1989 period. However, especially because neither the original turn-of-the-century flag desecration controversy nor the Vietnam-era controversy have ever before been the subject of an in-depth study, it gradually became clear that attempting to compile a comprehensive account of the American flag desecration from its origins through the 1989–90 dispute would produce—and in fact at one point did produce—a volume so large that it could not be feasibly priced, read, or probably even lifted.

Fortunately for me, and, I hope, for my readers, editor Peter Kracht of Westview Press encouraged me to carve out of my original manuscript—which ran 1,400 pages in typescript—a smaller book that would primarily treat the origins and development of the flag desecration controversy leading up to 1989, while including in Chapter 5 a lengthy summary of the 1989–90 dispute in order to provide historical completion to the study. Again, fortunately for me and I hope for my readers, Kent State University Press subsequently agreed to publish what was, in effect, the second half of the original manuscript as a separate book that focuses on the 1989–90 debate, and which will be published under the title of *Burning the Flag: The Great 1989–90 American Flag Desecration Controversy.*

In the process of writing what turned out to be two separate books on the history of the American flag desecration controversy, I collected approximately 30,000 pages of documents and eventually put together yet a third volume consisting of an edited and annotated collection of documents selected from these sources, which had provided the raw material for my research. This third book will be published by Syracuse University Press under the title of *The American Flag Desecration Controversy, A Collection of Key Documents from the Civil War to 1990.* (Three documents from this collection—a model law that became the template for many of the flag desecration laws that were passed by all of the states between 1897 and 1932 and the texts of the 1968 and 1989 federal flag desecration laws—are printed as an appendix to the book because their exact contents are critical to much of this narrative.) Happily, all three presses have agreed with me that these books complement, rather than compete with one another, and therefore have kindly pursued their individual volumes while still encouraging me to continue working on their scholarly "brothers."

This book is primarily intended as work of descriptive, rather than prescriptive, history and its main goal is simply to provide an accurate account of the origins and development of the American flag desecration controversy. However, like every one of the hundreds of people I interviewed in connection with my research for this and the allied books, I have my own views about this subject. As I have no doubt that my views have occasionally crept into or, at any rate, certainly influenced, the body of the manuscript, even before they are made crystal clear at the very end of the book, I feel that my readers are entitled to know what my bias is on this extrememly disputatious topic, if only so that they may be put on guard.

In short, while flag desecration strikes me as a generally highly counterproductive political tactic—one that mostly alienates people and makes them turn away before they have a chance of grasping any particular message that such conduct seeks to convey—I also have no doubt that it is a form of "symbolic speech" that is completely and correctly protected by the First Amendment to the U.S. Constitution. Moreover, even if that were not the case—for example, had the Supreme Court ruled differently in 1989–90—it should be so, because the right of vigorous and even highly offensive expression lies at the heart of democratic theory.

Perhaps the most eloquent statement of this argument was made by Supreme Court Justice Robert Jackson, writing for the majority in the 1943 case of *West Virginia Board of Education v. Barnette,* which struck down laws requiring compulsory flag salutes and recitals of the Pledge of Allegiance by American school children. This case is discussed at some length in Chapter 2 because its principles, more than that of any ruling, created the legal framework for the subsequent Supreme Court flag desecration decisions of 1989–90. Justice Jackson wrote in words whose eloquence reflected the importance of the subject matter that:

Those who begin coercive elimination of dissent soon find themselves ex-
terminating dissenters. Compulsory unification of opinion achieves only
the unanimity of the graveyard. It seems trite but necessary to say that the
First Amendment to our Constitution was designed to avoid these ends by
avoiding these beginnings. ... The case is made difficult not because the
principles of its decisions are obscure but because the flag involved is our
own. Nevertheless, we apply the limitations of the Constitution with no
fear that freedom to be intellectually and spiritually diverse will disinte-
grate the social organization. ... Freedom to differ is not limited to things
that do not matter much. That would be a mere shadow of freedom. The
test of its substance is the right to differ as to things that touch the heart of
the existing order. If there is any fixed star in our constitutional constellation, it is that no official, high or petty, can prescribe what shall be orthodox in politics, nationalism, religion or other matters of opinion.[2]

Political philosopher Alexander Meiklejohn has expressed this same
argument as it is applies in a series of concrete situations. As he has
written, the true meaning of freedom of expression is that:

[If] on any occasion in the United States it is allowable to say that the Constitution is a good document it is equally allowable ... to say that the Constitution is a bad document. If a public building may be used in which to
say, in time of war, that the war is justified, then the same building may be
used in which to say that it is not justified. If it be publicly argued that conscription for armed service is moral and necessary, it may likewise be publicly argued that it is immoral and unnecessary. If it may be said that
American political institutions are superior to those of England or Russia
or Germany, it may, with equal freedom, be said that those of England or
Russia or Germany are superior to ours. ... When a question of policy is
'before the house,' free men choose it not with their eyes shut, but with
their eyes open. To be afraid of ideas, any idea, is to be unfit for self-government.[3]

The many, overwhelmingly sincere, people who express different
views on the subject of the legalization of flag desecration generally
make two major arguments: that symbolic destruction of the flag is a
form of "conduct," whereas the First Amendment protects only the
printed or spoken word; and that, in any case, the flag is so important,
so special, so unique that, if need be, an exception should be made,
where it is concerned, from principles that would otherwise apply (that
is, few people who wish to ban flag desecration would likely advocate
forbidding destroying copies of the presidential seal, models of the Lincoln Memorial, or pictures of American bald eagles).

With regard to the first argument, I would respond that all forms of
communication, including oral and written speech, are ultimately
"symbolic" (since letters and words have no meaning by themselves,

but only represent other things) and they all involve conduct—opening one's mouth, printing and circulating a book, and so on. Unless flag desecration results in burning down a building or blocking a public street, it is, in practice, just as "purely" symbolic and purely expressive as are other forms of communication and therefore deserves equal protection. If the argument that only "pure" speech and writing are protected by the principles of constitutional democracy was accepted, then people who use sign language would have no rights, and neither would actors, dancers, musicians, painters, movie producers, or anyone else who communicated in any other way. I do not think this is the kind of world implied by the concept of democracy.

The argument that a special exception should be made for the flag is alluring on first glance. In fact such an exception would destroy the entire principle upon which democracy is based, as explained above by Justice Jackson and by Professor Meiklejohn: the right to vigorous debate and the expression of even the most hateful points of view and those that cut to the "heart of the existing order." In the words of Harvard University Law Professor and former Solicitor General Charles Fried, in arguing before Congress against a constitutional amendment exempting outlawing flag desecration from the protection of the First Amendment, "The man who says you can make an exception to a principle, does not know what a principle is; just as the man who says that only this once let's make 2+2=5 does not know what it is to count."[4] Having made "just one" exception for physical desecration of the flag, making another for verbal abuse of the flag would follow logically, and from then on one could easily justify outlawing extremely vitriolic criticism of the president, of the government, and so on.

Even putting these arguments aside, it seems to me that there is simply no need to seriously think about exempting flag desecration from constitutional protection. The massive adverse reaction to the 1989–90 Supreme Court rulings demonstrated conclusively that individual incidents of flag desecration do not in any way damage the feelings of the vast majority of the population for the flag, or diminish the patriotic feelings of the American people—the only grounds that could be logically advanced for forbidding such conduct.

Gregory Lee Johnson, whose conviction for a 1984 Dallas flag burning was overturned by the Supreme Court, thereby sparking the 1989–90 uproar, probably did more to promote love of the flag and American patriotism than any single individual in the last twenty years. Even had this not been the case, as *Washington Post* columnist Judy Mann has pointed out, when a flag is burned, "the sum total of the damage is a burned flag. No one is deprived of liberty or justice."[5] To the extent that Johnson's action had harmful consequences, in my view, it was only be-

cause of the huge amount of energy devoted to trying to ban flag desecration in the wake of the Supreme Court ruling setting him free. That
energy could have been more usefully devoted to solving the far more
real problems of this nation, whose neglect—as I try to point out in the
closing pages of this book—largely fostered the insecurity and anxiety
that probably mostly fueled the 1989–90 flag desecration controversy
in the first place.

Having made this point, I fully realize that, as the author of this and
allied books about the flag desecration controversy, I am myself contributing to this phenomenon. In defense, I can only suggest that the
one good thing to come out of the 1989–90 controversy is that the
country had the most vigorous debate within recent memory over the
meaning of fundamental democratic principles. I believe such discussion is at least occasionally necessary to maintain a democracy in good
health, just as a periodic vigorous intellectual and physical workout is
needed to keep both brain and body in good condition—even if most of
us try to avoid such experiences whenever possible because they can be
very taxing. At any rate, in this manner, at least, both I and the country
owe Gregory Lee Johnson a minor debt. He has forced us to think about
fundamentals. And I hope that this book will force my readers to do so
yet again.

Scattered portions of this book have appeared, usually in considerably different form, in two previously published articles, and I hereby express my appreciation for permission to make use of this material from
"The Great 1989–90 Flag Flap: An Historical, Political and Legal Analysis," *University of Miami Law Review*, 45 (September 1990), pp. 19–
106; and "The Vietnam War Flag Flap," *The Flag Bulletin*, 153 (July-
August 1993), pp. 142–75.

Robert Justin Goldstein

List of Abbreviations

AAUP	American Association of University Professors
ACLU	American Civil Liberties Union
AFA	American Flag Association
ALI	American Law Institute
AMVETS	American Veterans (of World War II)
DAR	Daughters of the American Revolution
FPA	Flag Protection Act
GAR	Grand Army of the Republic
HJC	House Judiciary Committee
ISU	Indiana State University
MCLU	Massachusetts Civil Liberties Union
MPC	Model Penal Code
RCP	Revolutionary Communist Party
RCYB	Revolutionary Communist Youth Brigade
SAIC	School of the Art Institute of Chicago
SAR	Sons of the American Revolution
SCW	Society of Colonial Wars
SDS	Students for a Democratic Society
SJC	Senate Judiciary Committee
SMAC	Senate Military Affairs Committee
UFL	Uniform Flag Law
USFF	United States Flag Foundation
VFW	Veterans of Foreign Wars

1

Origins of the American Flag Desecration Controversy, 1890–1907

T HE AMERICAN FLAG played a very minor role in the political, or even in the decorative, life of the United States until the Civil War. Only the outbreak of the Civil War transformed the flag into a genuinely popular, and frequently displayed, symbol of the nation, or, more precisely, of the North, in its struggle to maintain the Union against the Confederacy, which, of course, had its own flag. The enhanced popularity of the flag continued, at least in the North, after the conclusion of the Civil War. However, this new popularity at first contained within it no widespread sense, of the sort so clearly manifested by President George Bush and many others during the 1989–90 "flag burning" controversy, that the Stars and Stripes should be regarded as a sacred or holy relic of any kind that could or should be used for what the Supreme Court in 1989 termed "only a limited set of messages."[1]

In fact, aside from the far greater general display of the flag as compared to the antebellum era, the flag's new popularity was mostly manifested by its increasing use by the emerging advertising industry as the nation modernized. Representations of the flag were used to help sell products of all sorts, including liquor, cigars, fruit, and even toilet paper. Additionally, the growing popularity of the flag was manifested by the increased frequency with which politicians were willing to use it, both symbolically and literally, for uses far more crass and profane than sacred.

What might be termed the iconization of the flag is historically quite recent and developed, not as a result of any gradually emerging spontaneous popular consensus that the flag should be treated as a sacred object, but rather as the result of a deliberate, extensive, and prolonged campaign engineered during the post-1890 period by a variety of veterans groups, mostly Union Civil War survivors, such as the Grand Army of the Republic (GAR), and hereditary-patriotic groups, such as the Daughters of the American Revolution (DAR) and Sons of the American Revolution (SAR), whose members claimed to be descendants of revolutionary fighters. As a result of this campaign, either (but not both) the U.S. Senate or House of Representatives passed bills to outlaw "desecration" (by definition the sacrilegious treatment of a holy object) of the flag on nine separate occasions between 1890 and 1943, and Congressional hearings on the subject were held approximately a dozen times during the same period.

Although it was not until 1968, during the Vietnam War, that flag desecration was outlawed by the national government, in a transparent attempt to suppress a particular form of antiwar dissent, between 1897 and 1932 every state passed its own flag desecration law. One of the historical descendants of Texas's original flag desecration law, enacted in 1917, was struck down (along with, by implication, the 1968 federal law and many, if not all, of the other state laws) in the famous (and to some infamous) 1989 U.S. Supreme Court decision of *Texas v. Johnson*.[2]

The original effort to outlaw flag desecration especially flourished between about 1895 and 1910, a time of rapidly increasing immigration and industrialization. During this period, many middle-class Americans of northwest European descent became alarmed over what they perceived as a rapidly growing threat to the cohesion of American society—and their own traditional dominance of that society—by a variety of forces, including immigrants from southern and eastern Europe, political radicals, trade unions, and upstart venal businessmen. To a large extent, the campaign to turn the American flag into a holy object represented an attempt by traditionally dominant groups both to assert their own position as the most "true blue" patriots, and to provide criminal penalties for those elements who—already suspiciously "un-American" by virtue of their political beliefs, ethnic or regional backgrounds, and occupations—refused to conform to their demands for proper reverence of the flag.

In a broader symbolic sense, the turn-of-the-century flag desecration controversy represented an attempt by traditionally dominant groups to use the flag as a sort of psychological lance to slay their perceived enemies, much as the display of the cross (to which the flag was repeatedly compared by the supporters of flag desecration laws) reportedly could force the mythological vampire Dracula to flee.

The 1989–90 flag desecration controversy was not the first, but in fact the third time that the issue of flag desecration became the focus of considerable debate in American society. Memories of the 1989–90 and, to a lesser extent, the Vietnam era flag desecration controversies are still fresh in the minds of many living Americans. However, the first flag desecration controversy, which centered around 1895–1910 but encompassed in a less intense sense the entire 1890–1943 period (from the first to the last passage by one Congressional house of flag desecration legislation until the Vietnam period), has been almost forgotten. This original controversy was virtually never even mentioned during the 1989–90 conflict, for example, even though it was this earliest dispute that largely "created" the twentieth-century iconization of the American flag.[3] This original controversy, therefore, not only laid, in a narrow sense, the legal and ideational groundwork for both subsequent controversies, but it created, in broader terms, the popular and political sense of the power and importance of the flag that has been dominant since the turn of the century. This unexplored and forgotten controversy therefore cries out for examination.

The Flag in the Antebellum and Civil War Eras

The approval of the stars-and-stripes design for the new American flag by the Continental Congress on June 14, 1777, aroused little public interest at the time, and during the following eighty-five years there were few signs of general interest in or display of the flag. In fact, the first newspaper report about the approval of the new flag design appeared only seventy-five days after the fact in the August 30, 1777, *Pennsylvania Evening Post*. The primary reason for the approval of a new flag was to designate and hopefully protect American ships at sea. Speaking in the early 1800s, Massachusetts Congressman Josiah Quincy warned, however, that the flag would be a meaningless symbol unless the new country maintained substantive naval power to back it up: making an argument similar in tone to that made almost two centuries later by those who argued that forbidding flag desecration would betray the substantive freedoms represented by the flag in order to protect a mere symbol, Quincy attacked those who spoke as if "a rag, with certain stripes and stars upon it, tied to a stick and called a flag, was a wizard's wand" when in fact "if you have no maritime power to maintain it, you have a name and no reality; you have the shadow without the substance."

Until the outbreak of the Civil War, the flag was displayed on land almost exclusively on federal government buildings and forts (such as Ft.

McHenry during the War of 1812, the setting for Francis Scott Key's penning of "The Star Spangled Banner," which was officially designated the United States national anthem only in 1931). Exhaustive collections of contemporaneous songs, prints, and drawings about the American Revolution include very few references whatever to the flag, and as late as 1794, according to flag historian Milo Quaife, "the vast majority of Americans never came in contact" with a flag. U.S. Army units continued to fly distinct regimental emblems until 1834, and the army fought under the American flag for the first time only during the Mexican War of 1846–48.[4]

During the antebellum period, the flag was not unfurled over American schools; as the director of the Betsy Ross house in Philadelphia noted during the 1989–90 flag desecration controversy, "It would have been unthinkable to fly an American flag at a private home. It simply was not done." Textbooks used inside the schools, and even Fourth of July oratory throughout the country, made few or no references to the flag. Examinations of various artifacts of popular culture during the antebellum period, such as textiles, china, glass, and wallpaper, disclose that although the flag was occasionally utilized as a motif, especially after the War of 1812, it was very markedly less popular than other themes such as, above all, depictions of George Washington, personifications of Liberty and Columbia, and even the bald eagle. As one historian has noted, by 1810 it was the eagle, not the flag, that had become the "country's most popular emblem and the universal badge of an American." Another historian, in a comment that could apply today to the flag but in fact referred to the eagle, declared that "probably no modern civilized nation has venerated its national emblem so much as Americans." Because general display of the flag was virtually nonexistent during the antebellum period, the first full-time American commercial flag manufacturer was not established until the Mexican War stimulated enough demand to make such a venture worthwhile. In short, as cultural historian Wilbur Zelinsky summarized, "During its early career, the national flag was remarkably unimportant to the citizenry at large."[5]

One of the clearest indications of the relative lack of importance of the flag during the antebellum period was the fact that there was no officially prescribed standardized length-height ratio, color order of the stripes, or even arrangement of the stars in the field (and there would not be until President Taft issued an executive order concerning such matters in 1912). Thus, the canton of stars rested on a red stripe in some flags but on a white stripe in others, the constellation of stars varied wildly in design, and even the number of stripes displayed was often inconsistent (although this latter aspect of the flag had been officially established by law).

Eighteen months after the flag was created, American emissaries abroad could not accurately describe it. As late as 1847 the Dutch government politely inquired of the American government, "What is the American flag?" A 1793 watercolor depicts an American flag with green and red stripes, containing a yellow canton with 13 crosses, while a Liverpool jug from about the same period displays a flag with yellow and blue stripes. In 1817 Congressman Peter Wendover of New York lamented to the House of Representatives that although, by law, the flag should then have contained 15 stripes, in fact a 13-stripe flag was flying over the Capitol, the nearby Navy Yard and Marine Barracks was displaying a flag with "at least" 18 stripes, and the previous Congress had sat under a 9-stripe flag. (In 1818 the number of stripes was permanently fixed at 13; previously the number of stripes corresponded to the number of states.)[6]

In addition to the lack of any standardized flag design, another clear indication of the lack of the flag's importance for the general citizenry before the Civil War was the fact that it was hardly ever used for the purposes of expressing symbolic political protest. Two of the very few instances in which the flag was used in an unorthodox manner to convey protest before 1861 occurred in Boston in 1854, when abolitionists flew flags upside down to protest the return of a runaway slave and their leader, William Lloyd Garrison, protested the same event by burning a copy of the U.S. Constitution while speaking in front of a backdrop of a flag draped in black.[7]

Although the popularity of the flag received at least minor boosts from the patriotic fervor stirred up by the War of 1812 and the Mexican War, only the outbreak of the Civil War, symbolically begun by Confederate troops firing on the American flag-bedecked Fort Sumter, South Carolina, transformed the Stars and Stripes into a true focus for nationalist feelings (although, of course, only in the North). As flag historian Robert Philipps has noted, before Fort Sumter the flag had been regarded as "peculiarly governmental property," but thereafter it became "the flag of the people"; similarly, an 1896 report by the Connecticut SAR declared that although before 1861 there had been "comparatively but little display" of the flag, with the outbreak of war, "all at once the people of the Northern States of the Union discovered that there was an American Flag and towns and villages, cities and county hamlets blossomed full-bloom with a most gorgeous display of the Red, White and Blue."[8]

The leading nineteenth-century historian of the flag, George Preble, summarized its dramatic change in status in a romanticized but no doubt reasonably accurate account:

> The fall of Sumter created great enthusiasm throughout the loyal states, for the flag had come to have a new and strange significance. ... One cry was raised, drowning all other voices,—"War! war to restore the Union! war to avenge the flag!" ... When the stars and stripes went down at Sumter, they went up in every town and county in the loyal states. Every city, town and village suddenly blossomed with banners. On forts and ships, from church-spires and flag-staffs, from colleges, hotels, store-fronts, and private balconies, from public edifices, everywhere the old flag was flung out. ... The demand for flags was so great that the manufacturers could not furnish them fast enough. Bunting was exhausted and recourse was had to all sorts of substitutes. In New York the demand for flags raised the price of bunting from $4.75 a piece to $28. ... Cincinnati, after the fall of Sumter, was fairly iridescent with the red, white and blue.

Numerous ceremonial flag raisings were conducted in the North shortly after the outbreak of the war. At one such ceremony in Boston on April 27, 1861, the well-known orator Edward Everett declared that the "flag of the country always honored, always beloved, is now at once worshipped, I may say, with the passionate homage of this whole people." At a flag raising ceremony that attracted 100,000 people at Union Square in New York City on April 20, 1861, the tattered remnants of the Fort Sumter flag were placed in the hands of a statue of George Washington; throughout the war, this relic was used as a fund-raising device, and upon the recapture of Sumter in 1865, the flag was returned and rededicated in an elaborate ceremony. Popular magazines like *Harper's*, which before the Civil War had paid little attention to the flag, even in connection with Fourth of July celebrations, now focused on it as the preeminent symbol of the nation. The popular northern anthem "The Battle Cry of Freedom" featured the line, "we'll rally round the flag, boys," and " Marching through Georgia" promised southern slaves that northern troops bore "the flag that makes you free." One of the most famous poems based on the Civil War was John Greenleaf Whittier's "Barbara Frietchie," in which the fictional heroine hangs a flag out of her window in Frederick, Maryland and speaks to occupying troops: "'Shoot if you must, this old gray head/But spare your country's flag,' she said." However, to Boston writer and abolitionist Lydia Maria Child, Lincoln's failure to order an immediate end to slavery made the flag only a symbol of slavery; in a letter written during the early part of the war, she declared, "May the curse of God rest upon it! May it be trampled in the dust, kicked by the rebels and spit upon by tyrants."[9]

In fact, the flag's new status in the North and the desperate passions invoked by the war quickly made the emblem, for the first time, both the object of organized and deliberate physical assault (among those who opposed the North) and the object of governmental efforts to punish such forms of symbolic dissent. On January 29, 1861, ten weeks before the outbreak of the war, President Buchanan's treasury secretary John Dix telegraphed to a clerk in New Orleans, with regard to an attempt by Louisiana to confiscate a revenue cutter, "If anyone attempts to haul down the American flag, shoot him on the spot." Nonetheless, upon the war's outbreak, American flags were publicly torn down in Richmond on April 18, buried in Memphis on April 21, and burned in Liberty, Mississippi, on May 10, in what seems to have been the first protest flag burning in American history. During Christmas of 1862, Confederates danced on American flags used to carpet the floors at a wedding celebration in Murfreesboro, Tennessee, shortly before the inconclusive Battle of Stones River fought nearby.[10]

While the Union was helpless to prevent such incidents in regions under Confederate control, punishments did occur where Union authority existed. In some cases vigilantes forced suspect individuals or organizations to display the flag: thus, in New York, Philadelphia, Trenton and many other cities mobs compelled newspaper offices and stores to display the flag, and, as historian Preble relates "haste was made to borrow, beg or steal something red, white and blue, to protect property with." In other cases, official measures were taken against those deemed to have desecrated the flag. Thus, in Union-controlled Nashville in 1865, a schoolgirl was court-martialed, fined $300 and sentenced to 90 days in a military prison for tearing down and trampling an American flag (although, on review, the penalty was remitted, essentially on the grounds that she had been entrapped).

The outcome was far more serious in New Orleans during the Union reoccupation, where William B. Mumford was hung before a large crowd on June 7, 1862, after being convicted of treason in a military court for, on April 27, 1862, pulling down, dragging in the mud, and tearing to shreds an American flag that had been hoisted over the New Orleans mint. The death sentence was confirmed on June 5, 1862 by the autocratic Gen. Benjamin Butler (whose harsh rule in 1862 as military governor of New Orleans earned him the nickname of "Beast" and caused President Lincoln to withdraw him after eight months). Butler had earlier issued an order on May 1, demanding the suppression of "all ensigns, flags or devices" representing any authority but that of the United States, as well as demanding the "utmost deference" for the "American ensigns" and "severe punishment" for those acting otherwise. In confirming the execution order, Butler effectively made his

May 1 decree retroactive to cover Mumford's action of four days earlier, at a time when Union authority had not been fully secured. He declared that Mumford had intended to incite "evil-minded persons to further resistance to the laws and arms of the United States."

Mumford reportedly met his death bravely and quickly became a Confederate martyr. The deposed and fugitive Confederate governor of Louisiana, Thomas Moore, referred to Mumford's "noble heroism" and, commenting on Mumford's reported refusal to save his own life at the last minute by swearing loyalty to the Union, declared that he had bravely scorned to "stain his soul with such foul dishonor" and "transmitted to his countrymen a fresh example of what one will do and dare under the inspiration of fervid patriotism." Moore added that he would neither "forget the outrage" of Mumford's murder nor let it "pass unatoned." In a December 1862 proclamation Confederate President Jefferson Davis termed Mumford's execution the "deliberate murder" of "an unresisting and non-combatant captive" and declared Butler an "outlaw and common enemy of mankind" who should suffer immediate execution by hanging in retaliation "in the event of his capture."[11]

The Post–Civil War Era and the Rise of Commercial Use of the Flag

The end of the Civil War was greeted with a "joyous delirium" of flag displays that covered "all cities, towns and villages over the length and breadth" of the North. The new popular status of the American flag, at least in the North, remained firmly entrenched among the general public and grew ever greater during the period between 1875 and 1900, fostered by, among other things, numerous historical commemorations, such as the 1876 revolutionary centennial, the 1879 centennial of Washington's inauguration and the 1892 Columbian Exposition in Chicago marking the 400th anniversary of Columbus's voyage of discovery.[12]

However, this ever-growing popularity of the flag by no means led, at first, to its being treated as anything like a holy relic or object. No laws placed restrictions on how the flag could be used and even advisory "flag etiquette" codes did not exist. Politicians thought nothing of continuing to print their names, portraits, and slogans on the flag, as they had been doing in a small-scale way since 1840. Thus, one flag used during the 1884 presidential campaign contained, printed on the stripes, the slogan, "For President James G. Blaine For Vice President John A. Logan 1884"; the canton not only featured 38 stars but also pictures of the two candidates. It was also standard for Union veterans to print the names of their regiments and the locations of battles they had fought in on the flag's stripes.[13]

But above all, the new popularity of the flag was manifested by its use or depiction, or the use or depiction of flag bunting or decorative designs using the flag's colors, for commercial reasons, as the advertising industry developed amid the rapid industrialization of the nation in the postwar period. The use of the flag for commercial purposes was strongly recommended by a leading reference book of the period dealing with such matters, *Browne's Trademarks*: "Color may be of the essence of a trademark of manufacture or commerce. ... National flags are sometimes blended with other objects to catch the eye. They are admirably adapted to all purposes of heraldic display and their rich, glowing colors appeal to feelings of patriotism and win purchasers of the merchandise to which they are affixed."

While most businessmen who used the flags to advertise their wares probably did not need to read Browne to give them ideas, had Browne walked down the street of any American city during the late nineteenth century he might well have decided that he had written a best seller. According to a pamphlet published in 1895 that vigorously complained about the phenomenon, in Chicago alone more than 120 separate types of commercial use of the flag could be viewed, including the decoration or advertising of bicycles, belts, breweries, burlesque shows, door mats, ballet dresses, fish houses, grocery stores, lemon wrappers, pool rooms, saloons, table napkins, tobacco dealers, and whiskey barrels. Another list, presented by a complaining group in a 1904 Congressional hearing, included coal sacks, chewing gum, fireworks, patent medicines, shooting galleries, awnings, trolley tickets, toilet paper, the costumes of prize fighters and of Uncle Sam, paper used to wrap fruits, cheese, cigars, ham, and soap, and the burning of flag patterns "into porcelain or crockery water closets and urinals." One advertisement surviving from 1878 depicted an Uncle Sam pointing to a large ham against the backdrop of a flag that has printed across the stripes, "The Magnolia Ham is an American Institution." Another "meaty" flag from the Centennial period contained only 13 stars, making up for this deficiency with the message printed across the white stripes, "Don't Cook in Warm Weather. Use Wilson Packing Co.'s Cooked Corned Beef, Ham or Tongue, in 2, 4 or 6 pound cans."[14]

Organizers and backers of the flag protection movement, which first emerged after 1890, repeatedly attacked those who they claimed were prostituting the flag for the greed of commercial gain, contending that display of the flag for advertising purposes would degrade its significance in the minds of the general population. Thus, the *Chicago Military News*, in an editorial published in the mid-1890s, suggested that the use of the flag for advertising purposes amounted to a proclamation that "the God of the people is Mammon" and declared that "if the flag is to be held in any degree of veneration it must not be made familiar to the sight as a medium of advertising." Similarly, the authors of an 1895 pamphlet that was the first major publication of the flag protection movement claimed that it was "because of the merchantable use to which copies of the national flag has been put that a great deal of the natural reverence and respect the flag should command is dissipated. ... The tender sentiment associated with ... decent use of the national emblem is sadly marred when we see it shamefully misused as an apron on labor day parades, and as a costume to bedeck stilt walkers, circus clowns, prize fighters and variety players or gaiety girls."[15]

Often spokesmen for the flag protection movement attacked commercial use of the flag in a highly vehement manner that clearly suggests, together with the general middle-class and upper middle-class nature of the movement's leadership, that they were at least partly motivated by the fear that their traditional position of influence in the United States, and indeed that "their" America, was being threatened by the growth of a new class of businessmen thrust forward by the post–Civil War commercial, industrial, and advertising revolutions. Thus, in an 1898 pamphlet, leading movement spokesman Charles Kingsbury Miller declared that:

> Commercial piratism has seized the flag and made it a universal agent for advertising their [sic] wares and patent nostrums, until the leperized taint of private gain seems to have blighted the sentiment of patriotic reverence. ... In the sunshine of peace, the soldiers in the ranks of commerce, waging their mercenary warfare for the capture of the almighty dollar, do not seek their inspiration in looking up to the national colors flying above them but in gazing down at the flag, printed on their trade-marks, which booms their wares, gains the coveted dollar and is then flung like an outcast into the dust of disrespect.

In subsequent pamphlets published in 1899 and 1900, Miller warned that the "jingle of gold and silver shekels" could not compensate "greedy tradesmen" for the "wound they give the national honor" by encouraging "the masses" to "disrespect" the flag. He complained that "our American banner flaps its advertisement-covered folds, in the murky atmosphere of our factory chimneys, as the commercial symbol of a nation whose highest ideal seems to be to sell the goods they [sic] manufacture, and to debase to this end anything which serves to proclaim their wares."

In 1902, Miller denounced the "clutch of sordid tradesmen" who had turned the flag into "an article of commerce" by using it as a "medium of deception and fraud to proclaim their defective merchandise, flimsy wares and adulterated goods." Such "unscrupulous" businessmen were engaging in a "species of barbarism," Miller proclaimed, and had "polluted" the flag, whose "sacred folds were never designed to be defaced with advertisements of beer, sauerkraut candy, itch ointment, pile remedies and patent nostrums, to serve as awnings, horse blankets, merchandise wrappers, pillow and footstool covers or as miniature pocket handkerchiefs, on which to blow noses, or with which to wipe perspiring brows."[16]

Similar, if usually less florid, rhetoric was a staple of the flag protection movement, especially during the 1895–1910 period. Thus, during the late 1890s the *Manchester Daily Union* thundered that the "most beautiful flag in the world" should be "freed from the contamination of trade" so that it could "continue to wave as a symbol of deeds of glory and not the almighty dollar." The conservative black leader Booker T. Washington echoed this sentiment, warning that the flag was being "degraded" into becoming the "emblem of the dollar rather than the emblem of liberty." Ralph Prime, the president of the American Flag Association (AFA), a coordinating organization for the flag protection movement, labeled the movement's opponents the forces of "commercialism in the effort of those who have no patriotism whatever" who expressed their feelings by their "low born desire to prostitute our flag." DAR Flag Committee Chairwoman Frances Saunders Kempster complained bitterly that the flag had been "contaminated by the greed of gain until it has been dragged down to the vilest associations" by those who had turned it into a transformer of "patriots' blood into traders' gold." She declared that such businessmen had "brought to our gaze by means of the glorious banner which had beckoned so many to wondrous deeds of valor, self-sacrifice and death" information about "liquors and tobacco, food and clothing, pocket handkerchiefs, napkins and door mats."[17]

Although the flag protection movement objected to all commercial uses of the flag, judging from the examples that the movement's proponents most frequently cited as examples of obnoxious uses, they appear to have been particularly exercised by advertisements that associated the flag either with specific conduct generally viewed as vice-ridden, such as the consumption of alcohol and tobacco products, or with bodily functions, especially those in any way related to sexuality or excretion. Thus, in testimony before the Senate Military Affairs Committee (SMAC) in 1908, Isabell Ball, chairwoman of the Flag Committee of the Woman's Relief Corps (a female auxiliary of the GAR), denounced as particularly objectionable the fact that depictions of the flag had been burned into "the bottoms of the washbowls, in the urinals and everything else in the Soldiers' Home," in Washington, D.C., that "you will find over here in [the] Georgetown [district of Washington] today, in a plumber's institution, rolls of toilet paper, every piece with the American flag on it," and that "you will find it on beer bottles named 'Old Glory'; you will find it on whiskey bottles named 'Old Glory.'" An 1895 pamphlet denouncing commercial uses of the flag published a drawing of a young woman draped in a flag with one breast bared as an example of what it said could be seen "in almost any variety theatre"; it declared that "too many of these indecent public exhibitors use the national flag as a drapery, back-ground or accessory." The pamphlet also featured a drawing of a flag-decorated tissue paper used to wrap lemons, which, it declared, was prized by "janitors who preserve (it) for unmentionable purposes."[18]

In a letter from Kempster to House of Representatives Judiciary Committee Chairman David B. Henderson on March 22, 1898, in which she urged passage of a flag desecration law, she especially stressed the offensiveness of the use of the flag to advertise such products as "intoxicating liquors, patent nostrums," and any other use that "takes the sacred emblem ... down to the lowest depths of indecency." Similarly, a January 1898 petition to Congress from Massachusetts Governor Roger Wolcott and other prominent officials of his state mentioned as examples of objectionable commercial uses of the flag the advertisement of "eatables, bottles of lager beer, cigar boxes and many other goods, and recently upon toilet paper."

The *Chicago Evening Post* especially objected to the use of the flag as a costume for boxers, asking, "Could there a greater profanation of the emblem of freedom or an act more pernicious than the ignoble use of draping Old Glory about the waist of a burly brute?" In a 1901 pamphlet, Miller expressed especial outrage that the flag could be found in the American-occupied Philippines draped on officially licensed "houses of objectionable reputation to advertise their traffic and attract soldiers to these abodes." Similarly, in testimony before the SMAC in 1902 AFA President Prime complained that in American possessions abroad the flag was used more commonly "on liquor saloons and houses of ill fame" than for any other purpose. He also voiced special objections that depictions of the flag were sometimes "burnt into the porcelain" of urinals and toilets and that two New Jersey breweries were using in their advertisements flags imprinted with the words, "Stands for the best beer."[19]

The Ideology of the Flag Protection Movement

Within this context, and above all originally in reaction to perceived excesses of the advertising industry, the first significant movement in

American history developed, fostered above all by organizations of Union veterans and by members of patriotic-hereditary organizations, to deliberately and systematically create a "cult of the flag," which would turn it into a sacred object to be used only in certain conditions and treated only in a highly reverent manner. Originally, the overriding focus of this flag protection movement, which developed slowly after the Civil War, was to obtain passage of a federal law outlawing flag "desecration." The peak of the movement's organizational influence was reached during the 1895–1910 period. For example, six flag desecration bills were introduced in Congress during the fifteen years following the introduction of the first such proposal in 1878, while between 1895 and 1910 about fifty such bills were proposed. Backers repeatedly referred to the flag as "sacred" and often lumped it together with the cross and the Bible as objects whose disrespectful treatment would amount to "desecration." Thus, the House of Representatives passed for the first time in 1890 a bill aimed solely at commercial advertising, "to prevent desecration of the United States flag." The House Judiciary Committee (HJC) had urged such action because the flag "should be held a thing sacred" and thus to "deface, disfigure or prostitute it to the purposes of advertising should be held to be a crime against the nation and be punished as such." In 1895, the first major publication of the flag protection movement declared that "the stars and stripes are heaven's benediction" and "its folds are sacred."

An 1898 pamphlet authored by Miller declared at one point that the flag "should be kept as inviolate as was the Holy of Holies in King Solomon's temple" and at another point referred to "those three sacred jewels, the Bible, the Cross and Flag" that "command national reverence." In a subsequent 1900 pamphlet Miller explicitly referred to flag reverence as a form of religion, declaring that the United States "must develop, define and protect the cult of her flag, and the symbol of that cult—the Star Spangled Banner—must be kept inviolate as are the emblems of all religions." In a 1901 pamphlet Miller made his viewpoint yet more explicit, holding as an example to Americans of "how deep in reverence one can hold the national colors" the practice of the Sitka Indians of Alaska, who had supposedly "discarded their totem poles" and "substituted in place of their grotesque poles the Flag of the United States, which they will use as a religious emblem."[20]

Similar religious comparisons were endemic in the flag protection movement. Thus, in 1900 the national Commander-in-Chief of the GAR, the largest organization of Union veterans and a leading participant in the flag protection movement, compared the flag, as had Miller, to the "Holy of Holies." The head of the New Jersey GAR declared that the flag should be "as sacred to all patriots and liberty-loving people as the Holy Bible." Former senator and ambassador to Spain Thomas Palmer proclaimed, "What the cross is to the Christian, the flag is to the patriotic American."

In an 1899 report to the DAR, Kempster declared that the flag had been "christened and hallowed" by a "prodigal outpouring of noble blood" and should be "held free and pure and sacred as the cross." Failure to protect it, she declared, would be "like watching undisturbed while sacred altars were dishonored, for upon which altar has greater, richer sacrifices been poured than upon this altar of our country, in defense of this flag of freedom?" Reporting to the 1907 DAR convention, Kempster invoked biblical imagery to refer to flag desecrators as a "throng of irreverent money changers, who reach out, even to our country's altar, for the beloved emblem placed there by immeasurable suffering, made sacred and holy by bloody sacrifice." A subsequent DAR Flag Committee Chairwoman, Mrs. John Hume, told the 1918 DAR convention that "what the cross is to our church, the flag is to our country." Testifying before the HJC in 1928, Gridley Adams, chairman of a coalition of groups opposing flag desecration, known as the Flag Conference, proposed Congressional adoption of an official "Flag Code," to include the declaration that the flag was "sacred to all the people, and second only to their creator."[21]

Clearly, the major thrust of the movement to prevent "flag desecration" was to transform the flag into a holy relic. The success of this theme, which was deliberately engineered beginning about 100 years ago, can be seen in the comments of cultural historian Wilbur Zelinsky, who, writing in 1988 about the significance of the flag in American life, noted that it had "pre-empted the place, visually and otherwise, of the crucifix in older Christian lands" and that "nowhere is the observation more apt than in the United States" that modern states have made their flag into a "literally holy object, the equivalent of the cross or the communion wafer."[22]

Aside from its sacredness, the leaders and backers of the flag protection movement ascribed many other positive qualities to the flag, usually connected to fervently nationalistic and often jingoistic views of the United States. Much of this aspect of what amounted to a full-fledged flag worship movement was captured by GAR Commander-in-Chief Lucius Fairchild, who praised the "loyalty that asks no questions" while telling the Connecticut GAR in 1887 that "our country, right or wrong ... is the kind of loyalty that we instill into the minds of our children." Thus, to leading movement spokesman Charles Kingsbury Miller, the emblem represented "the ideal government of all humanity" and was the "Flag of Destiny" whose "bright folds resplendent with victory" inspired the "hearts and hopes of men." GAR Commander-in-Chief Albert Shaw declared in 1900 that in its "original and sacred form and color" the American emblem was the "oldest and most beautiful flag in the world."

According to an 1895 sermon by a Chicago clergyman, J. Q. A. Henry, "The loyal American believes that Old Glory is the brightest, most blessed, and most benign of all national emblems of all time; that it symbolizes the holiest hope of human-kind concerning civil and religious liberty, personal freedom and national independence; that it emblazons the climacteric point of progress and purity, equality and fraternity." Kempster, in addressing the 1903 DAR Convention, also lauded the flag in terms typical of those used by many in the flag protection movement, in which the emblem was associated only with the most lofty of American ideals and never with any injustices: "Our flag has not its like on earth. It is not the banner of the reigning despot. It does not shield the misdeeds of self will and tyranny. It does not shelter rank and caste and luxury, nor the sacrifice of the poor and industrious." Kempster's successor as DAR Flag Chairwoman, Mrs. Jacob Dickinson, quoted to an HJC hearing in 1913 from an essay that declared the flag uplifted the "eyes and hearts" of children by its "glowing colors and splendid promise," since under its protection lay "opportunities unknown to any other nation."[23]

In the eyes of leaders and backers of the flag protection movement, the flag's many glories, virtues, and benefits were not restricted only to Americans or to the physical limits of the United States. Indeed, according to one movement supporter, the American flag "is recognized by all the people of the earth as the handsomest flag in the universe." AFA President Prime declared in 1905 that the flag had "been carried to the utmost parts of the earth, carrying liberty wherever it has been thrown to the breeze," and that "Americans cannot fail of a feeling of pride and satisfaction, nor restrain the swelling of patriotism in the breast, when we contrast the meaning, in far distant lands, of ours and other flags displayed together." According to DAR Flag Committee Chairwoman Dickinson in 1911, when the American flag was "unfurled in the darkest savage districts of the far-off Philippines" its impact was "awesome" as it "seemed to present to them all that liberty and protection of person and property could guarantee a dependent and benighted race."[24]

According to flag protection movement spokesmen, the flag stood only for the purest of motives and actions. Thus, DAR Flag Committee Chairwoman Alice MacFarlane told the 1915 DAR convention, in words that probably would have rather surprised American blacks and Indians, not to mention Mexicans and Filipino rebels, that the flag had "never waved in behalf of tyranny, aggression or injustice," but had been "unfurled in more movements for the protection, the liberty and the elevation of man than any flag that ever waved." Twenty years earlier, and only three years before American annexation of the Philippines, the first major publication of the flag protection movement had made similar claims, declaring that the emblem was a "flag of peace" that had

> never been carried by an army of oppression, which went forth for conquest, animated only by greed of gain; it has never floated cruelly over scenes of ruin, plunder and carnage for the sake of ministering to the ambition of kings. But where high principles were in danger, where the liberties of its humblest subject was touched, where oppression of tyranny dared intrude, there the stars have always blazed with a wrathful flame and its red stripes have symbolized the punishment our country's enemies should receive at our hands. It means all that is good and true and pure and beautiful in a land of freedom. It is worthier of self-sacrifice and heroic devotion than any goddess of the oldest time.

At the 1898 national GAR encampment, Commander-in-Chief John Gobin celebrated America's victory over Spain by hailing the flag's display over foreign lands as "indicative of a higher civilization and a purer evangelization," while the GAR Chaplain-in-Chief thanked God for supplying a flag "to carry for civilization and to make the nations which have been blackened by superstition and darkness, brighter and more beautiful."[25]

Leaders and backers of the flag protection movement often attributed extraordinary powers to the emblem, predicted the most wonderful outcomes if Americans truly loved and expressed their devotion to the flag, and warned of the most dire consequences if flag desecration were allowed to flourish or go unpunished. In the early 1890s, *St. Nicholas*, a children's magazine, published poems glorifying the flag that transmitted sentiments typical of the flag protection movement: "Each stripe has a meaning you yet cannot guess; Each star is more sacred than words can express. ... This blessed banner overhead possesses heavenly powers!" GAR Commander-in-Chief William Warner declared in 1889 that if all American schoolchildren were "imbued with a reverence for the flag and all it represents" then "the future of the Republic is assured," while former New York Congressman Cornelius Pugsley told a 1923 New York City Flag Day celebration that, "No rallying point should be so effective to combat evil and dangerous tendencies in our national life than respect for our flag and our country." According to members of the Woman's Relief Corps speaking in the 1890s, the mere presence of flags in schoolhouses marked "a grand step toward making brave, manly boys and womanly girls" and its effect upon immigrant children "has been to make them enthusiastic Americans."

This latter claim was elaborated upon by a school principal named Chandler around 1890, who declared that if immigrant children had held up to their "gaze" not only the story of American heroes, but also "that flag on which the stars seem real, on which the white lines are the symbol of the purity of these heroes, and those of red their patriot blood, shed in defense of our country, we shall be rewarded with the pleasure of witnessing the great and beautiful transformation scene in making the immigrant ... an American citizen, who has broken the fetters which the despotism of the old country has wound around him, and who feels himself the freeborn equal of any man on the globe." Sometimes the flag apparently even had a magical effect akin to that of Mao Tse-tung's "Little Red Book" during the Cultural Revolution of the 1960s; according to one GAR member speaking in 1892, if children learned "to add and subtract and multiply under that flag" they would "do it a good deal better."[26]

While reverence for the flag promised the most miraculous results for the nation and its citizens, failure to protect the flag from desecration, flag protection movement leaders warned, would result in the most dire calamities. Thus, Miller declared flatly in 1899, "Flag [protection] legislation is essential to our welfare as a nation," because disrespect for the flag "may ultimately cause the government itself to tremble on its foundations." A group of Spanish-American War veterans endorsed this claim, stating that, "Every indignity put upon the emblem of freedom endangers our liberties." Similarly, according to the 1914 report of the DAR Flag Committee Chairman, when the flag "is trampled in the dust and no longer respected, then freedom and justice will be at an end." Former socialist John Spargo told a meeting of the SAR in 1923 that when the flag no longer commanded "the reverence and homage of our citizens, then this nation will pass from anarchy to oblivion." According to a legal brief filed in 1940 as part of an effort to force all school children to salute the flag, if refusals to salute became widespread such "demonstration of disrespect to our government" would ultimately cause the spirits of the entire nation to become "shaken and demoralized."[27]

Allowing disrespect for the flag was seen as leading directly to the most threatening forms of violence and instability. According to a pamphlet published by Miller in 1898, when the memories of the 1894 Pullman strike and the widespread marches of the unemployed and other manifestations of unrest that marked the 1890s were still fresh, tolerating disrespect for the flag "encourages in the leaders of mobs and misguided strikers of labor unions" a general "spirit of lawlessness and license," resulting in rampant "outlawry and hoodlumism" as well as "anarchy and murderous labor riots."

According to a 1900 statement by Brig. Gen. Irving Hale, the vice-president of a Spanish-American War veterans organization, flag desecration was a "crime more heinous in its ultimate effects than theft, arson, or murder, as it strikes at the root of law, order and government." A Washington newspaper declared that, "Anything that tends to destroy our respect for the national emblem bears the earmarks of treason." Shortly after the 1901 assassination of President William McKinley, Miller claimed in a new pamphlet that acts of flag desecration amounted to "open text-books from which the youth of this land are learning their lessons of disrespect for the flag of the United States and the government it represents"; he added that the McKinley assassination was "encouraged by the assassination of the sacred character of our flag." Similarly, in a 1916 article, Roger Wood, Assistant United States Attorney in New York, blamed those who offered "insults" to the flag for planting the "seed" that bore fruit in the brain of McKinley's assassin.[28]

In the eyes of at least some members of the flag protection movement, no penalties could be too harsh for such dangerous acts. Thus, during a Congressional hearing conducted in 1918 amid World War I, Michigan Rep. J. M. C. Smith termed flag protection legislation "as necessary as the espionage act," and declared "I wish we had more men like" Civil War Treasury Secretary Dix who "said if any man hauls down the American flag ... he should be shot on the spot." Congressman Wheeler chimed in to suggest that any man "who would wipe his hands on the flag" was an "enemy of this country" and the appropriate response should be to "either shoot him or lock him up."[29]

The 1896 Presidential Campaign and Opposition to Political "Misuse" of the Flag

Although an embryonic flag protection movement was clearly evolving by the time of the 1895 publication of a pamphlet entitled "The Misuse of the National Flag of the United States," its original focus was entirely the perceived commercial abuse of the flag and at first showed relatively few signs of significant popular or organizational support. However, the perceived political abuse of the flag in the 1896 presidential campaign and a series of resultant incidents in which the flag was physically assaulted gave a major new impetus to the movement. These incidents resulted in such an upsurge of support among patriotic and veterans organizations in late 1896 and 1897 that in early 1898 these groups formed the AFA as a coordinating organization that had the sole purpose of fostering flag protection legislation.

As previously noted, politicians had been using the flag to a limited extent for partisan purposes in presidential and other campaigns at least since 1840, often physically attaching their names and political slogans to the emblem. However, during the bitterly contested 1896 presidential campaign between Republican candidate William McKinley and Democratic-Populist candidate William Jennings Bryan, such use by the McKinley forces reached previously unknown proportions, amid what is generally considered the first presidential campaign run as a modern mass advertising effort. Much as ninety-two years later when Republican candidate George Bush physically and symbolically embraced the flag and suggested that Democratic candidate Michael Dukakis was less than fully patriotic, the 1896 McKinley campaign enveloped itself in flags and clearly suggested, both by slogans and symbols, that the Bryan forces were out to crush the "American way of life." In effect, physically waving the flag in 1896 symbolically replaced "waving the bloody shirt," the post–Civil War Republican tradition of linking the Democrats with the disloyalty of secession.[30]

Beginning with the 1896 Republican convention, McKinley's campaign manager, Mark Hanna, distributed buttons simply containing a replica of the American flag as symbols of support for McKinley, thus equating the candidate and his campaign for retaining the gold standard with the flag. Once the campaign began, Republican campaign officials purchased and distributed, literally by the traincarload, millions of flags for use at their rallies. Hanna organized a "Patriotic Heroes Battalion" of well-known Republican Civil War generals and other veterans, who toured throughout the Midwest, averaging seven stops daily and attracting crowds of thousands as they oratorically linked the Republican party and McKinley to special devotion to both the flag and Union. The heroes battalion travelled on a special train that bore the slogan "1896 is as vitally important as 1861." The train was bedecked with two thousand yards of flag bunting and equipped with two thirty-foot collapsible flagpoles designed to hoist huge flags during station stops and a cannon for firing salutes.[31]

The climax of this political flag campaign was October 31, during the weekend before the election, which Hanna declared to be a national Flag Day in honor of McKinley (at that time June 14 was not generally recognized as an annual Flag Day, as it was to be shortly, largely as the result of the flag protection movement and its allies). On October 31, huge Republican-organized demonstrations and rallies, especially backed by upper middle-class conservatives who feared Bryan's alleged radicalism, were held in major cities such as Chicago, San Francisco, and New York. They featured mass displays of flags and the symbolic linking of patriotism with the causes of McKinley and "sound money."

As the *Chicago Tribune* noted, the idea was that people should "unfold Old Glory" and thus demonstrate "their opposition to the Popocratic [a reference to Bryan's support from both Populists and Democrats] policy which tends to discredit it." *The Critic,* a liberal magazine less favorably disposed to the GOP, commented acidly a year later that the Republicans had in 1896 effectively claimed "the monopoly of patriotism and a sort of divine right to the flag."[32]

According to Stanley Jones, an historian of the 1896 campaign, the October 31 "flag day" demonstrations were prepared by the "dignified, the respectable, the well-to-do" who "joined in the preparations with an air of conviction and sober purpose" as though "they were entering a crusade or rallying for war." The largest demonstration, a parade of 100,000 people witnessed by another 750,000 in New York, was organized by the Business Men's Sound Money Association. According to the *New York Tribune*'s account:

> The flag was everywhere. It flaunted from every window; it waved from every portico; it flew from every roof; it floated over almost every street, and many times in every block. The marching thousands trampled between walls of human faces that were almost entirely folded in the stripes and dotted with the stars, while every man in the whole vast line carried a flag of his own. ... Many of those who marched yesterday have known what it is to march in war under the same flag that covered the city in its folds yesterday all the day long.

In Canton, Ohio, McKinley campaigned from his front porch on "flag day" by addressing a delegation of Cleveland workers, telling them that the flag was a "holy banner" and that he was "glad to know that the American workingmen have arrayed themselves on the side of country, patriotism, peace, progress, protection and prosperity." Earlier during the campaign, McKinley had clearly linked his opponents with the cause of disloyalty to the union and with the labor turbulence of the 1890s by declaring, "Let us settle once for all that this government is one of honor and of law and that neither the seeds of repudiation nor lawlessness can find root in our soil or live beneath our flag."[33]

Faced with this implied and often overt assault upon their patriotism, the Bryan forces feebly suggested that Democrats join in the October 31 demonstrations by flying the flag solely as a tribute to that emblem. Far more importantly for the development of the flag protection movement, in perhaps a dozen or so incidents Democrats who were enraged by McKinleyite slurs upon their patriotism vented their anger by tearing down or otherwise assaulting flags that the Republicans were using as part of their attempt to monopolize patriotism. Thus, in one such incident reported in the *New York Times* on November 1 (in words that read a bit too pat and melodramatic to be entirely believable), pro-Bryan forces in Sedalia, Missouri, became "wild with rage" upon spotting a McKinley demonstration and snatched an American flag from the hands of "Little 'Ollie' Wheeler, the five-year old daughter of Samuel Wheeler, who had been singing sound money songs." The flag snatcher then reportedly burned the flag along with some McKinley literature, supposedly causing one Bryan supporter to throw away his Bryan button and declare, "This is a disgrace and I'll never be caught in another Bryan crowd." Although at least by implication the vast majority of 1896 flag incidents were perpetrated by Bryan's supporters, in at least one case Bryanites were the targets: According to the *Omaha World Herald* of November 1, a picture of Bryan and an accompanying flag were fired upon during a parade.[34]

According to a collection of about a dozen such flag "desecration" incidents of 1896 reported by the National Flag Committee of the DAR (the Committee was formed shortly after election day, apparently largely in response to them), other examples included the following: In Council Bluffs, Iowa, a man on horseback reportedly fired a shotgun at a large American flag festooned with a political banner, resulting in return fire that killed the assailant's horse and wounded the assailant, who escaped; in Hammond, Indiana, a large flag bearing a partisan motto was reportedly torn down from a private residence and dragged in the mud; in Milwaukee, an unadorned flag flying from a political club was allegedly torn to shreds and trampled into the mud; in Janesville, Wisconsin, flags were rotten-egged and torn; and in Chicago a large number of flags were supposedly used as floormats and spittoons at the headquarters of a political party.

A few additional cases of alleged physical flag desecration incidents subsequent to the 1896 campaign were reported by Charles Kingsbury Miller in a series of pamphlets that he published between 1898 and 1902. In 1899, Miller claimed such incidents were "continually occurring" and that the daily press had given "numerous instances" during the very preparation of his pamphlet. He cited reported cases of flags torn down and destroyed in Chicago and Sioux City, Iowa; the seizure and trampling or dragging in the dirt of flags in Jersey City, New Jersey, Wallace, Idaho, and Philadelphia; the use of a flag as a church doormat for muddy shoes in Washington, D.C.; and the defacing of a flag on a ship in New York. In other pamphlets, Miller added accounts of eggs tossed and shots fired at flags bearing pictures or names of political candidates in Chicago, missiles hurled at a flag in Scalp Level, Pennsylvania, and the tearing of flags during a patriotic parade in Boston and from a storefront in East Boston.[35]

While the total of twenty or so flag "desecration" incidents reported in 1896 and soon afterwards seem to have had little practical significance or impact upon the growing public reverence for the flag, they did greatly spur concern among patriotic and veterans groups, and led directly to a considerable growth of the flag protection movement. Thus, AFA President Prime, addressing his organization in 1902, declared that "it was the presidential campaign of 1896, I am forced to believe, which intensified to the greatest extent the desire to secure by some means the safety of the flag," as flags to which political material had been attached were "ruthlessly torn down and trailed in the dust by those who cared not for it but who resented the appropriation of it for such uses." In 1907, Prime told the AFA that "acts of outrageous desecration" of the flag had "culminated in that presidential campaign of 1896," when abuses of the flag had "roused liberty loving and patriotic people to put an end to such forms of desecration and your association was one of the results of such experiences in that period."

Similarly, when a special Committee of the Commissioners on Uniform State Laws, consisting of representatives of the various states, met in 1913 to recommend the text of a uniform state flag protection law to replace the hodge-podge of existing state laws, it reported that "legislation on this subject arose from the condition of things in 1896." The committee explained that during the election campaign of that year the flag was used "for a variety of purposes," including "as a political emblem by all the political parties," as a result of which "outrages occurred in all sections of the country," as "in the excitement and anger generated at that time the flag so used was torn down and torn in pieces and trampled in the dust." The committee reported in a distinctly secondary manner and in far less detail that "at this time also a spirit of commercialism was rampant, and nothing was sacred, not even the flag, from uses of advertising merchandise."[36]

The events of 1896 were the focal point of much of the immediately subsequent demands for flag protection legislation, especially those by the DAR. Thus, in an 1897 petition to Congress calling for a national flag desecration law, the DAR's Milwaukee chapter, which spearheaded the organization's efforts in the flag protection movement, mentioned commercial use of the flag only in passing, but printed an apparently complete list of the 1896 politically related incidents, while claiming that "many" additional "similar occurrences are known to have taken place" and that they indicated that "the evil is widespread" and "the feeling is apparent everywhere that the flag can be treated with disrespect intentionally, and without fear of punishment." At about the same time, forty-two residents of Hilton, Pennsylvania petitioned their state legislature in 1897 for a law to punish those who would "take down, pollute, injure, remove or in any manner damage or destroy any flag." The Hilton petitioners did not even mention advertising abuse of the flag, instead urging legislative action because the flag had been "during the past year insulted and polluted, torn down from private flagstaffs and dwellings, dragged through the mud and the filth of the streets, an insult to patriotism, an outrage to civilization, and a crime against a nation—the greatest in civic virtue—and developed manhood in the World."

The *Terre Haute Evening Gazette* complained that "the use of the national flag as a party emblem" had "converted" it "into a political nose rag," while the *Indianapolis News* declared, "Political parties should cease using the flag as advertisements. What is there commoner than the American flag, with portraits of political candidates, suspended across the streets and from trees?" The writer of a letter to the editor printed in the *New York Times* of October 5, 1904, complained of such political flag displays and declared that he would never vote for any candidate who so misused the flag, as the emblem was the "property of the whole people, not of any one party" and "there is no surer road to revolution than the desecration of the flag!"[37]

Other spokesmen and organizations in the flag protection movement stressed both commercial and political flag misuse as more or less equally major reasons why legislation was needed to keep the national symbol from harm. Thus, an 1898 report of the SAR Flag Committee chaired by Prime denounced not only those who would use the flag in advertising for "selfish and unpatriotic purposes," but also those whose "partisan, political and unpatriotic sentiment" would allow the emblem to be used for "advertising political candidates." Prime declared that people must be educated to see the flag as a "sacred emblem, not to be used for any unholy or mercenary or partisan purposes" but to be "kept pure by patriots for patriotism and for country."

Similarly, in 1898 and 1902 pamphlets, Miller declared that the flag's "sacredness" had been "encroached upon" both by the "great political parties and the janizaries of trade" and abused equally by "avaricious tradesmen and crafty politicians, who turn it into a campaign banner for rival political clubs, a mop for the floor of barrooms and other despicable uses." In 1899, Miller gave examples of ever more ingenious types of both kinds of abuse: the "debasing" selling of "the flag on stockings" and the publishing, during a recent Chicago mayoral campaign, of hundreds of thousands of posters with pictures of the flag together with one of the candidates, including some small cardboard versions with brass eyelets, with the notice, printed on the back, "Please tie this to your horses [sic] head [for use as blinders]."[38]

The Flag Protection Movement and Fears of "Un-Americans"

By late 1896 the fundamental concerns and targets of the flag protection movement had seemingly been set—the prevention of misuse of the flag, for either commercial or partisan purposes, by essentially mainstream advertisers and politicians who might seek to associate the symbol with their generally respectable, if profane, activities, and thus might sully the holy character of the flag and provoke physical assaults upon it by those who disagreed with their causes. But shortly after the flag protection movement's relatively new focus on partisan misuse developed from the 1896 campaign, additional potential (although largely imaginary) threats to the symbolic physical integrity of the flag began to be increasingly stressed by the movement.

These newly perceived threats to the flag—highly revealing as to the real fears and motivations behind the movement—gradually began to eclipse the earlier expressed concerns about the actions of essentially "respectable" groups, such as businessmen and ordinary politicians. These new and increasingly stressed threats came from groups that movement leaders clearly viewed as "un-American" threats to the integrity, not only of the flag, but of the country itself, and especially to the traditional leadership of and deference shown to longstanding elites such as themselves: political radicals, the labor movement, and the "new" immigrants from such allegedly "unassimilable" regions as southern and eastern Europe who dominated American immigration patterns after 1880. These perceived emerging threats to the flag were the same forces that were blamed for the general turbulence that had rocked and in many ways emotionally dominated American society since at least the 1877 railroad riots, which were followed by other crises such as the Haymarket affair of 1886, the 1892 Homestead Strike, and the Pullman Strike and mass unemployment marches of 1894. All these disturbances had occurred against the background of almost constant recessions or depression since 1873 and were accompanied by a sweeping industrialization and urbanization of American life, the rise of the modern labor movement, and a vast increase in immigration from regions other than the traditional northwestern European sources.[39]

Collectively these developments transformed American society and politics in the post-Civil War period and, inevitably, created new social forces that threatened the role of precisely those traditional middle-class and upper middle-class elites who led the flag protection movement. The patriotic-hereditary societies that constituted one of the two major elements in the movement had, not coincidentally, virtually all been organized in the last years of the nineteenth century—the SAR was formed in 1889, the DAR in 1890, and numerous similar groups at about the same time, mostly differentiated from each other only by their own arcane criteria for membership. Clearly such groups wanted to assert their alleged special identity as "original" Americans by mining what historian Arthur Schlesinger Sr. has termed "the unearned increment of ancestral reputations," along with reasserting their role as traditional elites who had "formed the socially ambitious local gentry in many an American small town" and felt especially threatened by the new immigration and other forces transforming American society and creating parvenu elites.

The second major force in the flag protection movement, veterans groups, and especially Union Civil War veterans organizations, led by the GAR (representing all Union veterans) and the Loyal Legion (restricted to Union officers), were led by individuals from similar social strata (although this was definitely not true of the general membership of the GAR—for example eighteen of the twenty-three members of one Ohio GAR post were illiterate). Both the patriotic-hereditary and Civil War veterans organizations viewed themselves as having a special charge and a special right to define what constituted proper Americanism—the hereditary groups because of their lineage and the Civil War veterans because of their successful defense of the Union. As Wallace Davies, the leading historian of the veterans and patriotic groups has summarized, by virtue of their military sacrifices, the Civil War veterans "thought that they had acquired a first mortgage upon the country," while the hereditary groups asserted their lineage to create "self-appointed roles" as the "guardians of the American past and interpreters of its ideals."[40]

Even before the flag protection movement gained major strength after 1896, superpatriotic spokesmen had stressed flag devotion as a major means of unifying American society against various "un-American threats." Thus, the virulently nativist Know Nothing Movement, which gained considerable influence with appeals to anti-immigrant sentiment in the 1850s, developed out of an organization entitled the "Order of the Star Spangled Banner." In 1888 the Rev. Dr. John Paxton accompanied the presentation by a New York GAR chapter of an American flag to City College of New York students with the words, "Whatever nation you belong to by birth, whatever tongue your mother taught, you, whatever your color or race, no matter, there is only one flag. Now let us come and gather under its blessed folds. Let us be tangled in the stars and covered with the stripes." A couple of years later, the Patriotic Order Sons of America, one of the earliest flag protection crusaders, defined its task as defending the country against those foreign-born radicals who wished "to terrorize the community and to exalt the red flag of the [1871 Paris] commune above the Stars and

Stripes." At about the same time, a prominent school principal described the task of American educators as taking the "mingling of all races" who came to the United States and welding their children "into one homogenous mass" of "loyal citizens of the republic" by such means as teaching them to "love, adore, reverence and defend that flag which for more than a century has rustled above the head of the American people."

Faced with the perceived threat of "un-American" immigrants, radicals, trade unions, and others, which seemed to have suddenly mushroomed during the last few decades of the nineteenth century, the flag protection movement clearly viewed what its critics referred to as flag "glorification" as a means of restoring unity and "order" to American society. Shortly before opposition to flag desecration became the major focus of the movement, many of its constituents and supporters also began drives to demand that all public schools display the flag and that the general population, and especially schoolchildren, engage in ever more frequent, elaborate, and formal rituals of obeisance to the flag, such as saluting it in school, standing up and baring one's head during public flag displays, and honoring the flag each year with special celebrations on June 14. For example, the GAR frequently donated flags to schools in elaborate ceremonies; by 1895 the GAR proudly reported that flags waved over two-thirds of the 26,588 public schools located within the twenty-one Grand Army departments (located, of course, exclusively in the north, since the GAR comprised only northern Civil War veterans).

In response to such pressures many of the states, beginning in 1890 with North Dakota and New Jersey, for the first time required that school buildings display the flag on a daily basis (instead of just on special holidays); by 1895 ten states had passed such laws. The first of many state requirements that schoolchildren salute the flag daily was enacted in New York in 1898, one day after the United States declared war on Spain; by 1908 twenty-six states and territories either required or encouraged such rituals. The flag consistently played a major role in the burgeoning pre-World War I "Americanization" movement, which stressed the general need to turn "un-American" immigrants into loyal citizens. Thus, in an elaborate "graduation" ceremony conducted as part of the Ford Motor Company's compulsory "English Melting Pot School" for immigrants, students dressed in their native costumes descended into a great pot which occupied the center of a stage and soon after emerged wearing neat business suits and waving small American flags.[41]

Although the actual number of incidents of physical flag desecration by political radicals, trade unions, and "new" immigrants during the pre-World War I era appears to have been miniscule, the leaders of the flag protection movement made as a major theme in their rhetoric after 1896 the alleged threat that such elements posed to the flag, and, by clear extension, to American society. As usual, Charles Kingsbury Miller used the most melodramatic and exaggerated language in outlining the threat to the flag posed by what many in the flag protection movement clearly viewed as a variety of virtually interchangeable "un-American" elements. Thus, in 1898 Miller declared:

> The multitude of uneducated foreigners who land upon our friendly shores are ignorant of everything pertaining to American institutions ... while the world's enemies, the anarchists, flock to this country. ... As a result of these changes we observe our flag no longer protected by the sentiment of a century ago, but treated with open disrespect. ... Our public officials, acting under a flag openly degraded, battle with the lath of a manikin against the spirit of lawlessness and license, which this disrespect encourages in leaders of mobs and misguided strikers of labor unions. ... The seeds of contempt sown by public disrespect have already sprung up and grown into plants, manifested in part by anarchy and murderous labor riots. These noxious weeds of disorder are spreading with the increase of our multifarious population. Experience of past centuries impels us to sink the emotional in common sense, to turn deaf ears to the spell binders who would bewilder us with their rhetoric, and for the future welfare of our country, sound a warning note in demanding that the desecration of the American flag be stopped by law, before our people discover that the clenched fist of lawlessness has become the mailed hand of defiance.[42]

Miller returned to similar themes repeatedly in his various pamphlets. Thus, in 1899 he claimed that the "battle cry" of the Pullman Strike had been "To hell with the government and its flag" and warned that "the lowest class of foreign born" Americans interpreted American liberty as "license" and had to be taught "lessons in domestic respect" or else the nation would find itself grappling "with a social problem that will bear a very ugly resemblance to the social upheavals with which monarchical governments have to struggle." In 1900, Miller warned that the country had become "the international dumping ground" for "hundreds of thousands of the lowest class of immigrants" from the "most poverty-stricken and lawless classes of humanity" who swelled "the populace who abuse the United States flag" and posed "a menace to the nation." Such elements, he warned, along with "the riotous elements of the labor organizations" and "Socialists, Anarchists, Nihilist, Populists, Tramps and Criminals" made up a "vast army of men who are ready for any and all kinds of disturbance." Fortunately, the remedy for these horrendous threats was quite simple, Miller suggested—the nation need merely keep the American flag "inviolate as the emblems of all religions." Miller began a 1901 pamphlet, published shortly after President McKinley's assassination (by a deranged native-born American, whose foreign-sounding name and self-proclaimed anarchist beliefs provoked a nationwide "anarchist scare") with yet another litany of doom, which could, supposedly, be resolved by flag protection legislation:

> The red flag of danger flies in America. Anarchy is rampant, striking down the chief magistrates of our nation—increasing pauper immigration is deteriorating our citizenship—railroad trains are robbed from the Atlantic to the Pacific slope—a scattered army of 200,000 tramps commit depredations—gigantic trusts and combinations stifle competition in every state in the Union—the emblem of our country is desecrated by commercial vandalism. ... A flag law is ... needed to end the abuses of our nation's emblem, which inoculates the minds of our large and mixed population, unable and untrained to discriminate between the government and its symbol, with contemptuous disrespect of the government which permits the desecration of its national flag. What will the present Congress do with the red flag of anarchy, and what action will they [sic] take for protecting the honor of the American flag?[43]

Although Miller's venom and hyperbole were rarely matched by other leaders of the flag protection movement, their rhetoric clearly indicated that they shared his fears. For example, in its report to the DAR in 1898, the Milwaukee DAR chapter defined the purpose of its proposed legislation as punishing "all forms of desecration of the national flag" and causing it "to be held in respect by our foreign-born nationals." While addressing the DAR in 1899, Milwaukee chapter member and national DAR Flag Chairwoman Kempster called for protection of the flag against the "fomenter of sedition" and the "anarchist" as well as "the children of those new to our country." In her 1904 report, Kempster clearly alluded to the labor movement as well to the dangers posed by immigrants and political radicals:

> We have but to look about us with open eyes and mind to see the necessity for this [flag desecration] legislation. The air is full of threatening and defiant discontent. Misleading names cover ugly, intolerant, malicious teachings. Our country, offering its widespread freedom as a shelter beneath which the oppressed of all lands shall find refuge, has nurtured good and evil-minded with the same impartial care; and in the liberty which was her generous gift to each and all she has given a weapon which is being prepared for her own hurt. ...We see approaching us, as a great threatening cloud, a vast organized body, developed under our fostering and forbearing Government, and controlling every means of our daily existence, which stands menacing and revengeful and demands the destruction of government and law.

In 1907, Kempster called for flag protection legislation so that the nation could

> say by its own command, to the illogical and visionary enthusiast, distressed by the disheartening ills of human kind, to the glib-tongued, blatant demagogue, with his incendiary teachings of hatred and dissension; to the crafty schemer, using the weakness and discontent of mankind as ground for the planting of poisonous weeds, to the malignant fomenter of sedition, with his extravagant vagaries, his hatred of law his defiant insults—Cease! Cease![44]

AFA President Prime, in his 1912 address to his organization, claimed that those guilty of "malicious outrages" against the flag had invariably been immigrants associated with "meetings and demonstrations of the labor movement," whose leaders therefore were obligated "to have a thorough house cleaning and to eliminate from their membership from one end of the land to the other all flag desecrators and all anarchists of every name, style and sentiment." Prime's distaste for the labor movement was demonstrated with unintentionally amusing clarity and irony in 1904–05 when he advocated that all AFA members and supporters refuse to buy any products tainted with flag advertisements; at the same time he turned verbal acrobatics to dissociate such product boycotts from general boycotting of merchants, a tactic viewed by conservatives as virtually subversive when used by trade unions in connection with strikes and organizational drives. Prime asserted that there was a "radical difference" between the "patriotic and justifiable refusal" to purchase a "particular article" that a merchant "offensively thrusts upon us," such being merely "the assertion of the American principle of freedom to do as we please" as opposed to the "reprehensible boycott" of the "merchant himself," which was a concept "utterly repulsive," "disgusting" and "one of the most wicked inventions of the age." That a general labor boycott of a merchant, in objection to his general operating principles, was a logical extension of boycotting a particular item because of specific objections to it, and thus might also be an example of the "American principle of freedom," never seems to have occurred to Prime.[45]

Although leaders of the veterans groups that formed part of the flag protection movement were considerably less prominent and vocal than were those of the SAR, DAR, and AFA, it is clear that fears of immigrants, radicals, and trade unions played a major role in the former groups' participation in the movement also. Thus, in 1889 GAR Commander-in-Chief William Warner proclaimed his organization "the great conservative element of the nation." During and shortly after the 1894 Pullman strike, the head of the Indiana GAR urged vigilance against "the encroachment of the anarchistic and socialistic tendencies so prevalent among us," and the head of the Ohio GAR declared that his organization had "its thumb on the button, with forty rounds ready, to defend any legal administration against anarchists or others who violate the law." In 1890, a leading veterans newspaper questioned what good might come to the United States from the "presence of our foreign born rotten banana sellers, thieving rag dealers, Italian organ grinders, Chinese washmen and Bohemian coal miners, whose aspirations would make a dog vomit?" In 1892, the GAR's "patriotic instructor" suggested that restrictions needed to be placed "upon that portion of the tide of immigration sweeping upon our shores which represents only the poverty and crime of other lands."[46]

Leaders of the flag protection movement went out of their way to highlight cases of alleged flag desecration that supposedly involved foreigners, radicals, or trade unions, as did newspapers accounts. For example, during hearings before the SMAC in 1902, when Senator Hawley referred to an incident in Boston where a man had reportedly been fined for making "a rag bag of the flag," Prime immediately declared, "I am glad to say he was not an American born citizen, if he was a citizen at all. He was a Russian." Similarly, in an 1899 pamphlet Miller complained about an alleged incident in New Jersey, where a "crowd of Italians" supposedly seized and trampled a flag, and a similar case involving "a Welshman" acting as a result of "the bitter feelings engendered by lawless labor unions." DAR Flag Chairwoman Kempster referred in her 1907 report to an undated incident where supposedly the "flag was greeted with hoots and hisses and ordered from the room, at a gathering of 4,000 members of a labor organization in San Francisco." The GAR's "national patriotic instructor" reported in 1912 on an alleged incident in Boston, where "in connection with the car strike," a flag was used as a "receptacle"; observers had reported that "in addition to money, from the vast crowd cigar butts and other filthy articles were thrown into the flag, forming a disgusting mass." An Associated Press dispatch printed in the *Chicago Record-Herald* of December 26, 1912, reported, in a completely matter-of-fact manner, that "Austrians" in Los Angeles who had torn an American flag to pieces had been intercepted by the police "who clubbed [them] into submission and arrested them."[47]

The Organizational Structure of the Flag Protection Movement

The first antebellum flag desecration bill was proposed in the House of Representatives in 1878. As early as 1890 such a proposal, aimed solely at commercial misuse of the flag, passed the House (without any debate and apparently without any committee consideration) with the support of the New York department of the GAR and several branches of the nativist Patriot Order Sons of America. However, nothing approaching a real movement dedicated to opposing flag desecration emerged until 1895. The movement mushroomed rapidly thereafter, especially in the wake of the 1896 election, gaining support from a wide variety of patriotic and veterans organizations.[48]

The founding father, or "Johnny Appleflag," of the flag protection movement was Philip H. Reade (1844–1919), a West Point graduate who fought for the Union in the Civil War and saw service in the Indian campaigns, the Spanish-American War, and the crushing of Aguinaldo's insurrection in the Philippines. Eventually he was promoted to brigadier general in 1911 after forty-four years of service. Reade was an avid participant in the activities of both the SAR and the Society of Colonial Wars (SCW), both organizations whose members claimed descent from American soldiers of the Revolutionary War and pre-revolutionary wars. Reade served as a historian for both organizations, personally claimed descent from twenty-four colonial ancestors, and published a number of short historical works, including three genealogies of his own family. His first involvement in the flag protection movement appears to have come in 1895, when as governor (president) of the Illinois SCW he oversaw on February 23 the passage of a resolution urging Congress to forbid commercial use of the flag and subsequently appointed on April 2 a committee to study the issue. Reade worked tirelessly to obtain endorsements for the flag protection movement, speaking and writing to a wide variety of organizations.[49]

Largely, if not exclusively, through Reade's influence, between 1897 and 1899 the national organizations of the DAR, the SAR, the GAR, and the Loyal Legion all passed resolutions in support of flag desecration legislation and formed national committees to further this cause. At Reade's personal oral or written urging, resolutions in support of flag desecration legislation were also passed by a variety of other national and local groups, such as the national commandery Regular Army and Navy Union of the United States in Chicago in February 1895, the Wisconsin SAR in May 1895, the Sons of the Revolution (not be confused with the SAR) in 1896, the Wisconsin National Guard in January 1898, and the Minnesota Historical Society in March 1898. Although Reade's role was essentially that of organizing catalyst rather than ongoing administrator and leader of the flag protection movement, perhaps because his military career often led to frequent geographical transfers, he continued to maintain an active interest in the issue, for example speaking about flag desecration at the national SAR conventions in 1914 and 1918.[50]

With Reade sowing the founding seeds, three separate major focal points for the flag protection movement emerged by 1897: the flag committees of the Chicago-based Illinois chapters of the SCW and the SAR, both led by Charles Kingsbury Miller; the Milwaukee chapter of the DAR, led by Mrs. Frances Saunders Kempster; and the New York Chapter of the SAR, led by Col. Ralph E. Prime. Miller, originally Reade's appointee as secretary of the Illinois SCW Flag Committee, soon became chairman of the SCW Committee as well as of the Illinois SAR Flag Committee and used those positions as a springboard for becoming a major national figure in the flag protection movement; he also served for a short time as a member of the founding AFA Executive Committee.

Miller was born in Lodi, New York, in 1850, and claimed descent from an English settler who arrived in Massachusetts in 1629, about whom he published a genealogical study. He founded an apparently highly successful newspaper advertising agency in Chicago, enabling him to retire by the age of fifty. Miller was perhaps the most prolific publicist of the flag protection movement, at least between 1898 and 1902, during which he published numerous pamphlets that demanded Congressional action, attacked perceived opponents of the movement in often vitriolic terms, and painted an apocalyptic picture of the United States as a country about to be swamped and degraded by mobs of flag desecrators comprised of mercenary businessmen, near-savage immigrants, bloodthirsty trade unions, and revolutionary anarchists and radicals—who individually and collectively posed a lethal threat to American democracy but who could be easily tamed if Congress would only provide penalties for flag misuse. Miller was an indefatigable correspondent and organizer on behalf of the flag protection movement, obtaining endorsements of its goals from scores of prominent politicians, military officers, and newspapers, and frequently writing to key congressmen urging them to act.

For example, in an 1899 pamphlet, Miller published endorsements for national flag desecration legislation from almost one hundred prominent Americans, including former presidents Grover Cleveland and Benjamin Harrison, former vice-presidents Levi Morton and Adlai Stevenson, four sitting cabinet members, New York Governor Theodore Roosevelt, half a dozen sitting and former ambassadors, the president of the American Bar Association, scores of prominent military officials, including Spanish-American War hero Adm. George Dewey, former and future Democratic presidential nominee William Jennings Bryan, college presidents from Yale, Harvard, Stanford, Princeton, Columbia, and the University of Michigan, and black leader Booker T. Washington. In a 1900 pamphlet, Miller published an additional twenty-five endorsements from prominent Americans, including President McKinley, and cited editorials supporting the flag protection cause from over sixty newspapers.[51]

In a letter to Miller quoted in the January 1903 issue of *The Spirit of '76*, a house organ for the patriotic societies, Reade hailed Miller's contribution to the flag protection movement and declared that the passage up until then of legislation banning flag desecration in over twenty states and territories had resulted "more through your efforts than those of any one man." Such praise apparently enraged AFA president and national SAR Flag Committee Chairman Prime, who believed it grossly exaggerated Miller's role, and who was already outraged by Miller's repeatedly published and bitter personal attacks on HJC Chairman and later House Speaker David B. Henderson. Miller viewed Henderson as personally responsible for blocking Congressional flag legislation (a probably exaggerated if not fundamentally incorrect impression), but Prime viewed Miller's venomous attacks on such a powerful Congressman as completely counterproductive. Prime publicly denounced and disavowed Miller on several occasions and almost certainly was responsible for excluding Miller from the AFA Executive Committee after 1902. Thereafter, Miller apparently ceased publishing his pamphlets, but he continued, in a far less high-profile manner, his interest in the flag desecration issue, for example speaking at the 1904 national SAR convention and maintaining his membership on the Illinois SAR and SCW Flag Committees at least as late as 1908.[52]

Given the proximity of Milwaukee to Chicago and Reade's known activism in Wisconsin, it is almost certain that Reade was at least indirectly responsible for the fact that the Milwaukee DAR chapter, under the leadership of Frances Saunders Kempster, spearheaded the DAR's interest in the flag desecration issue. Kempster was born Frances Saunders in Ann Arbor, Michigan, around 1860 and was first married to a John Fraser, who left her a widow by 1891. In 1892, she married Walter Kempster, a Civil War veteran, who by the time of the marriage had become one of most prominent physicians in the country, appearing as an expert witness on insanity at the trial of Charles Guiteau for the 1881 murder of President James Garfield and eventually serving as Milwaukee health commissioner between 1894 and 1898. Although Mrs. Kempster claimed descent from a Revolutionary War privateer ship captain when she applied for DAR membership in 1894, it seems likely that her interest in genealogy and history was at least partly due to her husband, who was active in veterans groups and something of an amateur historian, publishing, for example, several studies about the history of the American calvary.[53]

The Milwaukee DAR chapter first called upon Congress to pass flag protection legislation on December 4, 1896, in the immediate aftermath of the 1896 election, and subsequently circulated an appeal to other DAR chapters to join its call. As a result, about eighty DAR chapters presented a joint appeal for endorsement of such a measure to the DAR national convention, which acted favorably on February 22, 1897. In July 1897, the DAR President-General appointed a national Flag Committee, which was headed by Kempster and dominated by the Milwaukee chapter until 1909. The Milwaukee chapter published at least three petitions to Congress for action between 1897 and 1899, stressing especially the 1896 incidents of physical assaults upon the flag. Kempster, like Miller, personally wrote to key Congressmen to urge passage of flag desecration legislation, and although the tone of her lobbying and publications had a much less hysterical and vitriolic tone than did Miller's, she also had run-ins with Prime, as will be discussed later. Kempster served as regent (president) of the Milwaukee DAR in 1902–04, but disappeared from the flag protection movement after 1909, apparently due to a nasty divorce. She died in 1927 after embarking upon a belated career as an artist, in which capacity she studied in Paris for four years and taught at the University of Utah in 1914–17.[54]

Although the Illinois SAR urged Congress to pass flag desecration legislation as early as March 1895, an action quickly applauded by the national SAR President-General, the flag protection movement gained widespread support within the SAR only in 1897. According to an account given in June 1899 by Ralph Prime, who by then was president both of the AFA and the national SAR Flag Committee, the SAR's interest largely dated from January 1897, when due to "some flagrant act of flag desecration" that "stirred to the soul" a member of the New York, or Empire State, chapter, that branch appointed a special Flag Committee. According to Prime, "the action of 1897, in the Empire State Society, SAR, marks a new departure and heralds the first success in the campaign" even though admittedly other flag committees "in the west [that is, Chicago]" had been already appointed, "whose existence was unknown." The Empire State SAR, represented by Prime, then successfully asked the national SAR convention meeting at Cleveland on April 13, 1897, to appoint a national SAR Flag Committee, which would have as its tasks "fostering public sentiment in favor of honoring the flag of our country and preserving it from desecration," initiating "legal measures to prevent such desecration," and joining with "other patriotic societies and committees of the same" to cooperate for such purposes.[55]

As a result of this resolution, a national SAR Flag Committee, chaired by Prime, was quickly appointed. At its first meeting, held in New York City in June 1897, the Committee unanimously decided to issue a call for a mass meeting of all existing flag committees of patriotic societies for the purpose of "securing united action in pursuing the common cause" of preventing flag desecration. This call resulted in a preliminary meeting of representatives of several flag committees in New York on July 15, 1897. It was followed by several other meetings, culminating in a mass meeting of flag committees held at the New York City Hall on February 17, 1898, at which the American Flag Association was formally established. The AFA's purpose was officially proclaimed to be coordinating "the efforts of all the members and the represented societies" in order to foster "public sentiment in favor of honoring the flag of our country and preserving it from desecration, and of initiating and forwarding legal efforts to prevent such desecration."[56]

At its origin, the AFA consisted of the representatives of thirty flag committees, including the national SAR Committee and committees of six state SAR chapters; the national DAR Committee and committees from five DAR chapters; the national Loyal Legion Committee and those of eight state Loyal Legion commanderies; and eight other committees representing an additional five other organizations, such as the Society of the War of 1812 and the National Society of Naval Veterans. According to the AFA's final published report of 1913, by then the organization had grown to include representatives of over one hundred flag committees, including the national SAR and eighteen state SAR Committees, the national DAR and twenty-three DAR Chapter Committees, the national and fourteen state Loyal Legion Committees, the national and eight other GAR Committees, five state chapters of the SCW, and committees representing another twenty patriotic groups, such as the United Spanish War Veterans, the Military Society of the War of 1812, and the Colonial Dames of America. In addition, the AFA also had in 1913 eighty-five individual memberships, a category that did not exist at its founding."[57]

The Executive Committee of the AFA consisted of a president, thirteen vice-presidents, and three other officers, elected at an annual general meeting held on June 14 (Flag Day) of each year, plus an additional thirteen or more persons to be elected either at the AFA annual meeting or by the other elected officials. The Executive Committee was entrusted with the "general management of the affairs of the Association when the Association is not in session," that is, except during the annual meeting, with a quorum of the Executive Committee set at four members. In practice, the AFA appears to have been dominated throughout its active life between 1898 and approximately 1913 by its sole president during this period, Col. Ralph E. Prime (1840–1920). Prime was born in Matteawan, New York. After being admitted to the New York bar, he enlisted as a private in Union forces at the outbreak of the Civil War and rose to the rank of lieutenant colonel. Prime fought in a number of battles, including Antietam, and was severely wounded at Gaines Mill. After retiring from the service due to his wounds, Prime returned to his law practice and served as city attorney of Yonkers and deputy Attorney General of New York. Like Miller and Reade, Prime published a book about his family's early history in the American colonies. According to a biographical sketch published by the SAR on Prime in 1902, due to his work with the AFA, "to him more than any other man perhaps is due the fact that the Stars and Stripes to-day are held in higher honor and greater respect than ever before." Similarly, in 1904 the chairman of the national GAR Flag Committee noted that Prime had "spent a great deal of his valuable time" on the flag desecration issue and "it is largely due to his untiring efforts that so much has already been accomplished."[58]

Since between 1897 and 1908 Prime served not only as AFA President but also as chairman of the national SAR Flag Committee, and because the AFA Executive Committee, especially in its early years, had a large number of SAR representatives, to a considerable extent the AFA seems to have been almost synonymous with the SAR, especially the SAR's New York and national Flag Committees. On the other hand, although the DAR participated in the AFA, it appears to have been frozen out of the AFA leadership—Mrs. Kempster never served on the AFA Executive Committee, for example. Because Prime lived in New York and the AFA headquarters was located there, the New York region was heavily overrepresented among the AFA leadership, no doubt largely due to the logistical difficulties of transportation and communication during the infancy of long-distance telephone service and in the preairplane age. Of the thirteen elected officers in 1902, for example, eight lived in New York, three served on the national SAR Flag Committee and another two were members of the Empire State SAR Flag Committee; of the twenty-two appointed Executive Committee members, fifteen lived in the New York area. Prime personally was a member and, apparently, also in most cases the chairman of an extraordinary number of affiliated committees. For example, in 1906, when the AFA had eighty-five affiliated Flag Committees, Prime belonged to six of them: the New York Committees of the Loyal Legion and the SAR, and the national Committees of the SAR, the Society of the Army of the Potomac, the Society of the War of 1812, and the Order of the Founders and Patriots of America. Prime was able to dominate the AFA no doubt mostly because he was willing to devote an enormous amount of time to the organization and most other members apparently were not. For example, minutes of the 1912 annual meeting reveal that, at a time when the AFA had eighty-five individual members and over one hundred affiliated Flag Committees generally consisting of thirteen members each, only forty-two persons attended, almost all of whom appear to have lived in the New York City area. Of the seventeen AFA officers, only Prime and three others attended; only one of the thirteen vice-presidents were at the meeting (President Taft was among the absent AFA vice-presidents).[59]

Prime devoted a considerable amount of his time to running the AFA and, especially given the low attendance at meetings and the rather minimal requirement of four Executive Committee members necessary for a quorum, he seems to have thoroughly dominated the organization. He appears to have tolerated disagreement poorly and jealously prized the AFA's preeminent role in the flag protection movement. Thus, Prime vigorously and repeatedly attacked Miller for undeserved self-promotion and counterproductive tactics and also, in considerably gentler terms, criticized the DAR for wrongheadedness. Prime's authoritarian tendencies seem to have led him to feel that he had a monopoly on the ability to accurately define patriotic behavior, as was perhaps most clearly displayed during a pair of incidents at the national SAR conventions of 1900 and 1903. After Prime made his 1900 report as national SAR Flag Committee Chairman, James Richardson, on behalf of the Committee on the Adoption of a National Banner for the SAR, proposed that the SAR adopt for its flag a banner with thirteen buff and blue stripes, with a white canton upon which the SAR gold-cross insignia would be embroidered. Prime vigorously objected that such a banner would be "an imitation of the flag of our country" and added:

We have been asking all over this country for flag legislation to prevent the use of that flag unlawfully, or any imitation of it, which by any means could deceive a looker-on and cause him to think it might be the flag of the United States. We have been striving for years to prevent advertisers from using just such flags, and I hope that we won't use it now as an advertisement ourselves.

Richardson, clearly stunned at Prime's remarks, responded:

Mr. Prime is Chairman of the National Flag Committee; I have the honor also to be chairman of the [SAR] Flag Committee for the State of Ohio. And I do not want the National Chairman of the Flag Committee to accuse me as State Chairman of the Flag Committee, of undertaking to defeat the object of that committee, in imitating the American flag. ... The Colonel is not color blind and he can see that buff and white are not an imitation of the [red and white stripes of the] American flag. There are no stars on the [white rather than blue] field, and how are you going to make a distinctive banner or flag with no device in it which involves colored cloth, without in some way copying something else?[60]

Prime's position prevailed in 1900, no doubt due to his greater prestige, and he again prevailed in 1903 when the situation was somewhat reversed. After listening to Prime's vigorous assault on flag desecration, delegate James DuBois complained that most Americans could not sing "The Star Spangled Banner" due to ignorance of the words and suggested that the SAR pass a resolution urging that "at least one verse of the 'Star Spangled Banner' be sung" whenever the flag was presented to an SAR meeting. DuBois asked, "Is it not high time that we wake up to a genuine appreciation of our Flag and of the sacredness of its character [by adopting such a ritual]?" However, Prime declared that although he had "as much respect as any one for the words" of the anthem, people did not sing it "simply because whoever wrote the melody wrote it beyond the compass of the American throat." Although during 1900 Richardson had in effect suggested that Prime's dogmatism about flag design flew in the face of reason, now Prime successfully argued against DuBois's position because, although "I honor the 'Star Spangled Banner,' ... I do think we ought to have a little common sense."[61]

Prime and the AFA were unquestionably the most prominent advocates for the flag protection movement between its founding in 1898 and about 1908 (although perhaps tied with Miller during his intense pamphleteering of 1898–1902). However, thereafter Prime's energies, which were virtually synonymous with those of the AFA, seem to have gradually declined, although the organization seems to have marginally survived his death in 1920. No doubt Prime's declining energies partly reflected his advancing age (he was seventy years old in 1910) and also perhaps his increasing interest in foreign travel (Prime's biographical sketch in *Who Was Who in America*, published after his death but certainly based on information he had supplied, noted that he had "crossed ocean 36 times," while a 1902 SAR sketch reported twelve such trips, suggesting at least annual trips between 1902 and 1920, one of which even led him to miss the 1907 AFA annual meeting). Even more significant in likely explaining Prime's declining energies with regard to the AFA was the fact that by 1905 the vast majority of states had passed flag desecration laws, while, as pointed out later, following the Supreme Court's decision in the 1907 *Halter* case Prime essentially lost interest in the flag protection movement's original goal of a federal law, therefore leaving him and the AFA with little to do (and probably also leading him to leave the national SAR Flag Committee chairmanship in 1908). At any rate, although Prime and AFA-supplied materials dominated a 1902 SMAC hearing and the committee's subsequent report of 1904, at Congressional hearings held in 1908 and thereafter on flag protection legislation no AFA spokesman appeared. Between 1900 and 1908 the AFA published a report every two years, but its next report did not appear until 1913, one year after a disastrous fire destroyed its office and records. Thereafter, the organization appears to have lost its significance entirely, although a *New York Times* article from 1923 indicates the AFA was still holding its annual meetings on June 14 at the New York City Hall.[62]

The original purpose of the flag protection movement was to obtain passage of a federal flag desecration law. In pursuit of this objective, the movement focused primarily on attempting to influence public opinion in general, through the publication of pamphlets and reports, and to influence key opinion leaders, in particular newspapers, prominent persons, and, above all, Congressmen, through letters, petitions, and personal contacts. Many of the movement's publications were distributed widely and at least in some cases received extensive publicity, making Miller, for example, something of a local celebrity in Chicago. For example, 3,000 copies of the first major publication of the flag protection movement, the Illinois SCW's 1895 pamphlet "The Misuse of the National Flag," were circulated, with copies sent to all Congressmen; all Supreme Court justices; President McKinley and his entire cabinet; all governors; the mayors, libraries, and postmasters of all major citics; editors of leading papers and magazines throughout the country; all major college presidents; and numerous clergymen, military officials, and patriotic and veterans groups. The Milwaukee DAR chapter circulated 2,700 copies of an 1897 circular, and the distribution list increased to 20,000 for Miller's 1898 pamphlet "Desecration of the American Flag and Prohibitive Legislation."[63]

These publications were supplemented by extensive personal correspondence and contacts and appear to have been highly successful in enlisting widespread endorsements by newspapers and prominent persons. Congressional archives for the 1898–1902 period, in particular, reveal frequent correspondence from Miller and Kempster to key members of Congress, and this correspondence and other references in various publications of the flag protection movement suggest at least a fair amount of personal lobbying with Congressmen. For example, Miller's correspondence indicates that he traveled from Chicago to Washington in early 1899 and spoke to a "number of gentlemen of prominence" about the flag protection cause; Prime's reports to the SAR indicate lobbying visits to Washington in 1898, 1899 and 1900, during which he conferred with a number of key Congressmen, including House

Speaker Thomas Reed and members of the Senate Judiciary Committee (SJC), including Chairman George Hoar; and in her 1899 report to the Milwaukee DAR, Kempster stated that after the annual DAR meeting of that year, held in Washington, she "called upon several members of Congress, and upon Senator Hoar, to learn their attitudes towards our bill." Published hearings on flag desecration were conducted by the SMAC in 1902 and 1908, and by the HJC in 1913, 1915, 1918, 1927, and 1928. In addition, according to various publications of the flag protection movement, the HJC held additional, unpublished, hearings on a number of occasions, apparently in 1898, 1904, 1909, 1910, and 1912.[64]

The Flag Protection Movement in Congress and State Legislatures

Although no national flag desecration law resulted from the early flag protection movement—the first such measure passed only in 1968 during the Vietnam-era flag desecration controversy—bills did pass one house of Congress, although not both, on nine different occasions between 1890 and 1943. Such bills passed the House of Representatives in 1890, 1928, and 1930; the Senate passed flag desecration legislation in 1908, 1913, 1914, 1918, 1941, and 1943. Although failing in its original primary goal of obtaining federal flag desecration legislation, the flag protection movement did obtain some minor victories at the federal level: in September 1899, Army Inspector Gen. Joseph C. Breckinridge, who was himself a member of the AFA Executive Committee, forbade the formerly authorized military unit practice of inscribing the name of battles it had participated in on the stripes of the flag; in 1903, the U.S. Commissioner of Patents, who was also the president of the Washington, D.C. SAR, adopted a new policy of refusing to register as trademarks any materials that made use of the flag, a regulation that Congress endorsed by law in 1905; and, shortly before American entry into World War I, Congress outlawed flag desecration in Washington, D.C., where Congress was the local governing authority. Two additional federal flag desecration measures were in effect during World War I only: in May 1918 Congress decreed the firing of any federal employee who criticized the flag in an abusive or violent manner and criminalized such behavior for all Americans, by outlawing all "disloyal, profane, scurrilous, or abusive language" about the "flag of the United States," the "form of government" of the country, the military and even military uniforms, as well as any language intended to bring such matters into "contempt, scorn, contumely or disrepute."[65]

While the flag protection movement failed to obtain its principal original goal of federal legislation, the number of Congressional hearings held on the issue, together with the numerous partial legislative successes and the minor victories noted above, suggest that the flag protection movement did have a significant impact on American politics, especially during the 1895–1918 period. This impact is particularly remarkable given the limited financial resources of the movement. In what is surely a commentary above all on the drastically lower printing and postal costs at the turn of the century, the total reported yearly expenditures by the DAR national flag committee were $38.59 in 1898–99, $17.33 in 1899–1900, and $11.94 in 1900–01. The AFA's total yearly expenditures seem profligate by comparison, ranging from $100 to $400.[66]

The failure of the flag protection movement to immediately obtain national legislation in the late 1890s quickly led its leadership to seek state flag desecration laws as a temporary alternative. In this goal the movement was spectacularly and ultimately completely successful, with thirty-one states (including New Mexico and Arizona territories, which became states in 1912) passing such laws during the early burst of movement activity between 1897 and 1905; all but three of the remaining states followed suit by 1920 and the last state fell into line by 1932. The first states to act during the 1897–1905 rush to passage were Illinois, Pennsylvania, and South Dakota in 1897, followed by two additional states in 1898 (New Hampshire and Vermont), five more in 1899 (California, Massachusetts, Minnesota, Arizona territory, and New York), one in 1900 (Iowa), a peak of six states in 1901 (Colorado, Indiana, Michigan, North Dakota, Oregon, and Wisconsin), four in 1902 (Connecticut, Maryland, Ohio, and Rhode Island), five in 1903 (Delaware, Maine, Missouri, New Mexico territory, and Utah) and five in 1905 (Idaho, Montana, Kansas, Nebraska, and Wyoming). Half of the laggards were southern states which acted under the combined impetus of fear and patriotism associated with the pre-World War I and World War I period and the postwar Red Scare; thus eight southern states passed flag protection laws between 1915 and 1919 (Alabama in 1915, Mississippi and South Carolina in 1916, Georgia, North Carolina, and Texas in 1917, and Arkansas and Florida in 1919). Other laggard states falling outside this pattern included Washington (1909), Louisiana (1912), West Virginia (1917), Oklahoma (1919), Nevada (1919), Tennessee (1923), Kentucky (1930), and Virginia (1932).[67]

In general, where flag desecration legislation succeeded in being reported out of state legislative committees, it usually passed within a short period, often less than a month, after it was first introduced. Typically such legislation was approved rapidly, or even completely without debate, on the legislative floor by overwhelmingly or, usually, unanimous votes. For example, in Vermont a flag legislation bill was introduced in the state senate on October 17, 1898, passed both legislative houses, and was signed into law by November 11 of that year; in Illinois a bill introduced in the House of Representatives on March 23, 1899, passed the House by a vote of 87–0 on April 4 and passed the state Senate by a vote of 44–0 on April 14; and in Minnesota a measure introduced on March 11, 1899, in the House passed that body by 71–0 on March 23 and passed the Senate by 41–0 on April 6. Where legislative votes were recorded, any voices at all in opposition were quite unusual; a survey of sixteen such votes reveals a grand total of three opposition votes, compared to almost one thousand in favor.[68]

The pattern of passage (or nonpassage) of flag protection legislation in state legislatures appears to have especially reflected two factors: on the positive side, state legislatures were especially prone to pass such measures where the flag protection movement had influential people "on the ground" who were willing to seriously lobby for bills; on the negative side, it is clear that, primarily for historical reasons associated with the Civil War, there was considerably less enthusiasm for all issues related to the American flag in the former Confederate states than elsewhere in the nation and that this factor blocked state legislation until southern states felt bound to the rest of the country by the threat of common enemies abroad and at home (due to the threat and outbreak of war during the 1914–18 period and the perceived threat of domestic radicals during the 1919 Red Scare).

The key role played by influential movement members in obtaining state legislative passage of flag desecration legislation was repeatedly cited by movement leaders. For example, in his 1902 report to the AFA, President Prime attributed passage of state legislation in Rhode Island to the efforts of AFA Vice-President Mrs. Charles W. Lippett, who was also Rhode Island state DAR regent and "the wife of one who had been the honored Governor of that state"; credit for success in Maryland was given to Edwin Warfield, the state SAR president who "gave personal attention and went to Annapolis and to the legislature." On the other hand, Prime told the AFA in 1903, failures resulted when flag desecration legislation "was not diligently, persistently and continuously attended to on the ground." He similarly told the SAR in 1904 that "it is exceedingly difficult for us who reside so far away to do this work alone" as there "must be on the ground earnest, zealous, painstaking and determined men who will take it up and push it in their respective localities."[69]

Prime repeatedly professed puzzlement over the South's embarrassingly obvious lack of early interest in the flag protection movement, telling the AFA in 1904, for example, that although an ocean-to-ocean "continuous and unbroken chain" of northern states had passed flag protection laws, none of the "so-called southern states" had entered the "patriotic column." Despite intense AFA efforts, he reported "none of them have listened to our appeal" and the AFA had not "succeeded in making an impression" even though "there is nothing political in the question and nothing sectional." Reporting to the SAR in 1901 on the failure to gain a flag desecration law in Texas, Prime lamented that "for some reason a suspicion appears to exist lest underneath this noble and patriotic purpose there should be underlying some vice." He told the AFA in 1907 that the South's failure to swing into line was not "due to any disloyalty," but resulted from "some other failing, which it is impossible to understand." Not only did the southern states consistently fail to pass flag desecration laws despite repeated AFA lobbying (until Louisiana succumbed in 1912), but not a single one of the AFA's twenty elected officers in 1913 lived in the South, and only two of the AFA's additional fifty executive committee members lived in former Confederate states. Of the almost sixty identifiable geographically based AFA affiliate organizations listed in 1913, only one, the Virginia SAR chapter, was located in a former Confederate state.[70]

There is plenty of additional corroborating evidence, not directly linked to the flag desecration issue, which suggests a general lack of southern interest in all issues related to the American flag around the turn of the century. For example, a report published in 1896 by the Connecticut SAR noted that the American flag was generally exhibited "throughout most of the northern states" but that "measures should be taken to secure a similar display in the southern states"; it added, reporting on the campaign backed by patriotic and Union veterans groups to require that all public schools fly the American flag, that "nearly every one of the northern states have passed such laws," leaving the obvious conclusion that southern states had not. Similarly, according to a historian of the GAR, its auxiliary Woman's Relief Corps was frustrated in its 1890s campaign to provide flags and promote flag rituals in the public schools "only by the complete indifference of southerners to its efforts." The passage by most southern states of flag desecration legislation after 1912 suggests that southern attitudes towards the American flag gradually changed as World War I approached; thus in 1907 the GAR's national patriotic instructor told the annual national encampment that the long-standing GAR campaign to have the states recognize June 14 as Flag Day was "beginning to find recognition in the south," although the general practice of displaying flags in schoolrooms was still reported everywhere "with the exception of those in the south."[71]

Although Prime expressed great puzzlement over the early southern failure to endorse the flag protection movement, the southern histori-

cal experience involving both the American flag and past northern disdain for the Confederate flag unquestionably explains this phenomenon. In short, the relative lack of enthusiasm in former Confederate
states for American flag protection legislation reflected the continuing,
strong influence of the Civil War during the pre-World War I period. For
many southerners, the American flag represented not freedom, independence, and political liberty, but oppression, occupation, and political manipulation. Many southerners had not only witnessed Union occupation troops flying the flag, but had also seen flag waving used,
along with "waving the bloody shirt," to repeatedly accuse the South of
treason during the post-Civil War period. As Scot Guenter, the leading
historian of the cultural and political uses of the flag in the nineteenth
century, writes, "The flag came to be included in the fiery rhetoric of
Republican politicians, who combined praise of the flag with 'waving of
the bloody shirt' as, in the decades following the war, they drummed up
memories of the conflict to humiliate Democratic opponents" and to
connect them "to treasonous action or support whenever possible."[72]

The general disinclination of southerners to support legislation con-
secrating the American flag could only have been increased by the major role played by Union veterans in the flag protection movement, especially because Union veterans organizations had bitterly attacked
post-Civil War southern efforts to honor the Confederate flag. As previously noted, both Reade and Prime had served in the Union cause, and
many others involved in the flag protection movement had also fought
against the South, including, on the AFA Executive Committee, Army
Inspector Gen. Joseph C. Breckinridge (not to be confused with former
vice-president and Confederate Gen. John C. Breckinridge); Maj. J.
Langdon Ward, who also headed the Flag Committee of the Loyal Legion, an organization of former Union officers; Rear Adm. Winfield
Schley; Col. Thomas Anderson; Maj. A. Noel Blakeman; and Gen.
Thomas Wilson. A very considerable part of the flag protection movement, including two of the most important four groups in the coalition
(the GAR and the Loyal Legion), consisted of Union veterans organizations; in 1906, over twenty of the approximately eighty-five AFA affili-
ates were either GAR or Loyal Legion chapters. By contrast, not a single
Confederate veterans organization was affiliated with the AFA.[73]

Union veterans and their organizations bitterly fought against any efforts to render homage to the Confederate flag during the late nineteenth century, a fact that legislators from the former Confederate
states undoubtedly still remembered during the early period of the flag
protection movement. In one widely publicized incident that to some
extent dominated American political life in 1887, the GAR had successfully led a campaign to overturn an order approved by President
Cleveland to return captured Confederate Civil War battle flags that

were in War Department custody. Denouncing Cleveland's order as "sacrilege," GAR Commander-in-Chief Lucius Fairchild proclaimed, in a statement that became famous, "May God palsy the brain that conceived it, and may God palsy the tongue that dictated it." Due primarily to the GAR campaign, Cleveland reversed his order (the flags were later returned without controversy by a Republican-controlled Congress in 1905). In 1890, the annual GAR convention demanded a law forbidding display of the Confederate flag on the grounds that such was an "affront to patriotism" that "encourages disloyalty," and the following year GAR Commander-in-Chief John Palmer ordered GAR members to boycott all demonstrations in which the Confederate "emblem of treason" was exhibited. Significantly, when Mississippi and Alabama finally passed flag desecration laws, they applied to both the American and Confederate flags.[74]

The exact provisions of the various state desecration laws varied somewhat, particularly before the AFA published a model bill in 1900, which, as revised in 1902, became the basis for a Uniform Flag Law (UFL) recommended in 1917 by the National Conference of Commissioners on Uniform State Laws and endorsed in 1918 by the American Bar Association (see Appendix, Document 1). In general they outlawed three major types of activities: placing any kind of markings, lettering, or pictures on the flag, whether for commercial, political, or other purposes, or displaying, selling, or distributing such flags; using the flag or representations of the flag in any form of advertising, such as selling a product with a picture of the flag on it or on an attached label, or depicting the flag in an advertisement for a product; and publicly mutilating, trampling, defacing, defiling, "defying," or casting "contempt," either "by words or act," upon the flag (with the "by words" provision clearly amounting to a sedition or secular blasphemy provision). By 1920, most of the state laws followed the AFA and UFL models in defining the term "flag" in a extraordinarily broad way, so as to include any flag, standard, ensign, or color, or any representation of such "made of any substance whatever" and "of any size" that "evidently" purported to be either "of said flag, standard, color or ensign of the United States or a picture or a representation of either thereof, upon which shall be shown the colors, the stars and the stripes in any number in either thereof or by which the person seeing the same without deliberation may believe the same to represent the flag or the colors or the standard or the ensign of the United States of America." Most states followed the AFA model in exempting any flag usage authorized by the federal government or the military, as well as flag depictions in newspapers and other publications, ornamental pictures, and stationary "disconnected from any advertisement."[75]

Within these basic parameters, there were many variations from state to state, especially since the flag desecration laws were frequently amended in some states (New York's law was changed at least seven times between 1904 and 1930, for example), although some state laws remained unchanged for sixty years or more. A few states, for example, omitted one or more of the three major types of provisions cited above, and a handful exempted from all of their provisions many or all political or patriotic flag usages. For example, the 1899 Illinois law exempted any flags used in art exhibitions as well as for "patriotic purposes"; the 1899 New Hampshire Law exempted flags "displayed with names, symbols, pictures or mottoes representing political parties" or used by "societies of a religious or fraternal nature"; the 1899 Maine law exempted flags used by political parties during presidential elections; the 1901 Colorado law exempted flags used in connection with "patriotic celebrations" so long as political advertising was not involved; the 1907 Pennsylvania law did not apply to "any patriotic or political demonstration or decorations"; the California law, which as originally passed in 1899 only banned attaching material to the flag, by 1913 had been amended to also ban physical desecration and using the flag for advertising purposes, but exempted flags "used in theatrical performances, and those carried by political parties or organizations"; and the 1917 Georgia law exempted flags used for "decorative or patriotic purposes."[76]

Probably the most vague and sweeping laws were the 1899 Arizona territorial statute, which outlawed any use that might "show disrespect to the American flag," and the 1903 New Mexico territorial statute (still in effect during the Vietnam era), which banned use of the flag "for any other purposes than the purposes for which it was designed by the Congress" and required that the flag be "used and displayed only in a seemly and decorous manner." Some of the oddest language appeared in the Iowa law, in effect in 1924 and for fifty years thereafter, which forbade people to, among other things, "satirize, deride or burlesque" the flag, by "words or act." The 1901 South Dakota law was the only pre-Vietnam era law that specifically outlawed burning flags. Although most state flag desecration laws provided maximum penalties of 30 days in jail and a $100 fine, a few were considerably more harsh, such as the one-year maximums in the 1901 Colorado and 1902 Maryland laws. This was above all true of the Texas World War I statute, which provided for penalties of up to 25 years in jail and remained in effect until the Vietnam War era (in 1970 the law's application resulted in a four-year jail sentence for a teenager who burned a piece of flag-like bunting); it was finally replaced in 1973 by the law that was struck down by the Supreme Court in the 1989 *Texas v. Johnson* flagburning case.[77]

2

The Interpretation and Application of State Flag Desecration Laws, 1899–1964

ALTHOUGH THE FLAG PROTECTION movement was spectacularly successful in obtaining passage of state flag desecration laws, a series of court decisions between 1899 and 1904 that either struck such laws down as unconstitutional or effectively emasculated them soon threatened to negate this achievement. Almost all of these cases involved challenges brought by commercial interests alleging that their private property rights had been infringed. In general, the early court decisions, which appeared to strike a fatal blow to the flag protection movement, either upheld such claims or struck down the state laws or particular prosecutions on extremely narrow grounds. Free speech claims were, generally, neither raised by those who challenged the laws nor cited by the courts. No doubt this reflected the fact that the cases usually centered on commercial rather than political issues and that those who challenged the laws probably correctly perceived that the courts were much more likely to be favorable to the claims of businessmen than to those of political dissidents. In any case, during the era of the emergence of the flag protection movement, modern free speech arguments were in their infancy, and it was not until 1925 that the U.S. Supreme Court held that the First Amendment even applied to legislation passed by the states (as opposed to federal laws).

State Flag Desecration Laws in the Courts

The first two court rulings that struck down state flag desecration prosecutions both originated in cases arising in Chicago in 1899 involving

47

use of the flag for advertising. Although Chicago, the home of Charles Kingsbury Miller, had been the original center of the flag protection movement, the strict enforcement of the state law that went into effect there on July 1, 1899, appears to have caused a significant backlash. Thus, on October 20, 1899, the *Chicago Inter-Ocean* (which in its June 14, 1895, issue had been one of the first newspapers to endorse a bill to protect the flag, which it termed "our covenant with destiny" and "the most sacred of symbols," to be used "honorably and holily") published an extraordinary story under the headline, "Flag Law a Hardship." The story reported that Chicago had been "terrorized" by more than 1,000 flag desecration prosecutions in less than four months, that the law was "already regarded as one of the most odious that ever crept into the Illinois statute book," and that "there is not a person in Chicago who is safe" since pictures of the flag in one illegal form or another "are really omnipresent in business places and homes." The *Inter-Ocean* cited as especially odious a peculiar aspect of the Illinois law, which directed that half of any fine resulting from a flag desecration violation would go to the complaining party, a provision it noted was designed to "stimulate prosecutions" and that reportedly had led "dozens of men" to start "making lists" of potential violators and had enabled some of them to make "large sums of money by this practice, and as they prosecute none but the poor and helpless the amount of suffering inflicted is immense."

The first Chicago decision declaring the Illinois law unconstitutional was relatively inconsequential, as it was handed down by a local judge on November 4, 1899, on the narrow grounds that the informer's fee provision was in conflict with both general principles of American law, as tending to promote strife between men, and also with the specific constitutional pardon power of the Illinois governor to remit fines and penalties. However, Circuit Court Judge Gibbons also indicated his low general opinion of the law, on the grounds that using the flag for advertising and other purposes simply did not "desecrate" it. Referring to another recently enacted state law that concerned flags, he asked, "If the common use of the flag is to abate veneration for it, why did our Solons pass a law making it compulsory for those in charge to fly the National emblem from the flagstaff of every schoolhouse?" He added that no law was needed to "make men patriotic" or prevent desecration since "every man in all this land vies with his neighbor in showing devotion, loyalty and reverence to the flag, and it is a reflection upon the names of Illinois' patriot dead to have enacted such a law."[1]

The second case originating in Chicago in 1899 that struck down the Illinois law was far more significant, both because the decision was handed down by the Illinois Supreme Court (on April 17, 1900) rather than a local court and because the decision was based on sweeping grounds. The court held that, among its other faults, the statute effectively deprived citizens of their personal liberty rights, under both the Illinois and federal constitutions, to legitimately pursue their profession by the use of advertising, and also that it exceeded the state's police powers since it was unrelated to promoting the social health, safety, welfare, or comfort. This case, *Ruhstrat v. People*, originated with a Chicago court conviction and $10 fines levied against two cigar merchants who used pictures of the flag upon cigar-box labels to advertise their wares.

In overturning the convictions, the Illinois Supreme Court held that the personal liberties protections of both the state and federal constitutions included the right to pursue an occupation, which encompassed the right to advertise a business "in any legitimate manner," including the use of pictures. The decision also held that the general police power that enabled the state of Illinois to legislate only extended to laws whose enactment was demanded by threats to the "public health, comfort, safety or welfare," that no such situation compelled the passage of a flag desecration law since placing a picture of a flag upon an advertising label was "harmless," and that therefore the state legislature simply had no power to "arbitrarily invade the personal rights and personal liberty of the individual citizen." Noting that flags were traditionally used to protect "a ship and its cargo" on the high seas, the court declared that it was "difficult to see" why "it should be a desecration of the same flag to use a likeness of itself upon a label or trademark in the prosecution of domestic trade or business." The court further suggested that Illinois was invading federal powers, since Congress, which had "taken jurisdiction of the subject matter of a national flag" by regulating its design, had not sought to ban advertising use of the flag, and because the federal patent office had approved trademarks that included pictures of the flag. (In 1903, as noted earlier, this policy was reversed.) Finally, the court held that the provision of the law that exempted art exhibitions using the flag was an unconstitutional form of class favoritism.[2]

Three further, if relatively minor, decisions handed down in 1904 cast further doubt upon the viability of flag desecration laws. On July 30, a Boston municipal court judge effectively struck down the broad definition of "flag" used in most of the laws by throwing out a prosecution for selling an item with a flag-like pattern in which the distribution of stars and stripes differed from official flags, on the grounds that such did not constitute a U.S. flag. In Colorado, what appears to have been the first prosecution involving the use of the flag for political dissent was also thrown out, apparently on the grounds of discriminatory prosecution. The case arose during a bitter 1904 strike, when two leaders of the radical Western Federation of Miners (including "Big Bill" Haywood, who was later notorious as leader of the Industrial Workers of the World) were arrested for printing a flyer captioned "Is Colorado in America?" Against the backdrop of a drawing of an American flag, the flyer textually protested repression of the strike by martial law and arbitrary arrests. The charges were dropped after Haywood produced in court scores of unprosecuted advertisements and circulars bearing the flag.[3]

In a third 1904 decision, in a case involving advertisements for cigars, the highest court in New York, the Court of Appeals, held unconstitutional a portion of that state's flag desecration law on the narrow ground that, by retroactively outlawing previously existing manufactured items bearing flag advertisements, the legislature exceeded its power by destroying "existing property rights." This decision, which was quickly remedied by a new New York law that only applied to goods manufactured after its passage, was not only extremely technical and limited in scope, but essentially overturned a far more sweeping lower court decision by the New York Appellate Division. The Appellate court had essentially adopted the position of the Illinois Supreme Court in the *Ruhstrat* case, holding that the advertising provision of the New York law banning the use of pictures of the flag "in no way relates to any one of the legitimate subjects to which the police power of the State extends," in that nothing about advertising involving the flag in any way degraded the emblem, and also that the law's exclusion of publishers, stationers, and jewelers was unconstitutional class favoritism. On the other hand, the Appellate decision had explicitly affirmed the legitimacy of the provisions involving physical flag desecration, including printing an advertisement upon, and therefore mutilating, the flag.[4]

By 1905, the collective result of these court decisions (especially the 1900 Illinois *Ruhstrat* case), verged on flushing the flag protection movement and its laws down the legal drain. However, in that year, the legal situation was suddenly turned around by a Nebraska Supreme Court decision, which was in turn upheld two years later by a U.S. Supreme Court ruling in *Halter v. Nebraska*, which seemingly definitively established the constitutionality of flag desecration laws. The *Halter* case involved convictions and $50 fines against two businessmen accused of selling a bottle of "Stars and Stripes" brand beer, upon which, in the words of the Nebraska indictment, "was attached and placed a label upon which was printed and painted a representation of the flag of the United States of America, to advertise, call attention to, decorate, mark and distinguish" the beer, in violation of the Nebraska state law and "against the peace and dignity of the state of Nebraska."[5]

The case was argued in both the Nebraska Supreme Court and U.S. Supreme Court almost exclusively on the question of whether or not Nebraska could legitimately regulate Halter's property rights under the general police power to safeguard public safety and welfare. Thus, Halter's attorneys argued in their U.S. Supreme Court brief that the Nebraska law unlawfully interfered with his rights to "pursue a lawful avocation in a lawful way without interference by the state," in particular by using the "flag in a respectful way in their said business for advertising purposes," and deprived him of the right to "earn a livelihood in the pursuit of a lawful and harmless occupation" and of his "inalienable" right to "pursue a lawful avocation in a lawful way without interference by the state."[6]

Halter's lawyers challenged the arguments that using the flag for advertising purposes either displayed contempt for the flag or threatened the public peace or any other valid state interest. Noting that American ships transporting goods for sales abroad flew under the American flag, they asked, "If the goods and wares beneath the folds of the flag cast no discredit upon it, what is there about a cut or picture of the flag painted or printed on such goods that would make the average American citizen bow his head in shame?" The lack of any threat to the peace posed by advertising use of the flag was demonstrated every day, they maintained, because "every merchant and druggist, every liquor and cigar dealer in Nebraska, sells goods over his counter without any disturbance every day in the year, in open violation of the law, and if there was any merit or truth in the contention that such use of the flag pro vokes breaches of the peace, the streets of our cities and towns would run red with blood."

Indeed, according to Halter's brief, the use of the flag had become as "much a part of our every day life as the air we breathe or the food we eat" and to forbid advertising use would therefore be "about on a par with a law enjoining the people from making any quotation from the Declaration of Independence or the Constitution of the United States for advertising purposes." In what amounted to a summary of their argument, Halter's lawyers asked, "How does a picture of the national flag on a bottle of beer, a box of cigars or any article of merchandise affect, directly or indirectly, for better or worse, the public health or the public welfare?" Halter's attorneys also argued that the American flag was a federal creation whose use could not be proscribed by the states and that the Nebraska law, by exempting the depiction of the flag, disconnected from advertising, by books and newspapers, amounted to discriminatory class legislation.

In response to Halter's arguments, Nebraska maintained that the use of the flag for advertising beer was an insult to the patriotic values of citizens and a provocation to a breach of the peace, and that its interests in protecting the public from such displays was a valid interest within the police powers of the state and as "legitimate a subject of legislation as property rights." In an argument remarkably similar to that made by the state of Texas before the U.S. Supreme Court eighty years later in the *Johnson* case, Nebraska declared that the state not only had the right to protect life and property per se but could also impose "penalties upon those who do not observe a decent respect for the patriotic, moral and religious sentiments and feelings of others." This interest fully justified banning advertising use of the flag, Nebraska argued, particularly because "patriotic sentiment for the flag and for the noble institutions it symbolizes is outraged by the appearance of the national emblem on a bottle of beer" and because such usage was bound to "incite indignant citizens to commit a breach of the peace" against the offender, especially as no soldier who had "fought for the flag and followed it for years" could pass a beer sign emblazoned with the flag "without an impulse to smash the sign." In short, Nebraska maintained, "Liberty must have gone to seed if there is now no power in the state to enforce a decent respect for the opinions of these patriotic citizens who believe that a beer sign is not a proper place to emblazon the stars and stripes."[7]

Nebraska's arguments were completely accepted and those of Halter were completely rejected in both the Nebraska and U.S. Supreme Courts. Furthermore, although the case involved only the advertising and not the physical desecration portion of the Nebraska law (and, as pointed out earlier, involved no claim of free speech), both courts clearly indicated in their decisions that any challenge to the physical desecration provisions would also have failed. Thus, the Nebraska Supreme Court, in explicitly rejecting the argument that no legitimate government purpose was served by flag desecration laws, declared that:

> Patriotism has ever been regarded as the highest civic virtue, and whatever tends to foster this virtue certainly makes for the common good. ... That contempt or disrespect for an emblem begets a like state of mind towards that for which it stands is a psychological law ... [which underlies] inhibitions against the irreverent use of sacred things [in religious practices and] may be justified [here] on the same principle. The flag is the emblem of national authority. To the citizen it is an object of patriotic adoration, emblematic of all for which his country stands ... and it is not fitting that it should become associated in his mind with anything less exalted, nor that it should be put to any mean or ignoble use. ... [The Nebraska law] is not only a valid piece of legislation, but one well-calculated to promote the common weal.

The Nebraska court also rejected the arguments of Halter and of the *Ruhstrat* court that the failure of Congress to ban flag desecration limited state action in this area and that the exclusion of some types of flag usage from the coverage of the law amounted to class discrimination, since "it is a matter of common knowledge that the use of the flag for advertising purposes offends the sensibilities of a large portion of our people," while the excluded acts, such as depictions of the flag in newspapers and on pieces of jewelry "disconnected from any advertisement" were "uses to which the most sensitive could not object."[8]

On March 4, 1907, the U.S. Supreme Court upheld the position of the Nebraska high court by an 8–1 vote. The Supreme Court's *Halter* decision was filled with patriotic oratory similar to that of the Nebraska court, and in effect provided an extraordinary official definition of how "true" Americans should feel about their flag:

> For that flag every true American has not simply an appreciation but a deep affection. No American, nor any foreign born citizen who enjoys the privileges of American citizenship, ever looks upon it without taking pride in the fact that he lives under this free government. Hence, it has often occurred that insults to a flag have been the cause of war, and indignities put upon it, in the presence of those who revere it, have often been resented and sometimes punished on the spot. ... [T]o every true American, the flag is the symbol of the Nation's power, the emblem of freedom in its truest, best sense. ... [T]o all lovers of the country it signifies government resting on the consent of the government, liberty regulated by law; the protection of the weak against the strong; security against the exercise of arbitrary power; and absolute safety for free institutions against foreign aggression.

The Court declared that Nebraska's exclusion of certain types of flag usages from the law's coverage were not "unreasonable or arbitrary." It also specifically rejected the claim that protection of the flag was a subject "exclusively" controlled by the federal government, instead declaring:

> [A] State may exert its power to strengthen the bonds of the Union and therefore, to that end, may encourage patriotism and love of country among its people. ... [L]ove both of the common country and of the State will diminish in proportion as respect for the flag is weakened. ... [Advertising usage of the flag] tends to degrade and cheapen the flag in the estimation of the people, as well as to defeat the object of maintaining it as an emblem of national power and honor. And we cannot hold that any privilege of American citizenship or that any right of personal liberty [or property] is violated by ... forbidding the flag to be used as an advertisement on a bottle of beer. ... As the statute in question had its origin in a purpose to cultivate a feeling of patriotism among the people of Nebraska, we are unwilling to adjudge that ... the State erred in its duty or has infringed the constitu-

tional right of anyone. On the contrary, it may reasonably be affirmed that a duty rests upon each State in every legal way to encourage its people to love the Union with which the State is indissolubly connected. ... It would be going very far to say that the statute in question has no reasonable connection with the common good and was not promotive of the peace, order and well-being of the people.[9]

The Failure of Federal Flag Desecration Legislation

Because *Halter* was the last Supreme Court decision squarely and explicitly expounding general principles relevant to the constitutionality of flag desecration legislation until the 1989 *Texas v. Johnson* flag burning case, it was repeatedly cited in many of the flag desecration cases that led to convictions between 1907 and 1989 (and was cited by Chief Justice Rehnquist in his dissent in *Johnson*). But while the *Halter* decision seemingly settled the question of the constitutionality of state flag desecration laws, at least for the following eighty years, it did nothing to remedy the flag protection movement's failure to obtain federal flag desecration legislation. This failure was to become a continuing and major sore point with the movement, one that was especially painful during the 1895–1910 period of the movement's greatest intensity and continued to nag with a gradually lessening importance until such a law was finally enacted during the Vietnam era flag desecration controversy.

The movement's failure to obtain a federal flag desecration law was particularly frustrating because between 1895 and 1910 its spokesmen repeatedly predicted imminent Congressional passage of such a law or, at the least, strong hopes for such. Thus, in her 1899 report to the Milwaukee DAR, Kempster reported, "I feel sure that the time is not far off" when a federal law would be enacted. In his 1902 report to the SAR, Prime declared the 1902 SMAC hearing had been "most satisfactory," with the "most pleasant assurances of action given," and indicated that "we are yet hoping" a law would be passed before that year's Congressional adjournment. Miller told the SAR Convention in 1904 that a federal measure "will likely be made into a law at the next [Congressional] session." And DAR Flag Chairwoman Dickinson told her 1912 convention that "we are nearer a federal flag law than ever before."

Dickinson's frustration at the continued Congressional failure to act was clearly reflected in her increasingly bitter rhetoric: She declared in 1912 that although she was "in no sense a suffragist," any "reflecting woman can but feel that it is because we are women and have not votes that we are put aside by fair promises like little children," and in 1913 she predicted success if the "noble law givers will condescend to consider a proposal from us poor deluded supplicants."[10]

The frustration of the flag protection movement's leaders—as their yearly predictions of Congressional approval were repeatedly deflated—was only increased by the contrast with their continuing overwhelming and ultimately complete success in the states, a contrast they found largely inexplicable and which remains somewhat puzzling today. Thus, in 1907 Prime told the AFA that it was "impossible to understand" why federal flag desecration legislation did not have "as friends every senator and member of Congress," and flag historian Peleg Harrison wrote in a 1906 book that "no good reason why it [a federal flag desecration law] has not been enacted can be given." Harrison expressed especial amazement at this failure because allegedly "no other national government allows its flag to be used for advertising purposes, or other improper uses," a claim movement leaders such as Miller and Prime also frequently made, but also a claim that seems to have considerably exaggerated the international prevalence of flag desecration laws. Thus, in 1900 Miller published a pamphlet entitled "The Crime of a Century: Desecration of the American Flag—The United States the Only Nation on Earth Permitting the Degradation of Her Flag." However, upon close examination, although some countries, such as Russia, Spain, and Italy, were cited as having specific bans on flag desecration, with penalties reportedly ranging up to 19 years in prison in Russia, many—indeed apparently most—countries were reported to have "no special legal provision," but allegedly could bring action against flag desecrators "under a general provision" of their laws.[11]

When leaders of the flag protection movement attempted to pinpoint the reasons for their failure at the federal level they generally focussed on several factors that probably did help block Congressional legislation but are almost certainly not the entire explanation: resistance from commercial and political interests who wished to continue to use the flag for their own purposes, resistance from key Congressional leaders, and divisions within the flag protection movement itself. Among the most common villains targeted for blame by the flag protection movement were advertisers and, to a slightly lesser extent, politicians, both of whom allegedly simply wanted to continue to exploit the flag for private gain. Thus, in the 1895 pamphlet that signaled the start of the flag protection movement, the authors declared that "aside from the bill poster agents and the parties who use the national flag as a trademark or label, we do not know of any active opposition." AFA President Prime, in his report to the 1902 SAR convention, focused on commercial opposition to flag desecration laws, attacking those who "love the dollar more than the land that gives them birth and sustains them" and those who had been able to "obscure and crush and strangle all that is virtuous and good and patriotic and loyal" thus defeating "in our legislative halls our brethren and compatriots who never succumbed to defeat in the battles of our country."[12]

In fact, unquestionably some of the opposition to advertising use of the flag, although often cloaked in patriotic language, was influenced by commercial considerations. Certainly it was no coincidence that most early challenges to flag desecration laws came from merchants who wanted to use the flag to advertise such items as cigars and beer. Other evidence of commercially motivated opposition to flag desecration laws can be found in Congressional debates and archives. For example, in opposing the advertising provisions of a flag desecration bill on the House floor in 1930, Congressman Ogden Reid of Illinois protested that the proposed legislation would even ban depicting the flag on calendars. He proclaimed, "We learned more about the flag than we would otherwise know from calendars and almanacs hung up in the old times in the stores and schools than by any other means." No doubt just as important a factor in his position, however, was his avowal, "These calendars are made in Joliet, in my district." An Iowa manufacturer similarly protested against proposed flag desecration legislation in 1941, writing to Vice-President Henry Wallace, a native Iowan, that the measure would be "extremely dangerous" as it would make it "even more difficult to inculcate the principles of patriotism and the veneration for the American form of government"—such as those the company had promoted in the past by publishing commercially sponsored "beautiful calendars in colors sometimes carrying the American flag," often in the context of depicting "fine works of art dealing with historical subjects."[13]

In addition to such evidence suggesting commercial opposition to flag desecration legislation, there is also evidence that the desire of politicians to continue to literally wrap themselves in flags played a role in the failure of federal legislation. For example, Republican SJC Chairman George Hoar, whose key position made him a crucial player in Congressional consideration of the issue, was quoted in a report issued in 1896 by the Connecticut SAR as having qualms on these grounds. Allegedly, Hoar stated that he had originally taken up the flag desecration issue "with a very earnest desire for some legislation," but as consideration of the issue progressed "the difficulties multiplied" and, in particular, he became "afraid that the great political parties of the country would not consent that the practice of hanging out the Flag with the names of the candidates attached should be abandoned." Two 1897 newspapers stressed such political motivations as likely to block federal legislation, arguing that the Republicans' use of the flag during the 1896 election demonstrated such efforts would be futile due to politicians' vested interest in using the symbol for self-advancement. The *Springfield (Mass.) Republican* suggested that there was little hope for banning the "prostitution of the flag to advertising purposes" so long as "a leading political party asserts an exclusive right to the flag to advertise itself during warm political campaigns," and the *Albany Argus* made a similar argument by referring to the recent parading of the flag as a "party device" by an American political party, "the one which claims a monopoly of patriotism and a sort of divine right to the flag."[14]

While the evidence clearly supports, at least to some extent, the contention of flag protection movement spokesmen that selfishly motivated commercial and political interests were blocking the passage of federal legislation, the failure of such interests to simultaneously block state laws suggests that other factors were involved at the Congressional level. One such factor, which flag movement leaders also focused attention on, was the often unexplained opposition of key committees and figures in Congress, that apparently resulted in the frequent failures of the House and Senate judiciary committees to report out flag desecration laws. Movement leaders unceasingly attacked the inaction of these committees, with key figures such as SJC chairman Hoar and Representative David B. Henderson, chairman of the House Judiciary Committee in the 1890s and Speaker of the House in 1901–03, the particular subjects of their wrath.

Kempster and Prime repeatedly criticized, in general terms, the failure of the judiciary committees to report out flag desecration legislation and often referred, although in relatively mild terms, to Henderson's reported opposition. Thus, in his 1899 SAR report Prime complained that Congressional flag desecration bills constantly "slept in the pigeon holes of committees of both houses" and "were sleeping the sleep from which there was to be no awakening." Similarly, Kempster's 1902 report to her Milwaukee DAR chapter lamented that then-Speaker Henderson was "well known to be opposed to action upon a flag law." Miller however, made his criticisms of Hoar, and especially of Henderson, far more often, more venomous, and by name, and seems to have developed a particular hatred of Henderson that became so intense and so public that eventually Prime effectively read Miller out of the movement for his allegedly counterproductive excesses. Miller seems to have become especially embittered by a comment that he repeatedly attributed to (and which was apparently never disavowed by) Henderson. Henderson, who represented Iowa, a highly agricultural state, was alleged by another Congressmen to have said that he "hoped the American people would continue to wrap hams in the flag, not to

teach patriotism, but to teach ham eaters to eat American hams."
Miller repeatedly quoted this remark and publicly termed it the most
"basedly degrading insult that has ever been offered to our national emblem."[15]

In April 1899, Miller wrote in a magazine article that Henderson,
along with Hoar, had "apparently forgotten that they occupy their position to carry out the will of the people instead of imposing their will on
the people," thereby forcing supporters of flag protection to turn to the
states, "weary of waiting on these indifferent chairmen, at whom the
contemptuous finger of a nation's shame has been pointed." In private
correspondence to another HJC member in April 1899, Miller termed
Henderson's "non-action" concerning a "wholly patriotic" measure
"something extraordinary" and claimed that "we are being continually
asked whether Col. Henderson is a foreigner." This latter thought publicly surfaced in a statement by Miller published in the *Chicago Evening Post* of December 18, 1899, which referred to Henderson as a
"Scottish-American" whose "obstinate indifference" had led "thousands" to ask "what antipathy has he to the flag?" Henderson's opposition could not represent the "courage of his convictions," Miller
avowed, since "according to his past record, he can smother [these] at
convenience to gain his own end." In a December 1899 pamphlet,
Miller accused Henderson of "ignorance or willful misrepresentation"
concerning the flag desecration issue.[16]

Miller continued these attacks for five years, between 1898 and 1902,
while serving as an appointed AFA Executive Committee member, and
although he apparently privately printed his pamphlets, they presented
the appearance of official AFA publications because they listed information about the AFA and the names of AFA officers on their last page.
By June 1902, Prime apparently decided that Miller had gone too far and
bitterly attacked him in his annual AFA presidential address (without
mentioning Miller by name but in a completely unambiguous manner),
as acting in a way "most injurious to our cause," as it was the "very
height of folly to antagonize those who we should be winning [over]."
Prime specifically referred to, and "disowned" on behalf of the AFA, a
recent published attack upon "one of the officers of the national Congress" that gave the impression of having "emanated" from the AFA
and which was issued "in violation of an express promise of its writer to
cease all such attacks." Prime announced that the AFA Executive Committee had forbade the "offender" from implying any "connection with
this association in any publication of any kind without the authority"
of himself or the Executive Committee, and Miller subsequently
ceased serving as a member (although he published at least one more

pamphlet in December 1902 minus the previous last-page AFA-related information).

In his 1903 AFA address, Prime suggested that Henderson's apparent continued opposition to the flag desecration cause primarily resulted from his taking offense at Miller's attacks. Prime declared, "We have witnessed, unfortunately, violent and unjustifiable personal attacks upon the high officers of the Government because they did not respond to the demands for flag legislation" and suggested that they were "so violent" that "self-respect and personal honor" had led to continued resistance, since "yielding would logically involve a charge of downright cowardice."[17]

There is some corroborating evidence that Henderson did in fact take deep offense at Miller's assaults. For example, Henderson personally marked "not to be answered" on a letter from Miller, dated May 26, 1898, which enclosed some of Miller's relatively mild early published criticism of Henderson (without mentioning him by name) for leaving all flag protection bills "regularly entombed" in the HJC. Another highly suggestive bit of evidence concerning Henderson's apparent pique at Miller was an April 19, 1899 front-page newspaper article in Henderson's homestate *Marshalltown* (Iowa) *Times-Republican* that was almost certainly inspired by Henderson and whose general tone was captured by its headline: "The Miller Method—Something More About His Persistent Efforts to Discredit D. B. Henderson—The Facts and Miller's Alleged Misstatements—How They Compare." The key sentence in the article flatly declared that "Miller was too intent upon destroying Col. Henderson" to "bother about facts that get in his way."[18]

While the dispute between Miller and Prime appears to have been the most bitter between leaders of the flag protection movement, minor squabbles between leaders and key organizations in the movement were endemic and were frequently cited by movement leaders as a major obstacle to their success at the federal level. Thus, Prime told the AFA in 1899 that the greatest single reason explaining the movement's failure at the federal level was "division among ourselves," as each flag committee "has attempted to work by itself, has made a fad of the particular form of words" in proposed legislation. Although the main task of the AFA was supposedly to coordinate the efforts of the flag protection movement, three years later Prime was still making the same complaint, namely that "every flag committee" had "some bill of its own" and insisted upon finding "in their particular bill the exact thing to be desired and will have [it] at all hazards or none at all."

In 1913, SAR Flag Chairman W. V. Cox continued to make the same complaint, declaring that a federal bill might be enacted if members of

the movement would "agree on some flag bill and work for its enactment instead of self-exploitation." In 1915, the SAR convention, in an
attempt to resolve this problem, endorsed a proposal previously approved that year by the DAR Flag Committee to have delegates from
the SAR, DAR, AFA, and representatives of other patriotic organizations interested in flag protection meet for the purpose of coordinating
their activities—which, of course, was precisely the reason the AFA
had been created almost twenty years earlier![19]

The constant disputes within the flag protection movement were
probably mostly the result of ego and turf battles between contending
leaders. For example, in 1899 Prime told the AFA convention that the
AFA was the "first ever" organization to unify the flag protection
movement and in 1903 he (clearly incorrectly) told the SAR convention
that the "first committee" in the "campaign in the defense of the
American flag against desecration" was appointed by the New York
SAR (in 1897). Meanwhile, in 1902 Miller (more accurately) proclaimed
that Illinois was the "first state in which the movement started [in
1895]," and in 1903 Kempster declared that it was the DAR that had
made the "first ever" appeal for an "adequate" flag protection bill.

Apparently referring to Miller, in 1903 Prime denounced those who
"take to themselves the credit of having procured legislation which
they have had nothing whatever to do with," citing in particular a
"merchant of patriotic articles." In 1904, Prime, who repeatedly
claimed credit for the AFA and himself for the flag movement's
successes, told the AFA of his regrets that there were "so many" in the
movement who were "far more anxious to be acknowledged to be the
first in this good work than to be very influential and potent" and declared that the "strife in such patriotic matter to be first, and to put the
personal pronoun I above everything else, is quite as lamentable as the
commercialism which desecrates the flag is lamentable." (At the end of
his 1904 speech, Prime used the "personal pronoun" a dozen times in a
single paragraph, declaring, quite truthfully, that the "mass" of the
AFA's work had "fallen upon me," taking "much of my time, much labor, a great deal of thought, and an enormous amount of correspondence," and giving himself the self-evaluation that "you have trusted
me implicitly, and I have not given you reason for disappointment.")[20]

On the surface, at least, the primary bone of contention during the
early years of the flag protection movement centered, as some of
Prime's statements quoted above suggest, over the exact form of correc-
tive legislation. Between 1898 and 1900 the DAR favored a federal flag
desecration law considerably more comprehensive than that favored by
the AFA and other participants of the flag protection movement, but after 1900 the AFA essentially adopted the DAR bill (although in an even

stricter form). These differences were the occasion for constant bickering between advocates of the various proposals, both in public and private. Thus, in a February 15, 1898 letter to HJC Chairman Henderson, Miller referred to the DAR's proposal as "too drastic" and expressed the hope that the "almighty may bless these noble women in granting them a broad judgment to unite in the support of a bill that will pass, or, at least, stand a fair chance of it." DAR Flag Committee Chairwoman Kempster wrote Henderson five weeks later to declare that her organization was "not insisting upon any special pet measure," yet simultaneously maintained that the DAR proposal was the "only one" with adequate provisions.

After the AFA changed its position, it was now Prime who told a Congressional hearing in 1902 that the AFA had "no particular zeal for our special bill as opposed to other bills" but that all other proposals were "deficient." In the meantime, Kempster bitterly told the 1900 DAR convention that the DAR's "wisdom" had been "proven more quickly than seemed possible," but that in the past the DAR's bill had faced "great opposition and condemnation from fellow workers for a flag law," who had provided "antagonism where we should have had assistance" and had declared that the DAR was striving for "impossibilities and ruining all chances for any flag law." In 1902, Kempster virtually crowed to the DAR convention that the AFA, which had at first "refused" to support a comprehensive bill, "has now for two years urged and presented for adoption by the states a flag law practically the same as our own," and in 1903 she seemed to suggest that sexism helped to explain the AFA's original stand, declaring that at first "we were met at every step by criticisms from our fellow workers of the sterner sex."[21]

Although members of the flag protection movement largely blamed their own squabbling on well-meant, if egotistic, excesses, they blamed actual opposition to flag protection, as represented by Henderson and alleged selfish political and commercial interests, on a simple lack of patriotism. Thus, the authors of the 1895 pamphlet, clearly addressing government officials, declared, "Your action regarding a bill to protect the national flag from debasing uses is the criterion, the test, of your patriotism. We ask. What are you going to do about it?" In calling for flag desecration legislation in an 1899 petition to Congress, the San Francisco Chamber of Commerce declared that the flag "deserves and should receive the highest respect from all true Americans." Miller entitled his pamphlet of March 5, 1898, calling for such legislation, "An Appeal to Every American in Whose Heart There is One Spark of the Ennobling Fire of Patriotism." In 1899, Brig. Gen. Harrison Gray Otis, the reactionary, powerful editor of the *Los Angeles Times*, pronounced that the need for flag protection was "so obvious that the question is hardly susceptible of discussion," and former envoy to Ecuador and former GAR department commander Archibald Sampson declared that "it seems only a traitor" would oppose a flag desecration law and that it was "incredible" that any Congressman "should find any pretext" for such behavior. Opponents of flag protection would suffer from the "voice of the people" who would be heard "ere long at the polls," Miller warned in a letter to Senator Hoar.[22]

Flag protection movement leaders apparently failed to consider the possibility that federal legislation did not succeed not because of opposition from the unpatriotic, the disloyal, and traitors, or because of internal movement squabbling, but simply because, for a variety of reasons, intelligent people of good will simply may not have been enthusiastic about the idea. However, this explanation is probably the most accurate answer for what admittedly does remain a bit of a puzzle, given the rapid and overwhelming passage of such legislation by the states. The apparent lack of enthusiasm at the federal level reflected a variety of motivating factors, including perceptions that the entire issue was not a serious matter worthy of Congressional action; that political and advertising use of the flag did not in any way desecrate it but instead promoted patriotism; that treatment of the flag was a matter that should be left to personal tastes that should or could not be regulated; that the flag protection movement was making a fetish out of the flag and placing symbolic obeisance above real improvements in the country that would foster voluntary respect for the flag; that the issue was properly a matter of state jurisdiction; and, for southern Congressmen, the previously discussed resentment over what they viewed as past mistreatment of the Confederate flag and unhappy recollections of the Civil War.

There are a number of indications that, fundamentally, many Congressmen simply did not view the entire issue of flag desecration as a serious enough issue to require their attention. For example, in a pamphlet published on March 5, 1898, Miller reported receiving a recent letter from a Congressman who declared that "a part of the members of the Judiciary Committee seem to have an entire lack of appreciation of the importance of the subject, as well as the absence of that education which inculcates respect for our national emblem." Similarly, Prime, in his 1899 report to the SAR, stated that trips to Washington over "two successive winters" to lobby for flag desecration legislation had completely failed "to call to life measures which slept in the pigeon holes" of Congressional committees, and that the "contempt of some [Congressmen], and sometimes of those who had followed the Flag on the field of battle was most disheartening. It is not well to commit to writing words that have been spoken on the subject."[23]

One of the clearest indications that at least some Congressmen, as well as some state legislators and to some extent many members of the flag protection movement itself, did not conceive of flag desecration legislation as truly critical to the nation's vital interest is that movement spokesmen repeatedly noted, with apparent understanding, the failure of legislative bodies to expend significant effort on flag protection measures whenever what might be termed "truly important" matters arose. For example, given the supposed importance attributed to flag protection legislation by movement leaders and their supporters, especially from the standpoint of preserving and fostering national unity, it would seem to logically follow that the outbreak of the Spanish-American War would intensify their efforts and speed up legislative responses. In fact the result was exactly the opposite. Thus, Prime told the April 1898 SAR convention, held two months after the war began, that "our minds and hearts have been too full to plan or continue the pressure for this [flag desecration] legislation." Meanwhile the Loyal Legion's Flag Committee chairman reported, in October 1898, that "until the difficulty with Spain developed there seemed to be an excellent prospect of securing the desired action from Congress" but that when war became "imminent, it became equally plain that it would necessarily so engross the whole energies and attention of Congress that further present effort of the Committee to secure its action would be wasted."[24]

In 1903, Prime told the SAR that Congressional consideration of flag protection had been "crowded out" by the "great political questions," while Kempster told the 1907 DAR convention that she had been repeatedly assured by "those who should know" that Congressional sentiment was favorable to her cause, but that "the urgency of momentous legislation is always pushing out of sight the questions of less immediate need." In 1909, SAR Flag Committee Chairman Thomas Vincent reported receiving a letter from the House subcommittee chairman handling flag desecration legislation relating that his hopes for considering a flag bill had been preempted by "work upon the Army and West Point appropriation bills." In 1912 Prime told the AFA the problem was the "all engrossing tariff legislation and legislation having political significance."

The Depression and World War II apparently had similar effects upon flag desecration legislation; thus, the DAR's Flag Committee report for 1932 indicated that the HJC chairman had advised not pressing for flag protection since the "minds of the members of Congress are in such a state of unrest and the entire country so weather beaten" that the prospects would be poor. And in 1943 the SAR's Flag Committee reported that "the work of this committee has been curtailed considerably, due to the fact that so many members had assumed duties which seemed more important."

The (generally temporary) failure of state legislatures to act on flag protection measures was also often attributed to the time required for "more important" matters, including the virtual outbreak of civil war in Kentucky over a disputed 1899 gubernatorial election and various other state political squabbles such as a disputed senatorial election (at a time when state legislatures elected senators) in Nebraska in 1901 that, Prime told the SAR, had "eclipsed everything else."[25]

Undoubtedly one of the reasons why many Congressmen and many other Americans did not see the flag desecration issue in the same light as did the flag protection movement's leaders was that the use of the flag in advertising, the initial target of a movement that sought in other ways to increase the display of the flag, simply did not degrade the flag in their eyes and, if anything, promoted the same patriotism, which was the ostensible objective of the flag protectionists. Such sentiments were previously noted in the decision of the Chicago court in 1899, which denied that advertising use of the flag would "abate veneration" for it, especially since the Illinois legislature had recently required that all schoolhouses display the flag in the hope that "common use" of it would have the opposite effect, and in the comments attributed to Congressman Henderson that selling hams wrapped in the American flag would promote American commerce. Similarly, in opposing passage of a flag protection bill on the Senate floor in 1896, Senator George Gray of Delaware declared his disagreement with attempts to "curtail the circulation of the American flag," as "it ought to have as wide a circulation as possible and we ought to have American industries protected by the American flag."

Prime lamented to the SAR in 1897 that, even when confronted by children with flag advertisements on beer barrels, Senators had seen "no impropriety in it." Even a 1896 report of the Connecticut SAR opposed restricting advertising use of the flag, declaring that "the more the flag is exhibited and displayed the better it will be for the whole country and that through it and its peaceful exhibition there will be developed a purer Americanism and more earnest love for the liberties which have been secured to us." The same report also quoted approvingly from Gen. G. E. Dalton, a Union Civil War veteran, who reported that his comrades "almost unanimously" felt "that the more the Flag is brought before the people, the more its representation is seen, the better. I think very few of them consider that the Flag is desecrated or the American Eagle is likely to lose a feather, from having the imprint of the same on any legitimate advertising, and I think it would be a sad day when the youth of the land should never see the Flag represented ... except when accidentally observed on some official document ... or flying over some public building." At least one branch of the GAR similarly dissented from the mainstream efforts of patriotic groups, petitioning Congress in 1898 to oppose flag desecration legislation on the grounds that the flag should be used "in all possible ways to bring it more prominently before the people" and that restricting "the rights of the people to the use of the flag is unjust and unpatriotic."[26]

Frequently coupled with objections to flag desecration proposals on the grounds that advertisements depicting the flag were harmless were objections that flag usage was ultimately a matter of taste and that people's taste differed—and in any case simply could not be effectively regulated by legislation (a position that ultimately amounted to declaring that the entire issue was not of great importance, since those who espoused it would certainly not have argued that whether or not people should steal, rob, forge, or murder was a matter of taste). Thus, SJC Chairman Hoar told the Senate in 1896 that, although he had voted to report a flag desecration bill out to the floor, "the more I think of it, the more there seems to be in the way of objection to any legislation upon the subject. ... It is a very difficult thing to deal with and whether it would not be better to leave it to the good taste and good sense of private citizens I very much question."

Similarly, in response to constituent mail urging action on a flag desecration bill, Congressman George Ray of New York, who headed the HJC subcommittee charged with considering the issue, responded in 1899 that it was "not desirable to legislate too much and it may not be wise to pass a law which declares in effect that the American people must be compelled by law to respect the flag." *The Independent,* a liberal popular magazine of the day, declared in 1903 that while some uses of the flag were "irrelevant and even ridiculous," such matters of taste were "not usually subjects for argument, still less for legislation. On the whole we prefer the flag to become commonplace rather than to be regarded as itself sacred, never to be torn down or burned up or handled with other than the purpose of patriotic motives." In 1935, New York City Mayor Fiorello LaGuardia vetoed a bill requiring the display of the flag at all indoor meetings, on the similar grounds that loyalty could not be compelled and that "patriotism can no more be instilled into a disloyal person by the forced presence of the flag than can the love of God be put into an atheist's heart by placing a Bible in his hand."[27]

An additional factor that helps explain the general reluctance of the Congressional judiciary committees to report out flag desecration legislation was the overrepresentation of southern Democrats on them. Al-

though Republicans controlled Congress almost continuously throughout the 1890–1930 period and therefore usually controlled the judiciary
committees, opposition to or lack of interest in flag desecration legislation among southern Democrats, for reasons explained earlier, probably made the Republican majorities reluctant to push such measures,
especially since the proposed laws would have limited political use of
the flag and because it was Republicans who had waved the flag most
effectively in political campaigns. At any rate, no doubt because southern Democrats were concerned about the potential role of the judiciary
committees in originating civil rights legislation, these committees
were constantly packed with Democrats from the former Confederate
states and such overrepresentation could only have acted as a drag on
flag desecration legislation.

For example, in 1896, four of the six Democrats on the thirteen-
member Senate Judiciary Committee and all seven Democrats on its
seventeen-man House counterpart were from the South; in 1910 southerners constituted five of the six Democrats on the fifteen-man Senate
committee and all six of the Democrats on the sixteen-man House
committees; and in 1920 six of eight Democrats on both the twenty-
three-member Senate and the twenty-member House Judiciary Committees were from the South. The high representation of the South was
far from typical of all Congressional committees; thus, in the House in
1900, while six of seven Democrats on the Judiciary Committee were
southern, the comparable figures were one out of six on the Invalid Pen-
sions Committee, three out of eight on Indian Affairs, three of six on Interstate and Foreign Commerce, one of five on Labor, two of five on
Manufactures and two of seven on Merchant Marine and Fisheries.[28]

Leaders of the flag protection movement recognized that they had a
problem with southerners on the Congressional judiciary committees.
For example, in a 1898 pamphlet, Charles Kingsbury Miller reprinted a
letter that he had recently sent to HJC Chairman Henderson taking issue with reports "that the Southern members of your committee object" to flag desecration legislation. It seems unlikely that mere coincidence explains that when the DAR chose a new Flag Committee
Chairwoman to replace Kempster in 1910 it selected Mrs. Jacob
Dickinson, who not only was the wife of the secretary of war but also
was from Tennessee. Addressing the HJC during a 1913 hearing, Mrs.
Dickinson pointedly denied being a "suffragette or a suffragist" while
noting "I am a southerner," and she stressed that at long last some of
the southern states had passed flag desecration laws and that the others
might "fall in line" if Congress acted.[29]

Ironically, while it was the very failure of Congress to pass flag desecration legislation in the late 1890s that caused leaders of the flag pro-

tection movement to vigorously lobby state legislatures to pass their own laws, success in the states quickly provided another argument for opponents of federal legislation. They argued that, since by 1915 almost all of the states had passed their own flag desecration laws, there was simply no reason for the federal government to duplicate such measures and that, in any case, the kinds of actions to be criminalized by flag desecration laws were rightly matters for state and local rather than federal jurisdiction. These arguments were especially powerful in the pre-New Deal era, in which federal jurisdiction was largely restricted to foreign and defense policy, delivering the mails, and regulating interstate and foreign commerce; in the absence of such later innovations as social security, federal aid to education, federal subsidies of public housing and highway construction, food stamps, and medicare, the ordinary citizen was rarely directly touched by the federal government. Few violations of law were federal crimes and only the largest cities even hosted federal courts.

AFA President Prime clearly had serious doubts about the need and efficacy of federal legislation after some of the states began passing their own laws. Thus, in 1898, he told the SAR convention that "some of us believe" that enforcement of flag desecration laws was "more simple and easy" if the states had jurisdiction, since state officials were "everywhere present," whereas federal courts and officials could often be found only "hundreds of miles distant" from potential places of offenses. After the Supreme Court's 1907 *Halter* decision upholding the constitutionality of state flag desecration laws, Prime essentially opposed any further attempts at passage of federal legislation, effectively putting the AFA out of business since with almost all states having such laws there was little left for it to do. Citing the Court's vague statement in *Halter* that, even if Congressional passage of a federal law "would supersede state laws of like character, it does not follow that in the absence of National legislation the state is without power to act," Prime argued that the Court had clearly indicated that any federal law would in fact supersede state legislation and would therefore weaken some state laws unless a federal statute incorporated all of the most restrictive provisions of all the state laws. Thus, in the AFA's last published circular in 1913, Prime warned against the "peril and danger" of any Congressional action that was not as "comprehensive and drastic as the most comprehensive of any" state law and urged active opposition to any such proposal as "otherwise all our work for sixteen years past will go to ruin." He soundly criticized the DAR, which had continued to strongly urge federal action on the grounds that state laws and enforcement varied drastically and that the flag was a federal symbol that Congress had created and therefore should protect. According to

Prime, who habitually lectured anyone in the flag desecration movement who dared disagree with him, "some of the noble women of our country" had to be "watched" because they allegedly approached Congress with their "patriotic desires uppermost and forgetful or thoughtless of all else" and were thus "meddling with a matter they do not understand."[30]

The jurisdictional argument—more that the issue of flag desecration was a matter for the states rather than that federal action might undercut the states—was probably the single most important barrier to Congressional action in the post-World War I period, since only a few states had failed to act by 1920. Thus, during a 1927 HJC hearing on federal flag desecration legislation, Representative Leonidas Dyer of Missouri indicated his sympathy for the principle involved, but declared that "the only point" that "would be seriously up for consideration by the committee would be the advisability of legislation, so far as Congress is concerned, or whether, or not, the question should be left to the states." During a 1928 HJC hearing, Representative Ira Hersey of Maine stated that the "trouble in the committee, more than anything else" was that a federal law would "take away from the States the right to legislate, when 46 of the States have done their duty in that respect; and hence the question would arise, Why pass a national law, when the states have passed laws on the subject?"[31]

Although by the World War I era southern Congressmen, like southern state legislators, presumably had become considerably more sympathetic to the American flag, southern Democrats remained drastically overrepresented thereafter on the judiciary committees (for example, in 1928 seven of nine Democrats on the House committee were southern). Because southern Democrats were particularly receptive to states rights arguments in general, it seems likely that persisting southern opposition to a federal flag desecration law continued to play a key role in blocking such legislation. This is especially clear in connection with the extremely strong opposition to a federal law by Representative Hatton Summers, a Texas Democrat who served for many years as chairman of the HJC or ranking minority member, depending upon which party controlled the House. The HJC files are filled with documentation of Summers' unyielding opposition, on states' rights grounds, to a federal flag desecration law. For example, in a June 23, 1941 letter to colleagues who had urged action on such a law, Summers wrote that, especially since all of the states already had flag desecration laws, he wished all Americans "in each of our communities" to feel that the flag belonged to them and that if flag desecration occurred "it is a finer thing" for local officials to prosecute the offender before a "locally chosen judge, with the people coming into the Court House to observe the trial, getting 'het up over it,'" than for "an appointed Federal Marshal to come from maybe a hundred miles or so, arrest the desecrator and take him to a Federal Court and have an appointed judge try him." Summers concluded: "I want these appointed officials to stay out of the picture and let the people take care of their own flag. It belongs to them and not to Washington. I would like to see a great deal more responsibility taken away from Washington and back to the people. In my judgment we have got to do that, or be governed by a great Federal Bureaucracy instead of a Democracy."[32]

Although most Congressmen (except for pre–World War I southerners) and others who opposed flag desecration legislation appear to have been fundamentally sympathetic to the movement, at the same time believing that the proposed legislation was misguided, a more basic critique came from a number of liberals and radicals. They essentially argued that the demand for flag protection reflected a fundamental confusion between symbol and substance and represented an attempt to suppress dissent and divert attention away from real ills in American society by turning the flag into the fetishistic worship object of a loud but ultimately phony superpatriotism. These sentiments were never publicly voiced in Congress, but it seems likely that, at least during the height of the Progressive Movement, some national legislators harbored and were influenced by such thoughts. During the late 1890s, the *Boston Herald* warned against the "worship of a textile fabric," and the *Springfield Republican* similarly demurred against a "foolish" excesss of zeal in the flag desecration movement that would end in "making a fetish of [the flag] and removing it from a very effective way of use."[33]

The *Nation*, a leading Progressive Movement magazine, used the occasion of the introduction of regular flag-related rituals in the New York schools in 1900 to refer acidly to those who fostered a "flag cult" of "old glorification" and "idiotic flag-fetishism" and believed that the mere sight of the flag should be a "signal for emotional hysterics." Terming the entire flag "glorification" movement "solemn nonsense" and completely unnecessary, the *Nation* opined that men had always "willingly died for their country without special instruction in color symbolism."

Similarly, the *Independent*, in a 1903 editorial entitled "The Flag as a Fetish," attacked the flag protection movement for what were deemed its excesses, satirically revealing that even worse flag abuses than those Miller revealed in his pamphlets were occurring: "The American flag has actually been sold, openly for money, on the streets of some of our cities! (In case this is doubted we will furnish names and dates.)" Furthermore, the *Independent* noted, the national anthem was regularly sung in theaters by "actresses whose characters were not above reproach," and coins bearing patriotic symbols like the American bald eagle were "often in the hands of irreverent and disreputable people" who sometimes used them for "the basest purposes." Worse yet, the post office operated "desecrating machines," which "at the rate of a thousand a minute," were defacing stamps bearing the pictures of great patriots like George Washington and even those of McKinley, "our martyred president," and postal officials who refused to "punch the head" of such patriots were threatened with losing their jobs. Another leading Progressive magazine, *The Public,* in 1913 denounced superpatriots who were then urging action to avenge insults to the flag abroad, declaring that for such people "the sacrifice of innocent lives and vast wealth is of little moment. The sole thing is to compel respect for the flag. The world must honor the flag on pain of death."[34]

Frequently, attacks on the flag protection and allied movements that argued the flag was being turned into a fetish were accompanied by arguments that such movements were fundamentally in error because they confused symbol with substance. According to this analysis, proponents of flag desecration laws did not understand that blind flag worship was devoid of any real meaning and that the only meaningful form of love for the flag could not be compelled by fiat, especially as it could only be earned by solving the country's ills and creating a nation that lived up to its ideals. In short, this argument went, those who really loved the flag and the country would devote their time to making the country a better place to live, not to mandating flag worship and outlawing flag disrespect, both of which were viewed as ultimately without any independent significance.

One argument involving the "substance over symbolism" theme was that by focusing so much attention on flag rituals and treating the flag as a sacred object, the flag protection movement was educating the American public, and especially schoolchildren, to revere the flag—but was not teaching them the fundamental principles that the flag stood for. For example, in 1899, Princeton Professor Woodrow Wilson declared that patriotism "does not show itself in the mere utterance of the sentiments of the lip." He expressed disapproval of creating a country with "schoolrooms full of children going through genuflections to the flag of the United States" unless they were also taught "what history has been written upon the folds of the flag," in particular that it was a "flag of liberty of opinion" (a principle that Wilson as president entirely disregarded in practice during World War I, when antiwar sentiment was aggressively suppressed by his administration). The purpose of patriotic teaching, Wilson declared in 1899, should be to teach "what is inherent and essential in the character of American institutions," and "we have forgotten the very principle of our origins if we have forgotten how to object, how to resist, how to agitate, how to pull down and build up, even to the extent of revolutionary practices if it be necessary, to re-adjust matters." He stressed that "you cannot compel a sentiment of [patriotic] sympathy [for the flag] unless you display the lovable quali-ties which inhere in the object which you would have loved."[35]

A similar argument to Wilson's was made in 1890, when agitation for school rituals was beginning, by Brown University President E. Benja-min Andrews. He argued that "true patriotic sentiment and purpose" could not be attained by "Fourth of July oratory or by the purchase and raising of flags," and that there was a danger that the "flag shall become a fetish" unless what was taught was "not the stars and stripes, but what the stars and stripes stand for: liberty, union, rights, law, power for good among the nations." In 1891, C. M. Waage made a similar point, maintaining that true patriotism as opposed to "blind submis-sion" could be achieved only by "education, not by inspiration," in-cluding particularly "knowledge of the duties of citizenship." As to pri-mary school students, Waage argued, "it may be enough to raise a flag over a school building and tell them a story about George Washington"; to older children such would "appear a farce." Chauncy Colegrove of the University of Chicago similarly warned in 1897 against identifying patriotism only with "drums and flags and bloody battles and military heroes and dying for one's country," as doing "more harm than good" by neglecting the more important topics of "democracy in government, equality in society, tolerance in religion and freedom in education."[36]

The most frequent point made by those who argued that the flag pro-tection movement focussed on symbol and ignored substance was that love of country could only occur when the country lived up to its ide-als, not through laws that regulated treatment of the flag. For example, in an article in *Arena* in 1898, Henry Foster warned against "artificial expedients" and "superficial and unavailing remedies" being used to promote patriotism such as flag desecration laws and flag rituals in the schools, since patriotism could not be compelled and such techniques would actually backfire when children grew up and realized that the flag had "failed to protect themselves" from social ills like rising crime and corruption, misgovernment, and social inequalities. "The average American citizen is not a fool," Foster wrote, "and when he comes to think it all over he discovers that the 'government' and the 'flag' con-cerning which he has been given such fine and lofty conceptions" in practice consisted of "hustlers for office and emolument who sit in up-holstered chairs, smoke high-priced cigars, and draw salaries several times larger than they could possibly earn by honest effort in any legiti-mate vocation." Foster concluded that only when good government and justice reigned, "then we shall have patriotism, then there will be no need of state and federal laws to protect the flag from overt insult or from being prostituted to commercial or partisan purposes. Then there will be no need of Gatling guns to protect public property by shooting down prospective mobs of our own people."[37]

Brown President Andrews similarly argued in 1890 that patriotism could not come "as the mere result of teaching," since one could not become an "enthusiast for my country, unless it is worthy of my enthusiasm." In 1906 the *Nation* made the same argument, declaring that true patriotism could not be taught by "shouting for the old flag" or banning use of the flag in advertisements or similar "hot house methods" that could create an "artificial and false" sentiment that would "stifle the noblest kind of love of country." Instead, the magazine argued, such sentiments cannot be taught but could only be "commanded by the country which deserves it," by such means as giving people "justice, freedom, and equal treatment before the laws."

The *Public* in 1913 similarly argued that "the truest lovers of the flag are not those who spring to their feet when the band plays the national air, or who pass laws against the display of the red flag, or who mob foolish labor agitators, but those rather who would remove from beneath it every form of social and economic injustice. When the last privilege has been abolished and all men stand equal before the law, it will not be necessary to compel anyone to respect Old Glory." The *Independent* gave a slightly different twist to this argument in 1914, proclaiming that even those who physically abused the flag in fact did no harm, since the flag was an "insensate piece of bunting" and "the virtue of the United States does not lie in cloth," although real harm was done to the country by those who sold "shoes with paper soles to the troops" or who voted "for an inferior candidate for Congress." The *Independent* urged that Americans "not waste upon this evanescent symbol the patriotic feeling now so much needed in more important ways," especially since the flag would likely soon join in the museum "its progenitors" like the "tribal totem worshipped by the savage."[38]

In 1903 the *Independent* made another "symbolism over substance" argument, which particularly targeted the hereditary patriotic societies, like the DAR and the SAR, who loudly proclaimed their love for the flag while restricting their membership to descendants of Revolutionary War colonists. The *Independent* declared that such a use of the flag was a "more serious" desecration than any misuse these organizations attacked, since by basing their membership on ancestry and attacking the influence of "foreigners," such organizations violated the fundamental principles of the country:

> If our flag stands for anything, it stands for opposition to hereditary privilege, the spirit of caste and exclusiveness, and all artificial distinctions and

eminences; and we confess that of the two, it seems less incongruous and distasteful to see a national emblem used to advertise a railroad, a patent medicine or a sugar-coated ham than to see it used to advertise the wearer as the thirty-second fraction of a Revolutionary hero. ... The revolutionary patriots did not fight for a 'flag.' They fought for freedom and good government, and they fought just as bravely under the sign of a tree or a rattlesnake or no flag at all as under 'Old Glory.' We hope, in spite of appearances, that their descendants will not neglect the reality in their zeal for the symbol.[39]

Perhaps the most bitter and developed attack on the flag desecration movement for stressing symbols over substance came in a 1915 pamphlet entitled "Our Flag and the Red Flag," authored by a socialist clergyman named S. S. Condo. Condo developed at great length the argument that the flag protection movement and its supporters deliberately sought to focus the attention of the American masses on flag worship for the express purpose of distracting them from the real ills of the nation and taking their eyes off the real "ball" of capitalist exploitation. Condo argued that the real desecrators of the flag were the "exploiters and oppressors of the laboring class," who "have made a fetish of our flag" even while they waved it over profits made from "child slavery, poverty, prostitution, political graft and rottenness." He declared:

> I know of no one thing that is more abused, misunderstood, prostituted and made to deceive the common people and serve the interests of capitalist exploiters, used in times of peace and war, to mislead the people than 'Old Glory,' and it is high time the working classes get wise about this idolatry. ... The American flag is a symbol that is used today chiefly to fool the voters and to whoop-it-up for patriotism and men will lay down their lives to preserve that symbol without considering in the least what those who wave that flag really stand for. ... Capitalist politicians are trying to blindfold the eyes of workingmen with our flag, while the capitalists pick your pockets and exploit you.

Not surprisingly, leading American anarchists like Emma Goldman and Alexander Berkman also argued that the entire issue of flag "glorification" was simply an attempt to divert mass attention away from the evils of capitalist exploitation. Goldman declared in 1916 and 1917 that "flag mania" and the attempt to "foster and force" patriotic sentiments upon a population that was already servile were especially ironic since they occurred in a government that "is hailed to be the world's greatest guardian of liberty, freedom of conscience, thought and expression." Berkman agreed, arguing in 1916 that, although the American flag might once have stood for "freedom of expression and political justice," it had become a symbol of "exploitation and militarism" as well as "prostituted justice and greedy capitalism." Referring to a one-month jail sentence recently handed out in a flag desecration prosecution, Berkman declared, "The very fact that men are sent to prison for 'desecrating' a rag proves that there is no freedom of conscience under that flag. No decent man or woman can respect the symbol of such tyranny." Radicals such as Goldman also periodically published artistic attacks upon flag "glorification." For example, the June 1912 issue of Goldman's journal *Mother Earth* featured a front-page cartoon of a corpulent capitalist forcing a flagpole down the throat of a chained worker, and the April 1916 issue of the radical journal *Masses* published a cartoon entitled "Patriotism," which portrayed a cleric, a businessman, and a politician wrapped in a flag while they stepped over a mass of corpses. Even flag-waving Broadway producer George M. Cohan (whose hit song "You're a Grand Old Flag" was originally titled "You're a Grand Old Rag," but was reworded in response to compaints that calling the symbol a "rag" amounted to desecration), seems to have recognized that the flag could be used to cover over or divert attention away from a multitude of sins: he noted that, "Many a bum show is saved by the American Flag."[40]

The Growing Focus on Political Dissent in the Post-*Halter* Era

On the surface, little significant change occurred in connection with the flag desecration controversy between the Supreme Court's 1907 *Halter* decision and the first passage of a federal flag desecration law in 1968, aside from the passage of additional laws in the laggard states, ending with Virginia's enactment in 1932. But, in fact, just below the surface very significant change gradually occurred, with the tense period leading up to American entry into World War I, the war itself and the postwar "Red Scare" of 1919–20 clear turning points in transforming the focus of the flag desecration issue. In short, although the flag desecration issue had originated in the late 1890s as a means of protecting the flag against essentially mainstream, and even arguably patriotic (if profane) uses, such as in advertising and political campaigns, by 1920 the focus of the flag protection movement had become overwhelmingly centered upon left-wing political dissent. Although the movement had originated as a means of protecting the flag against perceived misuse, whatever its origin—and in practice such misuses rarely originated among political dissenters—by 1920 the central focus of the movement was upon political dissenters, who in practice almost invariably were associated with the political left.

This transformation in the focus of the flag protection movement can be clearly traced in at least three areas: changes in the targets of state flag desecration prosecutions, changes in the rhetoric used by the movement, and changes in the language of proposed federal statutes. In each case, the original focus on advertising and mainstream political misuse of the flag, although not disappearing entirely, sharply decreased, to be replaced by an overwhelming focus on left-wing political dissenters, such as pacifists, militant trade unionists, and, especially after the 1917 Bolshevik Revolution in Russia, upon perceived Communists.

This shift can be most easily demonstrated with regard to post-*Halter* flag desecration prosecutions, although it is impossible to give a comprehensive accounting or analysis of such. (The vast majority of such prosecutions do not appear in legal reference works because, after *Halter*, the cases generally did not raise fundamental constitutional issues and convictions were rarely appealed beyond local courts; furthermore, with the major exception of the *New York Times*, newspapers from the pre-World War II period have generally not been indexed, ruling out another means of potentially tracking them.)

Nonetheless, judging from cases that were reported in legal references and in the *New York Times* and a few other scattered sources, the overwhelming majority of flag desecration arrests and prosecutions in the post-*Halter* period was directed against people who engaged in acts clearly associated with political dissent, while only a tiny fraction were directed against advertisers or mainstream political parties who had incorporated the flag in their commercial or political campaigns. Thus, with the major exception of the Haywood incident in Colorado recounted earlier, virtually all of the pre-*Halter* flag desecration cases involved alleged commercial misuse of the flag. However, of the total of about fifty-five flag desecration incidents uncovered between 1907 and 1964, about forty-five clearly involved perceived political dissent and only about five involved advertising use of the flag. (The remaining cases were ambiguous or did not fit either category, such as the 1917 arrest of a man for tying a flag to materials sticking out the back of his car and a 1958 conviction, ultimately overturned on appeal, in which the distributors of an Illinois magazine were prosecuted for publishing a picture of a woman naked except for a flag strategically placed over her pelvic region.)[41]

The overwhelming focus of post-*Halter* flag desecration enforcement on incidents with political significance is further highlighted by the clustering of cases around the World War I/Red Scare and World War II periods, which were accompanied by intensified patriotic-nationalistic fervor and decreased tolerance for dissent. Thus, of the approximately forty-five 1907–1964 flag desecration incidents that clearly targeted political dissent, about thirty-five occurred during the 1914–20 and the

1939–1945 periods, that is, about 80 percent of incidents occurred during less than fifteen of the almost sixty years involved. It is possible that more politically significant flag-related dissent actually occurred during the highly charged World War I/Red Scare and World War II eras, and that therefore the larger number of incidents during these periods simply reflected this fact. However, it is definitely not the case that the few post-*Halter* advertising-related prosecutions is a "misleading" reflection of an actual end to commercial use of the flag in response to flag desecration laws, rather than to a decreasing interest in pursuing such technically illegal activities.

There is plenty of evidence from the 1907–1964 period that large scale commercial use of the flag continued, although probably declining for a time, as the authorities increasingly looked the other way. Spokesmen for the flag protection movement incessantly complained during the post-*Halter* period that advertising violations of the state flag desecration laws were not being prosecuted—in fact this was a major argument they put forth for passage of a federal law—and frequently reported that they had intervened directly to encourage alleged transgressors to mend their ways, apparently due to a lack of official interest. Thus, in 1916 DAR Flag Committee Chairwoman Alice MacFarlane reported receiving numerous accounts of "many varieties of [flag] desecrations" including flag aprons worn by waiters, flag dresses, flag labels on brooms, and flag table covers, paper napkins, paper tablets, pillows, and candy and bread wrappers.[42]

Typically, flag protection spokesmen reported, informal requests to alleged violators resulted in apologies and an immediate end to the desecrations, although this was not always the case. Thus, in her 1916 report, MacFarlane related that one Ohio DAR chapter alone had "closed 150 cases of desecration" and "the majority of the desecrations reported were made through ignorance and not intentionally and were discontinued as soon as informed [by DAR members] they were transgressing." On the other hand, in 1931 the SAR's Flag Committee reported that, when a flag company was contacted to complain about use of the flag on its letterhead "for advertising purposes," in response "an abusive letter was received in which we were told that we were busybodies and that 'our obtuseness would be pitiable if it were not so tragic,'" but that nonetheless the letterhead would be changed "so that people without brains will not imagine" the flag was being misused.[43]

One especially clear example of the rapidly decreasing official interest in prosecuting commercial use of the flag can be found in the drastically changed tone of New York officials concerning this subject between 1900 and 1917. In July 1900 the *New York Times* reported that, due to the issuance of instructions from the district attorney concerning enforcement of the New York flag desecration law, New York City police would "summarily" haul down any kind of flag advertising, whether political or commercial, that the police would "frown" upon those merchants who sought to attract customers "by decorating their stores, factories and innumerable billboards with American banners," and that newspapers would not even be able "to announce in red letters, on a background of American flags, the victories of our troops over the Chinese [during the Boxer Rebellion]."

However, in 1917, when American entry into World War I was accompanied by an outburst of enthusiastic, although often illegal flag usages, such as the selling of gloves and hosiery with flag stitching reported by the *New York Times* on April 11, the New York City district attorney announced that "in such a time as the present, when the spirit of patriotism is everywhere apparent, such a law [that is, the flag desecration statute] should not be construed too technically" with regard to any "proper [that is, patriotic] use" of the flag.[44]

World War II was accompanied by another outburst of commercial uses of the flag that, as during World War I, virtually never led to prosecutions, even though a federal publication clearly indicated that they often transgressed the law. According to a 1941 Commerce Department pamphlet, written before Pearl Harbor, Americans had increasingly desired to display their patriotism amidst the "crescendo of warfare abroad," and in response, jewelers, textile manufacturers, and others had "exploited" such feelings, "deliberately or in ignorance of the common norm, beyond bounds of good taste and even beyond the limits of the law." That such commercial uses of the flag continued during and after World War II was clearly indicated in 1952, when the national Better Business Bureau felt compelled to issue a report entitled, "The Use of the Flag in Advertising," which warned that all states banned such usage.[45]

In fact, after World War II, even patriotic groups seem to have generally stopped complaining about nonpolitical violations of flag desecration laws and, as will be described in later chapters, during the height of the Vietnam War period and beyond, despite the essentially unchanged language of most flag desecration laws dating from the *Halter* era, massive commercial use of the flag, along with large-scale technically illegal "patriotic" flag usages, went completely unprosecuted while "dissenting" flag usages led to hundreds of prosecutions. Among the very few instances in which nonpolitical flag usages attracted objections during the post-World War II period, complaints were voiced in 1959–60 when it was discovered that 48- and 49-star flags, made obsolete by the admission of Alaska and Hawaii to the Union, were turning up in bales of rags, some of which were exported to Haiti for use as cleaning rags, curtains, and other things. In an attempt to limit or halt such incidents, new customs regulations were imposed requiring licenses to export U.S. flags. In 1963, a shipment of 202 bales of rags were impounded from a Polish freighter when five flags were found in the consignment. In 1964, a Long Island merchant withdrew some boys jackets from sale after a customer complained that the pockets were lined with flag material (apparently from cloth containing then-obsolete 48-star designs).

One clear sign of the almost vanishing interest in commercial flag use came in 1962, when the American Law Institute (ALI), a nongovernmental organization of prominent judges, lawyers, and professors closely intertwined with the legal establishment, proposed in its Model Penal Code (MPC) that all references to such be deleted from state laws, because "Whatever may have been true [previously], it is scarcely realistic today to regard commercial exploitation of the national emblem or colors as a serious affront to popular sensibilities," and if any regulation of "this sort of activity" was needed, "it belongs outside the penal code."[46]

Aside from a gradual lessening of interest by the authorities and patriotic groups in commercial flag use, prosecutions for nonpolitical flag misuse probably also declined soon after the 1907 Supreme Court *Halter* decision at least partly because government officials and the patriotic organizations could not agree on exactly which sorts of flag uses were banned and which weren't. While *Halter* clearly upheld banning commercial use of the flag, it did not define exactly what such forbidden use consisted of. Therefore, the interpretation of state laws was thereafter left largely up to state legal officials. However, when puzzled manufacturers asked state attorney generals for advice on how to interpret the desecration laws, they frequently received conflicting interpretations. For example, the Michigan, New York, Louisiana, and Wisconsin laws banned all depictions of flags in connection with advertisements. Yet Michigan's attorney general issued an opinion in 1941 stating that pictures of flags could nonetheless be legally used in advertisements for flags, since such usage complied with the law's intent to "foster sentiments of patriotism," without the "slightest danger" of "causing any desecration of the flag"; the Louisiana attorney general issued a similar opinion in 1940. But New York's attorney general, in 1940, and Wisconsin's attorney general, in 1918 and again in 1959, forbade such advertisements, with the latter explaining that the state legislature could have easily made such an exception in "clear and unequivocal language" had it wished to but had not.

Similarly, despite virtually identical language in the state laws, in 1917 the West Virginia attorney general advised companies that it would be legal to sell flag belt buckles, as well as "Bing Bang" guns that used paper flag representations, yet the same products were forbidden by the Maryland attorney general in 1918. The Iowa attorney general banned even printing reproductions of flags in newspapers in 1917, while other states such as Maryland, West Virginia, and New York raised no objections to such usage (which, in fact, technically violated most state laws, which banned depicting flags on any "merchandise") so long as the flag pictures were not part of advertisements. In 1915, the Massachusetts attorney general issued a truly bizarre opinion that authorized the printing of depictions of the flag upon the "covers of books, papers or magazines," but only if they were "used or intended solely for artistic or ornamental purposes" and "in no way used or intended to attract attention" to the printed materials "as it is offered for sale."[47]

If state authorities could not agree on what constituted proper flag usage, neither could the patriotic organizations. For example, at the 1904 national DAR convention, a member received applause when she complained that just outside the meeting room flags were being improperly draped on tables and souvenirs were being placed on them for sale ("I call that desecration of the American flag!" she proclaimed). In 1916 the DAR Flag Committee reported that the flag should never be "used as a covering unless it is placed over an altar" and "nothing should rest upon it but the Bible," yet at the 1912 AFA meeting President Prime proudly told members that they could find for sale nearby engrossed copies of the Gettysburg Address placed on top of a table draped with the flag. In 1916, the DAR's Flag Committee hailed the display of "floral" flag parks as providing a "patriotic appeal to all beholders," but in 1918 the same Committee denounced such "floral parks" because "our colors must not touch the ground" and the floral flags "could easily be trod upon." A 1917 book on flag usage reported that the federal government had "encouraged sailors and soldiers to have their national flag colored into the skins" for identification purposes, but that for civilians to do this "is considered disrespectful to the flag." According to one tally, by 1920 over twenty different "flag codes" were being circulated by an equal number of patriotic organizations. This situation eventually led to a conference of such groups in Washington in 1923–24, which developed a common code of "flag etiquette" (which was endorsed by Congress in 1942, but only as a solely voluntary code without any penalty for violations). But even the adoption of the flag code did not end quarrels between patriotic groups over correct flag etiquette. Thus, although the flag code prescribed burning as the proper means of disposing of worn flags, in 1960 the New York chapters of the American Legion and the Veterans of Foreign Wars got into a nasty public dispute over whether such burnings should be performed publicly or privately.

Similarly, while none of the other patriotic groups voiced objections to flag stamps during the post-World War II period, the United States Flag Foundation (USFF), a quasi-successor to the AFA, repeatedly complained that canceling such stamps was a clear violation of all state flag laws. In a letter to the *New York Times* in 1957, for example, USFF Director General Gridley Adams bitterly charged the Eisenhower administration with forcing "upward of a hundred thousand ex-GI's" employed by the postal service to "smear with their daubing brushes or canceling machines that very flag for which they offered their lives." In a 1953 book, Adams suggested that the flag stamps reflected Communist infiltration of the Post Office.[48]

The growing focus of the flag protection movement during the post-*Halter* period on suppressing political dissent was especially demonstrated during World War I, when several states drastically increased their penalties for violating flag desecration laws, and the federal government, as noted earlier, passed a wartime statute that outlawed verbal criticism (although not physical desecration) of the flag. Thus, the original Texas American flag desecration law, enacted in March 1917 (although a 1913 law protected the Texas flag), shortly before the United States entered World War I, carried a rather typical penalty of up to 30 days in jail and a $100 fine. However, in the so-called "disloyalty act" of March 11, 1918, penalties of two to 25 years in jail were provided for anyone who used "any language" calculated to bring the flag into "disrepute" or who publicly or privately physically damaged or "cast contempt" upon the flag; the key provision of this law remained in effect in Texas until 1973 and resulted in a four-year jail term for a 1970 flag burning. In Louisiana and Montana, the modest flag desecration jail sentences originally included in their respective laws of 1912 and 1905 were increased during World War I to five and 25 years respectively. The Montana law, passed in February 1918, became the model for the federal Sedition Act of May 1918, which outlawed "disloyal, profane, scurrilous, or abusive language" about the "form of government," the constitution, the military or its uniforms, and the "flag of the United States," as well as any language intended to bring such into "contempt, scorn, contumely or disrepute."

The federal law, which expired in 1921, carried penalties of up to 20 years in jail and a $10,000 fine and also required the immediate firing of any federal employee who "in an abusive and violent manner criticizes" the flag, although presumably a 20-year jail term would have in any case interfered with their employment. Another World War I federal action concerning flag desecration occurred shortly after American entry into the war in April 1917, when the Justice Department announced that any alien found "abusing or desecrating" the flag "in any way" would be subject to "summary arrest and confinement" as a "danger to the public peace or safety" under wartime emergency regulations.[49]

Altogether, of the forty-five or so politically oriented flag desecration cases reported in legal references, the *New York Times*, and scattered other sources between 1907 and 1964, almost half involved simply oral disrespect for the flag. The largest single cluster of such prosecutions occurred during World War I. Thus, in two April 1917 cases in New York City, one man was sentenced to 20 days in the county jail for using profane language about the flag (despite a futile attempt to prove his patriotism by wearing a flag in his buttonhole during a court appearance), and another was sent to the workhouse for a month for "making improper remarks" about the flag. Also in April 1917, an Indiana baker was fined $5 for saying "to hell with the flag" in a local bar, and a Wisconsin man was fined $50 for "slurring" the flag. In March 1918, a New York City woman was jailed for six months for displaying a German flag and hauling in an American flag that a neighbor had placed in her window, while declaring, "To hell with the American flag. I want my own flag."[50]

In what was apparently the first speech desecration case in which a conviction was upheld by a state supreme court, in 1918 the highest court in Kansas affirmed the conviction of a man who, in a blacksmith shop, had "expressed a very vulgar and indecent use of the flag" and whose "exact language" was reported to be such that it "should not find a permanent place" in the court's findings. The Kansas court found that a blacksmith shop was a "public place" (the Kansas law declared it illegal to "publicly defile, defy or cast contempt" on the flag), and that the defendant's language was so vile that "it is hard to conceive of language that would express greater contempt for the flag. ... The man who uses such language concerning it, either in jest or in argument, does not have that respect for it that should be found in the breast of every citizen of the United States."

In 1942, the Arkansas Supreme Court upheld a similar conviction in the case of a man who was sentenced to one day in jail and a $50 fine for calling the flag a "rag" without eyes, ears, or mouth and refusing to salute it when he was asked to do so as an apparent condition for obtaining relief supplies. The court majority found that, especially given the context of obtaining relief supplies from a "most generous government," the defendant's conduct "convincingly demonstrated in public" a "contempt for the flag." However, the chief justice bitterly dissented, arguing that the finding was especially inappropriate as the country was then engaged "not only in a war of men, machine and materials, but in a contest wherein liberty may be lost if we succumb to the ideologies of those who enforce obedience through fear and who would write loyalty with a bayonet."[51]

Unquestionably the most extreme penalty for oral flag desecration resulted from a case brought under Montana's previously discussed World War I law. E. V. Starr was arrested under the law for refusing a mob's demands that he kiss the flag (a favorite wartime vigilante punishment for the allegedly disloyal) and for terming it "nothing but a piece of cotton" with "a little paint" and "some other marks" on it that "might be covered with microbes." Starr was given the unbelievable sentence of 10 to 20 years at hard labor in the state penitentiary, along with a $500 fine. In a habeas corpus proceeding, Federal District Court Judge George M. Bourquin termed the sentence "horrifying," but declared himself powerless to overturn it, since the state law was clearly constitutional under the *Halter* precedent. Bourquin declared that the sentence justified George Bernard Shaw's comment that war hysteria had made the French courts "severe," the English courts "grossly unjust," and the American courts "stark, staring, raving mad." At the same time, Bourquin declared that the "unlawful and disorderly conduct" of the mob was itself "calculated to degrade the sacred banner and to bring it into contempt" and that "its members, not he, should have been punished." He suggested that they had been hypocritically "masquerading as superpatriots to divert attention from their real character" as "heresy hunters" and "witch burners."[52]

A 1942 decision of the Maine Supreme Judicial Court appears to have been the only case in which a conviction for oral insult to the flag was overturned on appeal, until the 1969 U.S. Supreme Court decision in *Street v. New York*, which effectively declared unconstitutional, on First Amendment grounds, the outlawing of spoken or written insults to the flag, but simultaneously ducked the question of the constitutionality of outlawing physical flag desecration. The Maine court seized on the technical definition of "public" to put aside the conviction of a man whose primary offense appears to have been making the hand motions of tearing up a nonexistent flag, after terming it a "rag" and declaring, "If I had an American flag here now I would strip it up and trample it under my feet." Although it is difficult to avoid the conclusion that the Maine court simply felt that a prosecution apparently brought for the imaginary tearing up of a nonexistent flag simply went too far, the court held that since the event occurred in a private home it did not violate the law against "public" flag desecration.[53]

Of the approximately forty-five politically related flag desecration cases uncovered between 1907 and 1964, slightly more than half involved physical abuse of the flag. For example, in 1914, a Dover, New Jersey man was arrested for allegedly throwing a flag to the ground and trampling it; in 1915 a New York City man was arrested after a mob beat him for allegedly tearing down a flag; and, during American participation in World War I, among the ten or so physical flag desecration arrests, a Trenton, New Jersey man was jailed for six months for spitting on a flag, another New Jersey man was arrested for cutting a flag to pieces and stomping on it, a New York man was arrested after a mob had attacked him for allegedly tearing down and trampling on a flag, two New York City woman were found guilty of disorderly conduct for sticking antidraft buttons and posters to flags, and two Ossining, New York men, identified as Scandinavian butlers, were arrested for allegedly shooting holes in a flag. (In another World War I case involving flag physical desecration, the authorities appear to have resorted to summary execution rather than to the courts: When a group later characterized as anarchists tore down a flag at a "loyalty" rally in Milwaukee on September 9, 1917, police opened fire, killing two of the alleged perpetrators and seriously wounding another; some of the anarchists reportedly returned the fire, leaving two of the police with minor wounds.) [54]

Among the handful of cases between the World War I and World War II eras involving physical abuse of the flag, a Los Angeles man was sentenced to 250 days in jail in 1925 for using a flag to wipe a shop window; two New York men were arrested in 1931 for carrying junk in a bundled flag; and in 1933 a left-wing radical speaker in Monticello, New York was arrested for allegedly blowing his nose with a flag and wiping his face and clothing with it. As World War II approached, there was a small flurry of cases involving alleged Axis sympathizers. For example, in 1940–41, an Italian alien in New York was fined $50 for flying a flag from an outhouse; a German-born young New Jersey woman was given a one- to two-year sentence to a reformatory for tearing a small flag from her motorcycle and throwing it to the ground while reportedly proclaiming her Nazi sympathies; and another alleged Nazi sympathizer was fined $30 for spitting on a flag. During World War II, a Wisconsin man who pulled down the flag at the house of a policeman was jailed for 60 days and fined $100 in 1942 by a judge who told him that "nothing can be permitted to hinder" the war effort, and a New York man was fined $50 in 1945 for displaying the flag in a reversed position in his delicatessen window.[55]

Only a handful of physical flag desecration cases were prosecuted between 1945 and the Vietnam War era. In one case with overtly political aspects, three members of a left-wing union were given 10-day jail terms for using a flag, during a 1946 New York City May Day parade, as a receptacle for collecting strike contributions. In 1948, a naturalized

Estonian living in Haverstraw, New York was sent to jail for 30 days for tearing down and mutilating a flag by a judge who declared, "If this had happened in your native country you probably would have been taken into the street and shot." In a 1951 case that provided a precursor of the some of the bizarre penalties imposed for flag desecration during the Vietnam War, two Illinois youths who were arrested for dragging a flag behind their automobile were ordered to recite the Pledge of Allegiance in court, to study a book on flag etiquette, and to attend public gatherings that featured flag ceremonies.[56]

During the entire pre-Vietnam War period, apparently only one prosecution for flag burning occurred. It involved a pacifist New York City clergyman named Bouck White, who presided over the "Church of the Social Revolution" during the period of increasing tension leading to American entry into World War I. White was originally charged, in March 1916, with violating New York's flag desecration law by circulating flyers advertising a lecture that included an antimilitarist cartoon depicting a flag on the ground near a bag of money with both objects entwined by a serpent bearing the legend "War." On the eve of his trial for this offense, the *New York Times* reported in a breathless front-page story published on June 2, 1916, that White had been observed by a reporter participating in a ceremony in which the American flag was burned, along with those of other countries, in a large kettle labelled "melting pot," amid hymns and calls for international brotherhood. White was found guilty and sentenced to 30 days in jail and a $100 fine for the original offense on June 2 by a judge who asked him, "Why don't you go off and live in some other country?"[57]

In March 1917, White was tried again for flag desecration in connection with the flag burning, along with ten other alleged participants. The basic defense offered by White (who acted as his own lawyer) and the other defendants was that they had not sought to disparage the flag, but rather sought to celebrate the brotherhood of all men. Thus, Bernard Raymond, the attorney for White's codefendants, declared, "I would rather mingle with lepers than defend these people if I thought they were disloyal to the flag." White, who asked himself questions during his appearance on the witness stand, stated that the attitudes of the flag burners during the ceremony had been "spiritual, majestic and reverential." Raymond Henkel, who was accused of having actually burned the flag in the "melting pot," declared that he loved the American flag and had acted only to symbolize in a "forceful manner" the "welding together of the people of the earth into a closer brotherhood. ... I place my allegiance to the flag second to the future state, in which humanity to man will be paramount. The American flag is supposed to represent the highest ideals of our people, but the greedy profit grabbers have changed that." During closing arguments, White proclaimed that, "instead of desecration, the flag never had received a more profound and mighty consecration," while prosecuting attorney Alexander Rorke declared, "If an American in his indignation had shot White dead on the night of the flag burning, I doubt if you could have found a juryman who would vote to convict him."

After five hours of deliberation, the jury found White, Henkel and one other alleged participant guilty, and acquitted the eight others who had burned non-American flags. Judge McIntyre praised the verdict, declaring that the jury had demonstrated "to the world" that the flag "must be revered and respected" and to aliens that "American institutions must be accorded proper respect, especially in these momentous days in the nation's history." White and the two others who were convicted were given the maximum sentence of 30 days, as McIntyre ignored the jury's recommendation of clemency and expressed regret that "I haven't the power to make this sentence a matter of years." Although all three of the guilty defendants were native-born Americans, McIntyre declared that he was sending to immigrants and others "the warning that hereafter it must be 'hats off to the flag.'" By a special order of the New York City commissioner of corrections, White and his fellow prisoners were directed to carry out a daily flag raising-and-lowering ceremony while imprisoned at the Tombs. As he hauled the flag up on his first day in jail, White declared, "It looks good to me but I wish my flag was there too." Queried, "What is your flag?" White responded, "The red banner of internationalism."[58]

The overwhelming concentration of post-*Halter* prosecutions upon forms of flag desecration associated with political dissent, as opposed to commercial misuse, is extremely strong evidence that the entire focus of the flag protection movement had changed by the World War I era away from flag *protection* towards *suppression* of what was perceived as radical political opposition. Additional evidence in support of this argument can be found in a shift in the rhetoric of the flag protection movement. Although, as previously noted at some length, antiradical rhetoric was associated with very early phases of the flag protection movement, the original impetus for and rhetorical stress of the movement was upon essentially nondissident forms of perceived flag abuse, namely the association of the flag with "mainstream" advertising and political campaigns. Although attention to perceived abuses in commercial use of the flag never disappeared from the rhetoric of the movement, after *Halter*, and especially after American entry into World War I in 1917, the Bolshevik victory in Russia shortly thereafter, and the 1919–20 Red Scare, the overwhelming focus of flag protection rhetoric became concentrated on the threat to the United States posed by left-wing radicals and the need to suppress their ability to express dissent through verbal or physical assaults upon the flag.

For example, in his 1912 address to the AFA, President Prime expressed shock at the "malicious outrages" committed against the flag by those who in a "spirit of lawlessness" had torn it down and trampled it and replaced it with "the red flag of anarchy and disorder." In her 1914 report to the DAR, Flag Committee Chairwoman Charlotte Allison called for a federal flag desecration law in order to "force the anarchist and law breaker to respect the symbol which floats over his land." In an editorial published on July 16, 1913, the *New York Times* declared that the "chief care" of patriotic Americans was that the flag be "treated with reverence" and therefore "when socialists, anarchists, syndicalists or other malcontents tear down our flag and trample it in our own territory, it is time to take action." In a subsequent editorial on April 27, 1916, concerning reports that the flag had been criticized at a meeting held in a public school, the *Times* urged that the schools be closed to "these discussions" since, instead of "wholesome topics of betterment," such meetings featured "tirades from socialists, anarchists, internationalists and agitators of all sorts." At a 1923 Flag Day (June 14) conference in Washington, D.C. called by a coalition of patriotic groups to agree upon a national flag code, Secretary of Labor James J. Davis warned that "disrespect for the flag" constituted one of the "first steps" towards a Communist revolution, and during commemorative ceremonies held the same day in New York, Louisiana Governor John Parker warned, "The Constitution is being attacked at its foundation by a long-haired, anarchistic Bolshevistic horde" while an "indifferent public is engaged in riotous jazz celebrations." In 1926, the DAR urged increased "reverence" for the flag to protect the country against "destructive revolution ... by the 'Red' Internationalists," while at about the same time, the United States Flag Association, a successor organization to the AFA, declared that protecting the flag was never "so vitally important" because millions of dollars were "being spent in this country for communistic and other anti-American propaganda."[59]

HJC hearings on proposed federal flag desecration legislation conducted after 1915 focused almost entirely on the need to suppress political dissent. Thus, in hearings held during World War I, Representative J. M. C. Smith of Michigan, the author of proposed legislation, declared action was needed because "this is absolutely a time, above all times" when "sedition should be suppressed." As an example of what his bill would outlaw, Smith gave as an example "swearing at [the flag] and expressing contempt for it, saying that the German flag is a better flag than ours." During a January 31, 1927, hearing, flag protection sponsor Representative J. Mayhew Wainwright of New York stressed that the need for a flag desecration law was clearly demonstrated by widespread "unrest" in the country, "with communistic and radical sentiment so prevalent and with open expressions of hostility to our form of government and to our constitution so freely voiced." During a subsequent lengthy House floor speech delivered on March 4, 1927, Wainwright termed flag desecration evidence of a "treacherous, treasonable, disloyal state of mind" that, unless "restrained, repressed and punished," might well lead to "the spread of pernicious doctrines" and lend "encouragement to those of revolutionary tendencies, of whom, alas, there are already too many among us."[60]

Among other witnesses at the 1927 hearing, DAR spokeswoman Mrs. Lowell Hobart urged action because radical groups were active in the nation's capital, teaching young children to "join with the people of Russia in overthrowing this government and having labor put in charge of everything." Capt. Paul Collins, a resident of Washington, D.C., stressed the need for flag protection because New York and Washington were "honeycombed with treason." As examples of such he recalled seeing the flag "draped around the cushion of a truck on which two negroes were riding," the appearance of "traitorous articles" in the American Legion magazine(!), such as one that advocated increased spending for education and decreased military spending, and, especially, the activities of noted Columbia University historian Carlton Hayes, whom he termed a "professor of treason" for reportedly giving a public lecture that ridiculed nationalistic excesses. Collins's remarks about Hayes led Representative William Bowling of Alabama to inquire, "Is there not some way by which [Columbia's] board of regents could get him out where he would have to make an honest living instead of what he is doing there?" Collins subsequently submitted a letter from New York Military Academy Superintendent Brig. Gen. M. F. Davis, who declared that Hayes was not "worth the ammunition of a firing squad" but that he should "be taken out by a vigilance committee and strung up to the nearest telegraph pole with a lariat that could be used again."

The leading proponent of Congressional action to combat flag desecration during World War II, Representative Bertrand Gearhart of California, repeatedly spoke on the House floor to demand such legislation, and invariably stressed the threat posed by political dissent that symbolically used the flag. Thus, in remarks entered into the *Congressional Record* on July 27, 1942, Gearhart demanded action against those who "desecrate, yea even spit upon the flag of our country," at a time when American soldiers "are laying down their lives in the far corners of the earth in defense of the glorious banner of this republic."[61]

As early as 1910, the repeated verbal linking of flag desecration with "un-Americanism," radicalism, and trade unions had become so pervasive that it became common for striking workers to march behind the banner of the flag in an attempt to establish their patriotic credentials and, perhaps also, to suggest that those who frequently sought to limit the rights of workers and often physically attacked peaceful strikers were the real "un-Americans." Thus, during a bitterly fought coal strike in Colorado in 1914, strikers carried a flag when they greeted the well-known labor agitator "Mother" Jones at a railroad station in January. After she was arbitrarily jailed strikers marched behind a flag to demand her freedom, only to be attacked by mounted troops with guns and sabers drawn, an event that led to headlines in the labor press such as, "Woman carrying American flag knocked down with butt of gun and flag torn from her hands by militiamen." During a textile strike in Passaic, New Jersey, which erupted amidst the Red Scare of 1919, strikers held a mammoth parade on March 17, led by army veterans holding American flags. And according to a standard history of the labor movement in Colorado, striking miners who were shot at by state police in 1927, with the result that five men were killed and another critically wounded, had marched "with the front rank carrying American flags, as was customary."[62]

Aside from the pattern of flag desecration prosecutions and the increasing emphasis on antidissident rhetoric during the post-*Halter* period, another indicator of the shift—away from the original flag protection movement's emphasis on mainstream political and commercial flag abuse towards primarily focusing on symbolic dissent—is a gradual change in the texts of proposed federal flag desecration laws that were approved by either the Senate or House (but never both) during the 1890–1943 period. Bills passed by the House in 1890 and by the Senate in 1904 both outlawed attaching any kind of advertising material to the flag, with the latter bill also outlawing physical flag desecration and using representations of the flag for advertising purposes.

However, in 1908, when the Senate considered a flag desecration bill similar to that passed in 1904, in response to concerns voiced on the floor about outlawing "innocent uses" of the flag, Senator Francis Warren of Wyoming, the floor manager, declared that the law would not apply to any "patriotic and loyal" purposes using flags; subsequently the proposal was amended before being passed to exclude all "banners or flags carried by military or patriotic organizations authorized by law." Similar or even broader exclusions for "mainstream" uses were included in bills passed by the Senate in 1913, 1914, and 1918, leading Senator Jacob Gallinger of New Hampshire to approvingly conclude in the latter year that the bill "excludes every valid use of the flag, but it precludes and prevents the use of it by those who want to desecrate it." Meanwhile, the proposed flag desecration law considered by the HJC in

1918 dropped all provisions outlawing flag advertisement, since, as its sponsor, Representative J. M. C. Smith explained, there were a "number of cases" where "very beautiful" depictions of the flag had been used for advertising purposes and he did not want to prevent such uses "where it is thoroughly for patriotic purposes. ... I do not think it should be prohibited for advertising if the purpose of the advertisement is a patriotic one."[63]

Flag desecration bills passed by the House in 1928 and 1930 did include advertising provisions, but their clear focus was suggested by provisions that not only outlawed physical desecration of the flag as in the past, but also, for the first time, forbade any display of "open or hostile contempt" for the flag, simultaneously excluding all cases where flag use was "purely and obviously for ornamental or patriotic purposes." The Senate bill passed in 1943 did not contain the "patriotic exclusion," but it also completely omitted the formerly standard provision barring the use of flag representations in advertisements (by far the most common form of commercial flag use). Instead it banned only physical desecration and the casting of "contempt," by word or act, upon the flag, along with placing of any markings, for any purpose, upon the flag. Gridley Adams, the chairman of the National Flag Code Committee, an organization representing more than 100 patriotic organizations, complained in writing to one HJC member that the changes had "cut out the very guts of what a flag bill should cover" and urged that the proposal be killed. "Few people today [physically] abuse a flag," Adams wrote, "while those who desecrate it in pictorial form are legion."[64]

The Fuzzy Line Between Outlawing Disrespect and Compelling Obeisance to the Flag

A growing emphasis on suppressing political dissent is clearly apparent in post-*Halter* flag desecration prosecutions, oratory, and statutory proposals approved by national legislative chambers. Moreover, this increasing focus of the flag protection movement also had what might be termed periodic "spillover" effects in the broader society, that reflected ever more clearly the political intolerance that increasingly formed the heart of the movement and which it generally fostered in what became its major long-term impact upon American society. During three of the greatest periods of domestic political tension in the United States between 1907 and 1945—World War I, the 1919–20 Red Scare, and the period leading up to and including U.S. participation in World War II—sentiments that the flag protection movement had stirred up, such as the conception that the American flag was sacred, that any true American would gladly pay homage to it, and that no true American would give greater homage to any other flag, especially one associated with radicalism and "un-Americanism," led to widespread demands that went far beyond the command that the flag not be desecrated. Often enforced by government authority, these demands included that the flag be kissed or saluted and that no flag associated with radical political opposition be displayed.[65]

In fact, the boundary between forbidding flag desecration and requiring flag obeisance was always a highly permeable one, as was demonstrated throughout the post-*Halter* period by periodic arrests for failure to show the demanded respect for the flag. For example, in 1922 a Des Moines, Iowa man was arrested (and subsequently severely beaten by his fellow inmates) for failing to remove his hat when the flag passed during a parade; in 1925 a New York man was fined $25 in a similar incident; and in 1930, two young women, who ran a Communist children's camp in Van Etten, New York, were sentenced to jail terms of 90 days each for "desecrating" a flag by refusing to hoist one at the order of a mob. In the Van Etten incident, the two women were charged after their camp was invaded by 700 local residents and Ku Klux Klan members who gave them a flag and demanded that they fly it and then essentially abducted them and brought them before a judge when they refused to do so. After the local district attorney authorized the filing of flag desecration charges and following a one-day trial, Justice of the Peace William Westbrook found the two women guilty and, according to contemporary newspaper accounts, declared that their sentences were intended "as a warning to Communists all over the United States that they could not trifle with the American flag or teach un-Christian doctrines."

In a foreign policy incident with a similar flavor, the failure of Mexican authorities to display proper respect for the flag was used an excuse to send American troops to that country in 1914, when the Wilson administration was seeking to oust the Mexican government led by Victoriano Huerta. Wilson insisted that Heurta demonstrate his remorse for the mistaken arrest of some American sailors by providing a 21-gun salute to the American flag, even though Heurta had previously ordered their immediate release and formally apologized to American officials. When Huerta refused to obey unless the American government returned the salute (a wry comment upon the fact that Wilson had refused to recognize his government), Wilson sent troops to occupy Veracruz, Mexico. According to Wilson biographer Arthur Link, as a result of this action, "in the eyes of the civilized world the President appeared ridiculous, as a person willing to make war over an obscure point of honor."[66]

The permeability of the boundary between outlawing flag disrespect and compelling flag respect became especially clear during periods of crisis. During World War I, scores of suspected political dissidents and, perhaps even more often, those suspected of insufficiently enthusiastic patriotism, were, as in the *Starr* case discussed previously, attacked by mobs that sought to compel them to kiss the flag. Government officials generally looked the other way or even joined in during these events and "no effort was made to catch those who took the law into their own hands." To give a few additional examples, in April 1917 a Wyoming man, who had praised the German Kaiser, was almost hung by a mob, revived by a city marshal, and then forced to kneel and kiss the flag; and a Chicago farmer who was similarly accused was also forced to kneel and kiss the flag, and then was arrested. In Iowa, those accused of failing to purchase sufficient liberty bonds were repeatedly brought before large crowds, compelled to kiss the flag and apologize, and assessed financial penalties by the authorities. In March 1917 five Delphos, Ohio businessmen were forced to kiss the flag by a mob of 400 people on threat of hanging, and during a mass antiwar demonstration in Boston on July 1, 1917, mobs of soldiers and sailors forced hundreds of socialists to kiss the flag as police stood by. (During the Great Depression, in one highly unusual "flagkissing" incident the usual roles were reversed as "establishment" figures were forced to kiss the flag, reflecting no doubt the generally "topsy turvy" politics created by the economic collapse: In April, 1933, when local officials in Primghar, Iowa attempted to evict a farm family for nonpayment of their mortgage, a crowd of local farmers beat back a force of club-swinging deputies and then terrified the mortgage holder's attorney into accepting a token payment and forced the attorney, the sheriff and all of the sheriff's deputies to kneel and kiss the flag in front of the local courthouse.)[67]

In a number of cases, governmental officials clearly encouraged the use of vigilante violence against those who were viewed as insufficiently devoted to the flag. For example, in 1917, after a Coast Guard recruiting officer knocked down a man who had allegedly wiped his hands on a flag placed at a recruiting station, the officer, a naturalized citizen, received a letter from the Treasury Department (which supervised the Coast Guard) commending him for the "spirit of loyalty and patriotism which impelled your ready defense of the national colors" and declaring that his actions provided "gratifying evidence of your assimilation of the spirit and best traditions of the country of your adoption." During a 1918 HJC hearing on flag desecration legislation, Representative J. M. C. Smith submitted, with apparent approval, a news account that reported how a New Haven man whose loyalty was suspect was forced to say "God bless Old Glory" and kiss the flag, but he "couldn't sing the Star Spangled Banner for his lips were too swollen and his voice was weak from whimpering. ... He is still in bed from the pounding he received." Smith also cheerfully reported on a "Cincinnati case where a person defamed the flag, and the White Caps took the man out, but they simply put hot oil on his head and obliged him to pledge his loyalty and they let him go again."[68]

During the 1919–20 Red Scare, official requirements for acceptable behavior with regard to flags was expanded beyond past demands for proper reverence for the American flag to outlawing the display of flags—usually but not only defined as red flags—viewed as subversive. Although these laws apparently led to only a handful of prosecutions— in New York City for example, local radicals did not attempt to test it further after police broke up a meeting in Central Park in 1919 and arrested the main speaker for disorderly conduct—the requirement that the American flag be treated with utmost deference while perceived opposition flags could not even be displayed demonstrated with unusual clarity that, by 1920, flag protection etiquette in practice primarily focused on suppressing dissent. Demands for the suppression of displays of red flags, the symbol of the international socialist and, after 1917, the Communist movement, had been gradually growing after 1900. Even before the Red Scare, a few states such as Rhode Island had forbidden such displays and some local authorities had effectively outlawed the red flag, as did East Liverpool, Ohio, where in May 1913 the Mayor ordered the red flag flying from socialist headquarters hauled down after vigilantes had repeatedly torn down and burned others. However, the anti-red flag movement exploded during the Red Scare, when amid absurdly exaggerated fears of an imminent Communist revolution in the United States, thirty-two states and a number of cities such as New York and Los Angeles banned the display of such flags.[69]

The official rationale for these measures was expressed by New York Mayor John Hylan, who in referring to foreign reports concerning the general "dangers of social upheaval," declared the United States was passing through "the most important and critical period of our history." He also said that red flag displays appeared to be "emblematic of unbridled license, an insignia for law breaking and anarchy." However, New York City Police Inspector Thomas Tunney was no doubt more accurate. He told a Senate committee that displaying red flags "simply enthuses [radicals], and they indulge in cheering and waving it in the air," with the only violent feelings resulting due to hostile onlookers, upon a "large number" of whom "it has the effect of creating a feeling that they would like to assassinate everybody carrying the red flag." One North Dakota dissident expressed his opinion of these laws by declaring that "the only animal who is afraid of a red flag has a fence around him."⁷⁰

The red flag laws typically carried penalties of up to $500 fines and six months in jail. Some of the red flag laws were extraordinarily vague, such as the Oklahoma ban on displaying any banners "indicating disloyalty or a belief in anarchy or other political doctrines"; the Wisconsin law, which forbade displaying any flag that symbolized a "purpose to overthrow, by force of violence" the American government; the New York statute, which outlawed displaying red flags to symbolize "any organization or association, or in furtherance of any political, social or economic principle, doctrine or propaganda"; and the West Virginia ban on displaying any emblem suggesting "sympathy or support of ideals, institutions, or forms of government hostile, inimical, or antagonistic to the form or spirit" of the American "constitution, laws, ideals and institutions." An early Massachusetts law proved so all-embracing that it technically forbade even the display of the Harvard crimson and had to be redrafted.⁷¹

In addition to the outbreak of forced flag kissings during World War I and the epidemic of red flag laws passed during the 1919–20 Red Scare, a third period that highlighted the intolerance spawned by the flag protection movement occurred during the late 1930s and the early period of American participation in World War II. During this period, hundreds of American children who refused to salute the flag (mostly Jehovah's Witnesses who acted out of religious convictions) were expelled from school. Moreover, in scores of incidents, mobs, often acting with official approval, attacked Jehovah's Witnesses because their opposition to saluting the flag was viewed as evidence of insufficient patriotism. By June 1940 school flag saluting disputes had developed in at least twenty states, and over 200 children had been expelled from school for refusing to salute the flag. This led one federal appeals court judge to sarcastically declare that, "Eighteen big states have seen fit to assert their power over a small number of little children."⁷²

In an atmosphere of increasing hysteria generated by the growing likelihood of American involvement in World War II, and as the Nazi spring offensive of June 1940 was overrunning France and the Low Countries, the U.S. Supreme Court greatly aggravated the situation with its decision in *Minersville School District v. Gobitis.* The Court upheld the legality of expelling children from school for refusing to salute the flag, on the grounds that the "flag is the symbol of our national unity" and "national unity is the basis of national security." The *Gobitis* decision was widely criticized in a variety of newspapers, magazines, and law journals; thus, *The Christian Century* magazine lamented in its issue of June 19, 1940, "It is bitterly ironical that a free government should inflict a penalty for refusal to salute a symbol of freedom." The ruling, along with American entry into the war in December 1941, helped to foster a new wave of expulsions of child Witnesses and a large and often extremely violent eruption of harassment, beatings, and arrests of adult Witnesses, with the refusal to salute the flag clearly the major, and now seemingly officially endorsed, "crime." The American Civil Liberties Union reported that, between May and October 1940, almost 1,500 Witnesses were the victims of mob violence in 355 communities in 44 states, and that no religious organization had suffered such persecution "since the days of the Mormons." Jehovah's Witnesses reported another 300 incidents and 200 arrests between December 1941 and December 1943. Before a June 1943 Supreme Court decision called a halt to compulsory school flag saluting, a total of 2,000 students had been expelled from school for refusing to comply with such demands.[73]

In one of the more egregious incidents directed against the Witnesses, seven of them were prosecuted in Connersville, Indiana in June 1940 for flag desecration, apparently because they had circulated literature opposing compulsory school flag saluting. Five pled guilty and were given light sentences; two who pled not guilty were subjected to new charges of "riotous conspiracy," resulting in two- to ten-year jail terms, which were eventually overturned by the Indiana Supreme Court as completely unsupported by the facts. Also in June 1940, a group of American Legionnaires and local police officials in Richwood, West Virginia forced a group of Witnesses to swallow large doses of castor oil, paraded them roped together before a large crowd before expelling them from town, and vandalized their cars. While the Witnesses were roped together, leaders of the mob attempted unsuccessfully to force them to pledge allegiance to the flag, as town Sheriff Martin Catlette read from the preamble to the American Legion's constitution, which proclaimed the purposes of maintaining "law and order," promoting "peace and good will on earth," and safeguarding and transmitting to "posterity the principles of justice, freedom and democracy."[74]

In short, the flag protection movement, which had originated primarily for the purpose of opposing essentially "mainstream" uses of the flag that were viewed as insufficiently reverential, ended up by primarily seeking to suppress political dissent, and by spawning movements that demanded ritual obeisance to the flag, even by those who did not wish to give it, and that sought to forbid any display of allegedly "subversive" flags. What had started out as a movement to protect the American flag from all forms of perceived misuse ended up primarily as a movement to suppress dissent and, at times, to forcibly compel symbolic allegiance to a flag whose primary virtue was held to be that it stood for freedom. Ironically—but from the standpoint of constitutional democracy, very, very justly—some of the worst and most undemocratic excesses spawned by the flag protection movement, namely the red flag and compulsory flag salute laws, led directly to Supreme Court decisions in 1931 and 1943 that established the basic legal principles that later logically compelled the Court in 1989 and 1990 to strike down all laws outlawing flag desecration.

In the 1931 case of *Stromberg v. California,* a red flag law prosecution, the Court effectively struck down all such laws, on the grounds that to forbid the display of emblems used to foster "peaceful and orderly opposition" to government was an unconstitutional violation of the First Amendment. This decision, the first Supreme Court declaration that symbolic speech was protected by the First Amendment, clearly established the general principle that symbols such as flags could be use to peacefully express political opposition and thus contained the seed of the 1989 *Johnson* decision. (Had the Court ruled otherwise, theoretically, southern states might have been able to legally ban display, in the aftermath of the Civil War, of even the American flag.)[75]

In the 1943 case of *West Virginia Board of Education v. Barnette,* the Court, citing *Stromberg* and other precedents, overruled its *Gobitis* decision of only three years earlier, now striking down compulsory school flag salute and Pledge of Allegiance requirements, on the grounds that a child required by state laws to attend public schools could not be forced by public authorities "to utter what is not in his mind." In a decision that seems to have been influenced by a change in the Court's personnel, by the Court's recognition that the *Gobitis* ruling had spurred widespread vigilantism, and by a turn for the better in Allied fortunes in World War II with the battle of Stalingrad and the successful Allied invasion of North Africa, Justice Jackson declared, in what remains probably the most eloquent and apposite paean to democratic principles ever penned by the Court:

> Those who begin coercive elimination of dissent soon find themselves exterminating dissenters. Compulsory unification of opinion achieves only the unanimity of the graveyard. It seems trite but necessary to say that the First Amendment to our Constitution was designed to avoid these ends by avoiding these beginnings. ... The case is made difficult not because the principles of its decisions are obscure but because the flag involved is our own. Nevertheless, we apply the limitations of the Constitution with no fear that freedom to be intellectually and spiritually diverse will disintegrate the social organization. ... Freedom to differ is not limited to things that do not matter much. That would be a mere shadow of freedom. The test of its substance is the right to differ as to things that touch the heart of

the existing order. If there is any fixed star in our constitutional constellation it is that no official, high or petty, can prescribe what shall be orthodox in politics, nationalism, religion or other matters of opinion.[76]

The *Stromberg* and *Barnette* rulings dealt with flags, but they did not directly address the issue of flag desecration—indeed the Court never dealt with that particular issue again between its 1907 *Halter* ruling and the Vietnam War era. Therefore, lower courts almost invariably upheld flag desecration convictions during the interim on the basis of *Halter*. However, the rulings helped to lay the legal foundations for the 1989–90 *Johnson* and *Eichman* rulings, which struck down all flag desecration laws, not only because they dealt with flags, but more importantly because they were keystones in an ongoing revolution in Supreme Court interpretation of the First Amendment—which is conventionally dated to the Court's 1925 ruling in *Gitlow v. New York*, in which the Court for the first time held that the First Amendment applied to the states as well as to the federal government. At the time of the *Halter* ruling, the issue in flag desecration legislation was primarily seen, as discussed earlier, as involving property rights rather than speech rights. In any case, in the pre-*Gitlow* era, the Supreme Court effectively left the states free to repress speech in any way they wished to and also upheld the constitutionality of highly repressive World War I federal restrictions on expression in such cases as *Schenck v. U.S.* and *Abrams v. U.S.* (both 1919 rulings upheld convictions in prosecutions resulting purely from peaceful dissident speech).[77]

By the 1960s, when the Court returned to the flag desecration issue, free speech claims had moved to the forefront of the argument of those who opposed restrictions on speech and symbolic conduct in which the flag was used to express dissent. This stress on free speech, as opposed to property rights claims, in large measure reflected the fact that the Court's rulings in cases such as *Gitlow, Stromberg* and *Barnette* applied the First Amendment to the states, brought at least some types of flag usage and other kinds of "symbolic" speech under First Amendment protection, and, as in the 1969 case of *Brandenberg v. Ohio*, established an increasingly broad interpretation of the meaning of "free speech" to encompass virtually any form of expression which did not concretely interfere with the rights of others and which did not pose an imminent danger of public disorder.

As will be discussed in greater detail in the next chapter, when the Court finally revisited flag desecration as a legal issue for the first time in sixty years, in the 1969 case of *Street v. New York*, it relied heavily upon *Stromberg* and *Barnette* to strike down any flag desecration law provisions that outlawed verbal disrespect for the flag, holding that such prior rulings had clearly established the principle that "under our Constitution the public expression of ideas may not be prohibited merely because the ideas are themselves offensive to some of their hearers." Subsequently, in the 1989–90 flag burning cases of *Texas v. Johnson* and *U.S. v. Eichman*, the Court, building explicitly on *Stromberg*, *Barnette*, and *Street*, declared unmistakably that the same principles that led it to forbid any attempt to ban oral disrespect for the flag in *Street* also applied to attempts to outlaw physical destruction of the flag for the purpose of expressing political dissent. Facing squarely a question that it had ducked in *Street*, the Court held that any distinction between "written or spoken words and nonverbal conduct" is "of no moment where the nonverbal conduct is expressive," because, "If there is a bedrock principle underlying the First Amendment, it is that the Government may not prohibit the expression of an idea simply because society finds the idea itself offensive or disagreeable." The line of Court principles and decisions that began with *Stromberg* and *Barnette* thus led directly to *Street*, *Johnson*, and *Eichman*. As political scientist William Lasser wrote in the aftermath of the *Johnson* ruling in 1989, the decision amounted to little more than the "next logical step" that "merely put the finishing touches on a line of constitutional doctrine stretching back over half a century" to the *Stromberg* case. In short, it was the very excesses of the flag protection movement that spurred the Supreme Court to establish the principles that later led the Court to declare unconstitutional the original purpose—the outlawing of flag desecration—which had given the movement birth almost exactly one hundred years earlier.[78]

3

The Vietnam War Era Flag Desecration Controversy, 1965–1974

JUST AS THE 1989–90 flag desecration controversy would be touched off by a single flag burning, two decades earlier a similar major flag desecration controversy was also essentially sparked by the burning of one flag. This earlier controversy was completely associated with internal American divisions over the Vietnam War. Therefore, it was not in the least coincidental that it was largely generated by a flag burning in New York's Central Park during one of the earliest massive antiwar demonstrations, held on April 15, 1967; similarly, it was no coincidence that the controversy peaked between 1967 and 1973, the years of greatest American intervention in Vietnam, and died down quickly thereafter.

The Central Park incident led directly to an achievement that had eluded the founders of the flag protection movement for seventy years—the 1968 Congressional passage of a national flag desecration law, which was hastily and poorly drafted, and passed in a climate of intense emotion (see Appendix, Document 2). By the time the Vietnam era flag desecration controversy faded away, along with the war, in the mid-1970s, perhaps as many as 1,000 flag desecration arrests had been made (mostly under state laws rather than the 1968 federal law), far exceeding the total of such incidents throughout all previous (and all subsequent) American history. However, due to the contradictory nature of lower court decisions dealing with flag desecration during the Vietnam period and due to the ambiguous and sometimes bewildering nature of a series of Supreme Court decisions (and nondecisions) dealing with the subject between 1969 and 1984, the legal status of flag desecration laws was in a state of complete constitutional confusion by the time of the 1984 Dallas incident that led to the 1989 *Texas v. Johnson* case. Since the *Johnson* decision inferentially struck down the 1968 federal statute and led to the passage of a new federal flag desecration law in 1989, which was in turn struck down by the Supreme Court's 1990 *U.S. v. Eichman* decision, the parallels between the flag burning incidents of 1967 and 1984 are quite remarkable: Both triggered waves of indignation, widespread demands for punitive legislation, and hastily and poorly drafted laws essentially aimed at the prevention of a highly unpopular (and to many deeply offensive) form of dissent that were eventually struck down as unconstitutional in landmark Supreme Court decisions upholding a fundamental democratic principle—the right to peacefully express political opposition, even in highly offensive and symbolic ways.

Origins of the Vietnam War Era Flag Desecration Controversy

The April 1967 New York flag burning and the reaction that it engendered was not the earliest indication that flag desecration was likely to become controversial again after more than twenty years of almost complete oblivion. There were a number of incidents beginning as early as 1965 that attracted a limited but steadily growing amount of publicity and demands for a federal flag desecration law. Thus, while in 1964–65 only three flag desecration bills were introduced in Congress, in 1966 thirty-four such proposals were made, and in the year of the Central Park burning over one hundred flag desecration bills were proposed. As will be pointed out later, what really distinguished the 1967 New York burning from earlier Vietnam era incidents was that, unlike the others, it was photographed and received massive press attention. In short, the 1967 New York flag burning both literally and metaphorically was the match that touched off a smouldering fire that was ready to ignite at any moment.[1]

Perhaps the greatest irony of the Vietnam War era flag desecration controversy was that it erupted just as interest in the entire subject of flag desecration had virtually disappeared, no doubt a reflection of both the general acceptance of pervasive flag use in advertising (as state officials had simply ceased enforcing their state laws banning such commercial use) and the virtual absence of instances of flags being symbolically used for political protest activities since at least World War II. As previously noted, in 1962 the American Law Institute had recommended a Model Penal Code that deleted all references to commercial flag misuse. Even more strikingly, in 1966, the National Conference of Commissioners on Uniform State Laws, which in 1917 had recommended a uniform state flag desecration law largely based on the AFA's

1900 model statute, withdrew its model law (see Appendix, Document 1). The 1917 model statute, which banned both commercial flag use and physical flag desecration, was disavowed in 1966 by the commissioners on the grounds that such laws had become "obsolete."

Perhaps the earliest sign that the flag was about to become the center of a contentious dispute during the Vietnam era came in August 1965, shortly after the introduction of American ground combat troops in Vietnam, when for the first time in decades a controversy over the commercial use of the flag received major press attention. The incident involved the Treo Company of New York, which was the manufacturer of a "Stars 'n Stripes" panty girdle featuring red and white stripes and blue stars on a white background. The product elicited vigorous denunciation from the DAR as "deplorable" and a "shocking caricature" of the flag. Under this attack from the DAR, the Treo Company announced that it would withdraw from the market the 3,000 girdles that were under assault. A spokesman for the company declared, "We will burn the damn things or send them to some foreign country where our flag isn't involved," in order to avoid allowing any organization to "spread comment that would be detrimental to us." According to the DAR's 1966 annual report, the incident received worldwide publicity and resulted in "hundreds of letters from patriotic men and women" praising the organization's action.[2]

The first incidents of protest involving flag desecration during the Vietnam era that attracted significant attention both came in March 1966. On March 16, during a Purdue University (West Lafayette, Indiana) chapter meeting of Students for a Democratic Society (SDS), reportedly held to recruit for a Chicago antiwar march, an apparent anarchist-pacifist guest speaker tore, spat, and trampled on a flag. The Purdue SDS chairman was quoted as saying that he was "shocked" at the incident but that the speaker was simply expressing his opposition to "all kinds of nationalism" and "to say no one may tear up a flag means there is no freedom to dissent." Although the Purdue incident received limited national attention, it was reported on the front page of the *Chicago Tribune* and created a furor in Indiana, where it was largely responsible for state legislative enactment of a new flag desecration law in 1967 that increased the penalty from a maximum $10 fine to a $1,000 fine plus one year in jail.[3]

In the meantime, during a black civil rights demonstration protesting conditions in black schools, on March 30, 1966, in Cordele, Georgia, an American and a Georgia state flag were hauled down from flagpoles at the Cordele courthouse. The American flag was subsequently ripped by protesters before an elderly black man grabbed the flags from the protesters, declaring, "I fought under this flag. You're not going to tear it up." Georgia Governor Carl Sanders quickly ordered state police into Cordele for the announced purpose of protecting the American flag. He proclaimed the incident had been "disgusting," adding, "In my judgment there is no greater outrage that can be perpetrated against our nation and our state," a pronouncement that by implication, at least, suggested that denial of equal educational opportunities or perhaps even a nuclear attack would, by comparison, be relatively minor matters. The flag ripping incident provoked a self-proclaimed "flag loving" Ku Klux Klan demonstration in Cordele on April 3, during which Klansmen sold automobile stickers reading, "God Bless this Flag," and Grand Dragon Calvin Craig proclaimed to a crowd, "If you can't protect this flag we will bring enough Klansmen to do it for you."

In May 1966, a 19-year-old Atlanta black, Rufus Hinton, was sentenced to the maximum penalty of six months each (to be served consecutively rather than concurrently) on two separate charges of flag desecration (one each for the American and the Georgia flag) stemming from the Cordele incident. Hinton's conviction was upheld by the Georgia Supreme Court, but was later overturned by the U.S. Supreme Court on unexplained but apparently technical grounds unrelated to the constitutionality or substance of flag desecration laws.[4]

Several days after the Cordele incident, the first Vietnam era flag burning was reported. On April 12, 1966, the *New York Times* reported that New York City licensing officials were investigating the Bridge Theater to determine whether to revoke its license in connection with the burning of an American flag in violation of New York state law during a performance on April 8. Theater producer Elsa Tambellini, who was represented by lawyer William Kunstler (who later represented the defendants in the 1989 and 1990 Supreme Court flag burning cases), readily confirmed that a flag had been burned during the production of an antiwar skit entitled "LBJ," which had been presented to a packed house of about ninety people. Tambellini defended the action squarely on First Amendment grounds, declaring that "LBJ" was a "very strong protest" against the Vietnam War, that the flag burning was directed against a "symbol of the extraordinary brutality that America has become," and that the licensing investigation was a repressive measure designed to punish the theater for its political viewpoint in a manner reflecting a "complete distortion of freedom of speech." New York City officials ended their investigation of the theater in December 1966, without taking any action and without explanation.[5]

During the nine months leading up to the April 15, 1967 New York City Central Park flag burning, four other flag desecration incidents received limited national attention. On June 6, 1966, Sidney Street, a 47-year-old black Brooklyn bus driver, who had been awarded a Bronze

Star for his heroism during World War II, was arrested in connection with burning a flag after he had learned of the shooting of civil rights activist James Meredith during a march in Mississippi. Although he was acquitted on a disorderly conduct charge, Street was convicted for violating the New York state flag desecration law, which, like most of the state laws, made it illegal to "mutilate, deface, defile or defy, trample upon, or cast contempt" upon the flag "either by words or act." According to the evidence and trial testimony that led to the conviction of Street by a New York City Criminal Court judge (sitting without a jury) on August 9, 1966, Street exclaimed to a small crowd that if "they let that happen to Meredith we don't need an American flag" and had also declared, "We don't need no damn flag."

During Street's trial and in subsequent proceedings before two New York appeals courts, which upheld his conviction, virtually the entire focus of both prosecuting and defense attorneys was whether flag burning was a constitutionally protected form of political protest, with minimal attention paid to Street's oral remarks. Thus, Street was represented by ACLU attorneys, who argued that flag burning was a "practical and effective way" to express political views, and New York's highest court, the Court of Appeals, in upholding the conviction on July 7, 1967 (three months after the Central Park burning), summarized the case as centering upon the question of "whether the deliberate act of burning an American flag in public as a 'protest' may be punished as a crime." In answer to this question, the Court of Appeals held that New York State could constitutionally forbid such action in order to "prevent a breach of the peace" and that the law had been properly applied to Street because his actions had amounted to an "act of incitement, literally and figuratively 'incendiary.'"[6]

Street's ACLU attorneys appealed his conviction to the Supreme Court, which by announcing its decision to hear the case on June 17, 1968, set the stage for its first consideration of the constitutionality of flag desecration laws since its only prior hearing of the issue sixty years earlier in the 1907 *Halter* case. However, unlike the *Halter* case, which involved advertising use of the flag and was argued and settled in terms of property rights (rather than free speech rights) versus the police powers of the state to regulate use of the flag, the *Street* case clearly involved political protest and, as in the lower courts, both sides focused on the fundamental issue of whether Street's action was a form of free speech protected by the First Amendment to the Constitution. Thus, Street's lawyers told the Court in their brief that flag destruction as a form of political protest could not be forbidden under the First Amendment because his action was purely expressive, with no harmful "by-products" (such as setting a building on fire or obstructing the streets) that the state could legitimately regulate. They added:

> If we concede that there are certain political symbols which are above desecration, we open the door to drastic suppression of our right to criticize the state. There is no logical differentiation between burning the flag and burning an effigy of the President. Our flag is really the effigy of a nation. As such, it is not immune from symbolic criticism.[7]

Street's lawyers added that any conviction based on the *possibility* that disorder might have resulted from his action could not stand either: Street's acquittal on the disorderly conduct charge demonstrated that his act had led to no disorders and suppressing expression merely on the basis of a possible, as opposed to an actual, breach of the peace, would open the door to forbidding a wide variety of expression based on speculation about the possible results. They also argued that the need to protect symbolic expression under the First Amendment was especially great because most people could not gain access to the mass media without engaging in "new, more dramatic forms of communication" than ordinary speech or press and that, in an age in which visual forms of expression were challenging the former primacy of the printed word, types of protest such as flag burning conveyed a message that could not be communicated as effectively in any other form. They declared, quoting the noted commentator Marshall McLuhan, that, "If, in fact, 'The medium is the message,' or at least an important ingredient of the message, this Court has [a] responsibility to insure that new, visual forms of communication receive the protection to which they are entitled."

In response to Street's argument, Brooklyn Acting District Attorney Elliott Golden, in his Supreme Court brief, defended flag desecration laws with rhetoric that was both clearly influenced by the general social turmoil of the late 1960s and highly reminiscent of the early days of the flag protection movement. Although supporting the New York law as a valid means of preventing breaches of the peace, which allegedly would likely be incited by flag desecration, the bulk of his argument fervently defended the state's right to prevent the communication of ideas that were deeply offensive to most people. Thus, he declared that flagburning amounted to "the disrespect of a needed and worthy symbol" and a "vivid reflection of disrespect for our institutions" and that it was "so patently offensive to, and 'sacrilegious' of, the deep traditional feelings of the American and the very spirit of this Country's history, that it would be unthinkable to shelter such conduct under the protective mantle of our treasured Constitution." According to Golden, "We cannot afford to experiment by permitting all acts and words denigrating to our basic philosophies to freely reach the market-place of ideas."[8]

Unlike burning an effigy of the president, an act he characterized as having a "political connotation," Golden declared that burning the flag amounted to an "offense directed at the *foundation* of government," an act equivalent to setting "fire to the Nation itself," and a "repudiation of everything, including the basic political spirit of the Country," that would lead to the "eventual, but almost certain, decadence of the Nation's spirit," threaten the "very foundations of a democratic way of life," and endanger "the structure of duly constituted government." He maintained, "Is not an act such as committed by [Street] one which will 'treasonably' lend aid and comfort to the enemy?" At one point Golden characterized Street's act as "no different than hurling a stone through the window of the White House, painting the latter black, while trespassing, or setting fire to the National Archives."

Golden repeatedly referred to the general social tensions of the late 1960s, for example in one extraordinary passage lumping Street's flag burning together with a broad assortment of symptoms of general social and political breakdown, including the assassinations of President Kennedy and Martin Luther King Jr., the "destroying of draft cards," "student riots," the "emergence of a 'hippie' generation," a rise in crime, and the "psychedelic adventures" associated with drugs such as LSD. In these conditions, which Golden said reflected the fact that a "significant" part of the population "either have chaotic and anarchic thought" or "harbor cold indifference," he maintained, "Can anyone of us, today, honestly and confidently, take the position that [Street's] act of defiantly burning the flag, if ignored and left unpunished, will not finally ignite the spark of conflagration and chaos tomorrow? ... It cannot be denied that to scorn a flag is to erode a nation from within!" Given these "critical times," Golden stated, New York viewed preserving "the dignity of this Nation's flag" as of "paramount importance." Therefore, Golden maintained, "The question of free expression must yield to the higher requirement" that the nation "survive in the hostile atmosphere of a tumultuous present-day history." Under the present circumstances, he declared, protecting the flag was a "vital need" that justified outlawing disrespect for it "over and above any immediate consideration of possible risk of breaches of the public peace which may be occasioned by such inflammatory behavior" and also warranted making "even the words by the appellant, in derogation of the flag, without more, subject to criminal punishment."

During oral argument before the Supreme Court on October 21, 1968, New York again maintained this latter point, declaring that Street could have been legitimately convicted even for using "only words" that expressed "contempt and hatred" for the flag. In its 5–4 decision of April 21, 1969, the Supreme Court seized upon this point to overturn Street's conviction on the narrow and strained ground that the formal charge against Street and the trial record did not preclude the possibility that he had in fact been convicted solely for his words. The majority opinion, written by Justice Harlan, was based firmly on the 1931 *Stromberg* red flag case and the 1943 *Barnette* flag saluting case, among other precedents. The majority completely avoided the issue of the constitutionality of outlawing *physical* flag desecration in the context of political expression, instead simply holding that a conviction possibly based solely on verbal remarks, in the absence of any evident threat to the peace or incitement to violence, could not be upheld. The Court declared, "It is firmly settled that under our Constitution the public expression of ideas may not be prohibited merely because the ideas are themselves offensive to some of their hearers," including even the expression of "distasteful" or "defiant or contemptuous" views about the flag. Having decided that Street's conviction was therefore invalid as possibly based solely on speech, Harlan added, the Court resolved to "resist the pulls to decide the constitutional issues involved in this case on a broader basis than the record before us imperatively requires."[9]

Despite its narrowness, the Supreme Court's decision in *Street* was something of a minor landmark, not only because it was the first high court opinion on flag desecrations laws in sixty years, but also because it clearly struck down the provisions contained in most state laws that outlawed contemptuous remarks about the flag. However, by explicitly avoiding the far more contentious issue of physical flag desecration, the Court initiated a pattern of failing to squarely face this question that would continue for the next twenty years, no doubt reflecting the court's desire to avoid or postpone the likely massive controversy that in fact did erupt in the aftermath of its 1989 *Johnson* decision. (In that case the Court struck down physical flag desecration laws by essentially, almost in passing, relying on *Street*, pointing out that symbolic physical flag protests were constitutionally equivalent to oral criticism of the flag, a logical point that hardly required twenty years of legal pondering to reach.)

The deep concern of the Court over the political explosiveness of the entire flag desecration issue was not only clearly reflected in the Court's strained argument that Street could have been convicted solely for his remarks (which logically implied that the New York Criminal Court judge might have conceivably found Street guilty of flag desecration for his speech, but not for the flagburning!), but also by a detour in the majority opinion in which Harlan departed from any required legal path in order to declare that "disrespect for our flag is to be deplored no less in these vexed times than in calmer periods of our history." This latter remark was retained in Harlan's opinion despite a private but futile protest from majority Justice Brennan, who lamented, "I have no idea what this means and ... [even] if I did, I still wouldn't like it".[10]

Consideration of the *Street* case caused severe turmoil within the Court. Immediately after the case was argued, a preliminary poll of the Court on October 28, 1968, revealed a 6–2 majority for reversing Street's conviction (which in fact was a 7–2 majority, as Justice Douglas abstained at the Court conference, apparently for tactical reasons, although his papers deposited at the Library of Congress make clear he strongly favored the preliminary majority view). However, during the seven months it took the Court to announce its opinion on April 21, 1969, Justices White and Fortas, who had originally voted to overturn the conviction, changed their minds, thereby changing a lopsided 7–2 majority into a narrow 5–4 majority. By late March, in fact, the prospect that Street's conviction would be upheld apparently was so strong that Douglas wrote (but never circulated) an opinion dissenting from such a possible ruling, on the grounds that "what one does with his own property seems to me to be his own business, so long as he does not imperil the lives or property of other people or use it to produce a riot." Meanwhile, Justice Fortas, who had circulated on December 11, 1968, an opinion concurring with the preliminary majority on the grounds that, although a conviction based on flagburning could clearly be upheld it was "impossible" to determine whether the conviction was based on speech alone, reversed himself in a memo to Justice Harlan on March 19. Apologizing for "inconstancy" Fortas declared that Street's conviction "was for the conduct of publicly burning the flag and not for the words used," and that "it is sensible to accept the realities of the facts."

At least some members of the Court minority were angered to the point of apoplexy by the majority ruling. In 1989, Duke Law Professor Walter Dellinger, who was a Court law clerk at the time of the *Street* decision, recalled during a Congressional hearing on possible responses to the 1989 *Johnson* ruling that the case caused the Court "true agony," and that Justice Black, who was in the minority, was more "emotionally affected" by it than any other case during his clerkship. According to Dellinger, Black felt "an enormous pull" between "first amendment theory on the one hand, and his very deep and genuine feelings about the flag on the other." According to a Supreme Court source who also worked at the Court in 1968–69 and who requested anonymity during a 1991 interview, Black at one point despairingly lamented to Chief Justice Warren that if Street's conviction was overturned, "Chief, next they'll be peeing on the flag."[11]

The four dissenters (Warren, Fortas, White, and Black) each wrote separate bitter dissents, which effectively accused the majority of rewriting the truth to avoid the fact that *Street* was a flag burning and not a verbal disrespect case and which firmly declared that statutes outlawing physical flag desecration were constitutional. Warren, who in the Supreme Court's private October 25, 1968 conference on the *Street* case was quoted by Justice Brennan as declaring that "the only question" was the constitutionality of outlawing flag burning, which he termed "conduct and not speech or symbolic speech," wrote in his dissent that the majority had searched the history of the case "microscopically" in order to settle it on "peripheral" speech grounds about which the trial record was "strangely silent," leaving "no doubt that [Street] was convicted solely for burning the American flag."

Warren suggested that, especially since the flag had recently "become an integral part of public protests," and flag desecration had become a matter of "widespread concern," the Court was obligated to face up to the issue. Warren aptly and presciently declared that both those "who seek constitutional shelter for acts of flag desecration perpetrated in the course of a political protest and those who must enforce the law are entitled to know the scope of constitutional protection" and the Court's failure to meet its obligation "encourages others" to test the issue "in the streets." Warren closed his twelve-page dissent by emphatically declaring that both state and federal governments "do have the power to protect the flag from acts of desecration and disgrace."[12]

Justice Black deleted from his published dissent his original intention to accuse the majority of an "extraordinary gymnastic feat" in its reasoning. However, he maintained the position that he had expressed at the Court's conference (that the conviction was based solely on the flag burning) and declared, "It passes my belief that anything in the Federal Constitution bars a State from making the deliberate burning of the American flag an offense." Justice White indicated agreement, declaring that the majority had "spun an intricate, technical web" and "ensnared itself in its own remorseless logic and arrived at a result having no support in the facts of the case or the governing law." White added that the majority's position that Street could have been convicted for speech alone could only have been written with "its tongue in its cheek," especially since such an interpretation assumed that Street could have been simultaneously acquitted for the burning. Justice Fortas avoided discussing the speech issue in his dissent, but implicitly assumed that the only issue was flag burning. He declared that physical flag desecration laws were constitutional because, under the 1907 *Halter* decision, although flags could be privately owned, such "ownership is subject to special burdens and responsibilities" because flag usage had "traditionally and universally" been "subject to special rules and regulations."[13]

While the *Street* case was making its way through the court system, and receiving relatively little publicity until the 1969 Supreme Court ruling, three additional flag desecration incidents were reported in the national press during the three months immediately preceding the April 15, 1967 New York Central Park flag burning. The incident that had the least impact was the arrest of four Yale University student actors, as well as their director, who were charged with flag desecration for allegedly using a flag as a blanket and shawl and throwing it on the ground and rolling on it during a March 1967 performance at a New York City theater. These charges were eventually dismissed in May 1967, at the request of the New York City District Attorney's office, leading Yale Drama School Dean Robert Brustein to express "delight" and the view that flag desecration laws should be struck down as unconstitutional "restrictions on artistic expression."[14]

Another flag desecration incident that took place during the immediate pre-Central Park burning period occurred on April 14, 1967 (the very day before the Central Park event), when Scott Chisholm, a thirty-one-year-old Canadian citizen and English instructor at Indiana State University (ISU) at Terre Haute, burned a flag during a class to suggest that symbols were not equivalent to what they represented, and that therefore one could burn an American flag without showing any disrespect for the United States. According to Chisholm, he had made this point in the abstract to his class on April 12, and when he arrived in class on April 14 he found a small flag and matches placed on his desk, which he termed "bait" and a "trap," and which led him to burn the flag on what he felt was a "dare." While burning the flag, Chisholm said later, he announced, "This is not to be misconstrued as an unpatriotic act, because I am not here involved in abstract questions about my government. What I am burning is merely a piece of cloth and a stick, a concrete object."[15]

Chisholm's action had only a modest national impact, no doubt lessened because it did not occur in the context of a public or antiwar demonstration and was not photographed, and above all because it quickly became swallowed up in the far more publicized burning that took place the next day. However, Chisholm's flag burning caused a furor in Indiana, where, within a few hours after the incident, he was summarily suspended, with pay, pending an ISU investigation for "unprofessional conduct." Governor Roger Branigin termed Chisholm's action an "outrage" that had left him "heartsick." During the next few weeks, the Chisholm affair was the subject of almost daily and often openly hostile news reports in the Terre Haute press. For example, in its first account of the incident, the *Terre Haute Tribune* described Chisholm as a "bearded" professor with the reputation of being a "poor teacher" who "wears his hair long" (although the paper published a picture of a bearded but clearly short-haired Chisholm) and who had been the "booster" of a "Bohemian-type coffee shop near the campus"—all words which in 1966 conjured up the image of a wild-eyed subversive, or, at the least, a left-wing radical.

During the following month, Chisholm received threats against his life; the *Terre Haute Tribune* endorsed Governor Branigin's assessment of the flag-burning as an "outrage" and praised ISU for its "swift initial" suspension; a Bloomfield, Indiana high school teacher who defended Chisholm was summarily fired by a unanimous vote of her school board, which acted after the local American Legion post demanded her dismissal and the local community was reported "in an uproar" over her statements; and an ISU art instructor resigned to protest "the handling of the Chisholm case." While the ISU investigation of Chisholm proceeded, some student spokesmen, including the local SDS chapter president, supported Chisholm, and the local chapter of the American Association of University Professors (AAUP) asked the national AAUP to investigate "unprofessional conduct" during the investigation by ISU officials, but most public comments were critical and demanded harsh action against him.

For example, Indiana Congressmen Richard Roudebush and John Myers both publicly denounced Chisholm and cited the incident as evidence that a national flag desecration law was required. Roudebush demanded that Chisholm be deported, while Myers told a Congressional hearing on May 17 that the incident "came as a shock which still hangs over the city of Terre Haute and, indeed, the entire state." Condemnations of and/or demands for the deportation and/or firing of Chisholm were also issued by the Terre Haute City Council, the local branches of the Mothers of World War II and the VFW, both the local and state American Legion branches, and other organizations. The state American Legion branch, claiming to speak for the "patriotic, loyal and law abiding citizens of this state," demanded that Chisholm be fired "for his disrespect for this county in time of great national strife," especially since he had burned a flag "on the very day" that an Indiana resident was killed in Vietnam "fighting for the rights which this flag desecrator was abusing."

In an action reported in the national press, Chisholm was in fact fired, for "poor judgment" and "unprofessional" conduct, by the ISU Board of Trustees on May 20, 1967, on a motion offered by ex-officio member Richard Wells, the state superintendent of public instruction.

In announcing the firing, an action taken despite a faculty recommendation that Chisholm be censured but not dismissed, ISU Board of Trustees President Wayne Crockett declared, no doubt correctly, that he knew of "no other instance in the history of American education in which a faculty member willfully burned an American flag in a classroom." After his firing, Chisholm issued a statement declaring that he had only intended to have his students "examine the images by which they live," since, as he reported he had told them, "To react solely to the object is irrational and when we become trapped by our symbols and do not think about the ideas they represent, we abandon reason and replace it with misplaced emotion." As Chisholm noted with great accuracy, "It is ironic to consider how true that statement has become." He concluded, "I am frightened that the substance of my lecture has resulted in such shattering truth. I have proved my point."

There is little doubt that the firing—which occurred less than two weeks after the HJC began the first Congressional hearings on a federal flag desecration bill in over thirty years in the aftermath of the Central Park burning—essentially reflected the University's fear of adverse public reaction to the flag-burning incident. (Ironically, Chisholm was never prosecuted under Indiana's flag desecration law, which in the aftermath of the 1966 Purdue University incident had been reenacted earlier in 1967 with a greatly increased penalty but was not yet in effect at the time of Chisholm's action.) For example, the faculty committee that investigated the incident reported that Chisholm's actions were related to his classroom material, that no evidence indicated any intent by Chisholm to express any political views whatsoever, and that all but one student witness indicated that they "were not disturbed by his act and that they understood his intent." Yet despite these findings the committee recommended censure essentially because Chisholm "brought embarrassment to the University," a finding completely irrelevant to academic considerations. Similarly, Trustees President Crockett declared in his statement of May 20 that Chisholm had been fired because he had caused "untold damage to the image of this University, and has subjected the entire staff to undeserved ridicule, criticism and suspicions." After the firing Crockett commented that he felt that ISU's "image" had been "aided" by the action.

An investigation of the Chisholm firing subsequently undertaken by the national AAUP concluded that ISU had, both procedurally and substantively, violated Chisholm's academic freedom rights and that the "intense publicity" the case received played a role of "major importance" in the University's actions. The AAUP investigation concluded that the University administration viewed the Chisholm incident "not in its pedagogical context as a classroom incident relevant to the subject of symbolism being taught, but as a public act which attracted wide public notice and hostile public reaction." In 1970, the AAUP formally censured the University for its firing of Chisholm.

Although the Chisholm affair received massive local publicity, the flag desecration incident that received the greatest national attention during the immediate pre-Central Park burning period was the December 28, 1966 filing of a complaint under New York's flag desecration law against Stephen Radich. Radich, the forty-four-year-old owner of a New York City art gallery, was arrested in connection with the display of sixteen sculptures and paintings by artist Marc Morrel that were clearly designed to protest the Vietnam War (for example, the exhibit was accompanied by taped antiwar music).

In what was in some respects a precursor to the 1989 "flag on the floor" Chicago art exhibit involving "Dred" Scott Tyler, which immediately preceded the subsequent 1989–90 flag burning controversy, Morrel, a twenty-nine-year-old ex-marine, incorporated representations of the flag in a number of his works. By far the most controversial of these was a sculpture displayed in a second-floor gallery window, in which a flag was stuffed with material shaped in a form suggesting a cadaver hanging from a noose, and a second sculpture, displayed inside the gallery, in which an erect phallus representation, covered with material resembling a small flag, was attached to the base of a large cross decorated in clerical-like garb. During eight years of litigation, which finally ended when Radich's original 1967 conviction was overturned on constitutional grounds by a federal appeals court in 1974, the case attracted enormous publicity, including a major article in *Life* Magazine, extensive continuing coverage in the *New York Times* (which, like *Life*, generally focused on the noose flag and omitted mention of the phallic flag), and three articles in *Art in America*, a journal for artists and art lovers.[16]

Radich (curiously, Morrel was not prosecuted for reasons that were never explained) was defended from the onset by the ACLU, which termed the prosecution a case of "cultural suppression" and declared, "What is at stake is the right of artists to freely express themselves and to use all the materials available to them." In one of the earliest full-fledged freedom of speech attacks on flag desecration laws, the ACLU maintained that New York officials were attempting to "sanctify the symbols of government" but could not do so because "the First Amendment protects the right to freely criticize the Government and all its institutions." Although Radich was not supported by any major American art institution or organization, such as the College Art Association, or the boards of any art museum, he gained the immediate support of many individual art dealers, artists, and critics, as well as a sprinkling of individual museum and school directors, such as Paul Mocsanyi, director of New York's New School Art Center. He wrote that Morrel had sought not to desecrate the flag but to "criticize those who pay lip service to the ideals for which the American flag is a symbol—and this has been considered in all civilized societies as the right of the artist." Radich himself warned that if his original conviction stood the freedom of art galleries "to show new work without police interference could be severely threatened," Morrel lamented that the conviction "depressed and disheartened" him because it "makes my works—and therefore my thoughts—illegal." On the other hand, the head of the United States Flag Foundation, which filed a separate civil suit against Radich for violation of the flag desecration law, declared, "You can't use the flag as a protest. It's just like you wouldn't murder your grandmother. The American flag is so high above everything—it's on a pedestal—that nothing should touch it." At least judging from Radich's mail, which was overwhelmingly hostile and included death threats, the Flag Foundation's position was the more popular.

Radich's trial was held on March 29, 1967, before a three-judge New York City Criminal Court panel, two weeks before the Central Park flag burning. Assistant District Attorney Gerald Slater maintained that the sculptures would arouse the public "to the point where there would be possible riot and strife" and therefore should receive no First Amendment protection. He denied the defense's contention that the state flag desecration law's explicit exclusion of ornamental pictures would also apply to sculptures since the legislature had taken "into consideration what objects would arouse the public wrath" and determined that "three-dimensional objects might and pictures might not," even if they were pictures of the same objects, because "for one thing a photograph in a book is not an animated object and cannot be touched" while a sculpture "can be touched, it can be seen and it is an object more likely to arouse the public wrath." Radich testified that the Morrel sculptures did not seek to express "contempt for the flag," as was required for conviction under the state law, but rather aimed at the "people involved" in supporting "aggressive acts," such as the support of "organized religion" for war that Radich felt was suggested by the penis-cross sculpture. *New York Times* art critic Hilton Kramer testified in support of Radich, arguing that while the sculptures were "rather feeble," they were nonetheless serious works of "protest art," with the phallic flag, for example, equating "social military violence" to "sexual excitement."

Radich was found guilty and sentenced to a $500 fine or a sixty-day jail term by a 2–1 vote in a verdict handed down on May 5, just three days before the scheduled beginning of the HJC flag desecration hearings. The court held that Radich had contemptuously displayed the flag, that New York's flag law was not unconstitutionally vague and that its "ornamental pictures" exclusion could not be held to encompass Morrel's sculptures or to invalidate the law on the grounds of arbitrary classification because "any contemptuous use of the flag comes within the purview of the statute, whether two-dimensional or three-dimensional." The majority held that the First Amendment's guarantee of freedom of speech did not include a "license to desecrate the flag" and, citing the Supreme Court's 1907 *Halter* decision, upheld the New York law as within the state's police power to outlaw acts that posed a "threat to public order."

Judge Amos Basel argued in dissent that the New York flag law was unconstitutionally vague. He also clearly supported Radich's free speech contentions, arguing that although "we may quarrel with his theme, disagree with his method, condemn his goal," the sculptures were clearly expressions of political protest, which Radich viewed in any case as not "showing contempt for the flag" but which instead attempted to show that American foreign policy was violating ideals such as liberty and equality—which Morrel supported and which the flag was supposed to stand for. Judge Basel anticipated by twenty years the Supreme Court majorities in the 1989 *Johnson* and 1990 *Eichman* cases by noting:

> No one would seriously argue [antiwar demonstrators] be jailed for expressing verbally or in writing what the artist here makes visual. I agree with defendant's art expert that the artist's talent is limited, his symbolism obvious, clichéd and lacking in imagination. I acknowledge he has chosen a means of expression in extreme poor taste and shabby in form. But is he to be punished for his lack of manners and his vulgarity when his intention is a serious condemnation of our present foreign policy?[17]

Radich's conviction was subsequently upheld by a unanimous vote (without written opinion) of a three-judge 1968 appeals panel of the New York Supreme Court, again by a 5–2 vote of New York's highest criminal court, the Court of Appeals, in 1970, and by a divided 4–4 vote (without written opinion) of the U.S. Supreme Court in 1971. The Court of Appeals majority, citing *Halter* among other precedents, essentially repeated the analysis of the Criminal Court majority. It stressed that the placement of the flag-noose sculpture "in a street display window" could threaten "preservation of the public peace," since a "reasonable" man would find this and the other flag sculptures acts of "dishonor." Such a desire to prevent breaches of the peace, rather than an attempt to "insure suppression" of dissident ideas, was the valid legislative purpose behind the New York law, the court held, and therefore, although "defendant may have a sincere ideological viewpoint," he "must find other ways to express it." *New York Times* art critic Hilton Kramer had testified at Radich's trial that he found the sculptures "feeble" yet nonetheless serious examples of protest art. He wrote that the court's opinion was "full of strange and frightening details," that it was a "frightening development" that threatened to lead to further prosecutions of "the display of works of art that protest the political policies of the government," and that if the court was correct that the Morrel constructions posed a threat to the peace "then our society is already far more fragile than even its severest critics have yet supposed."[18]

Court of Appeals Chief Judge Stanley Fuld, supported by another judge, issued a bitter dissent, an action redolent with irony since he had written the Court of Appeals decision upholding Street's conviction (later overturned by the Supreme Court), an opinion that was literally thrown in his face by the Radich majority. Fuld argued that while Street's public flag burning had posed a genuine threat to public order, the same could not be said of artistic constructions "displayed in the quiet surroundings" of an art gallery, especially since the sculptures amounted to "three-dimensional political cartoons." The state could not "legitimately punish that which would be constitutionally protected if spoken or drawn," Fuld declared, "simply because the idea had been expressed, instead, through the medium of sculpture." Such a prosecution, Fuld maintained, amounted to "nothing more than political censorship," because it was clear that the sculptures were "singled out" for prosecution "not because the flag was used," but "solely because of the particular political message" they sought to deliver.[19]

In November 1970, while Radich's fate was being considered on appeal to the U.S. Supreme Court, a show of "flag art," featuring such items as flag miniskirts, flag cookies, a flag penis (entitled "Yankee Doodle Keep It Up"), a flag in a toilet, and a flag stuffed in a fire alarm box, was held at the Judson Memorial Church in New York City as a "challenge to the repressive laws governing so-called flag desecration." The show, originally planned to run six days, was forced to close down one day early when the New York District Attorney's office (which had ignored an opening-day flag burning) raided it on November 13, seized the phallic flag, threatened to confiscate other exhibits if the show continued, and arrested, on flag desecration charges, three artists (none of whom had produced the confiscated work) who were involved in putting together the show. The Judson Church minister declared in a sermon delivered two days after the raid that, "when the flag becomes a sacred idol we are on the way to a tyranny." A committee formed to protest the Judson Church arrests declared that the arrested artists believed that all Americans had the "right/duty to register their political and moral beliefs using the people's flag in any and all ways one sees fit short of hurting or harming another human being" and in particular that "if the flag can be used to sanctify killing it should be available to the people to stop killing."

At a protest rally of several hundred New York artists on December 1, 1970, many audience members wore canceled flag stamps to point out the federal government's institutionalized, massive program of "flag desecration." During the trial of the "Judson Three," art critic Lucy Lippard declared that the meaning of the flag penis was that "a nation that won't let its people use their flag as they see fit is a prick." The Judson Three were convicted and given a choice of 30 days in jail or $100 fines, with their final fate on appeal made dependent by mutual agreement on the outcome of the *Radich* case.[20]

During oral arguments before the Supreme Court on February 22, 1971, Radich's ACLU lawyers stressed free speech arguments, declaring that "under our system of government, it cannot be a crime for a citizen to cast contempt upon any symbol of government" since such "inevitably involves the communication of an idea." The basic issue, they argued, was "whether our flag, originally designed to symbolize our heritage of freedom, has now become a totem whose worship can curb the very freedom it is supposed to represent." New York District Attorney Frank Hogan replied that the First Amendment only protected freedom of "the press" and "speech" and that "an actual flag in the form of a male sexual organ, or a hanging effigy, is neither 'speech' nor 'the press.'"

A group of influential members of the art world, including the director of New York City's Museum of Modern Art, submitted an amicus brief on behalf of Radich and declared that convicting him would make the flag a "fetish" and that it was illogical to "treat paintings and sculptures differently from speech and writing." On March 24, 1971, much to the astonishment of observers like *New York Times* Supreme Court reporter Fred Graham (who, in the aftermath of the *Street* decision, had written that it was a "foregone conclusion" that the justices would rule that "painters and sculptors are as fully protected by the First Amendment as any person who expresses ideas") the Supreme Court issued a 4–4 ruling (with Justice Douglas not participating) without any written opinions, which upheld the lower court conviction. (Under Supreme Court rules a tie vote results in an affirmance of the appealed case.) Art historian Carl Baldwin concluded that the lesson of the *Radich* decision was that artists would be "generally well advised to think twice before expressing satirical or dissident sentiment with allusions to the flag; many seem to be guiding themselves accordingly."[21]

Normally a Supreme Court decision would foreclose any further legal efforts, as a federal district judge held nine months later in response to a habeas corpus petition to release Radich. However, the U.S. Court of Appeals for the Second Circuit held in 1972, in a highly technical ruling (which was later substantively upheld in a different Supreme Court case), that, because the Supreme Court had not actually handed down an opinion in the *Radich* case and upheld the New York Court of Appeals only by virtue of its tie vote, Radich had not yet been given his right to seek one substantive adjudication of a claim to a violation of constitutional rights in the federal courts. On November 7, 1974, the most litigated flag desecration case in American history finally came to an end after eight years when Federal District Court Judge John Cannella granted Radich's habeas corpus plea in an extraordinarily long, well-researched, and vigorously argued opinion, which held the New York flag desecration law had been unconstitutionally applied to Radich in violation of his free speech rights. Heavily depending upon the then very recent and highly ambiguous Supreme Court decision in *Spence v. Washington*, in which a flag desecration conviction for taping a peace sign to a flag and displaying it from a window had been overturned, Judge Cannella held that the Morrel sculptures had clearly involved a form of symbolic speech raising First Amendment concerns. He declared that, as in the *Spence* case, the Morrel sculptures had clearly not destroyed or permanently damaged a flag (as in a flag burning, which he suggested might therefore raise additional issues). Rather, they had harnessed the flag's symbolic power, "in all of its communicative majesty, unalloyed and undiminished," to transmit political views by simply transferring "the symbol from traditional surroundings to the realm of protest and dissent."[22]

The fundamental point on which Cannella took issue with the Court of Appeals majority was his holding that, while preventing breaches of the peace was a valid state interest, an examination of the trial record revealed the lack of "any objective evidence whatever which would sustain the conclusion that a breach of the peace was either likely to occur, or an imminent result" of the display of the Morrel art constructions "in the privacy" of a "second floor art gallery," especially since the exhibit had been under way for two weeks without incident before Radich was arrested. When fundamental constitutional rights were at issue, Cannella held, "the state must demonstrate more than a mere speculative or hypothetical possibility of disorder" and although the flag is "dear to us," when "our interests in preserving the integrity of the flag conflict with the higher interest" of protecting basic rights, "the latter must prevail, even when it results in the expression of ideas about our flag and the nation which are defiant, contemptuous or unacceptable to most Americans."[23]

While the *Radich* case was making its way through the courts, artist Marc Morrel's flag art became the subject of yet another prosecution, although one that was far less prolonged. In March 1969, Morrel's exhibit "Flag in Chains," consisting of two flags sewn together, stuffed with foam rubber, and encircled by an iron chain, was seized by the county sheriff in Macon County, Illinois, where it had been available for viewing on request only at the Decatur Art Center. Two Art Center officials were charged with flag desecration, found guilty, and fined $75, but the Illinois Supreme Court, while avoiding basic constitutional issues, reversed the convictions in March 1972 on the grounds that the Illinois flag desecration law was designed to prevent breaches of the peace and that the evidence against the defendants failed to indicate "any immediate threat to public order or safety."[24]

The Impact of the Central Park Burning and the 1967 House Judiciary Committee Hearings

At the time of the April 15, 1967 New York City Central Park flag burning, Sidney Street's flag burning conviction was on appeal in the New York courts, Stephen Radich was about to go on trial in New York in connection with Morrel's flag constructions, four Yale University students had just been arrested for flag desecration during a New York theater performance, Rufus Hinton's conviction for ripping an American flag in Georgia was on appeal before the Supreme Court, and Scott Chisholm had, literally the previous day, burned a flag in his classroom in Terre Haute, Indiana. All of these events, plus the other 1966–67 flag desecration incidents described above, had been the subject of increasingly frequent denunciations in Congress and, as previously noted, by 1966 the number of flag desecration proposals introduced in Congress had skyrocketed to thirty-four. Especially vocal in the early (pre-Central Park) Vietnam era campaign for a federal flag desecration law was Representative Richard Roudebush of Indiana, a former VFW national commander, and Representative James Quillen of Tennessee, both of whom denounced flag desecrators on numerous occasions in 1966 and early 1967. For example, on July 20, 1966, Roudebush declared that, amid a growing wave of domestic "anarchy and disrespect for law and order," surely the nation could preserve the flag's "respect and dignity at home" if it was asking young Americans to "fight and die for this symbol abroad."[25]

Among other vocal Congressional supporters of the early Vietnam era campaign for a federal flag desecration law was Representative

Edwin Edwards of Alabama, who declared on April 5, 1966, that Congress would be "foolish and naive" if it underestimated the "Communist involvement in these incidents of agitation and strife" fomented by "subversives" and "hard core agitators" who deviously used the "same freedom symbolized by the flag they would desecrate" to carry out their "treasonable acts." Representative Maston O'Neal, whose Georgia district included the site of the Cordele flag ripping, told the House on April 6, 1966, that the incident reflected the "determined efforts" of "anti-American agitators" to "destroy America from within while operating under the guise of civil rights workers." And Representative John Ashbrook of Ohio, who on July 28, 1966, denounced the ACLU's constitutional defense of flag desecrators, declared that "it is unconscionable that anyone except Communist sympathizers and those who would destroy our nation" would take such a stance, although he conceded that the Supreme Court would "probably uphold their twisted, weird theory which they propound in this offensive, unpatriotic and despicable beatnik-type protest."[26]

In demanding a federal flag desecration law during the pre-Central Park period, Congressional backers introduced into the *Congressional Record* evidence of support from numerous newspapers and civic and patriotic organizations, including the *Bristol Virginia-Tennessean* (which referred to flag desecration as "near-treason"), the *Nashville Banner* (which lamented increasing incidents of flag desecration by "subversive characters" operating in an "era of rampant hooliganism and apparently privileged subversive mischief"), the *Stars and Stripes* (which proclaimed that only the "infinitesimal minority who have been guilty of Flag desecration" could oppose a federal law), the Catholic War Veterans, the Veterans of World War I, the American Coalition of Patriotic Societies, the American Veterans of World War II and Korea, and the VFW.

The VFW argument for a national flag law was typical in its response to the criticism that no additional legislation was needed since all states already had flag desecration statutes: VFW Commander-in-Chief Andy Borg declared in August 1966 that "the flag belongs to all the American people and thusly should be protected by national legislation" and that federal action was required to show that the nation was "sick and tired of the American flag being burned, stomped upon, torn apart and villified by communist inspired peaceniks and others." Borg's successor, Leslie Fry, proclaimed on April 4, 1967, eleven days before the Central Park burning, that "nearly all Americans—except the defilers and peaceniks"—would support a federal law to suppress such "heinous acts." The DAR also renewed its long-standing quest for national flag desecration legislation following the Central Park burning. The annual DAR convention passed a resolution expressing "indignation" over the incident and DAR Flag Committee Chairwoman Mala Crittenden declared that the event had "shocked the nation." DAR President-General Mrs. William Sullivan devoted a special column to supporting federal legislation in the June-July 1967 *DAR Magazine* (although in a bizarre display of ignorance of the DAR's role in originating such demands seventy years earlier she referred to the recent incidents as the "first time in the history of the United States" that the flag had been desecrated). The SAR also joined the campaign for a federal law, with a special resolution passed at its May 1967 convention.[27]

Clearly, the April 15, 1967 Central Park flag burning simply struck the spark on a flag desecration tinder box that was already on the verge of exploding into a national issue. The incident took place in the Sheep Meadow section of the park during a massive antiwar demonstration involving almost 200,000 protesters, and it was not even reported at first in most news accounts. For example, there was no mention of the flag burning in reports about the demonstration published on April 16 in the *Chicago Tribune,* the *Washington Post,* or the *Detroit News;* the *New York Times* buried a brief reference to the incident near the end of a lengthy story.

The major reason why the Central Park burning became such a cause célèbre, far outstripping the impact of the previous 1966–67 flag desecration incidents, was simply that, unlike any of the earlier cases (except for the Radich exhibit), photographers were on hand to record it. (However another photographic impetus to Congressional action may have been the placement on the front page of the April 8, 1967 *New York Times* of a picture of peace demonstrators burning an American flag in Paris during Vice-President Humphrey's visit there to place a wreath at the French Tomb of the Unknown Soldier). On April 16 the *New York Daily News* plastered one of the resulting pictures across an entire inside page, while the *Washington Star* published a picture of the burning on its front page. In subsequent days these pictures were republished in a number of outlets, including the May 1, 1967 issue of *U.S. News and World Report* and the May 21, 1967 *New York Times.*[28]

The Central Park incident and especially pictures of it were repeatedly cited during the subsequent Congressional debate as the most important factor which led to the 1968 enactment of the first federal flag desecration law in American history. Thus, commenting on the furor caused by pictures of the burning, Representative Louis Wyman of New Hampshire told the HJC on May 10, 1967, that the number of flag desecrators was "very limited," but "it is not the number of actors, it is the wideness of distribution of the public impression of a single act that is the crux of the problem for Congress." Representative Albert Watson of

South Carolina declared on the House floor on April 18, 1967, in an argument that scores of his colleagues would echo, that the flag burning would cost the lives of many American soldiers. According to Watson, "A picture is often worth a thousand words" and the widely published flag burning photo would give America's enemies in Vietnam "renewed psychological strength" and lead them to "push the war further under the false impression that these demonstrations prove there is no American consensus for the war." (Of course, that increasingly proved to be the case despite such arguments, which virtually amounted to declaring that America could only effectively fight for "freedom" abroad by suppressing all dissent at home.) Representative Dan Kuykendall of Tennessee asked during House floor debate on June 20, 1967, in an argument that could justify outlawing a great many things, "Which is the greater contribution to the security of freedom: The inspiring photo of the marines raising the flag at Iwo Jima or the shameful pictures of unshaven beatniks burning that same flag in Central Park?"[29]

While the Central Park burning was by far the most frequently cited incident during the subsequent Congressional hearings and debate, the *Radich* case and, to a lesser extent, some of other previously discussed incidents were also occasionally mentioned. Thus Representative Alexander Pirnie of New York euphemistically referred on the House floor to the Radich penis-cross as a flag desecration "too grotesque and obscene to be described," and Representative Richard Poff of Virginia referred to the same exhibit as a "flag in a posture of obscenity which the propriety of this debate will not permit me to describe." Representative Seymour Halpern of New York offered, during both hearings and floor debate, to show his colleagues photos of the Radich exhibit, depicting what he termed an "obscene and pornographic" portrayal of the flag, and Representative Jamie Whitener of North Carolina termed Halpern's color photographs "one of the most impressive bits of evidence" offered to the HJC.[30]

The especial significance of the Central Park burning was that it dramatically increased public and Congressional demands for action—such as Representative Albert Watson's previously quoted April 18 House floor statement and North Carolina Representative L.H. Fountain's declaration on April 19 that antiwar protests, "organized chiefly by known and admitted members of the Communist Party," only gave "aid and comfort to the enemy and cost many more American lives," and that the Central Park flag burning "borders very close to treason." As a result, HJC Chairman Emmanuel Cellar of New York, a civil libertarian who had previously refused to hold hearings on federal flag desecration legislation on the grounds that existing state laws sufficed, was forced to publicly reverse himself four days after the Central Park burning. Cellar's April 19 decision to schedule hearings, to be conducted by a subcommittee chaired by Representative Byron Rogers of Colorado, especially reflected growing threats that proponents of a flag desecration measure would force a bill onto the House floor without committee consideration or hearings, through a legislative maneuver known as a discharge petition. And, not coincidentally, Cellar's promise of forthcoming hearings came on the same day that what would soon become a tidal wave of flag desecration prosecutions for relatively benign, nondestructive activities began, when a Delaware man was indicted for flying an American flag in a position subordinate to a United Nations flag.[31]

By the time the HJC subcommittee began its hearings on May 8, Chairman Rogers had already publicly proclaimed his support for enacting a federal flag desecration bill in order to prevent insults "to the people of the United States and especially to our men in Vietnam who are giving their lives to protect our freedom." Although most Congressional hearings are not reported in the press, the Rogers hearings were prominently reported in newspapers across the country, including front-page treatment in the *Washington Post* and in both daily papers published in Terre Haute, the site of the recent Chisholm flag burning. (On the other hand, the *Detroit Free Press* may have suggested its view of the proceedings by placing its story on the comics page.) By the time the hearings opened, over sixty House members had proposed flag desecration legislation, and by the time the hearings closed the number had mounted to over one hundred. Most of their proposals were identical, making it illegal to "publicly mutilate, deface, defile, or defy, trample upon or cast contempt" upon the flag "either by word or act," and calling for penalties of one year in jail and $1,000 fine (although some versions provided penalties of up to five years in prison and $10,000 fines).

During five days of hearings between May 8 and June 5, 1967, the subcommittee received oral or written statements supporting a flag law from a parade of over five dozen members of the House, who vied with each other in denouncing flag burners and proclaiming their love of the flag. Also supporting legislation were spokesmen from veterans and patriotic groups such as the VFW, AMVETS, the American Legion, and the American Coalition of Patriotic Societies. Not a single Congressman submitted a statement opposing legislation and only a handful of witnesses were heard who took such a position: a spokesman for the ACLU, several law professors, and an obscure instructor from Bowling Green State University.[32]

While the House Republican Policy Committee endorsed flag desecration legislation on May 2, the Johnson administration demonstrated a clear lack of enthusiasm for the idea. Attorney General Ramsey Clark, in a letter sent to HJC Chairman Cellar on May 8, stated that the desirability of passing a federal flag desecration law was a "question for the Congress," but noted that all fifty states already banned flag desecration and suggested that "ideally, we would look to the States for effective enforcement of their laws against such local conduct." Clark added that although "we are deeply hurt" when the flag is "dishonored," the number of flag desecrators was "infinitesimal, a handful among 200 million," and that even in the unlikely event that "substantial" numbers of such people should emerge "all history shows a mere statute" could not provide a remedy. The "real tragedy" of flag desecration was "not the loss of the flag" but the fact that some Americans had "so little love for country or confidence in its purposes, or are otherwise so thoughtless or insensitive that they want to burn the flag." Clark promised to "vigorously prosecute" offenders if Congress nonetheless chose to pass a federal law, but urged that any statute delete any references to making it illegal to "defy" the flag or to verbally desecrate the flag (that is, to "cast contempt" upon the flag "by word") on the grounds that the courts would likely strike such provisions for vagueness or for violation of the First Amendment (as the Supreme Court in fact subsequently did in the 1969 *Street* case). Testifying before the Rogers subcommittee, Assistant Attorney General Fred Vinson Jr. (the son of a former Supreme Court chief justice) characterized Clark's letter as making it "clear that our position is not one of opposition," but took no issue with Representative Poff's retort that it was "equally clear" that the Johnson administration's stance was "not one in vigorous support of legislation."[33]

On June 5, the Rogers subcommittee approved a bill by a 6–1 vote, with Representative John Conyers casting the sole opposition vote. The following day the bill was favorably reported by an overwhelming, although not unanimous, voice vote of the parent HJC. The HJC bill followed the advice of Attorney General Clark, and omitted making it a crime to "defy" or verbally desecrate the flag, while adding language to specifically outlaw flag "burning." The HJC majority report declared that the bill had been "occasioned by a number of recent public flag-burning incidents" and was justified because "public burning, destruction and dishonor of the national emblem inflicts an injury on the entire Nation" while forbidding such actions imposed "no substantial burden on anyone." On June 20, the House of Representatives approved a flag desecration bill after a five-hour debate by a vote of 385–16 as, the *Washington Post* reported, "symbol-minded members, including some who have hardly ever cast a yea vote for any legislation, fell over each other grabbing for microphones to get on record in favor of the bill." Over five dozen Congressmen supported the proposal during the House debate, while only ten opposed it.[34]

The House action was prominently reported in newspapers across the country (other news accounts published on June 21 reported House passage of a bill extending the draft for four years and the five-year jail term given heavyweight boxing champion Muhammad Ali for refusing conscription). For example, the *New York Times* published its account on the front page. Most newspaper stories stressed an embarrassing parliamentary snafu that became apparent only after the House had completed action on the bill—due to complications on the House floor that apparently no one understood until it was too late, the term "burning" was accidentally omitted from the text of the enacted bill. The result was that, although the entire impetus for the legislation was to outlaw such events as the Central Park incident, the bill as passed failed to specifically outlaw flag "burning."

Although this omission was essentially meaningless, since the bill as passed by the House outlawed casting "contempt" on the flag by various means of physical assaults that surely encompassed burning, Representative Cornelius Gallagher of New Jersey, who had just voted for the proposal, immediately suggested a "bill burning." Representative Theodore Kupferman of New York fumed that the House had "spent the whole day" discussing "what happened in Central Park" and then "come to a conclusion which does not at all cover the very point that was raised initially." News reports published across the country on June 21 carried headlines such as "Flag Bill Lacks Key Clauses," "House Leaves Out Key Word in Flag Bill" (in a *Chicago Tribune* story published on the comics page, the same spot chosen by the *Detroit Free Press*), and "House Burning over Flag Goof." An Associated Press story began by reporting the House had "passed legislation against flag burning—sort of," while the United Press International account led by referring to House members as "red, white and blue with embarrassment."[35]

Although the omission of "burning" in the House bill was eventually remedied, this fiasco seems to have considerably deflated the political interest in the federal flag desecration bill. Even mainstream conservative and moderate publications ridiculed the House action. Thus, *Life* magazine, in an editorial entitled "Oratorical Overkill on the Flag Bill," referred to the House debate as marked by "heights of confusion and depths of platitudinous bombast," while a *Time* magazine news story characterized the House discussion as "almost wholly devoted to the oratorical flights that Congressmen usually relegate to the file drawer marked Independence Day." Although the Senate restored "burning" to the bill, it did not take up the measure until a year later, on June 24, 1968, and the Senate passed the bill without any debate, without even a roll call vote, and virtually without public notice. The *New York Times* reported the Senate's action in a one-paragraph item published on page 32. After the House accepted the Senate's restoration of "burning" and other minor changes on June 25, without any debate or roll call vote, President Johnson signed the first federal flag desecration law in American history on July 4, 1968, an action completely unreported by most of the press and noted in the *New York Times* only in a tiny item on page 40.[36]

The 1968 law made it illegal to "knowingly" cast "contempt" upon "any flag of the United States by publicly mutilating, defacing, defiling, burning, or trampling upon it," with violators subject to a penalty of up to $1000 in fines and/or one year in jail (see Appendix, Document 2). The law defined "flag" in the expansive manner typical of most of the existing state laws:

> any flag, standard, colors, ensign or any picture or representation of either, or of any part or parts of either, made of any substance or represented on any substance, of any size evidently purporting to be either of said flag, standard, colors or ensign of the United States of America or a picture or a representation of either, upon which shall be shown the colors, the stars and the stripes, in any number of either thereof, or of any part or parts of either, by which the average person seeing the same without deliberation may believe the same to represent the flag, standards, colors or ensign of the United States of America.[37]

The Debate over the 1968 Federal Flag Desecration Law

The same arguments that were to be made in 1989–90 among the advocates and opponents of flag desecration legislation were made in 1967–68 during Congressional hearings and floor debate. Above all, the major argument for the law was that the flag was a unique and special symbol of America, and especially American freedom, and that although the right to dissent was sacred, burning the flag simply went "too far." Thus, Representative John Hunt of New York proclaimed that flag desecrators "have crossed the line—they have gone too far—they have overstepped the bounds." Representative Quillen declared that the flag has "always been the symbol of freedom and liberty," but "there are bounds in which" such freedom should be exercised and "when anyone goes so far as to desecrate our beloved flag ... he has gone too far." Representative Jake Pickle of Texas proclaimed that "these young punks have gone too far." Senator Strom Thurmond of South Carolina argued that flag burning was the act of a "traitor" who "transgresses the bound of responsible dissent." Representative James Delaney of New York termed flag desecration a "clear transgression of the bounds of reasonable dissent"; Representative Charlotte Reid of Illinois argued that flag desecrators "go far beyond the bounds of propriety in rational dissent"; and Representative Hale Boggs of Louisiana termed flag desecrations "outrageous acts which go beyond protest and violate things which the overwhelming majority of Americans hold sacred."[38]

Like Boggs, many Congressmen termed the flag "sacred," and like Senator Thurmond many referred to flag desecrators as "traitors" and flag desecrations as acts of "treason." Numerous other epithets were applied to flag desecrators, who were described by various Congressmen as "a smelly bunch of unwashed creeps," "un-American," "dirty, unwashed, unshaven beatniks," "rabble," "a small group of misguided malcontents," fomenters of "depravity," "goons and gooks and hoods," "misfits," "irresponsible demonstrators and bold publicity seekers," "skilled, semi-professional agitators," "questionable citizens," "unwashed, irreverent gangs" of "anarchists," "crackpots and lunatic fringe demonstrators," "irresponsible louts," "young punks" and fomenters of "bush league anarchy," "traitors who are urging anarchy," "misguided mobs and collegiate reactionaries," "rats," "fellow travelers" and "pinkos," "buzzards," "unthinking hoodlums," "unspeakable persons," "no-goodniks," and "dirty, long-haired Communist-led beatniks." Pennsylvania Supreme Court Justice Michael Musmanno set some sort of record for invective in his HJC testimony, terming flag burners variously "miserable wretches," "vile America-hating hooligans," and "treasonous" agitators "fit to conspire with Communists who would force our freedoms into the straightjacket of Bolshevistic dictatorship."[39]

The damage and threat caused by flag burners was claimed to be immense. Many Congressmen, like Representative Kuykendall of Tennessee, claimed that flag burners were encouraging the enemy in Vietnam and thus prolonging the war and committing acts "very close to treason." Representative Edna Kelley of New York termed flag burning "a direct attack on the sovereignty of the United States" that "tears at the very core of our democratic society" and "is a form of destruction of the basic values and principles of our Government." Representative O'Neal of Georgia similarly equated flag desecration to an "actual assault upon the country" and urged Congress not to wait until "the country is at the point of revolution" before acting. Representative William Colmer of Mississippi said flag desecration amounted to "stabbing at the very heart of the Republic," and Representative E. Y. Berry of South Dakota agreed, arguing that flag burners were "setting fire to the institutions, beliefs and laws of our Nation as well."

The *Detroit News* compared flag desecrators to those who would assassinate a politician or blow up a bridge to make a political point. The

Jackson, Michigan *Citizen-Patriot* portrayed their actions as similar to breaking a church window or punching someone in the nose as a form of political expression, analogies that compared purely symbolic actions that solely expressed opinions to actions with concretely observable harmful physical effects. Pennslvania Supreme Court Justice Musmanno urged that flag desecration trials "have priority over all other trials" because flag burnings were a "national security matter," since "those who put a match to the flag ... apply an acetylene torch to the police stations, courthouses and Federal and state capitols."[40]

Although attempts to increase the federal penalty to five years in jail and a $10,000 fine failed by a 40–155 vote in the House, a number of Congressmen urged virtually no limits on punishment for flag desecrators. "Nothing's too strong for them," declared House Armed Services Committee Chairman Mendel Rivers, who claimed flag desecrators were "extending and lengthening the war in Vietnam" by giving "hope to the Hanoi government that this government may fall." Representative James Haley helpfully suggested, "Load a boat full of them and take them 500 miles out into the ocean and handcuff them, chain the anchor around their neck and throw them overboard and tell them to swim" to a country "whose flag they can respect." Representative Quillen, citing the Civil War directive of Treasury Secretary Dix, declared that "in earlier times it was thought better to kill" flag desecrators and averred that "anything short of a firing squad" would be "agreeable to me."[41]

Justice Musmanno inadvertently explained not only why flag burning upset so many people, but also why suppressing it was a direct assault on freedom of expression. He asked, "How could demonstrations against American policy be more vividly and dramatically manifested than by burning the very flag of the United States?" Many Congressmen, even while usually claiming that they only sought to regulate conduct and not suppress dissent, similarly made it clear that in fact the real offense of flag burners was their expression of dissident political views, which, as Representative Howard Pollock of Alaska described, "insult the honor and dignity of the United States." Thus, Representative Rivers claimed that he did not wish to "stifle the voices of dissent," yet declared that he objected to flag desecrators who "show contempt for certain policies which the United States is pursuing." Representative William Brock of Tennessee made the repressive purpose of banning flag desecration legislation crystal clear when he declared that attacks upon the flag were a "direct assault upon all of the principles and values" which Americans cherished, and that therefore "respect for our country and our flag...must be forthcoming" even if it had to be "enforced by threat of fine and imprisonment."

Representatives Charles Gubser and Craig Hosmer, both of California, and William Stanton of Ohio all described the purpose of the legislation as punishing "disrespect" for the flag or the nation. Representative Frank Horton of New York said "flag burning assaults the memory of thousands of Americans," and Representative E. Ross Adair of Indiana defined the offense of flag desecrators as that of demonstrating "actual hostility to the things for which our flag stands." Representative Richard Fulton of Tennessee termed flag desecration an "irresponsible expression of dissent." Representative Claude Pepper of Florida espoused a formula for suppressing all unpopular dissent, declaring that, although flag desecrators "have a right to their opinions," the majority also have "a right to ours" and the minority "must not be permitted to abuse the freedom of others" by engaging in "public and overt acts of disdain and contempt for the beliefs and traditions of the majority of Americans." The *Christian Science Monitor*, which was to strongly oppose the 1989 federal flag desecration law on First Amendment grounds, displayed a similar lack of sensitivity to the value of dissident political expression in 1967, declaring that the proposed law banning such behavior did not "greatly differ from numerous other bits of legislation designed to restrain acts which are offensive."[42]

That the 1967 bill was targeted precisely at dissenting thought was especially made clear by the fact that it only outlawed flag desecration that cast "contempt" on the flag. As Representative James Corman of California explained, "The thing we object to is not the burning of the physical flag itself, it is the burning of the flag for the purpose of casting contempt upon it or something which it symbolizes." Representative Andrew Jacobs of Indiana stressed that when "the American Legion, for example, in a ceremony to lay flags to rest, burns the flags it is an act of the highest kind of patriotism," and therefore a properly drawn bill would only punish flag burning such as those "disrespecting the policy in Vietnam." Floor manager Rogers specifically assured the House that patriotic groups could continue to burn worn-out flags "in a dignified way" without worry.[43]

Little serious attention was paid by backers of flag legislation to constitutional issues, other than endlessly repeated declarations, such as the one by Representative Kelley that freedom of speech simply did not include the "right to desecrate or destroy our national standard." Any arguments to the contrary, Representative William Randall of Missouri proclaimed, were "tommyrot, baloney, pure hogwash," or, in the more refined words of Representative Benjamin Blackburn of Georgia, "sheer and utter nonsense." The few Congressmen who even attempted to go beyond the flat assertion that symbolic flag desecration was not protected speech mostly argued, as did HJC subcommittee chairman Rogers, that (quoting the HJC majority report) since the bill only outlawed the "physical dishonor or destruction" of the flag, but not verbal criticism, it therefore did not "prohibit speech, the communication of ideas or political dissent."[44]

A few Congressmen additionally advanced the notion put forth by Representative Roudebush that all privately owned flags were somehow "property that belongs to millions of other Americans and thus [destroying them] is violating the rights of these millions." Representative Don Clausen of California argued that banning flag desecration could be justified as aimed not at suppressing dissent, but at maintaining the peace, since such acts would "be apt to provoke a public disturbance." A few Congressmen even advocated outlawing verbal criticism of the flag as well as physical desecration. Thus Representative O'Neal, warning of the need to suppress "an embryo Communist revolution going on in this country today," declared that "it is high time that we were prosecuting some of these people for sedition, and I would have no worries about the first amendment." When he was asked during the HJC hearings what it would mean to make it llegal to "defy" the flag, a term included in his draft bill, O'Neal at first confessed "you have got me there," then opined, "I can conceive of somebody standing on a platform and hurling one curse after another at the flag."[45]

As would be the case in 1989–90, flag burners were especially criticized for, as Representative Clausen and Senator Alan Bible of Nevada argued, respectively, desecrating "the very symbol of that which permits them to demonstrate" and seeking to "malign the very system that protects them and offers them the right to demonstrate." According to Senator Bible, flag desecrators were somehow even guilty of abusing and defiling "the constitutional rights of all Americans to speak freely, to assemble peaceably and to petition for a redress of grievances." Representative Pollock similarly declared "they are undermining the very system that assures them the freedom to dissent." Representative Kuykendall argued that the "symbol of liberty" could not be destroyed "without destroying liberty itself," and Representative Taylor proclaimed that flag desecration could not be allowed because the flag was a "symbol of our determination to remain free." Representative Edwards of Alabama and Representative Robert Sikes of Florida extended this peculiar logic to, respectively, reach the conclusions that suppressing the right to symbolically desecrate the flag was actually required to "preserve the right to dissent" and to "declare that we are serious about our belief in freedom." Representative Herbert Burke of Florida urged his colleagues to "rededicate ourselves to the principles of freedom and justice for which [the flag] stands" and ensure that it would "long wave over the land of the free" by providing "each future flag burner" with "the gift of time for meditation and reflection behind bars." Representative Philip Philbin of Massachusetts urged outlawing flag desecration because the country required the "unity, loyalty and unquestioned allegiance of all Americans." But it could be even more powerfully argued, as the Supreme Court eventually would in 1989–90, that flag desecrators were in a peculiar way celebrating the system by using their constitutional rights and those seeking to outlaw symbolic protest using the flag were willing to destroy the substance of the right to dissent, while hollowly celebrating only the symbolism of the flag, but not the concrete freedoms it represented.[46]

The Vietnam War hovered over the entire flag desecration debate, with backers of the flag desecration law repeatedly claiming that passage would support American soldiers fighting for "freedom" and dying to protect the flag and that tolerating flag burners would undermine morale and prolong the war by encouraging America's enemies. On May 2, 1967, for example, the House Republican Policy Committee endorsed a federal flag desecration act by declaring, "It is strange indeed to see on the same day, in the same newspapers, pictures of American young men facing danger and death in Vietnam, and pictures of other American young men burning their Nation's flag in the safety of an American park." Representative Speedy Long of Louisiana declared that the main purpose for passing a flag law would be to "give our men in Vietnam the moral support which might well mean the difference between life and death." Representative Odin Langen of Minnesota argued that, "At a time when American soldiers are engaged in a war halfway around the world, Congress should not hesitate to insure proper respect and protection for our national flag at home."

The Louisiana legislature (which almost exactly one hundred years earlier had seceded from the Union and sought to violently overthrow the American government and its flag in order to uphold wealthy planters' "freedom" to own slaves) similarly petitioned Congress to act to stop "seditious elements" from engaging in "reprehensible, loathsome and disgusting" acts of flag desecration while the "valiant defenders of Freedom" were fighting "the insidious hordes of atheistic communism" in Vietnam. Representative Colmer asked, "How can you expect American soldiers to go on the firing line, to bleed and to die for the cause for which we have sent them over there, when at the same time they read and hear about these acts of sedition and sabotage and, yes, treason in my book, that are going on in this country?" Representative Edward Gurney of Florida termed the "endless" numbers of flag desecrations "nothing short of traitorous" and "all the more loathsome occurring as they do" while other Americans were "giving their lives to protect the precious rights for which the flag stands" including, "ironically," the "right to dissent that protects its defilers." Similarly Representative W. J. Bryan Dorn of South Carolina termed flag burning especially "shocking" since Americans were dying in Vietnam "to secure the freedom of even those who would burn the flag" (which was a backhanded way of conceding that those who sought to suppress dissent at home were in fact betraying American soldiers fighting for that freedom abroad).[47]

Representative Quillen unquestionably spoke for most supporters of federal legislation by declaring that "in Vietnam, our men are dying this very minute for this flag" and that "if our flag is worth dying for, it is worth protecting." Thus, Representative Pepper of Florida claimed that, "On a thousand battlefields, in every part of the earth, in the dark depths of every ocean and in the skies which lie about the earth, brave Americans have valued that flag above life and limb and liberty and all else they valued." This argument was echoed by Gen. William Westmoreland, American commander in Vietnam, who termed flag burning "unpatriotic" since "thousands of men have died for that flag, and they are still dying for it in Vietnam." In fact, the argument that soldiers were dying for "the flag" hopelessly confused the flag's symbolism with the substance of what it symbolized and, if taken at face value, insulted the patriotism and intelligence of millions of American soldiers, who surely fought for their country and what it stood for, and not to preserve the physical integrity of millions of pieces of patterned cloth. As Representative John Culver of Iowa aptly commented, "It would be the greatest tragedy if our patriots" succeeded in Vietnam, "only to discover that politicians had legislated away their freedoms here."[48]

As in 1989–90, the smell of political pandering hung heavy over the 1967–68 Congressional debate. Representative Roudebush told the House that his mail and no doubt that of other Congressmen demonstrated that the public was "disgusted" with flag desecrators and "this is our chance to show the people back home that we do honor the American flag." Representative Dominick Daniels of New Jersey stated that in "my four terms in this House" he had never before heard his constituents "speak with one voice as they have on this issue." Representative Robert McClory of Illinois supported a flag desecration bill partly on the grounds that "the hundreds of letters we have received as well as the scores of editorials" demonstrated that "such conduct is socially offensive to the public" and "hence there is a vital national interest in this legislation." Representative Randall declared that in his congressional district anyone who voted against a flag desecration bill would be in "such an untenable position as to make it futile" to even run for reelection. Representative Joe Waggoner of Louisiana proclaimed that he could "not see how anybody could be against" flag desecration legislation "and still profess to be loyal Americans." As if on cue, Representative Lionel Van Deerlin of California openly confessed that he was voting for the bill although it was "bad" and "unnecessary," because it was "not important enough" to risk allowing "zealots and know-nothings who are always prepared to find evidence of disloyalty in positions that happen to disagree with their own" to make the question a "prime issue in my campaign for re-election."[49] (In a 1990 interview, Representative Don Edwards, who voted against the 1967 measure but supported a similar law in 1989 in an effort to defeat a proposed flag desecration constitutional amendment, blamed his 1967 stance for costing him 20,000 votes in the 1968 election. "For years," Edwards recalled, "kids came up and said, 'My mommy says you don't love the flag.'" Edwards said that Representative John Dow of New York lost his seat in 1968 due to his vote against the flag law, although Dow himself, also interviewed in 1990, recalled, "Just how much that affected me losing the election, I don't know, it undoubtedly had something to do with it. I don't recollect the vote as an overwhelming matter in the election." Dow recalled one direct result of his vote against the flag law was that "in one town in my district they had scheduled me to speak at the July 4 celebration and the people who sponsored it called up and said they couldn't stand to have me under the circumstances.")

Concerning the political implications of the 1967 flag bill, one anonymous Congressman was quoted by *Newsweek* as saying, "It's a great bill to vote for. We'll let the courts worry about the constitution." HJC Chairman Cellar termed the measure a "bad bill" of doubtful constitutionality, while explaining his ultimate support for it by declaring, "Who can vote against something like this? It's like motherhood." Among the handful of Congressmen willing to publicly speak out against the measure, Representative Robert Eckhardt of Texas lamented that "many Members, who in their hearts oppose this legislation, will yet vote for it for fear of being branded friends of the flag burners." Representative John Conyers of Michigan similarly expressed concern that due to the "very political nature" of the question, he doubted that "any argumentation, any logic or any court decisions" would lead members to oppose a flag desecration law. Representative Robert Kastenmeier of Wisconsin complained that, especially since all states already had similar measures, among the main functions the new law would serve would be to "provide empty rhetorical ammunition for the flag wavers" and "feed irrational demands for conformity" amid "a general climate of war hysteria."[50]

Just as the arguments for the 1968 law prefigured those advanced for the 1989 Flag Protection Act, so the arguments against it resembled those to be advanced against similar proposals and constitutional amendments twenty years later. Aside from criticizing proponents for political pandering, opponents of the flag law above all stressed that flag desecration, although highly distasteful, was essentially a form of political expression protected by the First Amendment, that the substance of constitutional rights was more important than protecting a symbol of those rights, that there were no substantial state interests unrelated to suppressing expression to be furthered by forbidding such behavior, and that love of flag and country could not be compelled. As opponents of a flag desecration constitutional amendment would later stress in 1989–90, Representative Jonathon Bingam of New York argued in 1967 that, "Respect for our flag and respect for our Constitution must go hand in hand." Senator Stephen Young of Ohio warned that those who sought to act against "misguided and stupid" flag burners would commit a greater offense to the Constitution than the flag burners committed against democratic principles. Young declared, "Let us remember that the flag is a symbol" while the Constitution was "more than a symbol," the "cornerstone of our liberties," with the First Amendment in particular requiring safeguarding against any "burning or desecrating" by "superduper, hysterical, self-appointed and proclaimed patriots." Representatives Conyers and Edwards protested, in dissenting from the HJC majority report, that the proposed legislation "would do more real harm to the Nation that all the flag burners can possibly do." It would "infringe upon what is certainly one of the most basic freedoms, the freedom to dissent," which was clearly the "real 'evil' at which the bill was directed." They rejected the majority's contention that flag burning "inflicts an injury on the entire Nation," instead declaring that, by unconstitutionally suppressing dissent, legislation "can only result in making dissent more widespread, more bitter and more valid." During floor debate, Edwards lamented the irony that Congress was about to use the flag as "an instrument to suppress free speech." Representative Eckhardt declared that "crime against a symbol" was unknown in American law and "it always will be so long as the first amendment" was effective, because attempts to outlaw symbolic conduct such as flag burnings were clearly designed to suppress "their thought content."[51]

Outside of the handful of Congressmen who publicly opposed the proposed federal flag desecration law on fundamental First Amendment grounds, a similar position was supported by the ACLU, about a dozen prominent law professors, and a number of major newspapers and periodicals, including the *New York Times*, the *Boston Globe*, the

Washington Post, Life, the *Nation, Commonweal,* and the *Christian Century.* Lawrence Speiser, director of the ACLU's Washington, D.C. office, noted that if flag desecration could be outlawed because it was "deeply offensive" to many or because it demoralized American soldiers in Vietnam, then the same argument could justify banning much verbal speech. But, Speiser maintained, in fact the First Amendment forbade such restrictions in either case, which could only tell the world of "our lack of confidence in the vitality of the flag and the deeper meanings of the nation." Similarly, Duke Law Professor William Van Alstyne warned that if Congress attempted to "armor plate" the flag it would only "confess by its deeds that those who claim that the flag does not stand for freedom may be right afterall." George Washington University Professor Monroe Freedman warned that, "In attempting to protect our flag from expressions of contempt, these bills themselves cast the utmost contempt upon the fundamental principles of our Government."

The *Washington Post* similarly declared that those who sought a federal law to outlaw flag desecration seemed "grossly ignorant" of the values, such as the right to dissent, which the flag stood for, and thus threatened to "do greater violence to the flag" than the "worst of the boorish oafs" who burned it, especially since such acts were only a "silly and ineffectual gesture" that did no more real harm than "hanging someone in effigy." The *Post* added that the few "disturbed and unbalanced" flag desecrators, who apparently "lacked the verbal facility and intellectual capacity to articulate a political argument in terms intelligible to literate persons," could never really "debase" the flag because ultimately it resided not in "a scrap of textile," but "in the minds of Americans when they think of all that is good in their nation." Therefore, such an image could only be disfigured by "acts and deeds unworthy of the principles for which it stands."

The *New York Times* also opposed the proposed flag law, as completely unneeded in the light of existing state laws, and as delivering the wrong message, since the flag is "a symbol of freedom, not herdlike conformity." The *Boston Globe* declared that respect for the flag would be meaningless unless there "was respect as well for the free and open kind of society it represents." Harvard Law Professor Arthur Sutherland denounced the proposed law as unconstitutionally suppressing dissent and likely only to create martyrs and damage the United States in world opinion, but tellingly felt compelled to conclude his letter to HJC Chairman Cellar by noting that he had just celebrated Memorial Day by flying a flag at his house "from sunrise to sunset."[52]

Aside from the fundamental freedom of speech argument, critics of the flag desecration law also attacked it on less central grounds. For example, a number of opponents argued that no flag desecration law could really obtain the desired end because it was impossible to compel people to feel patriotic. Thus, Representative William Fitts Ryan of New York warned that "to undermine the precious liberties which the flag represents would indeed cast contempt upon the flag," especially since in any case "history shows that it is not possible to legislate patriotism or morality." Similarly, Representative George Brown of California argued that outlawing flag desecration simply would not accomplish anything because love for the flag could not be legislated and "love and respect that is not freely given is without meaning." Noting that the Soviet Union had recently decreed a two-year jail term for flag desecrators, Brown said that if coerced respect were meaningful, then, since the proposed American law provided only a one-year penalty, the Soviet law "should make a Soviet citizen twice as respectful of his flag as the American citizen will be of his." Instead of attempting to compel respect for the flag, Brown concluded, the Congress should "instead, freely give our allegiance to the great principles embodied in our Constitution which set individual liberty as the touchstone of human progress." Whitney Smith, Director of the Flag Heritage Association, declared that the flag would be "respected when respectable, reviled when disrespectable" and that "no law, fine or jail term will coerce a man into honoring a flag he believes to have been dishonored by the nation it stands for."[53]

Several Congressmen ridiculed the definition of "flag" contained in the proposed legislation. Representative Brown warned that the definitional language was so vague that it might outlaw throwing a "red, white and blue egg at a picture of the president" and, comparing the proposal to the infamous 1798 Sedition Act, suggested that passing the law might eventually lead to making it illegal to "doodle a mustache" on pictures of politicians. Representative Ryan also attacked the proposed definition: He displayed a red-white-and-blue beach towel to the House and he asked if it would violate the law, and he asked the same question about a cigar that opened up to display a flag, if it "was smoked and burned." (During the HJC hearings, Representative Roudebush had stated that anyone who threw a flag-towel onto beach sand and then placed their "wet body" on the towel would be guilty of "a desecration," and Judge Musmanno had suggested that sitting on a pillow embroidered with a flag should be an offense, but that it would be all right to own such a pillow "if it is a matter of respect and not merely physical lounging.") Similarly, Representative James Scheuer of New York warned that the bill would make it illegal to "swat an insect" with a publication that contained a flag image, and asked, "What about the act of a Federal [postal] employee who takes a great big black [cancellation] stamp and with a massive swing of his arm obliterates the image of a flag?"[54]

Critics of 1967–68 flag desecration legislation also argued, as their counterparts would in 1989–90, that the handful of flag burnings hardly justified Congressional action. Thus, Representative Scheuer termed the bill an "overkill" of "classic proportions" to "an insignificant number" of "irresponsible extremists who count for naught in our society" and declared that Congress should not "rise to meet the bait of every irresponsible who finds a new way of making a bloody fool out of himself," especially since "we are not in the business of legislating honor, dignity, good taste or good sense," and should instead be "considering how we can put into reality" the freedoms that "the flag stands for." Similarly, Representative Benjamin Rosenthal of New York lamented that "because a couple of kids in Central Park" engaged in a "stupid act," Congress was acting as if "the whole foundations of this nation are shaking to the point that we are spending a entire afternoon on a bill of this type"; the "real 'evil' at which the bill is directed is opposition to the war in Vietnam," he complained, but tolerance of such dissent, "even irrational dissent, is at the very heart of our form of government." Representative Patsy Mink of Hawaii argued that no flag burning could really harm the nation, as the "frenetic fringes" of patriotism who would "curb the blessings of freedom alleged," but, if she was wrong, then "no mere $1,000 fine or year in jail would be punishment enough."[55]

The Vietnam era flag desecration bill was also attacked, as the 1989 law would be, as distracting the country from real issues and "real" rather than "symbolic" desecration of the country. Thus, *Commonweal* remarked sarcastically, "Seeing as nothing can be done about the war in Vietnam or rampant racism here, why not at least begin with respect for the flag?" The *Christian Century* demanded:

> Should we not ask who, other than a few radical and impetuous students, is really desecrating [the flag]? If the flag represents, as we believe, not material and military America, but the political faith and aspiration of its people, who is desecrating those? We have some candidates: the stinking ghettoes into which big cities pack frustrated, embittered helpless Negroes; ... the disgraceful life the nation imposes on American Indians, Spanish-Americans and migrant workers; the humiliations to which the nation still subjects the aged and insane; the preoccupation of the country with power and pleasure. ... Then there is Vietnam. ... While our Congress argues about people who burn a bit of bunting, the United States scorches land, blows up humble homes and burns thousands of people to death or until they pray to die. That, more than anything else, desecrates our flag. ... How agitated we become when someone insults our flag, but every day

in a hundred different ways we defile it, trample its spirit, drag through the dirt the principles it represents. If we do not try at home and abroad to redeem what the flag represents, then it will become a meaningless token, an idle gesture, a fiction. And when that happens, the flag will be beyond desecration.

As the flag desecration controversy continued and in some ways reached new heights by 1970 (as will be discussed later), the *Nation* made a similar argument, declaring that:

People opposing a war in which the United States is illegally and immorally engaged and which it is carrying on with a brutality unprecedented in American history are the ones who are really trying to protect the flag from desecration. Mutilating a particular flag is the act of an individual, but the devastation of countries like the two Vietnams, Laos, and Cambodia defiles the flag in the deepest sense.[56]

4

Flag Desecration Laws in the Courts During the Vietnam War Era

T HE 1968 federal flag desecration law did not end incidents of flag desecration: In fact, the 1968–1974 period saw an explosion of flag desecration prosecutions unprecedented in American history, of which all but a handful were brought under state laws rather
than under the new federal measure. As a result of the same climate
that led to passage of the new federal law, about ten states revised their
own flag desecration laws between 1967 and 1969 by drastically increasing existing penalties. For example, in addition to the 1967 Indiana revision previously discussed, Alabama, Oklahoma, and Illinois,
each having previously penalized flag desecration with up to 30 days in
jail and a $100 fine, increased their maximum punishments to between
two and five years in jail and $3,000 to $10,000 fines. At least one city,
Kent, Ohio, passed its own flag desecration law, in 1970, providing a
penalty up to one year in jail and a $1,000 fine, after a student burned a
flag on May 4, 1970, the day that four Kent State University students
were shot to death by Ohio National Guardsmen during an antiwar protest.[1]

Although many states increased their penalties for flag desecration in
the late 1960s, the basic elements of the overwhelming majority of the
state laws were essentially intact from the original enactments of the
1900–20 period: In general, they outlawed placing any marks or pictures of the flag, forbade any flag usage for commercial purposes, and
banned any physical destruction of flags or any "act or words" that publicly cast "contempt" on the flag (as previously discussed, the "words"
provision of state laws was effectively struck out by the Supreme
Court's 1969 *Street* decision). Almost all of the states also retained extremely expansive definitions of what constituted a "flag," as in the

law in effect in New York in 1966, which included, in addition to flags per se, pictures and representations of flags of "any size" and of "any "substance," as well as any representations that included the flag's "colors, the stars and stripes, in any number thereto" such that a person seeing the object "without deliberation may believe the same to represent the flag." (Compare the 1968 federal statute in Appendix, Document 2.)[2]

Because most flag desecration prosecutions were "unreported" (local trial court proceedings that are not appealed as well as many that are generally not published or "reported" in standard legal references), it is impossible to uncover exactly how many such cases were tried or what percentage of them were successfully prosecuted. However, the *Christian Science Monitor*'s unsourced 1973 estimate that "some 1,000" flag desecration cases had been prosecuted during the Vietnam War period is almost certainly an underestimate, as New York City ACLU attorney Burt Neuborne told a reporter in 1972 that he had personally handled over 300 such cases. Contemporary accounts differed wildly as to the general outcome of these prosecutions. For example, the ACLU reported in September 1970 that it was generally "winning the [flag] cases," but a law review article published at about the same time concluded that lower courts had "consistently upheld the constitutionality of the state and federal statutes" and law review essays published in 1971 and 1974–75 declared, respectively, that "state courts have traditionally upheld flag desecration convictions" and that "the majority of lower courts" had upheld the professed state interest in "protecting the flag as a symbol of the nation."[3]

My own comprehensive survey of the sixty flag desecration cases that were "reported" and definitively adjudicated between 1966 and 1976 shows that about 60 percent of these cases ultimately culminated in acquittals. Acquittals were increasingly likely after 1972, when American ground combat involvement in Vietnam began to decrease markedly and there was a growing general consensus that the war was an error. Thus, cases reported between 1966 and 1972 resulted in about 55 percent acquittals, but acquittals occurred in almost 70 percent of the cases reported during the following four years. The reported cases were divided into four basic types: flag burnings, such as in *Street* (9 cases); "wearing" the flag or flag simulations, usually as a trouser's seat patch, but also occasionally as a poncho, shirt, vest, and so on (16 cases); "superimposing" symbols, usually the "peace sign" (a trident surrounded by an oval) over the flag or a portion of it (15 cases); and a wide variety of miscellaneous charges, which included such diverse incidents as the Radich art exhibit, publishing a picture of a burning flag, driving a car painted with the flag's colors, pouring paint over a flag, and displaying a flag at half mast in an inferior position to the United Nations flag (20 cases).

Acquittals were far less common in prosecutions involving the literally and figuratively most inflammatory charge of burning the flag (only three of the nine cases, with two of the acquittals on highly technical rather than fundamental First Amendment grounds), than the incidents involving wearing the flag (55 percent acquittals), superimposing symbols on it (85 percent acquittals) or miscellaneous offenses (60 percent acquittals). In a 1991 interview, New York University Law Professor and ACLU attorney Neuborne, who had handled numerous New York City area flag desecration cases during the Vietnam War era, recalled that, "We were able to pretty much control [win cases in] everything except burning, but, especially after the Supreme Court refused to review several flag burning convictions in the mid-1970s, we advised people that 'If you burned the flag there wasn't anything we could do for you.'"[4]

Where prosecutions led to convictions, the prosecution and the courts generally relied upon one or both of the same two interests later advanced by Texas in the 1989 *Texas v. Johnson* Supreme Court case, which touched off the 1989–90 flag burning firestorm: first, that protecting the flag as a symbol of the nation furthered the state's interest in fostering unity and patriotism; and second, that tolerating flag desecration would likely lead to public outrage and disturbances, and therefore banning such conduct furthered the state's interest in preserving the peace (although, in fact, one survey of all flag desecration incidents reported in the press or in legal rcferences between 1915 and 1969 uncovered only 15 incidents of actual or "threshold" breaches of the peace in a total of 95 cases). Generally, courts that rendered or upheld convictions in flag desecration cases maintained that neither of these interests fundamentally conflicted with First Amendment rights because (at least after the Supreme Court's 1969 *Street* case) it was held that dissidents could still verbally express any views they wished, that the forbidden acts were "conduct" rather than speech, and that the government had valid interests in fostering patriotism and maintaining the peace that were independent of any impact the laws had upon dissident expression.[5]

For example, in the 1972 flag burning case of *Deeds v. State*, the Texas Court of Criminal Appeals upheld the conviction and the state law largely on the basis of a valid state interest in forbidding acts that degraded the "flag's symbolic value" and weakened its "unifying effect," declaring that "since the flag symbolizes the entire nation, not just one particular philosophy, the state may determine that it be kept above the turmoil created by competing ideologies." Such restrictions might "incidentally" limit expression, the court held, but Deeds could still "express his views in an alternate forum" and only "conduct, not speech" was prohibited. Similarly, in the 1974 flag burning case of *State v. Farrell*, the Iowa Supreme Court upheld a conviction on the grounds that Iowa had a "viable State interest in preserving the physical integrity of the United States flag as an unalloyed symbol of our country" and that Farrell's action had "permanently and contumaciously in a public place destroyed our symbol of patriotism, of pride in the history of our country and of the service, sacrifice and valor of millions of Americans" and therefore "manifested a total disregard for the flag as a symbol of patriotism and by the same token espoused disunity."[6]

In the 1971 case of *State v. Saulino*, an Ohio municipal court convicted a man for publicly driving a truck decorated on one side with a painted American flag with a large face of Mickey Mouse replacing the field of stars; it held that the government's interest in "preserving the loyalty and patriotism represented by the flag" justified the Ohio flag desecration law, since this interest was "unrelated to the suppression of free expression" and Saulino retained the right "to express his views in any manner whatsoever by way of speech." In the 1973 case of *Delorme v. State*, which involved wearing a flag patch on the seat of a pair of trousers, the Texas Court of Criminal Appeals upheld a conviction on the grounds that wearing a "flag or part of it on that part of the clothing covering the human fundament [anus], a part of the human body universally and historically considered unclean and the object of derision and scorn and the reference to which in a certain tenor is often the source of fighting words, was a clear act of defilement." The court added, "Such a use of the flag would degrade and cheapen it in the eyes of the people, as well as defeat the object of maintaining it as a emblem of national power and honor." In upholding a similar conviction, an Ohio appellate court in the 1972 case of *State v. Mitchell*, declared that attaching a flag patch to the "crotch seam of a pair of jeans is to 'defile' in the common usage of the term." According to the court, such usage was a "far cry from the use made by a patrolman who wears [a flag patch] on the sleeve of his blouse or attached to a shirt covering his breast" since "on the defendant's pants it is effectively 'trampled upon' by the posterior of the wearer, as effectively in fact as if it were under his feet."[7]

In upholding flag desecration convictions as legitimate attempts to prevent breaches of the peace, courts often cited (as did Chief Justice Rehnquist in his 1989 dissent in *Texas v. Johnson*) a phrase from the 1907 Supreme Court decision in *Halter*, which declared that, "It has often occurred that insults to a flag have been the cause of war, and indignities put upon it, in the presence of those who revere it, have often been resented and sometimes punished on the spot." Thus, in *State v. Waterman*, a conviction for wearing the flag as a cape was upheld, even without any evidence of actual or threatened disorder, by the Iowa Supreme Court, on the grounds that the state's interest in "preventing breaches of the peace which result from reactions to any attempted defilement of the flag has long been recognized." In *People v. Cowgill*, a 1969 case involving wearing a flag as a vest, a California appellate court upheld a flag desecration conviction because, even though no breach of the peace had occurred, at "another time a disturbance may well have resulted from defendant's actions." A federal district court held in *Sutherland v. DeWulf*, a 1971 flag burning case, that public flag desecration had a "high likelihood" of causing a breach of the peace, and was inherently an act of incitement as "fraught with danger ... as if a person would stand on the street corner shouting derogatory remarks at passing pedestrians."[8]

As in the *Radich* and *Street* cases discussed in the preceding chapter, defense attorneys in flag desecration cases frequently launched frontal First Amendment attacks on the state or federal law involved. For example, in attacking New York's law in a case involving "superimposing" the "peace symbol" over the flag's field of stars, defense lawyers declared:

> In a free society, no person should be compelled to make a ritualistic obeisance to a trapping of the state, whether by being ordered to salute it or by being ordered to observe a series of taboos concerning its display. The effect of either form of compulsion is to raise a state trapping to the secular equivalent of a religious icon. ... our flag as the emblem of a free society must symbolize, paradoxically, the right of free men to deal with it as their consciences dictate. Those who would ignore that paradox, inherent in the very nature of freedom, are the true, if inadvertent defacers of our national symbol.[9]

Similarly, in *Smith v. Goguen*, a Massachusetts case involving wearing a flag patch on the seat of the pants and a conviction that was ultimately overturned by the U.S. Supreme Court in 1974 (as discussed more fully later) on the grounds that the law involved was unconstitutionally vague, defense lawyers maintained that although Goguen "may have meant to show that he believed that America was a fit place only to sit on" or even to have expressed "more vulgar" ideas, nonetheless his conduct "was purely related to the expression of ideas," even if "unpopular or unpatriotic, about the flag or about the country it symbolizes." They argued that a long series of Supreme Court decisions, including the 1931 *Stromberg* ruling protecting the display of red flags, the 1943 *Barnette* decision forbidding compulsory flag salutes, and the

1969 *Street* ruling striking down laws that outlawed verbal disrespect for the flag, had established that

> whether one is compelled to respect a flag by saluting it or by observing a series of taboos concerning its use or display, the overriding state interest underlying both forms of compulsion is identical—the maintenaince of respect for a symbol of the state. Such an interest has been measured by Mr. Justice Harlan in *Street* and by Mr. Justice Jackson in *Barnette* and has been found wanting. It has no place in a society dedicated to political and religious toleration.

In particular, Goguen's attorneys argued, his conduct had amounted to "symbolic speech," just like the display of red flags which had been protected in the *Stromberg* ruling, and which was just as clearly protected under the 1969 *Street* decision, since there "appears to be no rational difference in state interest between regulation of words and regulation of acts which relate to the flag." In effect, Goguen's lawyers declared, Massachusetts wished to enforce a doctrine under which "it is permissible to use the flag as a symbol of national unity, but to use it to suggest national disunity or dissent will result in imprisonment," a distinction that would "paradoxically endanger the very freedom which the flag is designed to represent."[10]

Although defense attorneys in flag desecration cases often raised such fundamental constitutional issues, acquittals clearly based on courts' endorsement of a First Amendment right to desecrate the flag for the purpose of symbolic expression were rare before 1980, no doubt at least partly because, as a Connecticut appellate court correctly noted in a 1971 case, "There appears to be a reluctance on the part of [the U.S. Supreme Court] to rule squarely on the first amendment issue." However, there were a few such cases. For example, in the 1970 flag burning case of *Crosson v. Silver,* a federal district court explicitly rejected "the existence of a constitutionally recognized state power to prohibit flag desecration based on an interest in preserving loyalty or patriotism" and therefore declared Arizona's flag desecration law unconstitutionally overbroad because it was not narrowly drawn to forbid only acts that might threaten the peace. The court held that a wide variety of flag displays clearly communicated a message, including both when the authorities flew flags at "half-mast at the death of a dignitary" and when a "young person ... desecrates his country's flag at an anti-war gathering," and that all such uses were protected under the First Amendment unless they inherently threatened to provoke disorders—"the proper concern of the state." (The defendant in the case was later convicted for the same flag burning under the federal flag desecration law, a conviction upheld by a federal appeals court against a challenge on both First

Amendment and double jeopardy grounds, with the Supreme Court refusing to grant certiorari.)

In the 1973 case of *People v. Vaughan,* involving a flag patch worn on the trousers, the Colorado Supreme Court struck down Colorado's flag desecration law on similar fundamental First Amendment grounds. The court held that the law was not limited to banning acts that threatened the peace but rather generally limited "the expression of ideas about the flag to patriotic expressions acceptable to those charged with the enforcement of the criminal law" and thus "attempts to impose a symbolic orthodoxy upon the people of Colorado." The court explicitly rejected the argument that the state had an overriding legitimate interest in "preserving the symbols of our democracy and setting limits of proper dissent," because such interests were in "direct conflict with the fundamental values protected by the First Amendment" and operated as "a direct restraint upon free expression."[11]

In the 1972 case of *Goguen v. Smith,* another trousers flag patch case in which violation of the Massachusetts law barring "contemptuously" treating the flag in public was alleged, a federal appeals court declared that it was "not within the constitutional power of a state to proscribe criminal penalties for failure to show proper respect for our flag by words or acts," since any such requirement would be "directed point blank at the expression of mere belief in particular ideas." The original trial court judge had sentenced Goguen to a year in jail, on the grounds that his action was "in vile contempt of the symbol of the republic." However, the appeals court held that if Goguen could be punished for his action, then so could those who "placed the flag in odd positions, or in conjunction with deprecatory symbols, gestures or slogans, or who merely display it while acting out or speaking that which many Americans might consider obnoxious," such as "holding a flag while making a face or a contemptuous gesture" or "spitting in the direction of a flag." Ultimately in this case, as discussed later, the Supreme Court also ruled for Goguen but based its ruling solely on the "vagueness" of the meaning of "contemptuously," a legal approach that stripped the case of any broad constitutional significance.[12]

In several cases courts struck down flag desecration convictions on the grounds that on the facts involved in them there was no real probability of a breach of the peace, a position that implied a rejection of the alleged state interest in protecting the symbolic integrity of the flag but avoided the discussion of fundamental constitutional issues evidenced in the above decisions. For example, in *State v. Kool,* the Iowa Supreme Court reversed a conviction involving the superimposition of a peace sign over the flag on such grounds, rejecting any claimed threat to the peace, since although someone might have been "so intemperate as to disrupt the peace because of this display," if "absolute assurance of tranquillity is required we might as well forget about free speech." Similarly, in *People v. Keough*, a 1972 case involving publication of a photograph that depicted a woman apparently unclothed save for a flag, a New York appeals court overturned a conviction on the grounds that no realistic threat was posed to the public peace. Likewise, in the 1970 case of *Korn v. Elkins*, a federal district court relied on similar grounds to order University of Maryland officials to cease attempting to forbid distribution of a student publication that included a photograph of a burning flag. (In another issue of the same magazine, the students included a flag decal along with a book of matches to protest the University's original action.)[13]

Most acquittals in flag desecration cases were based on extremely narrow grounds that totally avoided basic constitutional issues. A number of convictions involving "wearing" of flags, "superimposition" of flags, and various other miscellaneous uses of flags were reversed on the grounds that no physical desecration had occurred, that no "contempt" had been displayed, or even that no real "flag" had been involved. For example, in the 1969 case of *State v. Saionz*, which involved wearing the flag as a cape, an Ohio appeals court found that since Saionz himself had not physically altered the flag to turn it into a cape, there was no evidence that he had "cast contempt" on the flag, because the court held that only an act of physical destruction could satisfy the "contempt" requirement of the state law. In *State v. Claxton*, a 1972 case involving wearing a flag patch on a pair of jeans, a Washington appeals court similarly ordered an acquittal because there was no evidence of any public mutilation or desecration of the flag as the state law required, especially since the law's purpose was held to be to prevent breaches of the peace. Similarly, in *Hoffman v. U.S.*, a 1971 case in which "yippie" activist Abbie Hoffman was charged under the 1968 federal law for wearing a shirt resembling the flag, the District of Columbia Court of Appeals threw out the conviction on the grounds that, by wearing his store-bought apparel, Hoffman had not personally engaged in the required physical destruction of a flag, especially since the "plain fact is that the shirt was not a flag." (Upon his original conviction, which brought with it a 30-day jail term and a $100 fine, Hoffman exclaimed, "I regret that I have only one shirt to give for my country" and termed the decision "ridiculous," since "everyone who wears an Uncle Sam suit is just as guilty.")

In *Franz v. Commonwealth*, a 1972 case involving wearing a flag vest, the Virginia Supreme Court overturned a conviction and one-year jail term (with nine months suspended) on the grounds that there was no evidence that Franz had either defiled the flag or intended to "cast contempt" upon it as required by Virginia law, even if his actions were "indiscreet, immature and thoughtless." Franz had testified that he found the vest and wore it because it was "cool," a factor that seems to have influenced the court along with the testimony of others whom the court said described him as a "former Cub Scout, a former Boy Scout active in his church, a loyal American citizen, and as one who worked well with colors, forms and objects."[14]

In *State v. Hershey*, a 1972 case involving a window display of a flag together with several unattached objects, including a goblet filled with a pinkish liquid and representations apparently intended to suggest blood dripping from the flag's red stripes, an Ohio municipal court reversed a conviction after finding that the facts could be interpreted as indicating a "respectful use of the flag for the purposes of political dissent" as much as a "contemptuous" use of the flag. In *State v. Kent*, a 1966 case involving display of a flag during an antiwar demonstration in which dollar signs had been substituted for the stars, a Hawaii circuit court ruled that there was insufficient showing of any attempt to dishonor the flag, especially since the defendant stated that he wished to gain respect for the ideals he felt the flag should represent and was, in fact, accusing others of symbolically desecrating it. In the 1971 "peace symbol" flag case of *State v. Liska*, an Ohio appeals court overturned a conviction on similar grounds, holding that Liska was only expressing his "aspiration for peace" and that this simply was "not a contemptuous act." In another "peace symbol" flag case, *State v. Nicola*, the North Dakota Supreme Court ruled in 1971 that since Nicola's flag had been specially manufactured with the peace symbol in place, he had never physically desecrated it, and that in any case Nicola's flag had never been the object of the state's law, which only protected real American flags as opposed to "any flag which may happen to have a prevailing scheme or idea of red and white stripes."

The Virginia Supreme Court issued a similar ruling in the 1972 case of *Herrick v. Commonwealth*, holding that the display of a specially manufactured flag that contained in its field twenty-six stars arranged to form a peace symbol was neither a real American flag, nor would it appear to be one "to a casual observer," and therefore did not violate the state law. In *State v. Hodsdon*, a 1972 case involving the display of the American flag in a position subordinate to the United Nations flag, a Delaware Superior Court held that no physical flag defilement as required by Delaware law had occurred. In *People v. Meyers*, a 1974 case involving allegations of lying on a flag in a park and then standing on it, an Illinois appeals court found the conduct did not constitute a public "trampling" of the flag as state law required.[15]

By 1974, flag desecration laws had been struck down as unconstitutional in whole or part in eight states, although except in Arizona and Colorado, as previously discussed, the legal grounds were essentially technical rather than fundamental: the particular language of the laws was held to be unacceptably vague or too broadly encompassing, as opposed to the principle that banning flag desecration was basically in conflict with the First Amendment. Thus, when the U.S. Supreme Court decided the 1974 case of *Smith v. Goguen* (discussed earlier as considered by a federal appeals court), involving a prosecution for wearing a flag patch sewn to the seat of a pair of jeans, the Court held that the Massachusetts law at issue, which outlawed "contemptuously" treating the flag in public, was unconstitutionally vague, although the Court ambiguously added that "certainly nothing prevents a legislature from defining with substantial specificity what constitutes forbidden treatment of United States flags."

As a direct result of this decision, a Pennsylvania flag desecration law with language similar to the flawed Massachusetts statute was declared unconstitutional in the 1974 case of *Commonwealth v. Young* by the Pennsylvania Superior Court, which noted that "we do not condone behavior which defiles the flag of this great nation, but the mandate of the United States Supreme Court is clear." The *Goguen* ruling was also a major reason cited by a federal appeals court for striking down New Hampshire's flag desecration law as unconstitutionally vague in the 1976 case of *Royal v. Superior Court of New Hampshire,* which involved a flag patch worn on a jacket that was partially covered with another patch (however, between Royal's 1970 arrest and the court decision, the New Hampshire statute had been replaced with a new law that eliminated the language found unconstitutional in *Goguen*).[16]

Two state flag desecration laws were struck down because of overly broad definitions of the term "flag." In *Alford v. Sacramento Judicial District,* a 1972 flag burning case, a California appeals court threw out the state law on the grounds that its (typical) flag definition was so broad that its coverage was "fixed only by the limits of one's imagination" and might outlaw even the destruction of a "martini toothpick mounted with a Flag designed to spear an olive" as well as the "deliberate trampling of a picnic napkin embellished with a picture of the flag and intended for the garbage can after use." Although the court's opinion was narrowly based on the law's flag definition, the court indicated that it would also take a dim view of a more carefully crafted law: "any person has the right to dislike the state within which he lives and to say so" and any "legislative attempt to force upon citizens a love for any particular state" would necessarily "do violence to the First Amendment."

In *Parker v. Morgan*, a 1971 case involving the wearing of a jacket with a sewn-on flag that had the words "Give peace a chance" superimposed on it, a federal district court similarly found North Carolina's law unconstitutionally vague and overbroad by virtue of its flag definition and provisions encompassing many behaviors that extended beyond what the court suggested was a constitutionally acceptable ban on the physical mutilation of flags. The state law was "an uncommonly bad statute," the court stated, first because it gave to the state control over "the colors red, white and blue and the depiction of stars and stripes" instead of restricting itself to the carefully "defined emblem itself," and secondly because it could be interpreted to even forbid a citizen to "turn thumbs down at the flag, or [to] stick out his tongue, or salute it with clenched fist," although in a democratic society "the right of protest includes the right to be derisive, disdainful, contemptuous and even defiant of government and what may be thought to be in a given context its symbols of authority." The court termed the law's flag definition "simply unbelievable" noting that:

> It seems to us that red, white and blue trousers, with or without stars, are trousers and not a flag, and that it is beyond the state's competence to dictate color and design of clothing, even bad taste clothing. ... Read literally, it may be dangerous in North Carolina to possess anything red, white and blue. Such a definition is a manifest absurdity. Since it is not suggested that the state has the slightest interest in singling out from the spectrum certain colors for unique protection, this definition alone is enough to void the statute. ... [Additionally] we think the line must be drawn at the point of contemptuous physical contact with the clearly defined flag and that physical protection of the flag itself is the outermost limit of the state's legitimate interest. It is absurd to say that one may verbally abuse the flag, but that he may not direct toward it a derisive gesture.[17]

Two other state flag desecration laws were struck down largely because courts held their language was so vague and overbroad that highly discriminatory enforcement was likely or possible. In *Long Island Vietnam Moratorium Committee v. Cahn*, a 1970 case involving buttons and decals that superimposed the "peace sign" over a portion of the flag, a federal appeals court held that the section of New York's law that banned placing any "word, figure, mark, picture, design, drawing, or any advertisement, of any nature" on the flag was unconstitutionally vague and overbroad in violation of the First Amendment. The court found that the law's broad language forbade "all kinds of posters, buttons, symbols, slogans, and emblems such as have been used for many years in election campaigns, patriotic movements and so forth." However, the court held that such usages involved espousing ideas, a "communicative activity which is protected by the First Amendment" that the "state has no valid interest in prohibiting" since they posed no threat to the peace, and that there was "no place in a free society" for seeking to ensure "proper respect for the integrity of the flag" if this required "worship of the flag by compelling a series of taboos concerning flag display." Above all, the court declared that the law was unconstitutional because, as a result of its vagueness, "no one knows what the statute means" and that:

> Because of its overbreadth the statute vests local law enforcement officers with too much arbitrary discretion in determining whether or not a certain emblem is grounds for prosecution. It permits only that expression which local officials will tolerate; for example, it permits local officials to prosecute peace demonstrators but to allow 'patriotic' organizations and political candidates to go unprosecuted.

In July 1974 the U.S. Supreme Court summarily (that is, without written opinion) affirmed the appeals court decision in *Cahn*, apparently on the basis of its own ruling four months earlier striking down on grounds of vagueness the Massachusetts law used in the *Goguen* flag seat-patch prosecution.[18]

The *Cahn* decision and the *Parker* decision striking down North Carolina's law were heavily relied upon by the New Jersey Supreme Court in declaring unconstitutionally overbroad part of New Jersey's flag desecration law in the 1973 case of *State v. Zimmelman*, involving the display of flags containing the "peace symbol" on an ice cream truck. The court held that the sweeping legislative ban on placing any markings on the flag would ban "the traditional as well as the extreme, the patriotic as well as the nonpatriotic, and the communicative as well as the noncommunicative" and that no "legitimate State interest" was served by such a prohibition. The court noted that, in practice, "patriotic slogans superimposed on flags or flag representations" had never been prosecuted, although extremely widespread, while Zimmelman's peace symbol flag, which he viewed as "respectful and patriotic," was prosecuted "presumably because it involved negation rather than affirmation of official administration policy," an outcome that the court deemed "intolerable in a democracy which values so highly the right of peaceful dissent." The *Cahn* decision was also relied upon heavily by a Florida appeals court in overturning a conviction for wearing a peace symbol flag on a helmet in the 1972 case of *Miami v. Wolfenberger*. Although the court made clear that it was not "in sympathy" with holdings that the First Amendment "protects the type of conduct" engaged in by Wolfenberger, the judges stated that they felt bound to follow such federal precedents since the defendant was "expressing his views" against the war. The court also noted that any other holding would make numerous "patriotic acts a crime," such as the showing of "television film of the American flag waving and our planes and ships superimposed thereon with the playing of the National Anthem."[19]

Discriminatory and Arbitrary Enforcement of Flag Desecration Laws

As many of the cases just discussed suggest, the general picture presented by the judicial consideration of the flag desecration issue during the Vietnam War era was one of chaotic, highly discretionary law enforcement and contradictory court decisions. Thus, in *State v. Waterman, People v. Cowgill,* and *State v. Mitchell,* wearing the flag, respectively, as a cape, a vest, and a patch on the seat of the pants, led to convictions, but in *State v. Saionz, Franz v. Commonwealth,* and *People v. Vaughan,* the same behaviors led to acquittals. Within a six-month period in 1971, the *New York Times* reported that a Massachusetts court had fined a woman $50 for wearing a flag patch on her pants seat and that a Kansas court dismissed charges resulting from an identical action, on the grounds that such behavior constituted "symbolic speech" that could not be suppressed and was in fact no different than displaying a bumper sticker with a flag and the slogan, "America: Love it or leave it."

An Ohio appeals court, in *State v. Kasnett,* upheld a lower court conviction of a man who wore a flag patch sewn on his back pants pocket, partly because wearing the flag "over the anus ... a part of the human body universally and historically considered unclean ... was a clear act of defilement," but the Ohio Supreme Court overturned the conviction, on the grounds that no physical damage had been done to the flag in question, and, in any case, as a matter of anatomy a patch over a pants pocket was not "over the anus." The Ohio Supreme Court declared that the intent of the Ohio flag desecration law was to ban physical mutilation of the flag and suggested that applying it to the use of the flag as clothing would raise the question, "Is a flag worn by a policeman over his heart, or on his sleeve, or on his helmet permissible, and the same flag worn by a student impermissible depending upon which part of his anatomy it is upon or near?" The court concluded that to avoid being struck down as unconstitutionally vague Ohio's statute must be interpreted to forbid only "contemptuous physical acts of destruction, mutilation, defilement or defacement of the flag" and that "the sole act of wearing it" could not fall within such terrain.[20]

In New York state, a Long Island man was fined $50 in 1969 for contempt of the flag for flying it upside down to signify his feeling that because of the Vietnam War the country was in a "distressed condition" (the arresting policeman paid $2 of the penalty when the culprit was only able to produce $48 in court). But a Mineola, New York woman, Elizabeth Hubner, was acquitted for precisely the same action the following year by a judge who declared that the display did not "in any way" indicate a "dishonorment or defiling of the flag" but was simply an expression that "she and the country was in distress." Hubner, the mother of two children who had won an American Legion good citizenship award while in high school, was handcuffed and fingerprinted when she was first arrested, and her husband had to bail her out with $500 cash hastily gathered from friends of hers when the local bondsman refused to provide bail. The *Hubner* case elicited widespread comment, leading one author to declare that it was a "mystery" that "a human being who has harmed no one's person or property in any way, is terrorized and treated like a criminal for the act of hanging one of her own possessions, a piece of striped cloth, one way rather than another." In the meantime, a nearby American Legion post that flew the flag upside down to protest the North Korean capture of an American ship was not prosecuted at all.[21]

In another set of New York cases, one man pleaded guilty to "contemptuous display of the American flag" and was fined $25 in 1970 for driving a car painted with stars and stripes, yet another man was awarded $2,750 in damages that same year when he sued for false arrest after being jailed for three days and having his car impounded for six weeks for the same offense. (A car painted with a flag motif also led to a prosecution in Chicago in 1971, where a young man originally charged with a felony offense of flag desecration carrying up to five years in jail was ultimately fined $25 for the misdemeanor offense of improper use of a flag, after five court appearances, by a judge who declared, as policemen wearing flag pins looked on, "I'm surprised at a nice boy like you doing something like this." The convicted miscreant lamented that he had thought he had simply done a "really good paint job" that "really dressed up the car. ... I don't believe it. I wouldn't believe it unless I were here, but it's happening to me.") In the Delaware case of *State v. Hodsdon*, flying an American flag in a position subordinate to that of a United Nations flag was found not to constitute flag desecration; yet in the Pennsylvania case of *Commonwealth v. Lorenc* the flying of an American flag below a Russian-style hammer and sickle flag by a businessman to protest the failure of a local school board to pay a bill led to an arrest (by a policeman who testified that he knew the display was illegal because of his "extensive Boy Scout experience") and conviction for casting contempt on the flag; the conviction was upheld by the Superior Court of Pennsylvania. In other Pennsylvania cases, however, convictions—arising from displaying flags with antiwar slogans emblazoned on them and from appearing at an army induction center draped only in undershorts and a flag to protest the possibility of ending up returning from Vietnam dead in a flag-draped coffin—were overturned by the state supreme court because the state flag desecration law specifically exempted from prosecution instances arising from flags used in any "political demonstrations."[22]

As previously pointed out, prosecutions for superimposing peace signs over the flag's field of stars almost invariably ultimately led to acquittals, but in *State v. Saulino*, superimposition of a picture of Mickey Mouse led to conviction. Displaying the flag over the artistic representation of an erect penis led to an acquittal in 1974 (after eight years of litigation) in *U.S. v. Radich*, but rubbing the flag over the genitals and using it as a handkerchief led to conviction in *Van Slyke v. State*. Burning the flag before 1983 generally led to conviction, but as discussed in the next chapter, after 1982 the same action always culminated in an acquittal, both in the lower courts as well as in the Supreme Court's 1989–90 decisions. In Dallas, within a three-month period in 1970, grand juries returned indictments for flag desecration in six cases involving trousers seat flag patches, yet refused to return indictments in two other apparently identical cases. A Dallas police spokesman, queried about these cases, said, "If there's a departmental policy in this area, I don't know about it."[23]

The most disturbing aspect of the flag desecration cases was the arbitrary manner in which such prosecutions were almost always only used against "peace" demonstrators. However, "establishment" and "patriotic" elements who wore flag pins in their lapels (including President Nixon and the White House staff and the police departments of Boston and New York City) or flag patches on their shoulders and placed flag decals on their windows and cars by the tens of millions, often in technical violation of flag desecration statutes, invariably were unhindered. President Nixon not only wore a flag pin himself, but personally congratulated a New York policeman who led the successful fight to change department regulations so that police could wear flag pins on their uniform. According to the Mayor of Macon, Georgia, the town police discovered that wearing flag patches deterred apparently patriotic criminals from assaulting them. He declared in January 1969 that since police had started wearing flag shoulder patches in July 1968, not a single officer had been assaulted, compared to 29 assaults during the first six months of 1968. "Some of our policeman have told me," the Mayor reported, "that people they were attempting to arrest gave indications they would have assaulted them and then they did not when they saw the flag on their shoulder."

Just in case anyone missed the message that the government felt that the flag could be used for symbolic reasons, but only to present a "patriotic" message, on July 4, 1970, Postmaster General Winton Blount announced that a new poster would be displayed in all post offices with a painting of the flag and the words, "This is our flag—be proud of it." Meanwhile, the Board of Freeholders of Burlington County, New Jersey, voted to place 200 flag decals with the message, "Our Flag: Love it or Leave," on all county-owned vehicles in July 1970, but then decided not to use them after it turned out that the Elks organization that had donated the decals refused, in an apparent display of their all-Americanism, to admit nonwhites as members.[24]

Whitney Smith, director of the Flag Research Center, summed up the situation in 1970 by noting that "commercial misuse" of the flag was "more extensive than its misuse by leftists or students, but this is overlooked because the business interests are part of the establishment." Similarly, articles appearing in the *New York Times* in 1971 noted that flag desecration laws were so broad that they could be used to punish virtually any alleged "abuse" of the flag but that "they have rarely been invoked against anyone except those who differ with prevailing ideas of patriotism" and that such targets were often "rebellious young people [arrested] for improper display of the flag on their clothing by policemen wearing flag patches or pins on their uniforms, while widespread commercial use of the flag is tolerated in advertisements and promotions."

A 1971 article in *Art in America* reached the same conclusion, noting that those arrested for flag desecration "are invariably critics of national policy, while 'patriots' who tamper with the flag are overlooked." A review of flag desecration cases published in 1971 in *The New Republic* concluded that "uneven enforcement" of flag desecration laws was "often intended to harass peace demonstrators and young persons with long hair and beards." *Time* magazine, commenting in 1970 on prosecutions for "wearing" the flag, noted that applying such logic, "Uncle Sam should be indicted first, followed by Roy Rogers and Dale Evans [popular entertainers who appeared on national television without incident wearing flag costumes in a clearly patriotic cause]." Similarly, *Commonweal* reported sarcastically in 1968 that clearly the "evil" of flag desecration was deeply rooted, since "decades of school children have been duped into picturing our national symbol as a shaggy, bearded type, disrespectfully clothed in flag-like togs, and irrelevantly known (that's the way these hippies talk) as 'Uncle'."[25]

In Albuquerque, New Mexico, all five flag desecration arrests that occurred in the summer of 1970 were targeted at persons who appeared to be "hippies" (one of whom received a six-month jail term for wearing a headband that contained an American flag; he testified a friend had given him the headband and had not known wearing it violated the law). Dallas police wearing flag patches on their arms arrested a man for wearing flags sewn into his trouser legs, while an Allegheny County, Maryland, man was sentenced to six months for sewing a flag to his pants, although police in nearby Prince George's County proudly displayed shirts with American flags sewn to them. Although Dallas grand juries usually (if not always) returned indictments in flag "wearing" cases, no indictment was returned in the case of a bank that used the flag in advertising, a clear contravention of the Texas flag desecration law. When asked to prosecute the bank, a Dallas assistant district attorney termed the issue "ridiculous" and "not in the spirit of the law," and the *Dallas Times-Herald* echoed this assessment, praised the bank for "trying to promote pride in the flag," and urged, "Keep her flying.") New York state prosecuted one man for driving a stars-and-stripes painted automobile along a highway that featured state billboards promoting New York potatoes, containing pictures of Governor Nelson Rockefeller superimposed over the flag and pictures of potatoes replacing the stars. In Chicago, a "countercultural" storeowner was arrested in 1970 for selling cocktail coasters imprinted with flag pictures, whereas other businesses were unmolested as they openly sold masses of merchandise imprinted with flags, ranging from stationary to rings and litter bags. One high-ranking Chicago police officer explained to a reporter that wearing a flag patch would be okay, but anyone using a flag as a shawl "would be in trouble."[26]

Occasionally these anomalies simply became too obvious to ignore. Thus, the charge against a Topeka, Kansas man for having a "peace flag" decal on his car was dropped after his lawyer pointed out that city police cars bore flag decals "defaced" by a "love it or leave it" slogan. Charges against five young Philadelphians for picnicking on a flag (they were originally detained on $25,000 bail each) were similarly dismissed after they brought to court cups, plates, and napkins with pictures of the flag, along with an 1862 photo depicting President Lincoln and Gen. George McClellan sitting at a flag-covered table and photos of actress Racquel Welch wearing a bikini, which displayed what *Time* magazine termed her "noteworthy anatomy cradled in the stars and snuggled in stripes." Before dismissing the charges, Judge Robert Latrone asked, "Is it worse for Racquel Welch to have the Stars and Stripes next to her bare anatomy than to sit on it? Do we condone that and prosecute these defendants? When she cloaks herself in the flag is she glamorizing the flag or desecrating it?"

In the Supreme Court case of *Smith v. Goguen*, the Court quoted a lawyer representing Massachusetts as admitting to a lower court that a "war protester who, while attending a rally at which it begins to rain, evidences his disrespect for the flag by contemptuously covering himself with it" would be prosecuted, whereas "a member of the American Legion who, caught in the same rainstorm while returning from an 'America—Love It or Leave It' rally, similarly uses the flag but does so regrettably but without a contemptuous attitude, would not be prosecuted." One young man who was prosecuted in Pennsylvania for wearing a flag patch on his trousers in 1970 apparently was well aware of the differential treatment accorded those using the flag in unusual ways: although he had been long-haired and "mod-attired" when arrested in 1970, when he appeared in court in early 1972 his lawyer stressed that the defendant was short-haired, conventionally dressed, and about to start employment in a "straight" job. When the judge nonetheless sentenced the defendant to 30 days in jail and a $100 fine for flag desecration, the young man fainted, and when he hit the floor, what turned out to be a wig hiding long, curly hair flew off his head.[27]

CBS television was afraid of legal difficulties and adverse public reaction arising from even broadcasting a picture of a "rebellious" person using the flag "improperly." So when "yippie" leader Abbie Hoffman was interviewed on "The Merv Griffin Show" on March 28, 1970, while wearing a shirt resembling the flag the network electronically "blacked out" Hoffman's face and body. (At the time Hoffman was, ultimately successfully, appealing a conviction under the 1968 federal law for a similar choice of costume worn earlier at a Congressional hearing.) When Hoffman first appeared on the screen he was wearing an overcoat, but as soon as he complained about being too hot and doffed it, he disappeared into a literal black hole (which Hoffman later termed a case of "electronic fascism"). Bizarrely, one commercial aired during the show featured a man in an Uncle Sam flag suit selling automobiles. CBS President Robert Wood went on the air shortly before the disembodied Hoffman appeared, explaining that CBS was "masking visual shots of the shirt" because it was concerned about "serious legal problems" and also desired to "avoid affronting many of our viewers." In fact, CBS's censorship triggered 4,000 telephone calls from angry viewers, some of whom pointed out that ABC had only two months before transmitted unimpeded pictures of flag-attired entertainers Dale Evans and Roy Rogers.[28]

The Vietnam War Era
Cultural War over the Flag

As previous references to policemen wearing flag patches and pins suggests, one of the results of the growing numbers of incidents in which flags were used to express political dissent was the emergence, especially in 1969 and 1970, of a counter-surge of "patriotic" flag displays. It was especially manifested by the widespread distribution and display of "flag decals," which hundreds of thousands of Americans pasted on their windows and their car bumpers (where, of course, they were subjected to "desecrating" influences from car exhausts, general atmospheric pollution, and severe weather conditions). Thus, press reports in 1969 and 1970 indicate that a total of over 70 million flag decals had been distributed, and that cloth flags were selling in record numbers. The most prolific distributor of flag decals was *Readers Digest* magazine, which mailed out a reported 49 million such stickers in 1969, and Gulf Oil, responsible for distributing 22 million decals; hundreds of thousands more were handed out, often as part of commercial promotions, by banks, service stations, and the Elks civic organization, whose flag decal featured a "love it or leave it" message. A cartoon in the October 24, 1970 *New Yorker* noted the subtle but growing peer pressure to display flags by depicting a business executive telling an employee that, "Naturally, X, the company doesn't care whether its employees have little flags on their desks or not. It's purely a voluntary thing. We just wondered why you happened to be the only person who hasn't got one." In 1970 folk singer John Prine satirized the growing cult of flag patriotism in a song entitled (and beginning with), "Your flag decal won't get you into heaven any more," with the second line, "It's already overcrowded from your dirty little war."[29]

Political scientist Seymour Martin Lipset explained the flag explosion by noting, "All sorts of traditional values are being challenged. In a certain sense, by having a flag on the car, you're saying that you're not a hippie, you're against campus demonstrations and that you believe in the traditions and values that are under attack." Similarly, the *Reader's Digest* vice-president for flag production explained, "It's a way for the ordinary fellow who works all day, has saved a little money and who leads an ordinary life to respond. It's a massive response to campus unrest, racial disharmony and all the other things that are wracking this country." Thus, a Chicago customer who visited a flag store in 1970 told a clerk, "I want a flag for my house, a flag for my car, and a flag sticker for my window. I want people to know that I'm sick of the kind of thing that's been going on in this country."[30]

Speaking from the opposite perspective, literary critic Alfred Kazin complained in 1970 that self-proclaimed patriots were displaying the flag to "cover up" the "fact" that over 40,000 Americans had died in Vietnam "for nothing" and to say to dissidents, "Hippie, long-haired nut, peace freak, Red slime, free-talking bastard, shut up, get off the streets, disappear." A *Village Voice* article sympathetic to the antiwar movement similarly lamented in 1970 that "the armies of the right, the rhetoricians of King and Country, have captured the stars and stripes and are defending it with Iwo Jima enthusiasm against the pinko, freako faggots on the left." *Chicago Sun-Times* cartoonist Bill Maudlin depicted a man covered in a flag bearing the slogan, "Obedience is patriotism," while another man told him, "It was designed as a flag, buddy—not as a blindfold."

Because displaying an unaltered flag became so identified with support for the "establishment," by 1970 at least some normally flag-flying Americans refused to unfurl their flags. Thus, a commentator in a religious journal lamented, "Today I feel uncomfortable if we put the flag out. Will someone think [this] means that I approve of the American position in Vietnam, the suppression of dissent and other official attitudes I consider uncivilized?" Similarly, a suburban Chicago father reported in 1970 that while he had regularly flown the flag on July 4, "Now all of a sudden we're afraid of being identified with the right-wingers or the hard hats or the people who hate the students. We'd like to fly our flag, but with people the way they are these days we just can't. That's a pretty sad state of affairs isn't it?"[31]

Others took a more utilitarian view of the flag. Thus, one college student explained his car flag decal by noting, "The police like this kind of thing and maybe if I'm speeding and they see the flag they won't pull me over," and a Berkeley coed with a flag knee patch said, "I just dig the colors. And I love stars. The flag's groovy from an aesthetic standpoint." Similarly, a New York fashion designer who in late 1967 sold, without any trouble from the authorities, twenty-five apparently illegal minidresses made from real flags, stated, "I don't feel unpatriotic. I like my country. And besides, the stars are so pretty on a blue background." A Texas youth who was subjected to a citizens arrest for wearing a flag sewn on his jeans (effected by two Houston prosecutors during a break from a trial in which they were prosecuting another man for wearing a seat flag patch), reflected the same sentiment, declaring, "I'm just wearing the flag of my country. What's the big deal?" Meanwhile, one flag manufacturer whose business and profits were booming declared, "Seeing all those flags fly just makes my spine tingle."[32]

By 1970, what amounted to a cultural war using the flag as a primary symbol was being waged across the United States. Thus, the *Village Voice* reported in a front-page story published on June 11, 1970, that the flag had become a "tragic icon, blindly worshipped, savagely ripped apart" and that "no one, any more, sees it flutter without the thought of blood and venom." The *Nation* similarly reported on June 29, 1970, that the flag had been "converted from a symbol of national unity into a symbol of disunity and bitter antagonism." In a lengthy cover story published on July 6, 1970, *Time* magazine lamented that the flag had "become the emblem of America's disunity" as the "defiant young blow their nose on it, sleep in it, set it afire or wear it to patch the seat of their trousers," whereas the response of other Americans was to "wave it with defensive pride, crack skulls in its name and fly it from their garbage trucks, police cars and skyscraper scaffolds." Alfred Kazin complained that the flag was being won "to divide our people, to start fights and to end conversation."

This civil war was perhaps best captured by two men quoted in *Time*: Arthur Stivaletra, an organizer of patriotic rallies, declared, "I see the flag as I see God: a supreme being," but a Southern Illinois University professor who was arrested for displaying a "peace flag" decal on his car lamented, "I'm willing to live with people who think the flag is sacred. But I'd appreciate it if they wouldn't lock me in jail if I don't feel the same way." Satirist Mike Royko noted on the eve of Flag Day (June 14) 1970 that the far right "will suspect that anybody who doesn't display a flag is in cahoots with Moscow" while the "far left will think that anybody who flies the flag is a latent concentration camp commander." Not surprisingly, the raging popular war over the flag was reflected in numerous aspects of general popular culture. For example, in the 1967 countercultural hit musical *Hair*, a singer complains in a song, "I fell through a hole in the flag/I got lost in the folds of the flag," and in one scene a flag is wrapped around one actor and used to "swing" another. These latter flag usages were cited along with brief nudity in the play, in unsuccessful attempts by city officials in Atlanta and Oklahoma City to ban productions of *Hair* from appearing in municipal facilities. And although Boston officials eventually lost a legal battle based on similar objections to prevent *Hair* from appearing anywhere in that city, the production was forced to shut down for six weeks while court proceedings dragged on. In 1968 folksinger Pete Seeger wrote a poem, "The Torn Flag," which refers to a flag that has been "used for wrapping lies" and "lies torn upon the ground" in a "flaming town." In the 1969 movie *Easy Rider*, one of the lead characters, who calls himself "Captain America," rides on a motorcycle, which is decorated in flag colors, and wears a jacket with a flag sown to the back of it; in the final scene of the movie his companion is shot to death by local "rednecks." (In the script to the film but not in the movie itself, "Captain America" places his jacket under his dying companion's head, so that he literally bleeds on the flag.) In the 1970 movie *The Strawberry Statement*, based on the 1968 student protests at Columbia University, the climactic scene shows police fighting with students in a gymnasium in which a huge flag is displayed; in several camera shots the combatants are shown literally fighting back and forth through the flag, which is thereby shredded both literally and metaphorically. The paperback cover of antiwar leader Tom Hayden's 1970 book *Rebellion and Repression* featured a photograph of a flag-wrapped police nightstick. On May 4, 1970, the day that four students were shot to death during an antiwar protest at Kent State University, *Time* magazine published a public-service ad entitled "Isn't it time we all did a little mending," which depicted a diverse group of people gathered around a tailor who is attempting to repair a battered flag.[33]

The American civil war over the flag climaxed in the spring of 1970 in the aftermath of the American invasion of Cambodia and the Kent State shootings. To protest these events, 20,000 antiwar demonstrators forced the governor of Massachusetts to lower the statehouse flag to half-staff; in New York City, on May 8 so-called "hard hat" construction workers, gathered behind a phalanx of flags and wearing flag decals on their hats, attacked and wounded student antiwar demonstrators and then stormed city hall, forcing officials to raise to full-staff a flag that Mayor John Lindsay had ordered lowered to half-staff. They also tried to tear down a flag flying over a nearby church in the mistaken impression that it was a Vietnamese communist banner. Throughout the rest of May, "hard hats" marched through New York's financial district displaying flags and carrying signs with slogans such as, "America, love it or leave it." Thus, the *New York Times* reported that, on May 15, several thousand "hard hats" marched with signs calling Lindsay variously a "rat, a Commy rat, a faggot, a leftist, a neurotic, an anarchist and a traitor." One "hard hat" told a reporter that he would kill his own son with "no compunction" if "he ripped the flag," since flag desecration was "the worst thing" antiwar protesters had ever done. Lindsay was reduced to pleading that citizens stop fighting over the flag since "the issue" was "the war and what it is doing to the nation" and Americans' commitment to "a common country and common principles" could only occur "by ending the controversy over the American flag."[34]

On July 4, patriots organized a special "Honor America Day" rally in Washington, D.C., attracting over 250,000 people who heard the well-known conservative clergyman Billy Graham denounce "extremist elements" who had "desecrated our flag, disrupted our educational system, laughed at our religious heritage and threatened to burn down our cities." According to an account in the July 13, 1970 *National Observer*, many of those attending the rally used flag designs for "everything from blankets to garters," yet "not one arrest was made"; a Justice Department lawyer explained that he would "hesitate to order arrests in a crowd like that for minor infractions" because "the resulting confrontation might have caused more damage than the flag desecration could have."

The "hard hat" incidents attracted widespread national attention. Thus, satirist Art Buchwald wrote a column about a flag salesman who demanded proof that prospective purchasers supported American foreign policy and whose flag models included those designed for "light combat" or "heavy fighting," including one with a metal flag pole tip "so when you hit someone with it it doesn't crack," and another with an eagle tip made "especially sharp so that when you lunge with it you can really do damage to the groin." Writing in 1971, cultural historian John Pullen declared that during 1970 the flag was the center of "more fist fights" than "constructive discussion. It used to be that when the flag went by, you got a lump in your throat; during this period you were likely to have got one on your head." Emotions were clearly still running high in mid-1971, when a San Francisco woman who smothered a flag set afire during an antiwar demonstration with her bare hands was featured as a hero in nationwide news accounts, appeared on numerous television and radio shows, received over one hundred congratulatory letters (including one from President Nixon), and was deluged with requests for dates, along with at least one marriage proposal.[35]

The contentious atmosphere surrounding the controversy over the flag during the Vietnam period appears to have affected a number of police, judges, juries, and prosecutors in ways that seem to have strongly prejudiced the cases against defendants in flag desecration cases. ACLU attorney Burt Neuborne, in a 1991 interview, recalled that when he talked to police who had made arrests for flag desecration during the Vietnam period, "It was amazing to me how deeply they felt. They had so internalized the flag as a symbol that they felt miserable about it. It was quite extraordinary how emotional they were about it." At least some judges and prosecutors were similarly emotionally affected by these cases or by their perceptions of public anger over them. Thus, when an Indianapolis art student was arrested for flying a flag upside down, the judge assigned to his case declared, "It looks to me like we have before us one of those young men who want to destroy our society"; a judge in another flag case refused to reduce a $3000 appeal bond, declaring "I'm not going to take the heat on this thing. There are a lot of people who think he got just what was coming to him." In the 1973 Texas case of *Renn v. State*, in which a student was given a sentence of 10 years probation for flying a "peace symbol" flag, the Texas Court of Criminal Appeals overturned the conviction due to prosecutorial misconduct, such as repeated references to the defendant as a "hippie," "anti-Christ," and "communist."[36]

In a 1970 Dallas case, which led to a four-year jail sentence for 19-year-old Gary Deeds for burning a piece of flag bunting, according to the recollections of defense attorney Robert Alexander in a 1990 interview,

Dallas County prosecuting attorney David Pickett, who had just returned from serving as a marine in Vietnam, acted as though "someone had personally attacked him" and a "whole lot of the case ultimately came down to the fact that Pickett felt so strongly about it." Pickett himself, in a 1990 interview conducted at his current office as chief prosecutor of the Dallas County organized crime division, maintained that Deeds "should have gone to jail" and that four years seemed to him a reasonable sentence at the time, but he conceded that "it might have been a little harsh now that I look back on it." Pickett, who publicly urged passage of a constitutional amendment to ban flag burning during the 1989–90 controversy, added:

> I have a lot of emotion invested in this thing. I had thirty years of believing that the flag was sacred [at the time of the Deeds trial]. You just didn't mess with the flag, I mean that's all there was to it. If somebody did, of course we felt like they definitely were traitors to this country. Even today I'm repulsed by the fact that this guy [Johnson] got away with burning the flag. I was so upset for a week [after the *Johnson* ruling], I get so emotional about that thing that I can't think straight.

Picket recalled that, shortly after prosecuting Deeds, he spotted a girl wearing a "flag bikini," and "I made it perfectly clear to her" that she could be in "legal trouble." Pickett said her response was that she was not desecrating the flag but "showing it off," but he added, "I didn't see that bathing suit again." Asked if he perceived the Deeds case as part of a threat of general societal disintegration during the late 1960s, Pickett responded:

> That's the way I looked at it. Of course, I was really emotionally involved in it. We were taking 50% casualties [in Vietnam] and every one of our fire bases over there had the American flag flying over it, every one, I won't forget either. Maybe I'm outdated, and I probably am, but I just don't understand how anybody can say that it is freedom of speech when you take that symbol and burn and destroy it. You can get the best constitutional lawyer in the world and lecture me for two, three, four weeks and it will never sink in.

If flag desecration was allowed, Picket asked, "What's my six-month-old son supposed to do, what's going to be his strength? If he goes in the military, what's going to hold him, what's going to bind him, what's going to inspire him, what's going to give him whatever it was that got me through my war, whatever it was that got my daddy through and his daddy? What's it going to be, the thought that, 'Hey, I'm over here fighting to give people the right to destroy the symbol of my country'?" Pickett termed the flag the "very essence" of America and declared, "If you destroy the flag, you're destroying the principles, you're saying the hell with those principles, they're not any good. A human being has got to have something tangible that we can get our hands on. A society must have rules and regulations that it abides by. If you destroy all the symbols of this country what do we have left? You might say we have the ideals left, but there's got to be something you can rally around."

Several courts that upheld convictions for flag desecration larded their opinions with extensive discursions on the historical and patriotic significance of the flag. For example, a federal appeals court in the 1972 flag burning case of *U.S. v. Crosson* referred to the World War II flag raising "in the-then hell hole of Iwo Jima," quoted from Whittier's poem about Barbara Freitchie, and declared that all adults remembered "standing stiffly at attention on hundreds of occasions to the gripping strains of the National Anthem." Another federal appeals court, in the 1971 flag ripping case of *Joyce v. U.S.*, declared that "there are few who are not appreciative of the blessings" represented by the flag and quoted at length from patriotic poetry and oratory, including astronaut James Irwin's remarks to Congress, in which he declared that his "proudest moment" was planting the flag on the moon. In a decision later overturned on appeal, an Ohio municipal court in the 1970 "peace symbol" flag case of *State v. Liska* declared that the defendant's beliefs and attitudes "do not conform with what is commonly thought to be the standards of the 'over 30' population," termed them "naive and an unconscious and unthinking mouthing of the political jargon of the new left," and urged him to "rethink his values before he becomes hopelessly enmeshed in political jargon and an illogical party line."

In *State v. Mitchell*, a 1972 conviction in a trousers seat flag patch case, the judge expressed outrage that the defendant had obtained a free high-powered defense from a public defender who had cited fifty-four case precedents and raised a "thoughtless incident" into a "gigantic constitutional issue." Such lawyering "could only have been purchased by a wealthy man," the court declared while claiming that the concept of equal protection of the laws needed "clarification when it reaches the point when the poor man gets more than the rich man, in exercising prudence, could afford to buy." New York University law professor Burt Neuborne, who defended many Vietnam era flag desecration cases as an ACLU lawyer, recalled in a 1991 interview that, during one of the numerous appeals of the *Radich* flag-art case (which, he declared, was "heard by more judges than any case in western history"), the judges asked to see the sculpture at issue, and it was "quite hilarious to see them recoiling in horror at a 7-foot flag penis."[37]

If police, prosecutors, and judges were affected by the emotionalism surrounding the flag during the Vietnam era, it seems likely that many juries were also. Dallas prosecutor David Pickett, in recalling the 1970

Deeds flag burning case in 1990, said that his major argument to the jury was along the lines of, " 'What price are you going to place on this kind of activity? You tell me and you tell the boys who are dying over there in Vietnam right now.' And the women [on the jury] just bit that hook, line and sinker. I was told that on the first jury vote the women voted for twenty years [the Texas flag desecration law, then the harshest in the country, had a maximum 25-year penalty]. It took a couple of strong men on that jury to get the sentence down to four years." Dallas attorney Stanley Weinberg (the trial court defense lawyer in the 1984 Dallas flag burning case that led to the Supreme Court's 1989 ruling in *Texas v. Johnson*) recalled, in a 1990 interview, that a jury member in the 1970 case of his client David Renn (who was given a subsequently overturned 10-year probated sentence for displaying a "peace symbol" flag), told him that the jury was heavily influenced by fears of adverse community reaction. According to Weinberg, a juror telephoned him after the case was decided "to say that the jury was going to walk him out there [acquit Renn], but for the fact that they were going to have to face the community, because they honestly didn't believe that he should have a prison sentence or a felony on his record because he was sincere." Similarly, John Nelms, who was the lead defense lawyer for *Deeds*, noted in a 1990 interview, conducted at his present office as chief prosecutor of the Dallas County district attorney's grand jury division, that because the case was "well-publicized, these jurors all had to go home to their own neighborhoods" and that, "They didn't want to see the people across the street or at the country club say, 'Why'd you let that little pinko commie off for.' There's that kind of pressure, very subtle, but it's there."

Peculiar Flag Desecration Prosecutions and Penalties

Before leaving the subject of the Vietnam era flag desecration prosecutions, mention should be made of some of the more bizarre incidents, arrests, and penalties of the period. In a number of cases, judges ordered what amounted to public apologies from flag desecrators. For example, Gary Wardrip, a Hartford, Indiana man who had used a flag as a curtain in his minibus, was sentenced in 1973 to spend three hours standing in a biting wind with a flag outside of city hall as a form of public penance and an alternative to a possible penalty of $1,000 and one year in jail. Wardrip was surrounded by a crowd of forty people and subjected to repeated shouts of "Commie"; after an hour he entered the courthouse to plead with the judge to mitigate the sentence, declaring, "I don't care what happens. I can't face the people outside." The judge decided to let

Wardrip complete the sentence inside the courthouse since he "would get better protection" there. Wardrip later told a reporter, "It tore me down—and my family. It was like the old days when they slapped you in the stocks. ... I'm just as American as anyone—I dig the flag. ... I'm fixing my van up real nice, I wouldn't put something in it that wasn't nice, too. I wanted to show my patriotism—honest."

In a 1974 incident, two teenage Ohio girls were ordered to publicly apologize in newspaper advertisements for burning a flag, and in addition were ordered to attend flag raising and lowering ceremonies at city hall for a week, to observe a curfew for six months, and not to communicate with each other for a year. A New York businesswoman avoided a sentence of up to one year in jail in 1970 for displaying a sign advertising, "American flag cigarette rolling papers—40 cents a pack," by agreeing to publicly apologize and to display a flag in her shop window.[38]

In another case involving public abasement, Martha Meyers, an Arlington, Massachusetts high school senior, was sentenced, on appeal, in 1970 to carry a large, fifteen-pound American flag on a three-mile march through Cambridge as an alternative to serving six months in jail for burning a flag in a classroom (a sentence pronounced by a judge who declared, "I'm sick of these protesters.") She was also banned from attending school by the Arlington school board "for her safety and the safety and general welfare of other students" following a special six-hour meeting, but was allowed to complete her work at home on condition that she not attend graduation ceremonies. According to news reports, Meyers carried the flag through Cambridge, accompanied by four court officers, with her head held high and a fixed facial expression in front of "hundreds of spectators" who "looked on in bewilderment." A former president of the Massachusetts ACLU declared that Meyer's sentence smacked "of the pillory and the stocks of 250 years ago," while the current president compared it to forcing adulteresses to wear a scarlet "A" on their foreheads in medieval times. The *New York Times,* in an editorial entitled "Pillory Revisited," suggested that the Massachusetts judiciary "might ponder whether the exposure of heretics to public scorn is the best way to create love and respect for the flag and the principles for which it ought to stand."[39]

In other bizarre flag penalties and prosecutions of the Vietnam War era, an Ohio man was originally sentenced to a $500 fine plus three months in jail, to be followed by two years of banishment from Athens County for wearing a trousers flag patch. (The conviction was upheld but the penalty was termed "clearly illegal" and replaced by a $200 fine on first appeal; when Ohio appealed the modification of the sentence, the Ohio Supreme court entirely voided the conviction.) A 16-year-old youth from Boston was banished from Alexandria, Virginia until the age of 21 after he was arrested there for wearing a flag vest (although a few days later Alexandria motorcycle police proudly escorted a man wearing an Uncle Sam suit with flag symbols as he marched past the city courthouse during a parade).

An Illinois teen-ager was arrested for wearing a red, white, and blue belt, while a Connecticut deputy sheriff who had been wounded fighting for the United States in World War II was fired in 1974 for turning his flag lapel pin upside down to express his feeling that Watergate and other events had left the country in "distress." In a case that was eventually dropped, a Pennsylvania student was originally held on $75,000 bail after displaying a flag painted on a sheet, with crosses and stars of David symbolizing war dead substituted for stars. An 18-year-old Minnesota man was given a three-month jail term after violating the provisions of his original sentence for wearing a flag shirt; the sentence had specified that he could not visit an area near the University of Minnesota campus (he also was ordered to attend naturalization proceedings and write an essay on the flag).[40]

In Johnson City, Tennessee, four police officers with flag patches on their shoulders and armed with a search warrant raided the house of a "hippie" college student at 7 a.m. after a passerby reported seeing a flag draped across a bedroom wall in sight of a window; charges of flag desecration were subsequently dropped on the grounds of lack of any violation of the law, but not before the student had been jailed for two days and missed three exams, thereby costing him an entire semester's work. Students at Hobart College in New York were arrested for washing a flag during a theater skit, and another New York student was arrested for flag desecration after he used a flag to keep warm when he could not start his car and had to walk back to his dormitory. An Indianapolis World War II veteran was fined $500 and sentenced to 180 days in jail for carrying his laundry in a flag, while a California teenager was sentenced to four months in jail and fined $250 for wearing the flag as a poncho. Another California youth, who used the flag as a beach towel, because, he said, "I didn't have anything better to lie on," was sentenced to 60 days in jail for "defiling" the flag, and additionally was compelled to write a 2,000 word essay on "What I think and feel the flag is to this country."[41]

An Amherst College junior, Robert Kingman, who had been arrested by five police dispatched in three cars, and was originally sentenced to a year in jail and fined $100 for wearing a flag patch on the seat of his shorts, on appeal was instead placed on probation until he graduated, fined $100, and required to write an essay on the American flag and "what it means to millions in this world" to be read during a naturalization ceremony. Kingman declared that a friend had given him the shorts and that he would have removed the patch if anyone had objected to it. Kingman's shorts remained impounded, but the appeals court judge declared that he had reduced the sentence because Kingman had "no record whatsoever" and the new penalty should insure that "he would never forget what he had done."

A Virginia man was sentenced to eight months in jail for burning a plastic flag replica while reading a poem during an arts festival, and three New York teenagers were sentenced in 1969 to raising and lowering a flag at their local town hall for 30 days after they admitted burning one. Another New York teen was sentenced in 1970 to performing the same chore in jail, while serving a month-long sentence for wearing trousers made from a flag. A Virginia man was sentenced to a year in jail in 1970 (all but three days of which were suspended) for wearing jeans with a flag patch sewn to the rear, after he told a judge that the patch covered a hole in the only clean trousers he had and that, "I've got nothing against the flag." Since the court confiscated the subversive trousers as part of the sentence he was to able to leave jail without violating public indecency laws only after friends brought him a new pair of jeans.[42]

In a case that amounted to a sort of conservative version of the *Radich* case, a Pittsburgh man was acquitted by a jury in 1974 of flag desecration in connection with an art exhibit in which, to protest the Supreme Court's 1973 decision legalizing abortion, a flag was glued upside down to a piece of canvas as a sign of distress, with a swastika painted across the stripes and a photo of aborted babies fastened to the field of stars. The judge told the jury that the key issue was whether the artist, William Mogush, had "intended to bring contempt on the flag." Mogush denied that this was his purpose, declaring that he had acted "out of love of my country, not hatred," and was only seeking to express the view that "in regards to basic human life, we're proceeding as Nazi Germany did."[43]

The harshest flag desecration penalty of the Vietnam War era was the previously mentioned four-year jail term given in 1970 to a 19-year-old Dallas man, Gary Deeds, for burning a piece of flag-like bunting in a Dallas park that had been the scene of repeated clashes between police and young people who had defied a city order not to swim in a creek that ran through it. Deeds testified that he burned the bunting, which he described as containing only 21 stars and 8 stripes, as a "theatrical display" and because he felt it "had been soiled by the policies of the country," such as "involvement in other countries and wars where it does not belong." He stated that "a soiled flag can be burned" and that he did not burn the bunting "as an insult to the flag," because "I love my country and the flag." Aside from Deeds, the only witness who testified at his trial was a Dallas policeman who reported that Deeds and a companion (who was also indicted but who never appeared for trial) had "strutted like a pair of peacocks" when others in the park applauded the burning; no evidence was introduced that the incidents occurred during or actually sparked any disorders.

Prosecuting attorney David Pickett urged the jury to pronounce a verdict that would "travel 7,000 miles to [Vietnam] where men are fighting," and his prosecutorial colleague Steve Tokoly urged the maximum 25-year sentence for Deeds, maintaining that it was "contemptible for anyone to claim love for the United States flag and then deliberately burn it." Defense attorney John Nelms appealed to the jury to give Deeds probation, because his action was the only way he could express his opposition to the Vietnam War since he was too young to vote. Nelms added that he was not saying that these motives were "good" and that if he had seen the incident, "I probably would have gone over and kicked him in the pants. But to convict him as a criminal and send him to prison for 25 years is wrong." When the jury issued its four-year sentence, after separate deliberations following its original finding of guilty, Deeds burst into tears and his mother ran from the courtroom sobbing. Pickett hailed the sentence as reflecting the "people of Dallas County," who don't "want to put up with things like this"; the *Dallas Morning News* also hailed the outcome, declaring that flag desecration was a "symbolic insult to the nation" as well as a "personal insult" to "most Americans," and termed the jury's sentence a "symbolic act of its own," which proved that "dishonoring a symbol that means so much to so many is playing with dynamite" and would hopefully deliver a message to "others contemplating similar acts of symbolic contempt." Deeds' conviction and sentence was upheld by the Texas Court of Criminal Appeals in 1971, and he served out his full four-year term.[44]

Twenty years after the Deeds trial, his two lawyers, John Nelms and Robert Alexander, and the lead prosecutor, David Pickett, all retained clear memories of the case in interviews conducted in Dallas in 1990 (attempts to locate Deeds in 1990 were unsuccessful). Pickett recalled, "We went on the symbolism argument, that what we have burning was, in fact, if not a perfect flag, a flag for the meaning that came out. What he was doing there, there was no question about it, his intentions were to burn the American flag." According to Pickett, Deeds was a "revolutionary-type kid, or his buddies were," and he was "trying to incite the crowd that was out there" in the park by "staging this burning." He added that when Deeds was arrested he was "wearing a jock strap made out of pieces of the American flag," and that when character witnesses appeared for Deeds during the sentencing phase of his trial, "I held that right in front of their faces" and "that didn't help" Deeds. Pickett recalled that Deeds' family members were "good, decent people" and "that's what made it so sad. Somewhere he had lost touch with his upbringing. That's what nailed him." Pickett said that years after the trial he saw Deeds waiting tables in a restaurant and Deeds "told me that he served every day of the four years." Pickett noted that he had tried "probably 400 jury trials," but that the *Deeds* case was one that "sticks out in your mind, you never forget"; Pickett attributed this to the fact that the case was a "sign of the times. It was a real struggle back then."

Deeds' attorneys also clearly remembered the case, but primarily because they viewed it as a terrible and unjust personal tragedy for their client. Lead attorney John Nelms related that he generally had "never been emotionally involved particularly in most of my cases," but that the Deeds case was different, because "I liked the boy, I liked his family, and I felt that the charge against him was unjust" because "if he desecrated anything I believe it was a piece of bunting that I don't think constituted a flag. What he did was next to nothing and certainly did not deserve the full power of the state to come down on him." Although Nelms, an ex-marine, said in 1990 that he believed a 30-day jail sentence would be appropriate for burning an actual flag, and that he favored a constitutional amendment to outlaw such conduct, "which is so emotionally charged that it would be a cause of homicide or something like that," he argued that the appropriate sentence for Deeds, given that he had no criminal record and had not burned an actual flag, should have been probation. "If Deeds had done almost anything else," Nelms argued, "possession of drugs, stealing a car, burglarizing a house, anything but armed robbery or aggravated sexual assault or murder, he would have gotten probation. I never dreamed at any time up to the moment I heard that verdict in my ears that there was even a remote possibility that he would go to prison."

Nelms termed the four-year jail term the "biggest shock that I've had as a trial lawyer. I've tried over 500 cases in jury trials and I couldn't believe that. This is probably the only case that I've thought about over the years. I have kind of a bathtub-type memory; when I get through with a case I usually pull the plug and it drains out." In this case, however, Nelms said, "I always remember the big soulful eyes of Mr. Deeds. I just always felt real sorry for the kid. He was about two to three years older than my oldest girl. I just always felt real bad about it. I still feel bad about it. If he had gotten probation it probably wouldn't have loomed so large in my memory, but the fact that he got such an outrageous sentence under such outrageous facts made it memorable."

Nelms attributed the sentence to the "very conservative" political climate of Dallas and the general "temper of the times" in the country, in which Deeds, whom he viewed as an "extremely believable and sympathetic type witness," was portrayed as a "no-account-commie-pinko-hippie." Nelms recalled that the effect of the sentence on Deeds' family was "just like they were hit in the head with a sledgehammer. I think they were destroyed by it. They were reeling. The boy [Deeds] was just like someone who's been in an accident, almost in shock." Nelms concluded, "The case was just a bump in the road for me, but for that kid, having to serve his four years, it was bound to have just a tremendous effect on the rest of his life. Once he went down as a convict, especially for four years, it would put a mark on him, it's hard to get work, and I'm sure it must have marked him psychologically, just the unfairness of it."

Robert Alexander, who handled Deeds' unsuccessful appeal to the Texas Court of Criminal Appeals, recalled the Deeds case in 1990 as "the most disturbing case" he was ever involved in during eight years as a lawyer, and as a modest contributing factor to his decision to leave the profession in the late 1970s. Alexander completely rejected Pickett's characterization of Deeds as a radical militant; instead he recalled Deeds as a "naive, innocent, teenager" who "believed in peace and love, he absolutely believed in them. In his mind he was making a gesture to indicate his unhappiness with America being at war in a foreign country and his unhappiness with police who would beat up on people just because they wanted to have fun and jump in the creek." Alexander recalled that when he first became involved in the case, "I couldn't believe that there was a felony crime of burning a flag," but that he soon realized that Dallas officials and the general community were not "willing to see that this was some fairly innocent prank at the worst and at the best someone with some perhaps muddled political ideas who was trying to make some sincere, but obscure statement." Instead, Alexander recalled, people insisted on viewing Deeds as a "pinko-commie-radical" who "was going to destroy America." According to Alexander, who described himself as a moderate Republican in 1970, people he ran into socially after he took the *Deeds* case "were really concerned that I would take it and just thought this was terrible. It was all confused in their minds with being unpatriotic, undermining the country, destroying the family, antireligion, for them it was all of a piece and so if they saw anybody who seemed to manifest any aspect of this phenomena, well, they might as well stand for all of it and they had to be stamped out."

Alexander related that the defense let Deeds "say a lot of things about himself" on the witness stand that "he probably shouldn't have, because he was so sincere and we thought when they see him they may think he's a damn fool but they're going to realize that this boy isn't going to bring down the government or anything remotely resembling it." Instead, Alexander ruefully concluded, when Deeds expressed political views such as his hopes for "a world without prisons, a world without hate, only love, like John Lennon's song 'Imagine'" the "jury hated that" and the cumulative effect was to "make them think that people like Gary had to be stopped." (Prosecutor Pickett characterized the same testimony as Deeds' indicating support for views such as, "Fuck America, release the prisoners, jail the judges.") Alexander concluded that while the jury wasn't "moved by Gary's sincerity, they were moved by Pickett's, and they thought, 'How dare Gary Deeds upset David Pickett, when David is such a patriotic young man and Gary was a pinko-commie?'" Like Nelms, Alexander termed the sentence a "real shock. We were just astounded that he did not get probation. We just never dreamed that they were going to send this baby-faced innocent 19-year-old to the penitentiary." Alexander termed the impact of the sentence on Deeds and his family "terrible," with the family "especially hurt that so many people, even some relatives, turned on them and would have nothing to do with them and told them how ashamed they should be of Gary."

Alexander related appealing the case to the Texas Court of Criminal Appeals on First Amendment grounds, but, as he remembered the oral argument, "The judges were completely uninterested in that line of argument. They didn't ask much. They had their minds made up." After the appeal was rejected, Alexander recalled, Deeds' family asked him to make no further appeals (to the federal courts):

> They allowed Gary to tell them that perhaps the best thing for all concerned would be if he just want to jail. I was pretty appalled because I had tried to make clear to them that it was not going to be easy for him in prison, it wasn't going to be like camp, and I sincerely thought that these laws contradicted everything I had learned in school about the First Amendment, and surely if I could just find some judges with some intelligence, education and detachment, that we could not put this boy in prison. The more I worked on the case the more I became convinced that it was simply punishment for communicating an unpopular idea and I was convinced that that had to be protected by the First Amendment.

As Nelms noted in his 1990 interview, Alexander was "a few years too early" in making this argument to the Texas Court of Criminal Appeals—the same court that was the first judicial body to overturn the conviction of Gregory Lee Johnson for the 1984 Dallas flag burning that was to make him famous. In yet another, almost bizarre, connection between the Deeds and Johnson cases, the presiding judge in Deeds' 1970 trial was John Vance, who was later to uphold Johnson's conviction as a Texas Court of Appeals judge and, subsequently, as the elected Dallas County District Attorney, was Johnson's unsuccessful chief protagonist before both the Texas Court of Criminal Appeals and the U.S. Supreme Court.[45]

The Supreme Court and the Flag Desecration Issue, 1969–1988

The greatest share of the responsibility for the confusion in the lower courts over flag desecration during the Vietnam War period, and during the entire subsequent period leading up to the Supreme Court's 1989 *Texas v. Johnson* decision, unquestionably rests with the Supreme Court itself. In the 1969 *Street* decision, Chief Justice Warren, in his dissent, quite literally pleaded with his colleagues to confront the issue of the constitutionality of laws banning physical flag desecration head-on, declaring that, "in a time when the American flag has increasingly become an integral part of public protest," it was the Court's responsibility to "confront that question squarely and resolve it." "[Both] those who seek constitutional shelter for acts of flag desecration perpetrated in the course of a political protest and those who must enforce the law are entitled to know the scope of constitutional protection." However, almost certainly due to the Court's accurate perception that the entire question of flag desecration was a political and legal hot potato—as the 1989–90 controversy amply proved—the Court refused to face the question "squarely" for two decades after ducking it in the 1969 *Street* ruling, instead handing down a series of vague, confusing, and sometimes contradictory legal signals concerning the issue.[46]

The *Street* decision was one of a series of Supreme Court rulings that made it clear by the late 1960s that, except under the most extraordinary and unusual circumstances, oral or written statements with political significance could not be criminalized, no matter how unpopular or offensive they might be. In *Street*, as discussed earlier, the Court had declared that this general principle encompassed the "freedom to express publicly one's opinions about our flag, including those opinions which are defiant or contemptuous." Other decisions during both the pre- and post-*Street* eras stressed that the First Amendment forbade outlawing even speech that deeply angered or upset people and, in fact, that such speech was especially intended to be constitutionally protected. For example, in the 1949 case of *Terminiello v. Chicago*, the Court declared that a basic function of free speech in a democracy is "to invite dispute," that "it may indeed best serve its high purpose when it induces a condition of unrest, creates dissatisfaction with conditions as they are or even stirs people to anger," and that speech "should be protected unless likely to produce a clear and present danger of serious substantive evil that arises far above public inconvenience, annoyance or unrest."

Similarly, in the 1964 case of *New York Times v. Sullivan*, the Court declared that "debate on public issues should be uninhibited, robust and wide-open, and that it may well include vehement, caustic and sometimes unpleasantly sharp attacks on government and public officials." In the 1978 case of *FCC v. Pacifica* the Court noted that "if it is the speaker's opinion that gives offense, that consequence is a reason for according it constitutional protection."

Furthermore, the Court established that, just as particular viewpoints could not be outlawed, neither was it permissible to outlaw the discussion of entire subject matters, regardless of viewpoint. Thus, in the 1980 case of *Consolidated Edison Co. v. Public Service Commission*, the Court rejected New York's attempt to forbid the Edison company from inserting political messages, including those relating to nuclear power, in monthly bills, holding that even though all such messages were forbidden, regardless of content, "the First Amendment's hostility to content-based regulation extends not only to restrictions on particular viewpoints but also to prohibition of public discussion of an entire topic." The Court also "rejected the suggestion that a government may justify a content-based prohibition by showing that the speakers have alternate means of expression."[47]

With regard to political speech, by 1969 the Court had indicated that there were only two exceptions to the general rule that no viewpoint could be criminalized. In the 1942 case of *Chaplinsky v. New Hampshire*, the Court created the so-called "fighting words" exception, which allowed the banning of personal insults that "by their very utterance inflict injury or tend to incite an immediate breach of the peace" and "are no essential part of an exposition of ideas, and are of such slight social value as a step to truth that any benefit that may be derived from them is clearly outweighed by the social interest in order and morality." Subsequently, in the 1969 case of *Brandenburg v. Ohio*, the Court, in a decision that considerably tightened previous "breach of the peace" exceptions to the general rule of protecting all political speech, declared that even advocacy of "the use of force or of law violation" could only be punished "where such advocacy is directed to inciting or producing imminent lawless action and is likely to incite or produce such action." In practice, the Court administered even these exceptions so tightly that they have had virtually no significance; for example, the Court has never upheld a single conviction using the *Chaplinsky* "fighting words" exception. And in the 1988 case of *Hustler Magazine, Inc. v. Falwell*, it overturned a libel conviction resulting from a quasi-pornographic caricature, declaring that, in public debate, insulting and even outrageous speech must be tolerated in order to provide "adequate 'breathing space' to the freedoms protected by the First Amendment" and that "an adverse emotional impact on the audience" could not justify restricting speech.[48]

Because the Court had established so clearly by 1969 that even the most offensive, unpopular, and provocative speech and writing was constitutionally protected, the only question concerning the constitutionality of outlawing physical flag desecration centered on whether such "symbolic" acts constituted the legal equivalents of speech and writing. As previously noted, in the 1931 *Stromberg* and the 1943 *Barnette* rulings, both flag cases, the Supreme Court had established that "symbolic speech" was, at least in some cases and to some degree, protected under the First Amendment; but until the 1989 *Johnson* case the Court repeatedly ducked the issue of whether physical flag desecration *was* a form of legally protected "symbolic speech." Between 1931 and 1970, the Court extended constitutional protection to a wide variety of types of symbolic speech, including the use of "opposition" flags to symbolize peaceful political dissent (*Stromberg*), the refusal to salute the government's flag (*Barnette*), and the rights to peacefully picket in labor disputes, to parade in support of civil rights, and to wear black armbands to school in opposition to the Vietnam War.[49]

Supreme Court justices not only viewed such "conduct" as essentially communicative in nature, but pointed out that "symbolic speech" might be the only way for the relatively powerless to gain public attention. Thus in the 1941 case of *Milkwagon Driver's Union v Meadowmoor Dairies, Inc.*, the court noted, "Peaceful picketing is the working man's means of communication," and Justice Douglas, dissenting in the 1966 case of *Adderley v. Florida*, noted that:

> Conventional means of petitioning may be, and often have been, shut off to large groups of our citizens. ... Those who do not control television and radio, those who cannot afford to advertise in newspapers or circulate elaborate pamphlets may have only a more limited type of access to public officials. Their methods should not be condemned as tactics of obstruction and harassment as long as the assembly and petition are peaceful.

Furthermore, the Court suggested that highly unorthodox and symbolic speech might especially deserve protection because it could communicate in an "emotive" way that ordinary speech and writing could not attain. Thus, in the 1971 case of *Cohen v. California*, the Court overturned the disturbing the peace conviction of a man who wore a jacket bearing the words "Fuck the Draft," declaring that words "are often chosen as much for their emotive as their cognitive force." "We cannot sanction the view that the Constitution, while solicitous of the cognitive content of individual speech, has little or no regard for that emotive function which, practically speaking, may often be the more important element of the overall message sought to be communicated." In any case, the Court added, "One man's vulgarity is another man's lyric."[50]

The Court also increasingly made clear that, just as ordinary written and oral political expression could virtually never be criminalized based on its content or because it was viewed as offensive or even posing a vague, potential threat to the peace, neither could symbolic political speech be restricted on such grounds. For example, in the 1969 case of *Tinker v. Des Moines Independent Community School District*, in which the Court overturned a ban on school children wearing black antiwar armbands, it declared that "undifferentiated fear or apprehension of disturbance is not enough to overcome the right to freedom of expression" and that to justify suppression of expression the government would have to show that its action was "caused by something more than a mere desire to avoid the discomfort and unpleasantness that always accompanies an unpopular viewpoint." In two other "symbolic speech" rulings in 1970 and 1988 that were to prove significant for the 1989 *Johnson* flagburning case, the Court respectively struck down, on the basis of unconstitutional discrimination based on content, a law that forbade the unauthorized use of military uniforms in dramatic productions, but only when such use "tended to discredit" the military, and a law that banned picketing close to embassies only when the picket signs tended to bring the foreign government target into public "odium" or "disrepute." In the latter case, the law was found to impermissibly focus "only on the content of the speech" and its "direct impact" on listeners."[51]

In short, by the Vietnam era, the Supreme Court had clearly recognized that "symbolic speech" could, in at least some cases, be a form of communication as equally protected by the First Amendment as ordinary written or verbal expression; in fact, in the 1969 antiwar armband case, the Court explicitly characterized the expression involved as "closely akin to 'pure speech.'" However, in other "symbolic speech" cases the Court made clear that symbolically expressive "conduct" was not always as protected by the First Amendment as was "pure speech."

Thus, in the 1965 case of *Cox v. Louisiana*, the Court "emphatically" rejected the "notion" that the Constitution granted "the same kind of freedom to those who would communicate ideas by conduct such as patrolling, marching and picketing on streets and highways" as to "those who communicate ideas by pure speech"; and in the 1968 case of *U.S. v. O'Brien*, the Court upheld a conviction under a law passed in 1965 to outlaw draft card burning, noting, "We cannot accept the view that an apparently limitless variety of conduct can be labeled 'speech.'" Although the 1965 law was passed after a Congressional debate full of references to draft card burners as filthy beatniks, communist stooges, and traitors, and was clearly intended to suppress a form of widely publicized dissent, the Court unconvincingly upheld it. It did so on the grounds that the law was not designed to hinder free expression but merely intended to facilitate the effective functioning of the draft (as though the draft administration did not retain copies of whatever information a draft card burner might destroy!)[52]

The real significance of the 1968 *O'Brien* ruling was that, for the first time, the Court established guidelines for determining when "conduct" could be constitutionally regulated where it was combined with an expressive element ("symbolic speech"). The Court declared that restrictions on mixed conduct-expression could be upheld where governmental regulation of the restricted conduct was within its "constitutional power" and furthered an "important or substantial governmental interest" that was "unrelated to the suppression of free expression" and "if the incidental restriction on alleged First Amendment freedoms is no greater than is essential to the furtherance of that interest." Given the nature of the *O'Brien* decision itself, in which political considerations seemed to outweigh legal ones, and the lack of clarity of the key phrases of the *O'Brien* guidelines, this test did not immediately clarify the legal confusion over "symbolic speech." Subsequently lower courts that applied *O'Brien* to flag desecration cases regularly ended up with different results under similar circumstances.[53]

During the two decades following the *O'Brien* ruling, it became clear that, in practice, the key phrase of its guidelines was the "unrelated to the suppression of free expression" clause. In short, when the Supreme Court found that the *intent* of a regulation of "symbolic speech" was not to suppress expression, it was virtually automatically upheld by applying the relatively lenient *O'Brien* requirement that the government's interest behind the regulation need only be found "important or substantial."

For example, in the 1984 case of *Clark v. Community for Creative Non-Violence*, the Court upheld a National Park Service ban on overnight sleeping in a Washington, D.C. park, as applied to a group that sought to protest homelessness; it held that the *purpose* of the regulation was not to suppress their political views but to avoid damage to the park and keep access to it open to others. On the other hand, the Court, in the 1988 case of *Boos v. Barry*, struck down a law banning picketing outside embassies when such conduct sought to bring public "odium" or "disrepute" upon the targeted foreign government. The Court declared that when the government's purpose in restricting symbolic speech was the suppression of expression, the government regulation could be upheld only if it was found "necessary to serve a compelling state interest" and therefore was to be "subjected to the most exacting scrutiny." In practice, as in the *Boos* case, if the Court found a regulation of politically oriented symbolic speech to be "content-based," (rather than to only "incidentally" affect expression in the "content-neutral" manner found in the *O'Brien* and *Clark* cases), it could not constitutionally survive the virtually impossible-to-meet "compelling" and "exacting" (as opposed to "important") state interest standard. This was because, in these circumstances, the regulated conduct was effectively treated as legally equivalent to "pure speech," which could only be criminalized if it posed a direct threat to the peace, as in the *Chaplinsky* and *Brandenberg* exceptions to otherwise virtually absolutely protected political speech and writing. As legal scholar Randolph Collins summarized in a 1991 article in the *American Criminal Law Review*, "As a practical matter, when the more lenient standard in *O'Brien* is applied, the statute is almost always upheld; in contrast, when the more exacting scrutiny is used, the statute is usually struck down."[54]

While the Court's approach to symbolic speech in general was gradually elaborated during the 1968–1988 period, the Court continually bobbed, ducked, and weaved to avoid squarely confronting the potentially politically explosive issue of physical flag desecration in particular, as it had in the 1969 *Street* case. Between the *Street* case and the 1989 *Texas v. Johnson* ruling, the Court wrote only two full-fledged opinions dealing with flag desecration and avoided the key issues in both of them. Furthermore, after *Street,*the Court invariably dealt with the literally and figuratively "inflammatory" issue of flag *burning* in particular by repeatedly refusing to grant appeals on all cases involving such conduct. The only two flag desecration cases that generated Supreme Court opinions during the two decades after the *Street* case were both issued in 1974. In the first of these, *Smith v. Goguen*, involving the conviction of a Massachusetts teenager for "contemptuously" treating the flag by wearing a flag patch on his trousers, a five-judge majority completely avoided the central First Amendment issue raised by flag desecration laws by issuing a technical ruling that the key "contemptuously" wording in the state law was unconstitutionally vague. In the other 1974 case, *Spence v. Washington*, involving conviction for taping a removable "peace sign" on a flag, the court also reversed, by a 6–3 per curium (unsigned) opinion, which again avoided squarely confronting the First Amendment issue—and was so garlanded with irrelevancies and minutiae that it had little clear precedential value.[55]

The *Goguen* case originated in January 1970 when Valerie Goguen, a 19-year-old Canadian who had lived in the United States for seven years, was arrested after a city councilman in Leominister, Massachusetts spotted him wearing a seat flag patch on his dungarees. Goguen told reporters that the only reason he was wearing the patch was to cover "the hole in my jeans," that he had not sought to "laugh at the American flag," and that, "If I knew there was a law against it, I wouldn't have done it." Nonetheless, Goguen was sentenced to the maximum penalty of one year in jail on February 23, 1970, after a nonjury trial before Leominister Judge Richard Comerford, who termed his action "in vile contempt of the symbol of the republic." A spokesman for the Massachusetts Civil Liberties Union termed the sentence "monstrously out of proportion to the crime." Goguen himself declared it "struck me kind of hard," and his mother lamented, "I know you have to respect the flag, but I didn't think they'd go that far."[56]

On April 15, 1971, Goguen's sentence was reduced to six months in jail after he was again convicted, upon exercising his right to a *de novo* jury trial, in Worcester Superior Court. Prosecutor John O'Connor urged the jury to convict, because "the American flag is not just a piece of cloth, but the American flag is America." To prove this he recited American history ranging from the American Revolution to Iwo Jima and Pearl Harbor, when he declared, "the only thing left on the [sunken battleship] Arizona as it went down is the American flag sticking up out of the water." On the other hand, Goguen's ACLU attorney, Evan Lawson, told reporters and unsuccessfully argued in court that the key issue was whether "the government can force citizens to show respect for a governmental token" or "establish a political sacred object" in "the land of liberty." In February 1972 the Massachusetts Supreme Judicial Court upheld Goguen's conviction on appeal, rejecting Lawson's challenge to the law based on free speech grounds and on the grounds that the "contemptuously" clause was unconstitutionally vague.

Goguen's luck began to change after his appeal entered the federal courts. On May 25, 1972, federal district court Levin Campbell overturned his conviction. Campbell declared that although Massachusetts could constitutionally ban "physically damaging the flag" with a "narrowly drawn statute" and Goguen had engaged in "silly conduct," the law was unconstitutionally vague, thus allowing the "police and the courts to pick and choose whom to prosecute and convict." Judge Campbell also found the law violated the First Amendment by going "well beyond prohibiting physical mutilation and destruction." He declared that the existing law could even be interpreted to allow prosecutions for verbal and "non-verbal insults" to the flag, "such as turning thumbs down or sticking out one's tongue at the flag," and possibly even for "failure to remove one's hat when the flag passes."

Following Campbell's ruling, the Charlestown, Massachusetts, American Legion chapter unanimously asked the State Department to deport Goguen. Earlier, Goguen had spent several days in jail after local bail bondsmen refused to help him and the original jury trial judge had refused to release him on personal recognizance while he appealed the case; finally a Massachusetts Supreme Court judge ordered him released, over the opposition of Worcester County officials who reported that Goguen had a criminal record, after Goguen's lawyer told the judge his client's record consisted of a conviction for "swimming in a reservoir." In a 1992 interview, Lawson recalled that Goguen was especially anxious to get out of jail because the other inmates and the guards sought to show that they were "patriotic" by "picking on him," including a threat by the guards to cut his waist-length hair.[57]

On December 14, 1972, a three-judge federal appeals court, declaring that "while the subject matter of this case is seat-of-the-pants, our analysis cannot be," unanimously upheld and broadened Campbell's decision following an appeal by Massachusetts. The appeals court found that the Massachusetts law was so unconstitutionally vague that it might criminalize "waving a flag during a speech critical" of governmental policy; "holding a flag while making a face or a contemptuous gesture; climaxing a speech by crumpling a flag; spitting in the direction of a flag; ... displaying the flag against a background surrounded with derogatory and condemnatory symbols and slogans"; and a variety of other acts. Especially since "those charged with violation" of the law had "seen unpunished hundreds, perhaps thousands of American citizens with American flags sewn to various parts of their clothes, or flying in frayed condition from radio antennas or automobiles, or used as advertising in store windows," the court continued, they could hardly be expected to "know that their similar actions" might "constitute contemptuous treatment."[58]

The appeals court also went well beyond the district court's holding to suggest that all flag desecration laws were inherently unconstitutional, in violation of the First Amendment, unless they were narrowly targeted "to prevent breaches of the peace." "[It] is not within the constitutional power of the state to proscribe criminal penalties for failure to show proper respect toward our flag by words or acts." Applying the Supreme Court's 1968 *O'Brien* draft card burning ruling, the court held that, because the flag was a "pure symbol," the purpose of the Massachusetts laws was "directly related to the suppression of free expression" beyond any concern with keeping the peace and that its evident intent to promote "loyalty and patriotism may not constitutionally furnish a justification for imposition of criminal penalties." Very directly anticipating the Supreme Court's 1989 *Johnson* ruling, both in approach and outcome, the appeals court declared that even if it "may be politically unpopular," the Constitution "required" the finding that "if verbal abuse of the flag cannot be proscribed in an effort to encourage respect for our national symbol," (as the Supreme Court had found in the 1969 *Street* case) then neither could "physical abuse which is visually communicative." Any such prohibition was "directed point blank at the expression of and mere belief in particular ideas" and ultimately sought to penalize "what the state considers an impure mind."[59]

Although the Supreme Court upheld the appeals court ruling that Goguen's conviction could not stand, its holding stripped the case of all First Amendment significance by finding that, since the Massachusetts law was so vague that it allowed "policemen, prosecutors and juries to pursue their personal predilections," it was unconstitutional on those grounds alone. Therefore, "there is no need to decide additional [First Amendment] issues." Only Justice White, in a concurring opinion that created a six-judge majority for Goguen, declared that the Massachusetts law should have been overturned, not because it was unconstitutionally vague, since "anyone with at least a semblance of common sense" would know that Goguen's seat flag patch was "contemptuous" of the flag, but because the law went beyond the valid purpose of seeking to protect the flag's "physical integrity" to additionally and unconstitutionally forbid using the flag only to communicate "ideas" that were "unacceptable to the controlling majority in the legislature."[60]

In a 1992 interview, Goguen's lawyer, Evan Lawson, still clearly recalled the case after nearly two decades, noting that "you don't get to the Supreme Court everyday" and "you don't forget a case like that." He related, "I tried to argue that the case was really about symbolism and that you could not talk about freedom of expression without recognizing the power of symbolism and that clearly the flag is the ultimate symbol as far as this country is concerned." Lawson said that although he was "concerned that I hadn't been able to sell it as a restriction on expression," the Supreme Court's decision was still of great significance. Although a First Amendment ruling would only have affected free speech jurisprudence, its ruling "set a precedent with far broader application since it applies across the board to all penal statutes in terms of the degree of specificity that you have to have so people can conform their conduct to what the law requires."

Lawson added that his most vivid recollection from the oral argument before the Supreme Court was that while Massachusetts was making its case, the late liberal Justice William Douglas was "just glowering" at them, but "while I was up there he was smiling at me." Lawson recalled that for years after the Supreme Court ruling he had an enlarged, framed newspaper clipping about the outcome on his kitchen wall and that "we had this guy who took out the garbage, and every week he would come in and look at that article, and shake his head and say, 'That's awful. You should take that down, you shouldn't be proud of that.' To me, that always symbolized the inherent contradictions of American society, a society built on individual expression and liberty and yet the people don't really want it."

In addition to the *Goguen* case, the other 1974 flag desecration case that elicited a Supreme Court opinion originated in Seattle, where Harold Spence, a 23-year-old photo finisher, was arrested on May 10, 1970, for displaying a flag from his apartment window to which he had affixed removable black plastic tape in the form of a peace symbol. Spence was convicted, first by a judge (who sentenced him to 90 days in jail, with 60 days suspended), and subsequently by a King County Superior Court jury (where the presiding judge, who said a large percentage of Americans regarded the flag as "something almost sacred," sentenced him to a $75 fine and a suspended 10-day jail term), for violating Washington's "improper use" flag law, which, among other things, barred placing any marks or designs upon the flag or displaying such altered flags in public view.

Spence testified that he had altered and displayed the flag in order to associate it with peace instead of violence and to protest the recent American invasion of Cambodia and the killing of four students at Kent State University. He added that he had not known that his act violated the law and that he had deliberately used tape that could be removed without damaging the flag. In a 1992 interview, David Allen, Spence's lawyer, recalled him as a "real nice guy" who was "a serious kid who was upset about Vietnam and wanted to make a statement" and "wasn't anyway on the radical fringe or anything like that."[61]

Spence's conviction was reversed by a 2–1 vote of a three-judge panel of the Washington Court of Appeals, on November 15, 1971, which held the state law unconstitutionally overbroad and in violation of his First Amendment rights. The appeals court held under the Supreme Court's 1968 *O'Brien* ruling that the Washington statute was directed solely at the "suppression of free expression" and was therefore just as constitutionally impermissible as the Supreme Court had found New York state's attempt to criminalize words critical of the flag in the 1969 *Street* case. If the government's interests in punishing such words were constitutionally insufficient, the appeals court found, "they would clearly be insufficient as to symbols used conveying the same meaning as the words themselves." However, on January 18, 1973, Spence's conviction was reinstated by a 6–1 vote of the Supreme Court of Washington, which cited the U.S. Supreme Court's 1907 *Halter* ruling and held that Washington's "improper use" law reflected the legitimate and nonsuppressive legislative purpose of "preserving the flag as a symbol of the nation and in keeping it free of extraneous adornment and alien markings and designs." The court held that the law at most imposed only a "miniscule and trifling" burden on Spence's First Amendment rights because he could still express his views by utilizing "thousands of other means," so long as he did not do so by placing them "upon a flag of the United States." The ruling evoked an extraordinarily bitter dissent from Associate Justice Finley, who termed Spence's action an "idealistic and courageous appeal for world peace" and denounced the majority ruling for "brusquely" and "myopically or arbitrarily" sweeping aside Spence's rights, thereby overturning the "better-reasoned, more rational" appeals court holding and indulging in the same kind of "reactionary, if not personally biased" reasoning that "perpetuated unconstitutional deprivations of fundamental liberties in the past," as in the legitimation of racial segregation in public facilities. To uphold such a deprivation because "other means" existed for Spence to express himself, Finley declared, was "not only highly irregular and unnecessary but arbitrary and oppressive."[62]

After Spence appealed to the U.S. Supreme Court, that body held by a 6–3 majority on June 25, 1974, that the Washington "improper use" flag law had been unconstitutionally applied to Spence in violation of the First Amendment. However, the Court's reasoning was so specifically tied to details of the case that its broader meaning, and therefore its general application to other flag desecration laws and prosecution cases, was, at best, highly obscure. Among the reasons the Court cited for reversing the conviction was that Spence had altered his own flag, rather than a government flag; that he had displayed it on private property by hanging it out of his apartment window, engaging in "no trespass or disorderly conduct"; that no evidence of a threat to the peace was apparent; that even the state of Washington conceded that Spence was "engaged in a form of communication"; and that "it would have been difficult for the great majority of citizens to miss the drift" of his expression. However, the Court's decision appeared to rest on its conclusion that Washington had prosecuted Spence in order to preserve "the national flag as an unalloyed symbol of our country" and that, even assuming for the sake of argument that the state had a legitimate interest in "preserving the physical integrity of a privately owned flag" for this purpose, no such interest had been "significantly impaired" because Spence did "not permanently disfigure the flag or destroy it." (This point led Justice Rehnquist, in a bitter dissent, to skewer the majority's avoidance of the key issue of the constitutionality of outlawing physical flag desecration in order to protect its symbolic value by suggesting that the majority's opinion seemed to suggest that Washington was only seeking "to protect the flag's resale value" and that therefore Spence "could be prosecuted if he subsequently tore the flag in the process of trying to take the tape off." In his original draft, Rehnquist accused the majority of verging on "pure flummery" in making such arguments, but he deleted this characterization from his published dissent.)[63]

Although the convoluted nature of the Court's opinion in *Spence* deprived it of immediate precedential value, tucked away in various parts of the ruling were several highly significant points that were eventually to lead directly to (and to reappear in) the 1989 *Johnson* flagburning holding. First, the court declared (in a footnote) that if Washington did have an interest in preserving the symbolic value of the flag, such an interest was "directly related to expression," and involved "no other government interest unrelated to expression." Therefore, at least "in the context of activity like that undertaken" by Spence, Washington's interest in passing its law could not be evaluated by the relatively lenient *O'Brien* test. While this cautious phrasing avoided any direct reference to flag burning, this was the first time that the Court had clearly stated that protest symbolically utilizing the American flag could be viewed as purely a matter of "expression." It logically suggested that flag burning would be also protected unless somehow permanently altering a flag could be regarded as legally different than temporarily altering one.

Second, (in another footnote) the Court "summarily" rejected the heart of the Washington Supreme Court's ruling, by rejecting the holding that the availability of alternative means of expression reduced the impact of the Washington law on Spence's First Amendment rights. In yet another highly significant point tucked away in the ruling, the Court produced its first real guideline for determining what constituted symbolic conduct that qualified constitutionally as "expression": whenever "an intent to convey a particularized message was present, and in the surrounding circumstances the likelihood was great that the message would be understood by those who viewed it."[64]

Both the *Spence* and *Goguen* rulings contained clear suggestions that the Court regarded most flag desecration laws as poorly written and overly broad, even if it was unwilling to confront them head-on. For example, in a footnote, the *Spence* decision referred to (without formally ruling on) the "nearly limitless sweep" of Washington's "improper" flag use law, which, if "read literally," would ban veterans from attaching "battalion commendations to a United States flag" and forbid newspapers from publishing "mastheads composed of the national flag with superimposed print." Similarly, the *Goguen* opinion, which struck down the "treats contemptuously" provision of the Massachusetts flag desecration law, declared that "casual treatment of the flag has become a widespread contemporary phenomenon" and that, "in a time of widely varying attitudes and tastes for displaying something so ubiquitous," it "could hardly be the purpose of the Massachusetts legislature to make criminal every informal use of the flag." Yet, the Court added, the existing statute "fails to draw reasonably clear lines between the kinds of nonceremonial treatment that are criminal and those that are not." The Court suggested that Massachusetts should "define with some care the flag behavior that it intends to outlaw" and that "nothing prevents a legislature from defining with substantial specificity what constitutes forbidden treatment" (which carefully avoided stating that the Court would necessarily uphold such better-drawn laws).[65]

The Court's studied avoidance of confronting the fundamental First Amendment issue clearly raised by the *Goguen* and *Spence* cases reflected considerable behind-the-scenes turmoil among the justices. Records deposited in the Library of Congress by retired justices clearly indicate that the Court majorities that overturned the two convictions were deeply divided as to whether to confront the constitutional issue squarely or to avoid it and that, in the end, majority opinions could only be obtained for the narrower approach. The records indicate that in the *Goguen* case, Justices Douglas, Brennan, and Marshall all wanted to strike down the Massachusetts law as violating the First Amendment; thus, at the November , 1973 Court conference following oral argument, Brennan declared (foreshadowing his majority opinion in *Johnson* sixteen years later) that the law amounted to a "governmental order that one idea," the "sanctity of the flag," could not be offset by another, such as "disrespect for what the flag is being used to represent," a position endorsed by Marshall, who said it was an "effort to make everyone conform." However, Justices Stewart and Powell were only willing to overturn the law on the basis of vagueness, leading Justice Douglas on November 21 to send a memo to those two justices along with Brennan and Marshall which noted that although "anyone can, of course, write his personal view, my concern at this time is whether we can get a Court [majority opinion]."[66]

The Court's behind-the-scenes turmoil in the *Spence* case was even more marked than in the *Goguen* case. At the Court's November 16, 1973 conference on *Goguen* Chief Justice Burger had strongly urged supporting the Massachusetts law on the grounds that respect for the flag was important because, "We have little to cling to in this country when trouble brews." However, at the Court's January 11, 1974 *Spence* conference he denounced the similarly worded Washington law as "foolish" and voted with six other justices to overturn Spence's conviction. Subsequently, Burger assigned the majority opinion to himself and circulated a draft opinion on May 29, 1974, which urged declaring the Washington law "unconstitutionally overbroad in its potential application to protected activity under the First Amendment." According to Burger's draft, the "extraordinary reach" of the law's terms "brings within its ambit a substantial range of legitimate activity respecting the flag," such as even barring the "taking, developing or printing for display of any photograph" or motion picture depicting a war hero standing in front of the flag, since both the flag and the person would subsequently appear "on the same [photographic] plane."

At the same time, Burger circulated a memo declaring that his draft opinion "does not fully satisfy me" and lamenting that the case involved "one of the minor 'thickets' that we have been drawn into." Subsequently, on June 3, Burger notified his colleagues that he was working on a new draft and followed this up the next day with the announcement that he had decided to change his vote entirely and to dissent from the Court majority. Subsequently, Powell wrote the majority opinion, but he refused to sign it despite the urging of Justices Stewart, Brennan, and Marshall that he do so rather than issue it as an unsigned, or *per curium*, opinion—which inevitably gave the impression that none of the majority justices wanted to take responsibility for it.[67]

Because *Street, Goguen,* and *Spence* all reversed flag desecration convictions, collectively they left the impression that the Supreme Court was reluctant to convict in such cases. But because all three decisions also avoided the fundamental First Amendment issue, they left the lower courts in a state of both freedom and confusion. If the view of the Court majority was left clouded in opacity, however, the strong and crystal-clear view of a significant Court minority—that flag desecration laws were unquestionably valid—was reflected in bitter dissents.

As previously noted, four justices vehemently argued that Street's conviction should have been upheld and that the government was clearly entitled to outlaw flag burning; similarly strong dissents were penned by three justices in both the *Goguen* and *Spence* cases. In *Goguen*, Blackmun and Warren argued that the "contemptuously" provision of the Massachusetts flag law was neither unconstitutionally vague nor aimed at punishing Goguen for any particular expression, but simply constitutionally punished him for "harming the physical integrity of the flag by wearing it affixed to the seat of his pants." This suggestion that Blackmun would uphold a flag desecration law that was not targeted at political dissent but sought only to protect the "physical integrity of the flag" would later pay a key role in the 1989–90 flag desecration controversy. In the *Spence* case (in which Blackmun voted with the majority to overturn a conviction for attaching a peace symbol to the flag, even though the Washington statute seemed aimed in part at protecting the same "physical integrity" he had found an acceptable goal in *Goguen*), Chief Justice Burger (after switching his vote) declared the Court should leave to "each State and ultimately the common sense of its people to decide how the flag, as a symbol of national unity, should be protected."[68]

In both cases, the most embittered and lengthy dissents were penned by Justice Rehnquist (joined in both cases by Burger and, in *Spence* only, by White), in what in retrospect can be seen as rehearsals for his impassioned dissent in the *Johnson* case fifteen years later. In *Goguen*, Rehnquist argued that the government was entitled to assert a "property interest," which could govern how individuals treated even privately owned flags, just as it could ban defacing currency, restrict the wearing of military uniform, or create and protect private "proprietary interests" through copyright laws. He maintained that what individuals purchased "is not merely cloth dyed red, white and blue but also the one visible manifestation of 200 years of nationhood." He also argued that the Massachusetts law "punishes a variety of uses of the flag which would impair its physical integrity without regard" to any "expressive conduct." Therefore, the government interests could be upheld under the *O'Brien* case as "unrelated to the suppression of free expression." As he would subsequently in *Johnson*, Rehnquist attempted to bolster his argument by quoting patriotic poetry and delivering a long paean on the history of the flag, ranging from the American Revolution to Barbara Frietchie, George M. Cohan, and Iwo Jima. He summarized this material by referring to the "deep emotional feelings" aroused by the flag "in a large part of our citizenry," which, he declared, "cannot be fully expressed in the two dimensions of a lawyer's brief or of a judicial opinion."

In *Spence*, Rehnquist cited the 1907 Supreme Court *Halter* ruling to underline his argument that the government was entitled to preserve the flag as "an important symbol of nationhood and unity" and that attempts to protect the "character, not the cloth" of the flag no more impermissibly burdened First Amendment rights than did laws against perjury, libel, copyright infringement, incitement to riot, or "the painting of public buildings."[69]

Concerning the Court majority's apparent unwillingness to tackle the flag desecration question head-on, New York University Law Professor Burt Neuborne, who helped defend both Goguen and Spence as an ACLU lawyer, declared in a 1991 interview that, even when reading *Goguen* twenty years later, "I can't stop laughing because I find it one of the most unpersuasive rationales that forbidding casting contempt on the flag doesn't give you adequate notice that putting a flag on your ass is outlawed." Neuborne further characterized the *Spence* ruling as reflecting "utter cowardice" by the Supreme Court, because "it was an absurdity that an important Supreme Court decision was decided on a per curiam opinion" and because "they were not prepared to come out with a reasoned exposition that could give guidance to anyone else. It read like it was written by one of the clerks." According to Neuborne, while the Court ducked the basic issues posed by the *Goguen* and *Spence* cases, the rulings ultimately reflected "the fact that they didn't want these kids to be convicted."

The confusion created by the Court's handling of the *Street, Goguen,* and *Spence* cases was only compounded by its actions with regard to other flag desecration appeals that reached it between 1969 and 1985. In one case, the Court handed down what amounted to an equally split "nondecision"; otherwise it simply refused to hear them altogether, in some cases leaving convictions standing, in others leaving standing lower court rulings that struck down flag desecration laws, and in all cases refusing to hear appeals when flag burnings were involved. As previously discussed, in the 1971 Radich art exhibit case, the only flag desecration case that the Court agreed to hear for twenty years after 1969, aside from *Goguen* and *Spence*, the Court split 4–4 (with Justice Douglas not voting), with the result that a lower court affirmation of Radich's conviction was left standing (although a federal district court overturned it in 1974 in a habeas corpus proceeding essentially based on the *Spence* decision). The *Radich* outcome shocked civil liberties lawyers, who were counting on Douglas as a certain vote to overturn the conviction. Thus, Professor Neuborne recalled in 1991 that Douglas's refusal to vote "stunned us, we thought we had five votes. If he had voted the way we predicted you wouldn't have had to wait until 1989 for a flag burning decision."[70]

In other flag desecration appeals brought to the Supreme Court between 1969 and 1985, the Court refused to hear more than a dozen cases, including *Cowgill v. California,* a state conviction for wearing a cut-up flag as a vest; *Joyce v. U.S.,* a federal appeals court ruling upholding a conviction for tearing a flag; *California v. Sacramento Municipal Court,* a California appeals court ruling declaring that state's law unconstitutionally vague in a flagburning case; *Cahn v. Long Island Moratorium Committee,* a federal appeals court decision declaring New York's flag desecration law unconstitutionally vague in a case involving flag "peace symbol" buttons; *Van Slyke v. Texas,* a Texas appeals court ruling upholding a conviction for using the flag as a handkerchief and simulating masturbation with a flag; *Royal v. Superior Court,* a federal appeals court decision overturning a conviction for wearing a flag seat-patch on the grounds that New Hampshire's law was unconstitutionally vague (based on the Supreme Court's similar action concerning a similar Massachusetts law in the *Goguen* case); and six different cases involving convictions for flag burnings by state and federal courts between 1972 and 1984.[71]

The Court refused to hear two flag burning cases on two different occasions in the mid-1970s, in a manner that both made clear how deeply split the Court was on the flag desecration issue and sent especially confusing signals about the majority's view (other than clearly signaling the majority's apparent terror of dealing directly not only with flag desecration in general but above all with *flagburning* in particular). On July 8, 1974, the Court refused to hear two different flag burning conviction appeals, *Sutherland v. Illinois* and *Farrell v. Iowa.* In both cases four justices (including Blackmun) indicated that they would summarily affirm the lower court convictions, while the five majority justices, without either agreeing to take the cases or making any finding, vacated the lower court rulings and ordered them to reconsider their findings in the light of the *Spence* ruling (and, in the *Farrell* case, also of the *Goguen* ruling).

In both *Sutherland* and *Farrell* the defendants had been convicted under state flag desecration laws for antiwar flag burnings, and in both cases the convictions had been upheld on appeal in 1973, in the *Farrell* case by the Iowa Supreme Court, and in the *Sutherland* case by an Illinois appellate court (from which the Illinois Supreme Court refused to hear an appeal). In both cases, the appeals courts had held that the state flag desecration laws were constitutional, at least as applied to flag burnings, by applying the same *O'Brien* test, which appeals courts in the states of Washington and Massachusetts had used to find their state flag laws deficient in the *Spence* and *Goguen* cases. In particular, both courts found that the state laws had the nonsuppressive, constitutional purpose of seeking to preserve the peace and that flag burnings were "highly likely to" or "could be reasonably expected to provoke a breach of the peace" (although no breach had occurred in either case, a fact the Illinois court seemed to attribute to the happenstance that the three convicted flag burners were all females).[72]

From a formal legal standpoint, the Supreme Court's 1974 orders that the lower court findings in *Sutherland* and *Farrell* be vacated and reconsidered in the light of its own intervening rulings did not necessarily imply that any particular outcome was desired by the Court's majority. However, especially since in both cases four dissenting Supreme

Court justices wanted the lower court convictions summarily upheld, and since the intervening *Spence* and *Goguen* rulings had both *over-turned* flag desecration convictions, it is difficult to avoid the impression that the majority wanted the lower courts to overturn the flag burning convictions even if they were not, to put it mildly, enthusiastic about undertaking such potentially explosive rulings themselves.

If, in fact, this is an accurate interpretation of the majority's wishes (as opposed to admittedly only reasonably informed speculation), both lower courts essentially responded by legally "telling" the Supreme Court that if it wanted to free flag burners it would have to undertake the task itself—and the Supreme Court majority subsequently declined to do so. Both lower courts reaffirmed their original findings, holding that nothing in the intervening Supreme Court rulings had invalidated the state's legitimate concerns over the risk to the peace posed by flag burnings. Thus, the Iowa Supreme Court, focusing on the loopholes that the U.S. Supreme Court had left in its *Spence* ruling, pointed out that whereas *Farrell* involved mutilating a flag by burning it "in a public place," *Spence* had only involved the "nonmutilative removable taping of a peace symbol on a flag then displayed on defendant's privately occupied premises." The Iowa Court added that it had become additionally convinced that the state flag desecration law served the further nonsuppressive purpose of "preserving the physical integrity" of the flag as "an unalloyed symbol of the country" and that Farrell had "manifested total disregard for the flag as a symbol of patriotism, and by the same token espoused disunity." When the defendants in both cases appealed once again to the U.S. Supreme Court, it refused to hear either appeal, although Justices Brennan and Douglas dissented from this refusal in both instances and were joined by Justice Stevens in the *Sutherland* case.[73]

The State Legislative Response to Vietnam War Era Flag Desecration Rulings

The Supreme Court's confusing legal signals concerning the fundamental legality of flag desecration laws between 1969 and 1984, and especially the Court's unwillingness to directly confront the First Amendment heart of the issue they posed, left lower courts, legal scholars, and state legislatures in a state of enormous confusion. Thus, when Federal District Judge John Cannella, in setting aside the flag art conviction of Stephen Radich in 1974, largely on the basis of the Supreme Court's *Spence* ruling, surveyed the findings of state and federal courts on the flag desecration issue, he accurately described a state of complete legal chaos. Thus, he noted:

In recent years, numerous courts, both state and federal, have been called upon to determine the relationship between statutes prohibiting acts of flag desecration and the First Amendment's guarantee of freedom of speech. Such consideration has produced diverse results, as both the state and federal judiciary have been unable to either agree upon the standard to be applied, or uniformly determine which conduct is to be protected and which is to be proscribed.

More specifically, Cannella noted that, with regard to claims that the government could legally protect the flag's "physical integrity" in order to preserve its status as a national symbol, some courts

> have found such interest to be sufficient ground upon which a criminal conviction for flag desecration might be predicated; others have dismissed this factor as insufficient to warrant abridgement of constitutional rights; while still others, applying an *O'Brien* test, have arrived at diverse results, finding either that such interest was so inexplicably intertwined with the ideas being expressed by means of the flag-related conduct as not to form sufficient independent basis for denying constitutionally guaranteed rights or not so inexplicably intertwined as to prevent its invocation.

Similarly, Judge Cannella noted in regard to the claim that flag desecration statutes served the valid state purpose of protecting the peace:

> Numerous courts have concluded ... that acts of flag desecration are, of themselves, so inherently inflammatory as to pose so great a danger to the public peace as warrants the state to act. Other courts have adopted the view that an act of flag desecration standing alone is insufficiently provocative to justify the imposition of criminal sanctions or abridge First Amendment rights; other objective evidence which demonstrates the imminence of public unrest, or a clear and present danger that a breach of the peace is likely must be adduced before a state may constitutionally act in a given case.[74]

Although, as Judge Cannella also noted, scholars writing in law journals during the 1968–1974 period were virtually unanimous that the Supreme Court should legalize flag desecration as a form of protected political protest (although often reaching this conclusion by different legal approaches), they were as equally baffled as the lower courts as to what the state of the law and Supreme Court intentions were, and this remained the case long after Cannella's 1974 opinion. For example, in a 1985 book, free speech expert Thomas Tedford concluded, based on the Supreme Court's repeated refusal to hear appeals from flag burning convictions after 1970, that it had made " 'perfectly clear' that it does not view mutilation or destruction of the flag to be symbolic expression deserving of the protective umbrella of the Constitution."

However, other legal experts reached quite different conclusions. For example, after the Supreme Court agreed to hear Dallas's 1988 appeal from the Texas Court of Criminal Appeals ruling overturning the 1984 flag burning conviction of Gregory Johnson, civil liberties lawyer Martin Garbus expressed astonishment that the Court would even consider such an issue: "Up to now, it seemed that the court had already said definitively that the use of the flag to express a political belief was perfectly acceptable, that such activity was protected by the First Amendment." The American Law Institute took an in-between position, concluding in 1980 that the Court's actions had left the "implication" that flag desecration "may be punished in at least some contexts."[75]

While judges and legal experts attempted to read the tea leaves of the Supreme Court's decisions and nondecisions, state legislatures in almost twenty states significantly revised their flag desecration statutes between 1970 and 1980, the first major overhaul of such laws since the 1900–20 period, in attempts to update them and overcome constitutional problems with existing laws that had been suggested by various Supreme Court or lower court rulings. Ironically, however, at least in retrospect, virtually every one of these state legislative revisions only succeeded in making their laws even less constitutional than they were previously, by making more clear than ever that they were aimed directly at suppressing political dissent. In essence, all of the major post–1970 revisions deleted provisions that had outlawed the use of the flag for advertising purposes and the placing of marks of any kind on the flag, retaining bans only on forms of flag usage unambiguously associated with political dissent.

Thus, Missouri's 1980 revised law read, in its entirety: "Any person who purposefully and publicly mutilates, defaces, defiles, tramples upon or otherwise desecrates the national flag of the United States or the state of Missouri is guilty of the crime of flag desecration." (The great majority of states outlawed desecration of the *state* as well as the national flag by 1980, while five southern states additionally banned desecration of the *Confederate* flag.) Another ten or so states made revisions like that of Missouri, which seem to have been modeled on the 1968 federal flag desecration law (although usually, if they were passed after the Supreme Court's 1974 *Goguen* ruling, as in the case of Missouri, they omitted the federal provision making the offense dependent upon intent to "cast contempt" on the flag).[76]

An additional eight or so states made revisions that were clearly based on the American Law Institute's 1962 MPC, which had suggested a text largely identical to the revised Delaware law, which read, in its entirety: "A person is guilty of desecration if he intentionally defaces, damages, pollutes or otherwise physically mistreats any public monument or structure, any place of worship, the national flag or any other object of veneration by the public or a substantial segment thereof, in a public place and in a way in which the actor knows will outrage the sensibilities of persons likely to observe or discover his actions." In Massachusetts, quite uniquely, the legislature in 1974 tried to get around the Supreme Court's recent *Goguen* ruling by rewriting the law to ban wearing the flag "on the lower half of the body" or selling any clothing with flags affixed intended for such wear. As the Massachusetts Civil Liberties Union (MCLU) pointed out, this revision was intended to forbid wearing the flag as a trousers-patch, while still allowing police to wear flag patches on their shoulders. The MCLU reported that it had considered recruiting some "go-go dancers" to perform at the State House "suitably displaying the flag above their waist, as a means of demonstrating the bill's idiocy," but it was spared from undertaking this activity when the proposal proved too much even for Republican Governor Francis Sargent, who pocket-vetoed the bill on the grounds that any attempt to "legislate respect for the flag is doomed to failure."[77]

The aim of the just-discussed revisions, which became law in about 40 percent of the states after 1970, was clearly, on the one hand, to delete all references to the use of the flag in advertising, since it was clear that few, if any, public officials had the slightest interest in prosecuting such uses. On the other hand the revisions attempted to conform with the Supreme Court's *Goguen* and *Spence* rulings and with lower court decisions which, as previously noted, had struck down more than a half dozen state flag laws, usually on the grounds of vagueness, by removing terms such as "contemptuous" as well as all other references to uses of the flag that were neither obviously permanently destructive nor clearly intended to convey political dissent.

The result was to restrict the banned activities to physical flag mistreatment of the sort almost exclusively used by political protesters, which made it increasingly and unmistakably obvious that the real purpose of the revised laws was solely to suppress political dissent and thus to ensure that eventually the Supreme Court would have to find them unconstitutional, as outside of the *O'Brien* guidelines. Furthermore, some of the revised laws were just as, or even more, hopelessly vague than were prior flag desecration statutes. This was most blatantly the case with the new statutes based on the MPC that typically were larded with virtually meaningless phrases, which eliminated any objective definition of exactly what was being criminalized by making such matters dependent not only upon whether undefined "substantial" segments of the public venerated the object to begin with, but also upon whether the actor "knows" that persons "likely to observe or discover" the actions would be "outraged" by the particular way the object was "polluted" or otherwise "mistreated."

One of the states that adopted a flag desecration revision based on the MPC was Texas, which in 1973 passed a new law that included "a state or national flag" as a venerated object, along with public monuments and places of worship or burial, and outlawed defacing, damaging or "otherwise" physically mistreating such objects "in a way that the actor knows will seriously offend one or more persons likely to observe or discover his action." University of Texas Law School Dean Page Keeton, who chaired the Texas Legislative Council Committee that recommended the change, told a reporter in 1970 that the revised law would punish flag desecration because such acts were "regarded as highly offensive conduct by the majority of the people."

The Texas law was actually a considerable improvement over the MPC text, because it did not include as a protected object anything that a "substantial" segment of the public venerated and it omitted the hopelessly vague "pollutes" language; it was also a considerable improvement over the existing state law, as it sharply reduced the draconian maximum 25-year penalty to a far more typical maximum penalty of one year in jail and a $2,000 fine. It was this 1973 revised law, whose reduced penalty seems to have partly been a reaction to the four-year jail term given Gary Deeds for burning flag bunting in Dallas in 1970, that was to be invoked against Gregory Lee Johnson for a 1984 Dallas flag burning and that was to lead to the Supreme Court's 1989 *Johnson* ruling.[78]

In a 1992 interview, Austin lawyer Seth Searcy, who served as staff director of the Texas Penal Code Revision project (which supervised the general criminal law revision in the early 1970s that incorporated the new flag law), did not recall that any particular attention was paid to the "seriously offend" language that was to become a major focus of attention during the 1989 flag desecration controversy. He added that those who drafted the law viewed it as a "disorderly conduct type statute," all of which "tend to be vague at the margins," and that the "seriously offend" phrase was probably "borrowed verbatim" from the MPC. Searcy could not recall whether the Deeds sentence played a role in the drastically reduced sentence for flag desecration, but added, "It may well have. Maximum penalties in the old penal code were extraordinarily harsh, like 20 years for marijuana possession, and we generally reduced them across the board."

The post–1970 flag desecration revisions in general made the state laws more overtly and clearly unconstitutional, as a matter of broad constitutional theory, because they were much more clearly targeted at specifically suppressing dissent than had previously been the case. Moreover, laws such as the 1973 Texas statute, which explicitly made the offense dependent upon whether or not people were seriously offended or outraged by viewing or learning about an incident, were most unconstitutional of all because the Supreme Court had made it clear that the criminality of expressions with political significance (unlike obscenity) could not be based upon such considerations. In its 1969 *Street* decision, for example, the Supreme Court had declared, with citations to several "symbolic speech" cases, that "it is firmly settled that under our Constitution the public expression of ideas may not be prohibited merely because the ideas are themselves offensive to some of their hearers." This statement was approvingly quoted by the Supreme Court in the 1974 *Spence* case, along with the comments that anyone offended by Spence's flag display "could easily have avoided" it and that the 1943 *Barnette* compulsory flag salute case had made clear that people could "not be punished for failing to show proper respect for our national emblem."

In an article in the March 1975 *Texas Bar Journal*, Dallas lawyer Walter Steele foretold the Supreme Court's 1989 *Johnson* ruling by warning state officials that the 1973 law was in serious constitutional trouble because of its "serious offense" wording. Citing the *Spence* case, Steele declared that to make a criminal offense depend "entirely upon the attitude of the person who views the conduct" was a "rather ephemeral criterion" and made the new Texas flag law "open to attack on the grounds that it is too vague and overbroad and on the ground that it infringes First Amendment liberties."[79]

Perhaps the greatest irony associated with the adoption of revised state flag desecration laws based on the 1962 ALI MPC was that by the time the ALI got around to publishing an explanation of the MPC in 1980 it was forced to concede that its model "desecration of venerated objects" law was probably unconstitutional as a result of intervening Supreme Court decisions. In its 1980 commentary, the ALI noted that the "essential rationale for the offense" was "to prevent outrage to public sensibilities," but also that the "desecration of venerated objects will often be undertaken for their communicative impact" and that when such objects were desecrated by their owners "the only state interest justifying criminal punishment is directly derivative from the communicative aspect of the actor's conduct." The commentary concluded that the Supreme Court's rulings in *Street, Spence,* and *Goguen* (especially *Spence*) suggested "far more doubt" about the proposed law, on these grounds, "than reasonably could have been anticipated at the time of its drafting" and that "at best" the model was of "doubtful" constitutionality as applied to the desecration of privately owned flags by their owners. In the meantime, however, Texas and a half-dozen other states had based their new flag desecration laws on a model that its own author effectively disowned in 1980.[80]

5

The Great 1989–1990 Flag Burning Controversy

WITH THE END of major American involvement in the Vietnam War by the mid-1970s, general interest in the entire subject of flag desecration rapidly diminished, no doubt greatly facilitated by the end of antiwar demonstrations and, between 1974 and 1979, the virtual disappearance of symbolic protests utilizing the flag. Even after a new spurt of flag burnings erupted in late 1979, they received virtually no national publicity—in fact the only such incident reported in the *New York Times* between 1979 and 1988 was the 1984 Dallas flag burning for which Gregory Lee "Joey" Johnson was convicted and which led to the Supreme Court's 1989 *Johnson* ruling.

Like the Johnson flag burning, virtually all of the post-Vietnam flag burnings involved members of the Revolutionary Communist Party (RCP), a small Maoist-oriented group. RCP members began to engage in such protests in late 1979, apparently inspired by the widely televised images of flag burnings conducted by the Iranian students who seized American hostages in Teheran. The 1984 Dallas flag burning for which Johnson was arrested was one of at least eight flag burning incidents between 1979 and 1984 involving RCP members. In five instances, flag desecration prosecutions and convictions followed, but in three of them, including the Johnson affair, the convictions were eventually overturned on appeal by federal courts on First Amendment grounds (although, except in the *Johnson* case, the judicial reversals came only after those convicted had already served out jail terms).[1]

Before agreeing to hear Johnson's case in 1988, the U.S. Supreme Court continued, in several of the RCP cases, its post–1969 posture of refusing to accept all appeals involving flag burning, with the result that about a dozen RCP members spent a total of about 10 years in jail in the 1980s for an "offense" that the Court was to eventually label constitutionally protected free speech in 1989. In one of these cases, *U.S. v.*

Kime, Justice Brennan foreshadowed his own majority opinions for the Court in the 1989 *Johnson* and 1990 *Eichman* cases by writing a blistering and devastating critique of his colleagues' refusal to hear an appeal from the eight-month jail sentences given to two RCP members who had burned a flag in Greensboro, North Carolina in 1980. They had been convicted under the 1968 federal law (see Appendix, Document 2), which forbade "knowingly cast[ing] contempt" upon the flag by "publicly mutilating, defacing, defiling, burning, or trampling upon it."[2]

In his dissent, Brennan declared that, applying the logic of the Court's own 1974 *Spence* ruling, the Greensboro flag burning was clearly expressive in nature and that the only possible government motive in banning such behavior was the invalid purpose, under the *Street* and *O'Brien* doctrines, of suppressing expression that challenged the government interest in fostering the flag's symbolic value, since there could be no "esthetic or property interest in protecting a mere aggregation of stripes and stars for its own sake." Further, Brennan noted, the terms of the 1968 law expressly made flag burning an offense only when it was done to "cast contempt" upon the flag, thus making the crime totally dependent upon the expression of a particular viewpoint. Brennan noted archly, "This is indeed a narrowly drawn statute; it is drawn so that everything it might possibly prohibit is constitutionally protected expression."[3]

In the lower courts, the U.S. Court of Appeals for the Eleventh Circuit also foreshadowed the 1989–90 findings of the Supreme Court in another one of the RCP flag burning incidents. In the 1984 case of *Monroe v. State Court of Fulton County,* in which two RCP members were sentenced to maximum one-year jail terms under the Georgia state flag desecration law, the convictions had been originally upheld by the Georgia Supreme Court and a federal district court. However, the Eleventh Circuit federal appeals court reversed on the grounds that the flag burning was presumptively protected "expressive" conduct under the *Spence* test and that Georgia's professed interests—the same interests cited by Nebraska in the 1907 *Halter* case and to be cited by Texas in the 1989 *Johnson* case—of seeking to protect both the peace and the symbolic value of the flag were neither "unrelated to the suppression of free speech" (thus ineligible for the lenient 1968 *O'Brien* test) nor "so substantial" as to justify overriding First Amendment interests. The appeals court cited the Supreme Court's 1943 *Barnette* flag salute ruling and held that there was "no significant difference" between government attempts to "compel the expression of respect" for the flag and government attempts to "prevent the expression of disrespect." Noting that in the 1969 *Street* case, the Supreme Court had held this to be true with regard to attempts to ban verbal disrespect for the flag, the appeals court concluded that "governmental regulation of nonverbal expression should be subject to the same limitations."[4]

With regard to Georgia's professed interest in maintaining the peace, the court held that the state had failed to demonstrate any "clear and present danger" of imminent public disorder, as required by the Supreme Court's 1969 *Brandenburg* ruling, or the sort of personal insults required by the "fighting words" doctrine of the 1942 *Chaplinsky* case. This ruling marked the first time that a federal appeals court had overturned a flag burning conviction squarely on First Amendment grounds; in 1985 the same court overturned, on identical grounds, yet another RCP-related flag burning conviction that had led to jail terms under the Georgia state law.[5]

The Case of Gregory Lee Johnson

When Gregory Lee Johnson was arrested for violating Texas' flag desecration law (officially known as the Texas Venerated Objects law) in Dallas in 1984, there was at first no indication that this incident would attract any more attention than the other RCP-related flag burning incidents of the 1979–1984 period. The Johnson affair originated on August 22, 1984, while the Republican National Convention was meeting in Dallas, Texas, to renominate President Ronald Reagan. Following a rowdy demonstration and march by about one hundred protesters through downtown Dallas, during which numerous acts of minor vandalism were committed, including the spray painting of walls of several buildings and the overturning of potted plants in the lobby of a bank building, a flag was burned in front of the Dallas City Hall. No disorders occurred during or after the actual flag burning.[6]

Dallas police, who had observed the entire march without taking any action, rounded up scores of protesters about half an hour after the flag burning, at first charging all of them, including Johnson, with disorderly conduct. All of the disorderly conduct charges were quickly dropped, but new charges were placed against a few of the protesters, including complaints filed against Johnson and three others for violating the Texas Venerated Objects law, which outlawed "intentionally or knowingly" desecrating a "national flag," with "desecrate" defined to mean "deface, damage or otherwise physically mistreat in a way that the actor knows will seriously offend one or more persons likely to observe or discover his action." The other protesters charged with flag desecration either pled guilty or failed to appear for trial and forfeited bonds. Ultimately, Johnson, a member of the Revolutionary Communist Youth Brigade (RCYB), the RCP's youth group, became famous because he was the only protester charged with flag desecration who chose to fight the charges and, especially, because he appealed his original conviction all the way to the U.S. Supreme Court.

Johnson was convicted by a jury on December 13, 1984, and sentenced to the maximum penalty of one year in prison and a fine of $2,000. Johnson's trial featured displays of open antagonism between Johnson and the prosecuting attorney, assistant Dallas County District Attorney Michael Gillett; both openly proclaimed their very different views of life in America. Although Johnson denied that he had personally burned the flag in Dallas on August 22, he appeared in court each day wearing an RYCB T-shirt, which featured a depiction of a man carrying a rifle; both in and out of court he proclaimed that it was "great to see the American flag go up in flames, a symbol of international plunder and murder reduced to ashes." For his part, Gillett repeatedly drew the attention of the jury to Johnson's political views and his T-shirt, at one point even asking Johnson to move his arms so it could be seen more plainly. When Johnson took the witness stand, Gillett focused almost all of his questions on Johnson's political views and repeatedly suggested that if Johnson didn't like the American political system "why don't you just leave" or "move to Russia."[7]

Although Johnson's trial filled more than 800 transcribed pages, remarkably little of the testimony focused on whether or not he actually burned a flag in Dallas on August 22, 1984. The vast bulk of the case Gillett presented focused on the generally disorderly nature of the protest march and Johnson's alleged leadership role. Although Gillett maintained that Johnson had personally burned the flag, he effectively conceded that Dallas' case was not strong on this point by telling presiding Judge John C. Hendrik that even if Johnson "physically himself did not" necessarily participate in all of the illegal events that occurred during the protest, because Johnson was present "our theory is that by his conduct and participation that he would be responsible for acts of co-conspirators and was acting as a party by aiding and encouraging this type of conduct." Johnson's volunteer ACLU lawyers, Stanley Weinberg and Douglas Skemp, maintained that their client did not burn the flag, but that even if he did such conduct was constitutionally protected "symbolic speech."

While this constitutional issue was effectively dismissed out of hand by Hendrik at the trial, it became the primary focus of five years of litigation that followed Johnson's conviction. At the first appeal stage, the Court of Appeals for the Fifth District of Texas upheld Johnson's conviction on January 23, 1986. The appeals court held that, although under the Supreme Court's 1974 *Spence* test Johnson's action was "symbolic speech" that required First Amendment scrutiny, the Texas law did not violate Johnson's First Amendment rights because Texas had overriding interests. Relying heavily on the 1972 ruling of Texas's highest court, the Court of Criminal Appeals, upholding the conviction and four-year jail term in the Vietnam era *Deeds* case, the appeals court declared that "acts of flag desecration are of themselves, so inherently inflammatory that the State may act to prevent breaches of the public peace" and that Texas had a "legitimate and substantial interest in protecting the flag as a symbol of national unity."[8]

However, the Texas Court of Criminal Appeals reversed Johnson's conviction by a vote of 5–4 on April 20, 1988, holding that the Texas Venerated Objects law had been unconstitutionally applied to Johnson in a manner that deprived him of his First Amendment rights. Rejecting its own earlier analysis in *Deeds* as inadequate due to subsequent Supreme Court decisions, notably *Spence* and the 1988 case of *Boos v. Barry*, the court not only found that Johnson had engaged in "symbolic speech," but that Texas had no compelling overriding interests that justified violating his First Amendment rights.

First, the court held that the Texas law was "too broad for First Amendment purposes" to be used properly to prevent breaches of the peace, both in general and in the case at hand, because by banning all flag desecration that caused only "serious offense" it outlawed "protected conduct which has no propensity to result in breaches of the peace." The court specifically noted that in the *Johnson* case there had been, according to trial testimony, "serious offense" but that no violence had been associated with the flag burning. Relying heavily upon and quoting extensively from the *Barnette* flag salute case, the court further rejected Texas's proffered interest in preserving the flag as a symbol of unity as inadequate to justify compromising Johnson's First Amendment rights:

> Recognizing that the right to differ is the centerpiece of our First Amendment freedoms, a government cannot mandate by fiat a feeling of unity in its citizens. Therefore, that very same government cannot carve out a symbol of unity and prescribe a set of approved messages to be associated with that symbol when it cannot mandate the status or feeling the symbol purports to represent. If the state has a legitimate interest in promoting a State approved symbol of unity, that interest is not so compelling as to essentially license the flag's use for only the promotion of the governmental status quo.[9]

The court further declared, citing *Barnette*, that for Texas to override Johnson's First Amendment rights in furtherance of its interest in promoting national unity it would have to demonstrate that Johnson's action posed a "grave and immediate danger" that the flag would lose its ability to "rouse feelings of unity or patriotism" and become devalued "into a meaningless piece of cloth." "We do not believe such a danger is present," the court concluded; therefore it declared that the Venerated Objects law was unconstitutional when "used to punish acts of flag desecration when such conduct falls within the protections of the First Amendment." The court specifically declined to address the question of whether Texas could prosecute flag desecrations that did "not constitute speech under the First Amendment" and therefore declined to respond to Johnson's urging that the statute be found facially invalid on grounds of vagueness, declaring that "our holding that the statute is unconstitutional as applied to this appellant renders a facial determination unnecessary."

In response to the Texas Court of Criminal Appeals ruling, Dallas County appealed to the U.S. Supreme Court, which announced on October 17, 1988 that it would hear it, thereby marking the first time since 1969 that it accepted an appeal in a flag burning case. Although the national media had paid virtually no attention to the *Johnson* case as it made its way through the Texas courts, and typically a Supreme Court decision merely to hear a case attracts little media attention, the Court's October 17, 1988 announcement attracted very considerable press attention. This was above all because a highly symbolic political controversy involving the flag had become a central issue in the 1988 presidential campaign, then less than three weeks away from election day.[10]

During the campaign, Republican Presidential candidate George Bush repeatedly dredged up a hitherto obscure veto that Democratic candidate Michael Dukakis had issued as governor of Massachusetts in 1977 against a law requiring daily public school recitation of the Pledge of Allegiance to the flag. Dukakis's veto was based on solid and diverse legal advice that the law was unconstitutional under the *Barnette* doctrine. Bush used this trivial incident to repeatedly, effectively, and unfairly impugn Dukakis's patriotism, asking at one point, with regard to his opponent, "What is it about the American flag which upsets this man so much?" Bush also habitually led his audiences in mass recitals of the pledge, surrounded his campaign stops and advertisements with flags, and visited Flag City U.S.A. (Findlay, Ohio) and even a flag factory.[11]

One reporter noted wryly of Bush that, "flags surround him on the stump like flowers at a mafia funeral," and another characterized his entire campaign as a cross-country version of the children's game "capture the flag." While Bush asked "from sea to shining sea" why Dukakis vetoed the 1977 bill, another reporter wrote, Dukakis responded by citing *Barnette*, giving an "answer that was scholarly, cogent and politically devastating." Bush stressed the pledge issue so much, in a campaign largely devoid of any substantive issues, that *Time* magazine declared in early October—shortly before the Supreme Court announced it would hear the *Johnson* case—that, "Five weeks after the Republican convention, the public can be certain of [only] two things about George Bush: he loves the flag and he believes in pledging allegiance to it every morning. But some voters may wonder what he would do with the rest of his day if he became president."[12]

Although much of the press was editorially critical of Bush for his stress on the pledge issue, the media willingly gave it massive coverage and the general consensus was that it played a major role in his election victory. Bush's apparent success in using the "flag issue" and his deliberate, seemingly cynical and misleading manipulation of it, together with the effectiveness of his so-called "30-second negative attack" ads, which suggested that Dukakis was soft on crime, were later to have profound repercussions during the 1989–90 flag burning controversy— indeed the specter of 1988 hung over the entire dispute. When, as President, Bush demanded passage of a constitutional amendment to override the Supreme Court's legalization of flag burning as a form of political protest, Democrats viewed his stand as simply an attempt to again cynically "capture the flag" for the Republican Party, but, remembering the "lesson" of 1988 and fearing "negative" ads in their upcoming races if they supported the Court, they were also determined not to be portrayed as less than 100 percent patriotic—as one reporter put it, "many Democrats swore they would never be outflagged again." As the *Washington Post* reported, with the 1988 election fresh in mind, Congressional Democrats "kept up a fusillade of pro-flag rhetoric" in the aftermath of the 1989 *Johnson* ruling, matching the Republicans "word for word" and talking "bar-room tough, essentially saying no Republican had better call them soft on the flag." Under these circumstances, the major focus of the immediate response to the *Johnson* ruling was to become, at least among politicians, *how* and not *whether* to override the Court, and the fundamental constitutional principles involved in the Court's decisions were virtually neglected as both parties battled to demonstrate their patriotism.[13]

Shortly before the *Johnson* case was scheduled for oral argument before the Supreme Court on March 21, 1989, another heated dispute over the flag erupted, this time centered on a student art exhibit in Chicago. The exhibit, by Scott "Dred" Tyler, was part of a large display of art by minority students at the School of the Art Institute of Chicago (SAIC). It featured a photographic collage, attached to a wall, of flag burnings and flag-draped coffins; on the floor in front of the collage was a flag and below the collage on the wall was a ledger in which visitors were asked to record their responses to the exhibit title, "What is the Proper Way to

Display the American Flag?" The flag on the floor was placed in such a way that patrons seemed invited to walk on the flag in order to write in the ledger. [14]

The Tyler exhibit set off a storm of controversy in Chicago, leading to weeks of protests. This tempest in a teapot led to the passage of resolutions of condemnation by the Illinois and Indiana legislatures, a cut-off of funds to SAIC by the Illinois legislature, and the passage of legislation banning putting the flag on the floor by the Chicago City Council and the Illinois legislature. One of the sponsors of the Chicago City Council action termed the Tyler exhibit the most "dastardly act in the history of this city." The largest demonstration protesting the exhibit, on March 12, attracted an estimated 5,000 people, including eleven Chicago aldermen, ten state legislators and a variety of other politicians, leading *Chicago Tribune* satirist Mike Royko to write that Chicago politicians had leapt into the controversy with glee "through the camera's first glare, while filled with hot air," speaking "through the night that our flag shouldn't be there."[15]

The Tyler exhibit attracted considerable national media attention and also denunciation by national politicians. Thus, President Bush termed the exhibit "disgraceful," and the U.S Senate passed, by a 97–0 vote on March 16, an amendment to the 1968 federal flag desecration act outlawing maintaining a flag on the floor. Republican Senate Leader Robert Dole, who was the main sponsor of the measure, declared, "I do not know much about art, but I do know desecration when I see it." (Subsequently, a similar provision was included in the Flag Protection Act of 1989, which Congress passed in October in an attempt to override the Supreme Court's *Johnson* ruling.) Five days after the March 16 Senate response to the Tyler exhibit, the Supreme Court heard oral argument in the *Johnson* case, an occasion that provided yet another opportunity for media focus on the flag desecration issue.[16]

Clearly, by the time the Supreme Court issued its ruling in the case of *Texas v. Johnson* on June 21, 1989, political, public, and media interest in the question of flag desecration had been "primed" to a degree unknown since the Vietnam War era. In its ruling, the high court upheld the decision of the Texas Court of Criminal Appeals, holding by a 5–4 vote that the Texas Venerated Objects law had been unconstitutionally applied to Johnson in violation of his First Amendment rights. Finally squarely facing the issue of the constitutionality of laws that forbade physical flag desecration, a question it had previously consistently ducked for twenty years, the Court's opinion, written by Justice Brennan, largely mirrored his dissent in the 1982 *Kime* flag burning case, as well as the prior ruling in *Johnson* by the Texas Court of Criminal Appeals, and the 1984 decision of the Eleventh Circuit in the *Monroe* case.[17]

Using its own 1974 *Spence* test for determining what constitutes "whether particular conduct possesses sufficient communicative elements to bring the First Amendment into play," the Supreme Court first determined that the "expressive, overtly political nature" of Johnson's conduct was "both intentional and overwhelmingly apparent." Next, the Court considered whether what it termed the "relatively lenient standard" of the 1968 *O'Brien* draft card burning case test was applicable to determine whether Texas's claimed interests could outweigh Johnson's First Amendment rights; the court had held in *O'Brien* that where "important or substantial" governmental interests are involved, the "non-speech" aspects of "conduct" which combine both "'speech' and 'non-speech' elements" can be regulated, so long as "the governmental interest is unrelated to the suppression of free expression."

In considering the two interests advanced by Texas, the need to protect the peace and to protect the symbolic value of the flag, the Court first held that, under the standards proclaimed in the 1969 *Brandenburg* and the 1943 *Chaplinsky* cases, "the state's interest in maintaining order is not implicated," since "no disturbance of the peace actually occurred or threatened to occur because of Johnson's burning of the flag." In practice, the Court held, the state's position amounted to the claim that all flag burnings posed a "potential for breach of the peace," which could justify suppression. However, such a position was held to "eviscerate" the *Brandenburg* doctrine—that only expression posing an imminent and likely threat to the peace could be legally forbidden—and to fly in the face of numerous precedents. (Compare the 1978 case of *FCC v. Pacifica*, which held that the very fact expression caused offense "is a reason for according it constitutional protection.")

Turning to Texas's second asserted interest, "preserving the flag as a symbol of nationhood and national unity," the Court noted that the state's apparent concern was that flag burning would convince people that "the flag does not stand for nationhood and national unity" or that "we do not enjoy unity as a nation." However, the Court pointed out, as it had previously declared in *Spence*, such "concerns blossom only when a person's treatment of the flag communicates some message," which meant that Texas's interest was related "to the suppression of free expression." Therefore, the "relatively lenient" *O'Brien* test was completely inapplicable. Instead, since Johnson's guilt depended "on the likely communicative aspect of his expressive conduct," and was therefore "restricted because of the content of the message he conveyed," the Texas statute was held to be "content based" and, under the doctrine of the 1988 case of *Boos v. Barry,* was therefore subject to "the most exacting scrutiny," requiring a demonstration of a "compelling state interest" to justify overriding Johnson's First Amendment rights.

However, the Court continued, since Texas essentially wished to prevent citizens from conveying "harmful" messages, such an interest violated the "bedrock principle underlying the First Amendment ... that the Government may not prohibit expression of an idea simply because society finds the idea itself offensive or disagreeable." Citing its previous holding in the 1969 *Street* case—that "a State may not criminally punish a person for uttering words critical of the flag," even the expression of "opinions which are defiant or contemptuous"—the Court declared flatly that Texas's attempt to distinguish between the "written or spoken words [at issue in *Street*] and nonverbal conduct ... is of no moment where the nonverbal conduct is expressive, as it is here, and where the regulation of that conduct is related to expression, as it is here." Furthermore, the Court declared that "the enduring lesson" of its past decisions, including *Spence,* that "the Government may not prohibit expression simply because it disagrees with its message, is not dependent on the particular mode in which one chooses to express an idea" and therefore the state could not "criminally punish a person for burning a flag as a means of political protest" on the grounds that other means of expressing the same idea were available.

Citing its own ruling in the 1970 case of *Schacht v. U.S.,* which struck down a federal law that banned unauthorized use of military uniforms in dramatic productions only when their use tended to "discredit" the military, and clearly following the reasoning of the Texas Court of Criminal Appeals, the Court specifically rejected the constitutionality of laws that would mandate that a symbol "be used to express only one view or its referents" and allow the government to "foster its own view of the flag by prohibiting expressive conduct relating to it." Further, the Court specifically rejected the creation of a "separate juridical category for the American flag alone," which would exempt the flag from the "joust of principles protected by the First Amendment." The Court concluded that the "principles of freedom and inclusiveness that the flag best reflects" would be reaffirmed by its decision: "We do not consecrate the flag by punishing its desecration, for in doing so we dilute the freedom that this cherished emblem represents."

The Response to the *Johnson* Ruling

The Supreme Court decision touched off what one newspaper termed a "firestorm of indignation" and what *Newsweek* termed "stunned outrage" across the United States. Certainly no Supreme Court decision within recent memory was so quickly and overwhelmingly denounced by the American political establishment. To some extent, at least, the reaction reflected massive and prominent media coverage, which by its very nature conveyed the implicit message that the Court had done something very bizarre. This implicit message was sometimes compounded by reporting to the effect that the Court had approved of flag burning, as opposed to its narrow legal ruling that flag burning was a constitutionally protected form of protest. (In fact, the Court majority had made clear its distaste for flag desecration, for example, expressing its belief that its ruling "will not endanger the special role played by our flag or the feelings it inspires" and that "nobody can suppose that this one gesture of an unknown man will change our Nation's attitude towards its flag.")[18]

Public and political reaction to the *Johnson* decision was, in any case, immediate, massive, and adverse. Within a week of the ruling, President Bush proposed a constitutional amendment to overturn it and 172 members of the House and 43 Senators sponsored 39 separate resolutions calling for such an amendment; the Senate passed a resolution 97–3 expressing "profound disappointment" with the *Johnson* ruling and approved an attempt to legislatively overturn it; the House of Representatives approved, by a vote of 411–15, an expression of "profound concern" with the decision and followed this up with a highly unusual all-night session devoted to speeches denouncing flag burners and the Court. According to Senator Strom Thurmond of South Carolina, the *Johnson* ruling had "opened an emotional hydrant across our country demanding immediate action to overturn it." Thurmond himself captured the emotional force of much of the criticism of the Court when he proclaimed to the Senate, "We must stand up for America. The flag, the flag. America, America. For us!"[19]

The bitter criticism of the *Johnson* ruling was by no means confined only to politicians and Washington. By July 4, both legislative houses in at least four states approved resolutions calling on Congress to pass a flag protection constitutional amendment and individual legislative chambers in at least another twelve states either took similar action or passed resolutions criticizing the *Johnson* decision. Scores of local governments across the country joined in demanding that the ruling be overturned. A poll published in the July 3 *Newsweek* indicated that 65 percent of the public disagreed with the Court's ruling and that 71 percent favored a constitutional amendment to overturn it, and by October 1.5 million people had signed petitions to that effect.[20]

In the end, both the legal and popular arguments critical of the *Johnson* ruling boiled down to this: the flag, as the most well-known symbol of "freedom" and the nation, was "unique" and "special" and that although dissent was a legitimate and critical part of the democratic process, desecrating the flag went "too far." Thus, in typical reactions by political figures, Senate Republican Leader Robert Dole declared that "freedom of speech is a constitutional guarantee that America holds dear, but we draw the line when it comes to our flag," and President Bush proclaimed that the flag was a "unique national symbol," that he felt "viscerally about burning the American flag," and that "as president, I will uphold our precious right to dissent, but burning the flag goes too far." The decision was also attacked as ignoring the wishes of the vast majority and condoning behavior that would damage the symbolic value of the flag and the strength of the country. Thus, the *Indianapolis Star* asked in an editorial, "Who will protect the rights of the millions who oppose destruction of the symbols of American freedom?" Senate Democratic Leader George Mitchell said the decision "devalued and cheapened" the flag, and an officer of the Seattle Veterans of Foreign Wars declared that, "When you destroy that flag, you destroy the principles of the country."[21]

Much of the popular criticism of the *Johnson* decision, especially in the immediate period after June 21, was couched in highly vitriolic terms. Representative Ron Marlenee of Montana termed the decision "treasonous" and, referring to the six marines depicted in the Iwo Jima Memorial, declared, "These six brave soldiers were symbolically shot in the back by five men in black robes." The Chairman of the South Carolina Joint Veterans Council called on Americans to write to their elected officials to demand that "this crap" be stopped, while conservative columnist Patrick Buchanan termed the decision an "atrocity" and the Court a "renegade tribunal" to which the American people should respond by putting "a fist in their face." The *New York Daily News* termed the *Johnson* decision "dumb" and declared it put the Court in "naked contempt" of the American people and displayed "pompous insensitivity to the most beloved symbol of the most benevolent form of government ever to appear on this Earth"; it also published a cartoon showing a figure resembling President Bush pouring gas on a pile of law books forming a pyre below five bound judges who were bearing copies of the "flag case," with the caption, "Anybody got a match?"[22]

The legal argument for upholding Johnson's conviction did not differ greatly from the popular argument. Texas, in its brief in *Johnson*, essentially argued that the flag was a "unique symbol, qualitatively different from any other symbol that this nation uses to express its existence," that this uniqueness made protecting its symbolic value override "any First Amendment rights an individual may have in expressive conduct," and that its symbolic value would be endangered by "its wanton destruction in a public context." Stripped down to its basics, this position, essentially legally anchored to the 80-year-old *Halter* decision, amounted to declaring that ordinary legal principles concerning freedom of expression simply did not apply where the flag was concerned; in fact Texas declared at one point that the flag was "sui generis."[23]

The four dissenting Supreme Court justices essentially adopted the "sui generis" position. Justice Rehnquist declared, in a dissent (joined by Justices O'Connor and White) that primarily consisted of quotations from patriotic poetry and recitals of incidents in American history involving the flag, that the "flag is not simply another 'idea' or 'point of view' competing for recognition in the marketplace of ideas" but a symbol viewed with "almost mystical reverence" by millions of Americans. At one point, to illustrate his argument, Rehnquist even noted, "The flag has appeared as the principal symbol of approximately 33 United States postal stamps and in the design of at least 43 more, more times than any other symbol." (He did not point out that canceling such stamps made the Postal Service the leading flag desecrator in the country by a factor approaching trillions.) Justice Stevens, in his separate dissent, pronounced that if "the ideas of liberty and equality ... are worth fighting for" then "it cannot be true that the flag that uniquely symbolizes their power is not itself worthy of protection and respect."[24]

Justice Rehnquist's dissent explicitly endorsed the concept that the views of popular majorities should be controlling with regard to the outlawing of behavior they viewed as abhorrent, and in doing so hopelessly confused the distinction between political expression and common criminality. He declared, "Surely one of the high purposes of a democratic society is to legislate against conduct that is regarded as inherently evil and profoundly offensive to the majority of people—whether it be murder, embezzlement, pollution or flag burning." Similarly, Justice Stevens compared Johnson's burning of the flag to spray painting "his message of dissatisfaction on the facade of the Lincoln Memorial" and putting "graffiti on the Washington Monument." This comparison of protecting the flag, which is primarily an idea and which concretely exists only in millions of representations, most of which are privately owned, to unique, publicly owned buildings, was also repeatedly made by Texas and its supporters. Texas, the dissenting justices, and many critics of the *Johnson* majority also argued that forbidding flag desecration placed only a minor burden on free expression because, as Texas stated, it "does no more than prohibit one form of conduct by which a demonstrator may express himself; there remain abundant alternative avenues of communication." Similarly, Justice Rehnquist, who declared at one point that flag burning was hardly expression at all but "the equivalent of an inarticulate grunt or roar," opined that the Texas law left Johnson with "a full panoply of other symbols and every conceivable form of verbal expression" that he could have used to convey his message "just as forcefully in a dozen different ways."

In political circles, the specter of President Bush's apparent success in using the "flag issue" during the 1988 campaign profoundly shaped the response to the *Johnson* decision. Although most Congressional Democrats opposed a constitutional amendment, they overwhelmingly joined Republicans in blasting the *Johnson* ruling, and their Congressional leadership led what ultimately proved in 1989 to be a successful fight to a enact a law that could, supposedly, circumvent *Johnson* faster than an amendment and simultaneously avoid officially "tampering" with the First Amendment. Privately, and sometimes publicly, Democrats frequently admitted that they both understood and, from a legal standpoint, even agreed with the *Johnson* ruling, but added that politically they simply could not be placed in the position of seeming to "oppose" the flag, especially out of fear of being targeted by the "30-second negative ads" made notorious during the 1988 campaign. Thus, when former Solicitor General Charles Fried told a House Judiciary Subcommittee that the court's decision was right and no action should be taken to override it, Democratic Subcommittee Chairman Don Edwards said, "Your point of view is the correct point of view, but it's such a [political] loser," and party colleague Congresswoman Pat Schroeder of Colorado said, "We're not talking about a purist world. We're talking about a very political world."[25]

Democrats across the country were also clearly affected by such political calculations. Thus, Kentucky State Democratic Senator Roger Noe declared that, "Given the kind of mud-slinging being used these days, I can envision seeing campaign ads with opponents who were not strongly supportive of the amendment being pictured as communist or pinko or un-American." California State Senate Democratic Majority Leader Barry Keene voted for a resolution supporting a constitutional amendment to ban flag burning to avoid what he termed a "deathtrap for Democrats"—even though he declared that the real desecration of the flag was the "shameful, cynical, tawdry, manipulative exploitation of the flag for political purposes." Keene lamented, "They know that their political trick will work because we can't take the risk of being thought unpatriotic." Under these circumstances, the major focus of the immediate response to the *Johnson* ruling, at least among politicians, became how, and not whether, to override the Court, and the fundamental constitutional principles involved in the Court's decisions were virtually neglected as both parties battled to demonstrate their patriotism.[26]

Despite the massive attack on the *Johnson* ruling, civil libertarians, hundreds of law professors, the American Bar Association, the American Society of Newspaper Editors, and an overwhelming majority of newspaper columnists, editorials, and editorial cartoons supported the decision as a clear and simple application of the fundamental principles of American democracy. President Bush was especially criticized for allegedly trying to repeat his 1988 presidential campaign strategy by sponsoring a constitutional amendment. Thus, a *Salt Lake Tribune* cartoon depicted Bush as an emperor, naked except for the flag, and the *Washington Post* showed a flag reading "politics first" hoisted over the American flag atop the White House. Other supporters of the *Johnson* ruling criticized politicians of both parties. Thus, radio personality and author Garrison Keillor suggested, "Any decent law to protect the flag ought to prohibit politicians from wrapping it around themselves." The *Philadelphia Inquirer* published a cartoon showing a Republican elephant and a Democratic donkey tearing a flag to shreds in a tug-of-war.[27]

Aside from lambasting politicians for pandering over the *Johnson* ruling and supporting the Supreme Court on the fundamental First Amendment issue, defenders of the Court also argued—echoing the position of some of those who were dubious about flag desecration laws in earlier eras—that there was no real flag burning threat to the country and therefore the whole issue was an absurd distraction from the country's real problems. Thus, Representative Walter Fauntroy (a nonvoting member representing the District of Columbia) termed the entire controversy "another example of misplaced priorities of too many of our national leaders and our people" since such issues as "affordable housing, adequate health care, education and the anti-drug effort" were "far more critical to the quality of life of the American people." A cartoon published in the *New York Daily News* illustrated this point by depicting politicians scrambling to get under a "flag amendment" tent to avoid a rainy downpour of "issues." The *New Jersey Record* portrayed a flag-covered bandwagon crowded with politicians and led by President Bush, with an attached sign reading, "Free ride for all politicians!! Tired of controversial issues? Hop aboard! No Risk!! Photo-ops galore!!"[28]

Another criticism of the drive to circumvent the Court was that there was no way to satisfactorily define such terms as "flag" and "desecrate" in either legislation or a constitutional amendment. Thus, a *Washington Post* cartoon showed a man rushing to stop his wife from burning the trash, because an envelope in the wastebasket had "an American flag [stamp] on it." A satirical column in the *Washington Post* suggested that all possibilities be covered by defining "desecration" to mean "subjecting the flag to damage, disrespect or funny busi-

ness"; anyone who, with regard to a flag, "misfolds, improperly laun-
ders, shreds, deep-fat-fries ...sneezes at, whips-chops-and-purees, wears
a hat in the whereabouts of ... [or] fails to get kinda misty at" would be
subject to up to two years imprisonment making license plates emblazoned with the motto "Land of the Free, Home of the Symbolically
Obedient." The column also proposed the establishment of a commission on "Symbolico-Devotional Malfeasance," to advise the government on "properly reverent behavior towards the Flag and Related Textile Entities."[29]

The Congressional Debate over How to Overturn the *Johnson* Ruling

Despite such arguments from defenders of the Court, in "realpolitik"
Washington, and even though the early intense and massive uproar
over the *Johnson* ruling died down considerably after about a month,
the only real debate quickly became centered upon whether or not it
would be possible to circumvent *Johnson* by a law, a position favored by
most Democrats, or whether a constitutional amendment would be required, a position taken by President Bush and most Republicans. The
Democratic Congressional leadership, most Congressional Democrats,
and a scattering of others, the most prominent of whom was the well-
known Harvard Constitutional Law Professor Laurence Tribe—all who
favored a law—noted that the *Johnson* decision struck down a Texas
statute that forbade flag desecration likely to cause "serious offense" to
observers, rather than, as the Court noted at one point, "protecting the
physical integrity of the flag in all circumstances," and further that the
Court had not never ruled on the latter type of law and might well uphold such a statute. This argument hung heavily on a weak, and ultimately constitutionally insufficient, rationale based on a passing reference in the *Johnson* ruling, ignoring what clearly seemed to be the real
focus of the Court's opinion: that Texas's professed interest in "preserving the flag as a symbol of nationhood and national unity" was "related
to expression" and emerges "only when a person's treatment of the flag
communicates some message;" that the government "may not prohibit
the expression of an idea because society finds the idea itself offensive
or disagreeable;" and that the government may not "foster its own view
of the flag by prohibiting expressive conduct relating to it" or by permitting "designated symbols to be used to communicate only a limited
set of messages," in particular by seeking to "criminally punish a person for burning a flag as a means of political protest."[30]

Despite the tenuous legal position advocates of a law to overturn
Johnson found themselves in, they nonetheless maintained that five

Supreme Court members might well uphold a so-called "content neutral" law that forbade flag desecration under all circumstances without reference to any "offensive" impact upon observers or the requirement that such action cast "contempt" upon the flag, as was the case with the 1968 federal law and many of the state flag desecration laws. Thus, according to the Senate Judiciary Committee report in support of such a law, it would focus "solely and exclusively on the conduct [as opposed to any intended message] of the actor" and protect the "physical integrity of flag in all circumstances," consistent with the alleged right of Congress to "protect symbols and landmarks," especially the "unique and unalloyed symbol of the nation," in recognition of the "diverse and powerfully held feelings of our citizens for the flag." Similarly, the House Judiciary Committee majority argued that the government could legitimately honor the "diverse and deeply held feelings of the vast majority of citizens for the flag" through the "protection of a venerated object in the same manner that protection is afforded to gravesites or historic buildings." The Senate Committee declared that, "When it comes to the American flag—that one symbol of the spirit of our democracy—we care more about protecting its physical integrity than about determining why its integrity has been threatened," and claimed—in what seemed to be an attempt to square the circle—that protecting the flag's physical integrity because "of what it expresses and represents" would pose no First Amendment problems because such protection was not designed to "censor or suppress the person who might attack it."[31]

Proponents of a statute added that it could be passed far more quickly than a constitutional amendment and would also avoid "tinkering" with the Constitution, thereby avoiding the possibility of opening up a "slippery slope" for subsequent infringement of the First Amendment. However, since proponents of a statute openly proclaimed that its advantage would be to more quickly bring about the same effect as a constitutional amendment, presumably the statutory approach would itself open up an even more "slippery" (because easier to accomplish) precedent for evading by legislative subterfuge Supreme Court decisions upholding unpopular constitutional rights. Many of the proponents of a statute also declared that they would back a constitutional amendment if the statutory approach failed in the Supreme Court, making clear that, for them at least, only tactics and not fundamental democratic principles were really at issue; their fundamental point was, as the Senate Judiciary Committee majority put it, that "the amendment process should be invoked as a last—not as a first—resort."[32]

From a political standpoint, the strategy of the statute proponents was clearly to hope that public and political pressure would cause at least one justice from the *Johnson* majority to uphold a supposedly "content neutral" law, especially since Justice Blackmun, who voted with the majority in *Johnson*, had suggested in the Goguen case fifteen years earlier that he would support the constitutionality of a law that provided general protection for the flag's physical integrity. Many backers of the statutory route also hoped that, by putting forth an alternative to a constitutional amendment, a "cooling off period" would take place, which would dampen Congressional fervor for an amendment since voting would be postponed until hearings could be held on the different proposals (as turned out to be the case, with hearings held during the summer and voting put off until September and October). The *Arkansas Gazette* no doubt expressed the private views of many statutory proponents when it declared on October 8, 1989, that a statute's only virtues were "negative ones—it's not as bad as [permanently disfiguring the Constitution with] an amendment, and it might lessen support for an amendment."[33]

In response to the backers of a statute, proponents of an amendment to override *Johnson* essentially argued (correctly, as it turned out) that no bill that sought to outlaw flag desecration could withstand Supreme Court scrutiny under the *Johnson* principles. The only result of passing an inevitably constitutionally defective statute, they argued, would be to generate litigation that, after a long delay, would result in returning to the alternative of a constitutional amendment. In the words of former judge and unsuccessful Supreme Court nominee Robert Bork, "After several years we would be right where we are now." Proponents of the constitutional amendment approach added that since the flag was "unique," there could be no "slippery slope," and that attempting to circumvent a Supreme Court decision by legislation would create its own "slippery slope" of bad precedent.[34]

Amendment backers also attacked proponents of the statute as hypocrites, because, as Republican Senators Orrin Hatch of Utah and Charles Grassley of Iowa noted in their dissent to the majority report of the Senate Judiciary Committee, the claim that the statute was intended to "neutrally" protect the flag against all physical threats to it appeared highly strained. "No one claims that we are interested in protecting the material, the thread and the dye in the flag. We protect the flag as a symbol, including against those who would desecrate the flag as part of political expression." They pointedly asked, in response to statute proponents who opposed an amendment as a threat to the First Amendment, "How is a statute which prohibits flag desecration in all or some instances not a threat to First Amendment principles, while a

constitutional amendment achieving the same thing is such a threat?"
Eight Republicans who dissented from the House Judiciary Committee
majority report urging support for a statute and opposition to an
amendment no doubt reflected much of the emotional fervor propelling
many proponents of the amendment approach when they asked:

> Why are we so reluctant to amend the Constitution to demand that flag
> desecration be prohibited? Is it too much to ask that those who call them-
> selves Americans be required to have respect for the flag? In this day and
> age, when it seems that perversion is accepted and morality a taboo reli-
> gion, perhaps this small mandate for freedom is not asking too much![35]

Amid the virtually hysterical reaction in the immediate aftermath of
the *Johnson* decision, it was widely predicted that a constitutional
amendment to outlaw flag desecration would quickly pass both houses
of Congress and be ratified by the states in record time. Thus, *New Republic* columnist Hendrik Hertzberg decried President Bush's proposed
amendment as "just another tactic for narrow partisan gain" but lamented that "it's hard to see at this point who's going to stop him."
Duke University Law Professor Walter Dellinger predicted "any
amendment that comes out of the Congress will be ratified faster than
any amendment on record." But even though Congressmen, during the
aftermath of *Johnson*, reported the vast majority of their constituents
who contacted them favored a constitutional amendment, by late July
press reports suggested a considerable lessening of public interest in the
entire issue along with increasing public acceptance of the argument
that the Constitution should not be hastily "tinkered" with, especially
if other alternatives were available.

Thus, Kansas Senator Nancy Kassebaum reported that although she
had been deluged with petitions demanding an amendment in late
June, by late July 60 percent of her mail on the issue opposed such action; Representative Ben Jones reported a similar shift in feelings
among his Georgia constituents, as the "issue has cooled and people are
more thoughtful" and "becoming more reflective about whether they
want to alter the constitution in response to this kind of stupidity."[36]

Whether due to a perceived cooling of public sentiment, to increasing
signs of growing "elite" opposition to a constitutional amendment,
such as a public letter to that effect signed by over 500 law professors in
October, or to growing acceptance of the argument that trying a statute
first was preferable to constitutional "tinkering," by October the drive
for a constitutional amendment, which had seemed unstoppable in late
June, was clearly sputtering. On October 19, the constitutional amendment was killed, at least for 1989, when the Senate defeated it by a vote
of 51 for and 48 against, with two-thirds of those voting required for ap-

proval. However, although the vote temporarily killed the movement for a constitutional amendment to overturn *Johnson,* one major reason for the amendment's failure was precisely that in the meantime both houses of Congress had passed the Flag Protection Act (FPA) of 1989, which clearly aimed at the same result as the amendment. The FPA passed with a combined vote in both houses in favor of about 465 compared to a combined vote against of about 50, with half of the FPA opponents indicating their vote reflected their belief that only a constitutional amendment would obtain their goal of banning flag desecration, and the other half (less than 5 percent of all Congressmen) opposed to any attempt to overturn *Johnson* on grounds of First Amendment principle.[37]

The FPA provided penalties of up to one year in jail and a $1000 fine for anyone who "knowingly mutilates, physically defiles, burns, maintains on the floor or ground, or tramples upon any flag of the United States" with "flag" defined as "any flag of the United States, or any part thereof, made of any substance, of any size, in a form that is commonly displayed."(See Appendix, Document 3.) In response to Republican complaints that litigation over the FPA would be prolonged and end up forcing Congress to consider a constitutional amendment again in several years after it was struck down, the law also contained an extraordinary provision mandating expedited review by the Supreme Court following any ruling on the FPA by a federal district court, bypassing the ordinary intermediate appeals process and also denying the Supreme Court its ordinary power to decide what cases to hear and when to hear them.[38]

The FPA specifically exempted from its provisions "any conduct consisting of the disposal of a flag when it has become worn or soiled." While this provision was a response to complaints from veterans or others who burned worn flags to dispose of them (the disposal method actually recommended in a voluntary flag code passed by Congress in 1942) and thus feared imprisonment for such disposal, it also seriously undercut the claims of FPA backers that the law would impartially protect the flag from desecration, regardless of motive. Ten dissenting members of the House Judiciary Committee, writing in support of a constitutional amendment, attacked the flag disposal exemption as opening up a "dirty flag defense" for future flag desecrators, while Democratic Senator Howard Metzenbaum declared, in opposing either a law or amendment, that under the FPA prosecutions would likely turn "upon the amorphous concept of whether a flag was sufficiently tattered to have warranted disposal." In fact, the FPA failed to provide any definition of what constituted a "worn or soiled flag" and also failed to define its other key terms, such as "mutilate," "deface," and "physically defile"—opening up the possibility of prosecutions like those of the Vietnam War era for wearing a flag patch on one's pants, superimposing the peace sign or a picture of Mickey Mouse on the flag, or even pinning ceremonial military awards on a flag. The FPA also failed to define what "any part" of a flag meant (a white star on a blue shirt?) or what "commonly displayed" meant.[39]

Testing the Flag Protection Act in the Courts

Although the purpose of the FPA was supposedly to end flag burnings, its immediate impact was to spur perhaps the largest single wave of such incidents in American history, as flags were burned in about a dozen cities shortly after the law took effect in late October. The Bush administration chose two flag burning incidents to prosecute, to test the law, one in Seattle and the other on the Capitol steps in Washington, D.C.

In parallel decisions handed down in the two prosecutions in early 1990, federal district court judges in Seattle and Washington, D.C. struck down the new law as unconstitutional when applied to political protesters, based on the principles of *Johnson* coupled with a finding that the FPA in fact was not "content neutral," either in the governmental interests that motivated it or in its text. Both courts essentially accepted the defense position that the *Johnson* case was controlling, because the defendants were all engaged in expressive conduct requiring First Amendment scrutiny and because, as Judge Barbara Rothstein noted in the Seattle case, the underlying government interest was "in protecting the symbolic value of the flag" and could not "survive the exacting scrutiny which this court must apply" under the *Boos* doctrine.

Thus, both judges rejected the vigorous arguments of the House and Senate in court briefs that the FPA could be justified on nonspeech regulation grounds, thereby qualifying for the more lenient *O'Brien* test. For example, the Senate's argument that the new law was "content neutral" because it had the allegedly nonspeech-related interest of seeking to protect the "physical integrity of the flag" in all circumstances was rejected as still based on a desire to suppress expression, such as, as Judge June Green noted in the Washington, D.C. case, "those viewpoints which are expressed through the symbolic destruction of the flag." Furthermore, Judge Rothstein declared, the law simply was not content neutral because it singled out for prohibition only conduct "generally associated with disrespect for the flag," allowing conduct that threatened the flag's physical integrity but did not "communicate a negative or disrespectful message," such as "flying the flag in inclement weather or carrying it into battle."[40]

While rejecting the House and Senate claims that the FPA should be subject only to the *O'Brien* test as reflecting a governmental interest in regulating nonspeech activity, both judges noted that the Justice Department's brief conceded that the "exacting scrutiny" of the *Boos* test was applicable because the government's purpose admittedly was to suppress expression in order to protect the flag's symbolic value. However, the two judges rejected the Justice Department's contention that the government's interest was "sufficiently compelling" to survive such scrutiny, even though the Supreme Court had rejected this position in *Johnson*, because since that decision "both the Congress and the Executive have pronounced the protection of the flag as a necessary policy goal" and their actions demonstrated the "compelling nature of the government's interest." This position was summarily rejected by both courts, which noted that the *Johnson* Court had pointed out that the protection of minority political dissent was a "bedrock principle" that was "situated at the core of our First Amendment values." "However compelling the government may see its interests, they cannot justify restrictions on speech which shake the very cornerstone of the First Amendment," Judge Green wrote. Judge Rothstein penned an equally eloquent defense of the First Amendment, noting that "in order for the flag to endure as a symbol of freedom, we must protect with equal vigor the right to wave it and the right to destroy it," that freedom of speech "is the crucial foundation without which other democratic values cannot flourish," and that although flag burning, however "repellant to many Americans, does not jeopardize the freedoms which we hold dear," American liberties would be threatened by "allowing the government to encroach on our right to political protest."

On March 13, 1990, Solicitor General Kenneth Starr invoked the extraordinary provisions of the FPA that required mandatory and expedited Supreme Court review of any final federal district court decision without need for intervening appellate court consideration. The Supreme Court quickly accepted jurisdiction of the cases (which were consolidated and henceforth known as *U.S. v. Eichman*) and scheduled a special sitting for oral argument on May 14 (even though its last scheduled hearing of oral arguments for its 1989–90 term had been previously set for April 25).

In his brief, Starr essentially called for the court to overturn its *Johnson* decision, noting, with considerable understatement, that the arguments he was advancing were "in tension" with *Johnson*. Seemingly discarding entirely the Congressional "content neutral" argument by endorsing the district courts' conclusions that the law was "based on a view that the flag stands for something valuable, and should be safeguarded because of that value," Starr first argued that nonetheless the Supreme Court should "reconsider" its *Johnson* holding that flag burning was "expressive conduct meriting full First Amendment protection." Instead, he maintained, the Court should hold that "physical destruction" of an American flag, an action "uniquely … anathema to the Nation's values" and constituting a "physical, violent assault on the most deeply shared experiences of the American people," should be considered outside such protection—as the Court had held with regard to certain forms of expression such as obscenity, child pornography, defamation, incitement to violence, and "fighting words."

Second, Starr argued, echoing the government's position in the district courts, that the Court should reconsider its *Johnson* finding that the government's interests were not compelling enough to overcome Johnson's First Amendment rights and that the flag had no special constitutional protection; this was the case, he maintained, especially in light of the "representative consensus articulated by the Congress and the President in connection with the enactment of the FPA of 1989" that the "flag of the United States, as the unique symbol of the Nation, merits protection not accorded other national emblems" because physical mistreatment of the flag inflicted an "injury to the shared values that bind our national community."[41]

In oral argument before the Court on May 14, Starr changed the emphasis of his argument considerably. Whereas in his brief the "content neutral" argument had been seemingly dismissed in a footnote as entirely lacking in substance, in oral argument Starr maintained that in the FPA Congress had carefully followed the *Johnson* guidelines to create a content neutral law that protected the physical integrity of the flag without "singling out certain viewpoints for disfavored treatment," much as governments could protect "houses of worship" or "the bald eagle" against destruction, regardless of what motivated such action. Starr also introduced an entirely new position in oral argument, claiming that flag burning failed to meet the *Spence* test of "expression," which required the delivering of a "particularized message," instead leaving a "major message gap" and resembling an "overload loudspeaker" or even the "mindless nihilism" that the *Spence* Court suggested was undeserving of First Amendment protection.[42]

In response, lawyers David Cole and William Kunstler, who represented the accused flag burners, argued in their brief and in oral argument that the district courts had correctly held that the *Johnson* principles governed the new case, especially since the FPA was by no means content neutral and the enactment of a Congressional law could not infringe basic First Amendment rights. Thus, they argued that Congress passed the new law essentially to preserve the flag's symbolic value, but that *Johnson* had determined that the government "may not criminalize flag burning" for such a purpose.

Further, they maintained, the FPA was not "content neutral" nor directed only at protecting the flag's physical integrity. They argued, for example, that the statute allowed "patriotic" conduct that imperiled the flag—such as flying it in a storm or in battle—while protecting the flag only from "those who would hurt it or cast it in a bad light," even if such action would not physically damage it (such as maintaining a flag on the floor, even under a glass cover). The very act of singling out the flag for special protection made the law "content based" and thus subject to strict scrutiny, the defendants argued, as would be immediately apparent if the statute had forbidden desecrating the "emblem of the Democratic party" instead of the flag. The defendants added that the government's urging of Court deference to Congress in this case would "leave the Bill of Rights to the whims of legislators," and would place "the sanctity of its official symbols above the reality of human freedom."[43]

In response to Starr's oral argument that flag burning did not deliver a "particularized message," Kunstler told the Court, "That's true of all non-verbal communication. ... You can't relegate non-verbal expression to the scrap heap." Responding to Starr's analogizing of flag desecration with child pornography or defamation as not warranting full First Amendment protection, Kunstler declared, "In the area of political speech, the government cannot make judgments of what is overly offensive or unimportant." In effect, Kunstler concluded in his oral argument, the government was seeking to turn the flag into a "golden image" that must be worshipped, but "once people are compelled to respect a political symbol, then they are no longer free and their respect for the flag is quite meaningless. To criminalize flag burning is to deny what the First Amendment stands for."

The Supreme Court's 5–4 decision in *U.S. v. Eichman*, upholding the lower federal court rulings and thus striking down the FPA as applied to political protesters, was handed down with extraordinary speed on June 11, 1990, less than a month after oral argument. The *Eichman* decision, again written by Justice Brennan, essentially followed the outlines of the *Johnson* decision and the district court opinions. It found that the *Boos* test of "most exacting scrutiny" must apply because the government's interests of protecting the flag's "status as a symbol of our Nation and certain national ideals" was related "to the suppression of free expression" and that this interest could not justify "infringement on First Amendment rights."

In moving towards this conclusion, the court declined to "reconsider our rejection in *Johnson* of the claim that flag burning as a mode of expression, like obscenity or 'fighting words' does not enjoy the full protection of the First Amendment." While conceding that the new law, unlike the Texas statute at issue in *Johnson*, "contains no explicit content-based limitation on the scope of prohibited conduct," the Court held the law was not exempt from strict scrutiny because it still suffered from "the same fundamental flaw" as the Texas law, namely that it could not be "justified without reference to the content of the regulated speech." This was held to be clear not only from the government's asserted interest in protecting the flag's symbolic value but also from the "precise language" of the law, which outlawed conduct which "connotes disrespectful treatment of the flag" even while exempting similar conduct involving the disposing of worn flags that are "traditionally associated with patriotic respect for the flag" and allowing the flying of flags in storms and "other conduct that threatens the physical integrity of the flag, albeit in an indirect manner unlikely to communicate disrespect."[44]

In rejecting the government's "invitation" to reconsider the *Johnson* holding that the government's interest in upholding the symbolic value of the flag could not infringe First Amendment rights in view of "Congress' recent recognition of a purported 'national consensus' favoring a prohibition against flag burning," the Court bluntly declared that, "any suggestion that the Government's interest in suppressing speech becomes more weighty as popular opposition to that speech grows is foreign to the First Amendment. ...Punishing desecration of the flag dilutes the very freedom that makes this emblem so revered, and worth revering."

The four-member dissent, penned by Justice Stevens, was considerably more tempered than the *Johnson* dissents, but otherwise made the same claim that the unique importance of the flag, such as its role in symbolizing "the ideas of liberty, equality and tolerance," justified infringing upon political expression to protect its "symbolic value," especially when there was no "interference with the speaker's freedom to express his or her ideas by other means." Aside from dispensing with patriotic poetry, the far calmer tone of this dissent was particularly marked in other ways. For example, whereas in *Johnson* Justice Stevens had compared flag desecration to placing "graffiti on the Washington Monument" and Justice Rehnquist had lumped flag burning together with murder and embezzlement, in his *Eichman* dissent Justice Stevens clearly repudiated such analogies: burning a privately owned flag "is not, of course, equivalent to burning a public building" as it "causes no physical harm to other persons or to their property" and its impact is "purely symbolic." Further, the *Eichman* dissent delivered a sharp rebuke to "those leaders"—apparently referring especially to President Bush and other supporters of a constitutional amendment—who had "compromised" the "integrity" of the flag by seeming to "advocate compulsory worship of the flag even by individuals whom it offends" or seeming to "manipulate the symbol of national purpose into a pretext for partisan disputes about meaner ends."[45]

The Response to the
Eichman Ruling

The *Eichman* decision sparked an immediate renewal of calls by President Bush and others for a constitutional amendment to prohibit flag desecration. Thus, Bush declared, "The law books are full of restrictions on free speech. And we ought to have this be one of them." In the immediate aftermath of *Eichman,* many predicted that a constitutional amendment would pass handily and rapidly. Thus, Republican House Minority Leader Robert Michel, an amendment advocate, predicted swift Congressional passage, asking rhetorically, "Who wants to be against the flag, mother and apple pie?" Harvard Law Professor Christopher Edley, the issues director for the 1988 Dukakis campaign, declared, "Opposition to the amendment may be noble, but it may take a miracle to stop it." Although opinion polls indicated majorities of about 60 percent or more of the public favored passage of a constitutional amendment, the intensity of public interest appears to have been far weaker in mid-1990 than it had been a year earlier. This factor probably played a key role in the amendment's demise when it was soundly defeated in both the House and Senate within two weeks of the *Eichman* decision.[46]

For example, Democratic Representative Richard Durbin of Ohio, who listed himself as undecided as of June 18, told the *Washington Post,* "The phone isn't ringing, the mail isn't coming in. The intensity of this is much lower than a year ago." No doubt at least partly as a result of this perceived lack of intense public demand for a flag amendment, almost all of the originally undecided Congressmen swung against the amendment during the post-*Eichman* period. Thus, an Associated Press survey completed on June 18 indicated 255 Representatives and 58 Senators for or leaning towards the amendment, 114 apparent opponents in the House and 24 in the Senate, and 65 Representatives and 18 Senators undecided. However, in the June 21 vote in the House there were 177 negative votes and in the June 26 Senate vote there were 42 negative votes, indicating that virtually all wavering Congressmen ended up opposing the amendment.[47]

Although Republicans, who overwhelmingly voted for the amendment, promised to make the flag controversy a major issue in the 1990 election campaign, by September 1990 the whole subject had disappeared as a subject of news or discussion, perhaps largely due to competition for public and political attention from the looming threats of a Mideast war, a serious economic downturn, and massive budget deficits. In any event, the flag desecration controversy was barely mentioned during the elections and has since disappeared entirely from the national political scene (although in numerous incidents that attracted only local media and political attention, alleged flag desecrators continued to be harassed and, in some cases, even prosecuted on a variety of often trumped-up charges, during the 1990–1994 period). Even the Supreme Court dissenters had no interest in revisiting the issue: Despite the fact that all four justices in the minority in the *Johnson* and *Eichman* rulings remained on the Court in October 1992, when an opportunity arose to reopen the flag desecration issue, fewer than the minimum required four justices voted to even hear an appeal from a Texas appeals court decision, which, on the basis of the Supreme Court's recent precedents, had struck down a 1989 Texas flag desecration law that had been modeled on the 1989 federal law.[48]

A number of often interconnected reasons help to explain why an issue that one Washington reporter termed "hot as a magnesium flare" in the summer of 1989 had become "politically lukewarm" by the late spring and early summer of 1990. Although superficially the FPA's proponents had been defeated when the Supreme Court struck down the law in *Eichman*, the deeper strategy of at least some of the statute's less enthusiastic backers—which was to put off serious consideration of a constitutional amendment in the hopes that passions would cool—succeeded remarkably well. At least in terms of intensity of concern, the public as a whole simply lost interest by June 1990 in an issue that not only had dragged on for a year, but which also had in a sense become— in an age of political concern over 30-second negative TV ads—a summer "rerun," a TV formula notorious for producing boredom. This was especially the case given that most Americans never saw anyone burn a flag except on TV and had never been more than symbolically affected in their daily lives by flag burners. Thus, an anonymous House Democratic leadership aide pointed out, "Put this up against whether or not people think they have got enough money to send their kids to college, and this isn't going to be an issue."[49]

These factors were probably further strengthened by negative public and vociferously hostile press reaction to the numerous overt political references made by Republican backers of the amendment in 1990, which sharply contrasted with the paucity of overt political comments in the aftermath of *Johnson* (even if everyone knew that politics hung heavy in the air). Thus, on the day of the *Eichman* decision, Senate Minority Leader Robert Dole of Kansas declared that a vote against a constitutional amendment "would make a pretty good 30-second spot" during the 1990 elections, and Marc Nuttle, executive director of the National Republican Congressional Committee, termed the fight over the amendment a "real opportunity" that "allows us to make a true comparison between parties and candidates." Such statements aroused sharp criticism on both sides of the political aisle and may well have "turned off" members of the public already cynical about the motives of politicians.[50]

Another factor that may well have strongly influenced the outcome in 1990 was that the entire argument was "framed" for public and Congressional consumption far differently than it had been the previous year, in a manner that made the case for not doing anything to seek to override the Supreme Court far more intellectually and political appealing. In 1989, the issue had been effectively "framed," as Republican Senator Strom Thurmond told his Senate Judiciary Committee colleagues, as what would be "the most desirable and effective approach to" overturn the *Johnson* decision. With the issue "framed" this way, the concept that the *Johnson* ruling should not be overturned at all never effectively entered the political arena in 1989, with the only question being passage of an amendment versus passage of a law. However, following the *Eichman* decision, with the statutory option effectively eliminated, opponents of an amendment, including many who had shown no compunction about legislatively diminishing freedom of expression the year before, got "constitutional religion" and "reframed" the issue as a battle of competing icons: the symbolic representation of liberty (the flag) versus the substance of liberty (the First Amendment).

Thus, on the day that *Eichman* was handed down, Senate Democratic Majority Leader George Mitchell of Maine, a critic of the *Johnson* decision and a supporter of the FPA, declared that he opposed a constitutional amendment to attain the same purpose sought by the statute, because the issue is "not the flag [but] whether we are going to amend the Bill of Rights." Democratic Representative Barbara Boxer of California, who had also voted for the FPA in 1989, similarly opposed a constitutional amendment in 1990, declaring that "there is a difference between voting for a law to ban flag burning and voting to change the Constitution" to obtain the same goal, because the Bill of Rights was "sacred" and "the greatest document of freedom in the world."[51]

This reframing of the controversy in 1990 to focus on protecting the Constitution rather than, as in 1989, on protecting the flag, was likely enhanced in its appeal by intervening international developments, notably the growing reform movement led by Soviet President Mikhail Gorbachëv and by the eastern European democratic revolutions of late 1989, which had prominently featured widespread desecration of national flags to support demands for greater freedom. (Thus, a book about the Romanian revolution was entitled *The Hole in the Flag*, a reference to the widespread tearing out from the center of the Romanian flag of symbols of the Communist regime.) The facts that flag desecration had been widely used in eastern Europe to express clearly understandable political views that were enthusiastically applauded by the American public, that the Communist foe in the Soviet Union, which had been traditionally viewed as the greatest symbolic foe of the American flag, appeared to be in a state of both growing collapse and rapid liberalization, and, it could be argued, that banning flag desecration would diminish American freedoms just as freedom was being expanded in the former communist totalitarian states gave powerful ammunition to opponents of the amendment in 1990.

Thus, Republican Representative Constance Morella of Maryland argued that, "At a time when Americans are celebrating the rebirth of political freedom in Eastern Europe and supporting the efforts of the Soviet and Chinese people to be free of political repression, now is not the time to tamper with this vital [first] amendment." Democratic Senator Tom Harkin of Iowa noted that Americans had not denounced protesters in eastern Europe for "cutting the Soviet hammer and sickle out of the center of their flags," but instead had "praised them for their act of political defiance" and for their "powerful act of political speech"; and Republican Senator Gordon Humphrey of New Hampshire similarly termed it "preposterous" that the Bush administration wanted to outlaw "the very same thing that we exulted in when it took place in Eastern Europe."[52]

Some Closing Words

Superficially, the movement to outlaw flag desecration in the United States, from its beginnings during the late nineteenth century through the Vietnam War era and the massive 1989–90 controversy, reflected American pride and patriotism. But, examined more carefully, and particularly given the lack of evidence that flag desecration has ever caused any concrete harm of any kind, it is difficult to avoid the conclusion that, just beneath the surface, these periodic eruptions have in fact reflected insecurity and doubt rather than pride and confidence, especially given their historical association with such events as the attempt to ban the display of red flags and to force unwilling schoolchildren and citizens to salute or kiss the flag. Just as more widespread repressive excesses, such as the 1919–20 Red Scare, the "McCarthy" phenomenon, and the massive abuses of the American intelligence agencies during the post-1940 period in surveilling and often attempting to disrupt the peaceful and legal activities of millions of American citizens, have frequently revealed a governing elite and large segments of the broader public which feared political dissent far more than they loved political freedom, the recurrent attempts to jail people for verbally or physically abusing American flags have similarly demonstrated that, at a fundamental level, a large segment of the American political leadership and citizenry is simply unwilling to accept, much less welcome, the very sort of unpopular political expression that the Constitution and the entire system of American democracy is designed to protect in a way that is supposed to distinguish the United States among the nations of the world.

The use of advertising involving the flag during the pre-World War I period, and the smattering of supposed incidents involving dissident symbolic use of the flag during that era posed no threat of any kind to American democracy—no more than did the single flag burnings in New York City in 1967 and Dallas in 1984, which led directly to the Congressional passage of federal flag desecration laws in 1968 and 1989. (Indeed, at the time the Dallas incident occurred it evoked virtually no public attention or reaction.) The real significance of the flag controversies that peaked during the 1895–1920, 1965–1974, and 1989–90 periods was not that flag desecration during these eras actually posed any real threat to anything, but rather in the reactions they evoked, reflecting the fact that these three major flag desecration furors all erupted during periods of grave and widespread doubts about and divisions over the fundamental health of American politics and society. In short, in all three periods, flag desecration or the threat of it in effect symbolically poured salt on an already wounded society rather than independently causing any real harm.

During the 1895–1920 period, traditional American elites and newly emerging business and political elites felt especially threatened by the rise of "new" immigrants, trade unions, and political radicalism as reflected in groups such as the Socialist Party, the Industrial Workers of the World, and, after 1917, the Communist Party. The Vietnam War era, which involved not only an eventually highly divisive foreign conflict, but also a perceived general rise in social disintegration as reflected in such developments as rising crime rates and the emergence of the youth "counterculture" and of militant black organizations, similarly caused enormous anxiety and feelings of insecurity among many members of the American political elite and large segments of the general public (feelings that clearly helped to elect Richard Nixon in 1968 and, eventually, help bring Ronald Reagan to power in 1980).

Although the early period of the Reagan administration was associated with a general sense of a return of American self-esteem (helping to explain the general lack of reaction to the RCP-associated flag burnings of the 1979–1984 period, including the Dallas incident of 1984 that only became a cause célèbre five years later), by the late 1980s there was a deepening sense in American society that the United States had entered a period of profound economic and political decline, both domestically and in terms of its power abroad and in the world marketplace. That perception, which would subsequently increase dramatically, strongly contributed to the defeat of President George Bush in 1992, despite the American military victories in the Panama invasion of early 1990 and the Persian Gulf War of early 1991. For example, such perceptions helped to make bestsellers out of books like Paul Kennedy's 1987 *The Rise and Fall of the Great Powers*, whose theme was that America was on the brink of a major decline, and a 1992 book whose title, *America: What Went Wrong?* is self-explanatory.

Thus, in analyzing the 1989–90 flag controversy, Terrence McDonald, history professor at the University of Michigan, noted that although in the twentieth century "it's always been a good idea for a politician to wrap himself in the flag," the post-*Johnson* flag eruption was especially "linked to the perceived decline in American power in relation to the rest of the world" since "when reality gets too hard to handle, you can fall back on symbols of nationhood." Similarly, Richard Madsen, a sociologist at the University of California at San Diego, declared that the 1989 flag controversy reflected "great insecurity about our own values and unity. Many people have a sense of America in decline, a sense of intractable problems from drug abuse to the environment. Under these conditions, people get doubly upset when the flag is desecrated."

No doubt another element that metaphorically added fuel to the massive 1989–90 flag desecration fire was the very fact that flag burning reminded many people of everything that they had disliked about the 1960s, providing conservative politicians in particular with both an attractive issue and a receptive audience. Thus, commentator Ronald Brownstein wrote in 1990 about the flag controversy that, "President Bush and the cultural conservatives in Congress are behaving like graying devotees of classic-rock radio stations: After all these years, they still can't let go of the 1960s." Similarly, historian Alan Brinkley noted in 1990 that the flag desecration uproar reflected the fact that although the "New Left may be all but dead ... the attempt to discredit it lives on" because "the continuing resentment of the radicalism" of the

Vietnam era "has been a staple of American conservative politics for more than 20 years." Also supporting the general "insecurity" theory as an explanation of the repeated episodes of anxiety over flag desecration, Brinkley added that democracies that are "secure in their identities and confident of their principles" rarely feel the "need to define patriotism by law" but that "given the conspicuous absence of either security or confidence in contemporary American culture, no one should assume that the flag issue has been put to rest for good."[53]

In assessing the 1989–90 flag burning furor, Democratic Representative Don Edwards lamented, "To think that a nincompoop in Dallas, Texas could do something that could trigger this reaction is rather distressing." Whether or not Gregory Lee Johnson was a "nincompoop," the "reaction" displayed both by the American public and, especially, the American political elite, to this incident and to earlier controversies involving flag desecration, certainly says some "distressing" things about the health of the American body politic in general and also about the lack of either basic political courage or basic understanding of fundamental democratic principles among the political elite in particular.[54]

Whatever one's view of the wisdom of burning flags, it can hardly be doubted that such behavior is a form of political expression that has no real adverse consequences. Every bit of evidence from all three major eruptions of controversy over flag desecration in American history suggests that, rather than diminishing the symbolic value of the flag in the eyes of the vast majority of the population, flag desecration has exactly the opposite effect; surely no one American has done as much for patriotism in recent times as has Gregory Lee Johnson. Even if mass flag burnings were to become everyday occurrences, by itself such actions could do no real harm, and indeed would probably provide a service to the political leadership by informing them that political grievances were spreading among the population and needed attention. In any case, sending flag abusers to jail is hardly going to turn them into patriots convinced of the wonders of American liberties or to produce any other positive effects.

Since burning the flag is a form of harmless political expression that is clearly protected by the fundamental charters of American democracy, the Constitution, and especially the Bill of Rights, aside from reflecting a collective public insecurity about the state of the country, the recurrent episodes of virtual hysteria over flag desecration also suggests one of the major reasons for that insecurity: namely, that the American political leadership, especially during the television era, is far too often consumed with symbols rather than substance and, either out of inability or unwillingness, has far too frequently preferred to engage in ultimately nonproductive and often divisive public relations extravaganzas about nonissues rather than to tackle real problems. As Senator Bob Kerrey of Nebraska pointed out about the flag desecration rumpus in 1989:

> Where does it lead? When you're all done arguing, what have you got? Have you built a house? Have you helped somebody? Have you created a better world? Have you fought a battle worth fighting? Or are you banging into the shadows on the wall of a cave? It seems to me there's nothing produced from it and you've divided the nation.

The *Seattle Times* similarly pointed out that, above all, the 1989 furor amounted to a distraction of attention away from real issues that reflected poorly about the quality of the nation's leaders:

> Into a nation plagued by inadequate housing, rampant drug abuse, a mammoth federal budget deficit and the growing specter of AIDS, those wonderful folks in Washington, D.C. have introduced a flag law. ... The real desecration of democracy occurs when people don't have places to live or work or adequate health insurance. ... Those kind of issues don't seem to play well in the nation's capital. Maybe it's because they require real statecraft and that's in a lot shorter supply than the hype and rhetoric that's been conjured up around a non-issue like flag burning.[55]

Although certainly the American people as a whole cannot escape some responsibility for the massive amounts of time and energy that has been devoted to fighting the "threat" posed by flag desecration, ultimately the American political leadership sets the tone and must bear the bulk of the blame. And if diverting public and political attention away from real issues and pandering to the public's worst instincts is in general a far-too-often instinctive reaction of American political leaders in the late twentieth century, a far more serious charge that can be brought against them—one with even greater potentially disastrous consequences for the nation—is that they apparently have little or no faith in or understanding of the most basic democratic principles, of a "free marketplace" of ideas, and of tolerance of even the most unpopular and offensive political dissent. This fundamental democratic lesson was elaborated with unequaled eloquence by Justice Jackson in the *Barnette* case: "If there is any fixed star in our constitutional constellation, it is that no official, high or petty, can prescribe what shall be orthodox in politics, nationalism, religion or other matters of opinion or force citizens to confess by word or act their faith therein." Applying this general principle to the specific issue of flag desecration, Judge Cannella, in his 1974 ruling that freed Stephen Radich in the case of the 1966 phallic flag art exhibit after eight years of litigation, declared:

"The flag and that which it symbolizes is dear to us, but not so cherished as those high moral, legal and ethical precepts which our Constitution teaches. When our interests in preserving the integrity of the flag conflict with the higher interest of preserving, protecting and defending the Constitution, the latter must prevail." It is a sad commentary that in the last decade of the twentieth century, during the bicentennial celebration of the Bill of Rights, that the American political leadership still needs to learn this lesson, and even more importantly, to reflect it in their daily actions and words.[56]

Notes

Abbreviations Used in Footnotes

A: *Atlantic Reporter*

AA: *Art in America*

AFA: American Flag Association, *Circular of Information* (date is given in each citation)

ALI: American Law Institute, *Model Penal Code and Commentaries* (Philadelphia: American Law Institute, 1980)

AM: *American Monthly Magazine* (magazine of the Daughters of the American Revolution)

BG: *Boston Globe*

BW: Bernard Weisberger, "The Flap Over the Flag," *American Heritage* (November 1990), pp. 24–25

CDN: *Chicago Daily News*

CKM 1898a: Charles Kingsbury Miller, *An Appeal to Every American in Whose Heart There Is One Spark of the Ennobling Fire of Patriotism* (Chicago, 1898)

CKM 1898b: Idem, *Why Do Our Legislators in Washington Not Give Us a Flag Law?* (Chicago, 1898)

CKM 1898c: Idem, *Desecration of the American Flag and Prohibitive Legislation* (Chicago, 1898)

CKM 1899a: Idem, "A Nation's Disgrace: Insults to the American Flag to be Stopped," *The Spirit of '76* (April, 1899), unpaginated

CKM 1899b: Idem, *Desecration of the American Flag: Our Nation's Disgrace* (Chicago, 1899)

CKM 1900: Idem, *The Crime of a Century: Desecration of the American Flag* (Chicago, 1900)

CKM 1901a: Idem, *The American Flag Dishonored at Home Loses the Respect of the Nations of the World* (Chicago, 1901)

CKM 1901b: Idem, *The American Flag Dishonored and Disgraced in America, Cuba and the Philippine Islands* (Chicago, 1901)

CKM 1902: *Desecration of the American Flag* (Chicago, 1902)

CR: *Congressional Record*

CR1: *Congressional Record, 1967*

CR2: *Congressional Record, 1989*

CR3: *Congressional Record, 1990*

CS: Charles Spain, "The Flags and Seals of Texas," *South Texas Law Review*, 33 (February 1992), pp. 215–59

CSM: *Christian Science Monitor*

CST: *Chicago Sun-Times*

CT: *Chicago Tribune*

CW: C. Waage, "Patriotism and School Education," *Overland Monthly*, 17 (April 1891), pp. 377–84

DAP: Document(s) in author's possession

DAR: Proceedings of the DAR Continental Congress (year is given in each citation)

DAR-M: Daughters of the American Revolution, Milwaukee Chapter, Recording Secretary's Book No. 3, June 4, 1902–May l, 1906 (in the archives of the Milwaukee County Historical Society)

DAR-R: Report of the Daughters of the American Revolution

DMN: *Dallas Morning News*

DN: *Detroit News*

DP: David Prosser, "Desecration of the American Flag," *Indiana Legal Forum*, 3 (1962), pp. 159–237

DTH: *Dallas Times Herald*

F.: *Federal Reporter*

FB: *Flag Bulletin*

F. Supp.: *Federal Supplement*

GAR: *Journal of the National Encampment of the Grand Army of the Republic* (year is given in each citation)

GLJ: Trial Transcript, *Texas v. Johnson*, No. MA8446013-H/J, County Criminal Court, Dallas County, Texas, November Term, 1984

HJC 1913: House Judiciary Committee, *Protection of the American Flag*, 62nd Cong., 3rd Sess., February 11, 1913

HJC 1915: Idem, *Desecration of the Flag*, 63rd Cong., 3rd Sess., February 10, 1915

HJC 1918: Idem, *To Preserve the Purity of the Flag*, 65th Cong., 2nd Sess., January 23, 1918

HJC 1927: Idem, *To Prevent Desecration of the Flag*, 69th Cong., 2nd Sess., January 31, 1927

HJC 1928: Idem, *To Adopt an Official Flag Code of the United States*, 70th Cong., 1st Sess., January 25, 1928

HJC 1967: Idem, Hearings on H.R. *271 and Similar Proposals to Prohibit Desecration of the Flag*, 90th Cong., 1st Sess., Serial No. 4, 1967

HJC 1967a: House Report No. 350, *Penalties for Desecration of the Flag*, 90th Cong., 1st Sess., June 9, 1967.

HJC 1989a: House Judiciary Committee, *Hearings on Statutory and Constitutional Responses to the Supreme Court Decision in* Texas v. Johnson, 101st Cong., 1st Sess., Serial No. 24, 1989.

HJC 1989b: House Report No. 231, 101st Cong., 1st Sess., 1989.

JH: James Hall and Walter Albano, *Selected Decisions on Flag Use, Flag Desecration and Flag Misuse* (Washington: Congressional Research Service Report No. 81–126A, May 18, 1981)

LAT: *Los Angeles Times*

LS: Leonard Stevens, *Salute! The Case of the Bible vs. The Flag* (New York: Coward, McCann & Geoghegan, 1973).

MD: Mary Dearing, *Veterans in Politics: The Story of the GAR* (Baton Rouge: L.S.U. Press, 1952)

N.E.: Northeastern Reporter

NAR: National Archives, Record Group 233

NUC: National Union Catalog

NYDN: New York Daily News

NYN: Newsday (New York)

NYP: New York Post

N.Y.S: New York Supplement

NYT: New York Times

P: Pacific Reporter

PH: Peleg Harrison, *The Stars and Stripes and Other American Flags* (Boston: Little, Brown, 1906)

RJG: Robert J. Goldstein, *Political Repression in Modern America: From 1870 to the Present* (Boston: G. K. Hall, 1978)

RP: Robert Phillips, *The American Flag: Its Uses and Abuses* (Boston: Stratford, c. 1930)

S.E.: Southeastern Reporter

S.W.: Southwestern Reporter

SAR: Sons of the American Revolution, *National Yearbook* (year is given in each citation)

SAR-C: Connecticut SAR, *Report on Desecration of the American Flag* (1896)

SAR-M: Sons of the American Revolution Magazine

SCW: National Flag Committee of the Society of Colonial Wars in the State of Illinois, *Misuse of the National Flag of the United States of America* (Chicago, 1895)

Senate Brief 1990: Brief for the United States Senate as Amicus Curiae in Support of Appellant, in the Supreme Court of the United States, October Term, 1989, *U.S. v. Eichman*, Nos. 89–1433 and 89–1434, April 1990.

SG: Scot Guenter, *The American Flag, 1777–1924: Cultural Shifts from Creation to Codification* (Rutherford, N.J.: Fairleigh Dickinson Univ. Press, 1990)

SJC 1989a: Senate Judiciary Committee, *Hearings on Measures to Protect the Physical Integrity of the American Flag,* Serial No. J-101–33, 101st Cong., lst. Sess., 1989

SJC 1989b: Senate Report 101–152, *The Flag Protection Act of 1989,* 101st Cong., 1st Sess., September 29, 1989

SLPD: Saint-Louis Post Dispatch

SM: Stuart McConnell, *Glorious Contentment: The Grand Army of the Republic, 1865–1900* (Chapel Hill: Univ. of N. Carolina Press, 1992)

SMAC 1902: Senate Committee on Military Affairs, *The American Flag,* 57th Cong. 2d Sess., Document No. 229, 1902

SMAC 1904: Idem, *Desecration of the American Flag,* 58th Congress, 2d Session, Report No. 506, January 29, 1904

ST: Seattle Times

U.S.: United States Reports

U.S.C.: United States Code

USN: *U. S. News & World Report*
VV: *Village Voice*
WD: Wallace Davies, *Patriotism on Parade: The Story of Veterans' and Hereditary Organizations in America, 1783–1900* (Cambridge: Harvard Univ. Press, 1955).
WP: *Washington Post*
WSJ: *Wall Street Journal*
WT: *Washington Times*
WWW: *Who Was Who in America, 1897–1942* (Chicago, 1966)
WZ: Wilbur Zelinsky, *Nation into State: The Shifting Symbolic Foundations of American Nationalism* (Chapel Hill: Univ. of N. Carolina Press, 1988)

NOTE: Citations to legal sources follow the standard form for legal citations. Thus, a citation to 189 *P.*2d 341 (1989) would indicate a reference to the case beginning on page 341 of volume 189 of the *Pacific Reporter,* second series, that was reported in 1989. A citation to 189 *P.*2d 341, 343 (1989) would indicate a reference to the same case and especially to information contained or quoted on page 343 therein.

Preface

1. *NYT,* October 21, 1993.
2. *W. Va. Bd. of Education v. Barnette,* 319 *U.S.* 624, 641 (1943).
3. Alexander Meiklejohn, *Freedom of Speech and Its Relation to Self-Government* (New York: Harper, 1948), p. 27.
4. Senate Judiciary Committee Hearings, *Measures to Protect the American Flag,* 101st Cong., 2d Sess., Serial No. j-101–77, 1990, p. 108.
5. *WP,* June 30, 1989.

Chapter 1

1. *Texas v. Johnson,* 491 *U.S.* 397, 417 (1989).
2. The *Johnson* ruling was subsequently reaffirmed and strengthened in the 1990 Supreme Court ruling in *U.S. v. Eichman,* 496 *U.S.* 310.
3. In the thousands of pages of Congressional hearings and debates and legal briefs written in connection with the 1989–90 controversy, the only extensive treatment of the turn-of-the-century controversy was contained in the amicus brief submitted to the Supreme Court in the 1990 case of *U.S. v. Eichman* by the United States Senate (Senate Brief 1990).
4. SG, p. 32; WZ, p. 202; Milo Quaife, *The Flag of the United States* (New York: Grosset & Dunlap, 1942), p. 100; Merle Curti, *The Roots of American Loyalty* (New York: Columbia Univ. Press, 1968), p. 132; BW, p. 24.
5. *WT,* July 4, 1989; Willis Johnson, *The National Flag: A History* (Boston: Houghton Mifflin, 1930), p. 95; SG, pp. 35–39, 50, 219; WZ, pp. 160, 200–202.

6. Geo. Henry Preble, *Origin and History of the American Flag* (Philadelphia: Nicholas L. Brown, 1917), pp. 468–69; SG, pp. 33, 36–37; Curti, p. 132; William Griffis, "The Flag of the United States," *The Independent* (July 4, 1912), p. 34; Quaife, p. 120.

7. James McPherson, *Battle Cry of Freedom: The Civil War Era* (New York: Ballantine, 1989), pp. 119–10; Michael Curtis, "Introduction," in Michael Curtis, ed., *The Constitution and the Flag*, Vol. 1 (New York: Garland, 1993), p. xx.

8. RP, p. 58; SAR-C, p. 4.

9. Preble, pp. 453, 456, 459–60; SG, pp. 68, 83; BW, p. 24–25.

10. SG, p. 64; Preble, pp. 474–76.

11. Preble, pp. 464, 471–474, 480–81; James Parton, *General Butler in New Orleans* (New York: Mason Brothers, 1864), pp. 352–53, 607–09).

12. Curti, pp. 191–92.

13. SG, pp. 50–53; Boleslaw and Marie-Louise D'Otrange Mastai, *The Stars and the Stripes: The American Flag as Art and as History from the Birth of the Republic to the Present* (New York, 1973), p. 208.

14. Browne, quoted in SG, p. 139; SCW, p. 6; SMAC 1904, pp. 3–4; Mastai, pp. 183, 202.

15. SCW, pp. 16, 21, 26.

16. CKM 1898c, pp. 21, 10–11; CKM 1899b, p. 3; CKM 1900, p. 3; CKM 1902, pp. 1–2.

17. CKM 1898c, p. 3; CKM 1899b, p. 14; AFA 1905–06, p. 16; SAR 1902, p. 172; *AM*, 1907, p. 455.

18. SMAC 1908, p. 10; SCW, pp. 9, 27.

19. NAR, HR 56A-F 19.2, HR 55A-H 12.6; CKM 1899b, p. 2; CKM 1901b, p. 3; SMAC 1902, pp. 5, 7.

20. *CR* (1890), p. 10697; HJC, "To Prevent Desecration of the American Flag," Report No. 2128, 51st. Cong., lst Sess. (1890); SCW, p. 15; CKM 1898c, pp. 4, 11; CKM, 1900, p. 5; CKM 1901a, p. 3.

21. SAR 1900, p. 94; AFA 1901–02, p. 16; CKM 1900, p. 7; *AM* 1899, pp. 903–04, 906; *AM* 1907, p. 457; DAR 1918, p. 80; HJC 1928, p. 27.

22. WZ, pp. 196, 243.

23. MD, p. 406; CKM 1901b, p. 3; CKM 1898c, p. 13; AFA 1900 No. 3; SCW, p. 26; *AM* 1903, p. 1297; HJC 1913, p. 5.

24. SCW, p. 28; AFA 1905–06, p. 10; *DAR-R*, Senate Report No. 371, 62nd Cong., 2d Session, p. 36.

25. DAR 1915, p. 1123; SCW, p. 25; SM, pp. 233, 236.

26. SG, p. 112; WD, p. 219; *NYT*, June 15, 1923; *CW*, p. 379.

27. CKM 1899b, pp. 3, 7, 13; DAR 1914, p. 1171; *CR* (1927), p. 5933; LS, p. 77.

28. CKM 1898c, pp. 11–12; CKM 1900, pp. 5, 7, 13; Roger Wood, "Abusing 'Freedom of Speech,'" *Forum*, 56 (July, 1916), p. 6.

29. HJC 1918, pp. 9–10.

30. See SG, pp. 133–35.

31. SG, pp. 134–35; Stanley Jones, *The Presidential Election of 1896* (Madison: Univ. of Wisconsin Press, 1984), pp. 291–93; MD, pp. 460–62; Lawrence

Goodwyn, *The Populist Moment* (New York: Oxford Univ. Press, 1978), pp. 280–82.

32. MD, p. 461; *The Critic*, October 23, 1897, p. 235.

33. Jones, p. 292; Goodwyn, p. 280.

34. Cited in Senate Brief 1990, p. 10.

35. Petition from Milwaukee DAR Chapter, 1897, NAR, HR 56A-F19.2 (much of this information is also included in an 1899(?) DAR pamphlet, "A Plea from the Daughters of the American Revolution"); CKM 1899b, pp. 1–2; CKM 1900, p. 9; CKM 1898c, p. 3; CKM 1902, p. 2.

36. AFA 1903–04, p. 27; AFA 1907–08, pp. 20–21; *Proceedings of the 23rd Annual Conference of Commissioners on Uniform State Laws, 1913–1914*, pp. 157–58.

37. NAR, HR 56A-F19.2; HR 55A-H12.6; CKM 1900, pp. 11–12.

38. SAR 1898, pp. 82–83; CKM 1898c, p. 4; CKM, 1902, p. 5; CKM 1899b, p. 2.

39. See generally RJG, pp. 1–60; John Higham, *Strangers in the Land: Patterns of American Nativism, 1860–1925* (New York: Atheneum, 1970).

40. Arthur Schlesinger, *The Rise of the City, 1878–1898* (Chicago: Quadrangle, 1961), p. 410; WD, pp. 354–55.

41. Higham, p. 58; *CW*, p. 378; SG, p. 105; David Bennett, *The Party of Fear* (New York: Vintage, 1990), pp. 110–16; Higham, pp. 147–48; BW, p. 26; Morris Sica, "The School Flag Movement: Origin and Influence," *Social Education*, 54 (October 1990), pp. 380–84.

42. CKM 1898c, pp. 7–8, 11–12.

43. CKM 1899a (unpaginated); CKM 1900, pp. 1, 4–5; CKM 1901b, pp. 1, 4.

44. *AM* 1898, p. 208; *AM* 1899, p. 906; *AM* 1904, p. 636; *AM* 1907, p. 460.

45. AFA 1909–13, pp. 47–48; AFA 1904–05, pp. 19–20, 25.

46. WD, pp. 293–94; SM, pp. 210–11.

47. SMAC 1902, p. 4; CKM 1899b, pp. 1–2; *AM* 1907, p. 458; *GAR* 1912, p. 159.

48. *CR* (1890), pp. 6736, 6944, 7016, 10697; WD, p. 220.

49. For biographical information on Reade, see *WWW*, p. 1014; NUC, vol. 483, p. 367.

50. For example, see *CT*, February 24, 1895; SCW, pp. 2, 5; *AM* 1897, p. 871; SAR 1895, p. 4; SAR 1897, p. 249; SAR 1914, p. 132; SAR 1918, p. 156; *GAR* 1899, p. 330; WD, p. 221.

51. For biographical information on Miller, see Louis Cornish, *A National Register of the Society of the Sons of the American Revolution* (Washington, 1902), vol. one, p. 1026, vol. two, pp. 351–52; NUC, vol. 384, p. 157. For endorsements of flag desecration legislation, see CKM 1899b, pp. 8–15; CKM 1900, pp. 9–16.

52. SAR 1904, p. 177; AFA 1907–08, pp. 36, 40.

53. Biographical information on Frances Kempster was supplied by a variety of sources, the most important being the DAR, where she is registered as member no. 5654, and the Milwaukee County Historical Society (DAP); information on her husband Walter Kempster can be found in a variety of standard biograph-

ical sources such as the *National Encyclopedia of American Biography,* vol. V, p. 21.

54. *AM* 1898, pp. 854–55. A summary of the DAR's involvement in the flag desecration issue can be found in DAR 1932, p. 202. The DAR's 1899 petition to Congress was published under the title *To All Who Love the Flag* (Milwaukee, 1899). Other evidence of DAR activity is located in NAR, HR 55A-H12.6, HR 56A-F19.2., in Kempster's reports to the Milwaukee DAR (DAR-M), in yearly DAR reports *(DAR-R)* published by the U.S. Senate and in the DAR's own published reports (DAR) of its annual DAR conventions.

55. SCW, p. 2; AFA 1900 (unpaginated); SAR 1897, p. 249.

56. SAR 1899, p. 97; AFA 1903–04, p. 2.

57. SAR 1899, p. 88; AFA 1909–13, pp. 52, 57–58.

58. Biographical information on Prime can be found in *WWW,* p. 996; Cornish, vol. two, pp. 387–88; NUC, vol. 471, p. 360; *GAR* 1904, p. 308.

59. AFA 1901–02, pp. 1, 24–25; AFA 1905–06, pp. 29–48; AFA 1907–08, p. 11; AFA 1909–13, p. 51.

60. SAR 1900, pp. 107–09.

61. SAR 1903, p. 124.

62. *WWW,* p. 996; Cornish, vol. two, pp. 387–88; *NYT,* June 15, 1923.

63. *Chicago Evening Post,* November 30, 1898, December 6, 1899; *Spirit of '76,* May 1898, p. 72; CKM 1898b, p. 3; SCW, p. 31; *San Francisco Evening Post,* November 30, 1898.

64. For example, see SAR 1898, p. 84; SAR 1899, p. 89; SAR 1904, p. 150; AFA 1905–06, p. 15; DAR 1910, p. 145; DAR 1913, p. 710; DAR-M, p. 108; NAR, HR 55A-H12.6.

65. AFA 1901–02, p. 15; SAR 1903, p. 115; SAR 1909, p. 114; Congressional laws of February 20, 1907 (33 Statutes 725), February 8, 1917 (39 Statutes 900), and May 16, 1918 (40 Statutes 553–54).

66. *DAR-R,* Senate Report No. 219, 56th Cong., 2nd Sess., p. 270; DAR-M, p. 253; AFA 1905–06, p. 28; AFA 1907–08, p. 13; AFA 1909–13, p. 55.

67. For a listing of states with the dates (often including month and day as well as year) of passage of flag desecration laws up to 1905, see PH, p. 383; a complete list of the year of original passage of all state flag desecration laws is included in "Flag Burning, Flag Waving and the Law," *Valparaiso University Law Review,* 4 (1970), pp. 362–67. For collections of the texts of early state flag desecration laws, see SMAC 1904, pp. 4–12; AFA 1903–04, pp. 10–24; AFA 1905–06, pp. 29–76; SAR 1912, pp. 112–17; AFA 1909–13, pp. 69–91; HJC 1915, pp. 10–15; SAR 1915, pp. 126–31; Bernard Kosicki, *Commercial Use of National Flags and Public Insignia* (Washington: U.S. Department of Commerce, Trade Information Bulletin No. 438, 1926).

68. This paragraph is based on a survey of published annual state legislative journals. For example, the material for Minnesota is based on the 1899 *Journal of the Senate* and the 1899 *Journal of the House* for the 31st session of the Minnesota Legislature.

69. AFA 1903–04, pp. 28, 41; SAR 1904, p. 150.

70. AFA 1905–06, p. 13; SAR 1901, p. 140; AFA 1907–08, p. 22; AFA 1909–13, pp. 1–4.

71. SAR-C, pp. 5, 14; MD, p. 475; *GAR* 1907, pp. 178, 180.

72 SG, p. 88.

73. AFA 1905–06, pp. 29–48. For biographical information on some AFA Executive Committee members, see AFA 1909–13, pp. 41–45.

74. WD, pp. 88, 265; MD, pp. 344, 410.

75. For the AFA model bill, see AFA 1900 (unpaginated). For the UFL, its background, and its adoption by various states, see *Uniform Laws Annotated,* vol. 9A (Brooklyn: Edward Thompson, 1951), pp. 32–38. For the 1918 ABA endorsement of the UFL, see *ABA Journal,* 4 (1918) pp. 528–30; *Report of the 41st Annual Meeting of the ABA* (1918), p. 82.

76. See the sources listed in footnote 67.

77. For the history of Texas flag desecration laws, see CS.

Chapter 2

1. *NYT, WP* (both November 5, 1899).

2. *NYT,* April 18, 1900; 57 *N.E.* 41 (1900).

3. *NYT,* July 31, 1904; Peter Carlson, *Roughneck: The Life and Times of Big Bill Haywood* (New York: Norton, 1983), pp. 70–75.

4. *People ex rel. McPike v. Van de Carr* (N.Y. Supreme Court, Appellate Division, 1904), 86 *N.Y.S.* 644; *People ex rel. McPike v. Van De Carr* (N.Y. Court of Appeals, 1904), 70 *N.E.* 965.

5. *Lincoln (Nebraska) Journal,* July 9, 1989; *Halter v. State,* 105 *N.W.* 298, (1905); Transcript of Record, *Halter v. Nebraska,* in the Supreme Court of the United States, No. 174, October Term, 1906, p. 3.

6. All material in these and the next few paragraphs is taken from Brief for Plaintiffs, *Halter v. Nebraska,* in the Supreme Court of the United States, No. 174, October Term, 1906.

7. All material in these and the next few paragrpaphs is taken from Brief of the State, *Halter v. Nebraska,* in the Supreme Court of the United States., No. 174, October Term, 1906.

8. *Halter v. State,* 105 *N.W.* 298 (1905).

9. *Halter v. Nebraska,* 205 *U.S.* 34, 35–37, 41–43, 45 (1907) .

10. DAR-M, p. 109; SAR 1902, p. 170; SAR 1904, p. 177; DAR 1912, p. 726; DAR 1913, p. 710.

11. AFA, 1907–08, p. 22; PH, p. 280; CKM 1900, p. 5.

12. SCW, p. 19; SAR 1902, pp. 171–72.

13. *CR* (1930), p. 3106; NAR, 77A-D20.

14. SAR-C, p. 4; *The Critic,* October 23, 1897, p. 235.

15. SAR 1899, p. 89; DAR-M, p. 252; CKM 1898c, p. 6; CKM 1898b, p. 4; CKM 1899b, p. 5; CKM 1902, p. 6.

16. CKM 1899a (unpaginated); Miller to Rep. George Ray, April 17, 1899, NAR, HR55A-H12.6; CKM 1899b, p. 4.

17. AFA 1901–02, pp. 29–30; AFA 1903–04, pp. 43–44.

18. Miller to Henderson, May 26, 1898, NAR, HR55A-H12.6.

19. AFA 1900 (unpaginated); AFA 1901–02, p. 9; SAR 1913, p. 101; SAR 1915, pp. 123, 125, 131.

20. AFA 1900 (unpaginated); SAR 1903, p. 114–16; CKM 1902, p. 5; *AM* 1903, p. 1295; AFA 1903–04, pp. 22–23.

21. Miller to Henderson, February 18, 1898, Kempster to Henderson, February 22, 1898, NAR, 56A-F19.2; SMAC 1902, pp. 6–7; *AM* 1900, pp. 963–64; *AM* 1902, p. 1229; *AM* 1903, p. 1295.

22. SCW, p. 17; Petition of San Francisco Chamber of Commerce, January 10, 1899, NAR, HR 55A-H12.6; CKM 1898a, p. 5; CKM 1899b, pp. 13–14.

23. CKM 1898a, p. 3; SAR 1899, p. 89.

24. SAR 1898, p. 84; *Journal of the Proceedings of the 14th Annual Meeting of the Military Order of the Loyal Legion of the United States*, 1898, p. 93.

25. SAR 1903, p. 114; *AM* 1907, p. 456; SAR 1909, p. 117; AFA 1909–13, p. 47; DAR 1932, p. 202; *SAR-M* (July 1943), p. 50; SAR 1900, p. 92; SAR 1901, p. 140.

26. *CR* (1896), p. 2334; SAR-C, pp. 15–16; Petition from Westfield, WI, *GAR* post, March 19, 1898, NAR, HR 55A-H12.6.

27. *CR* (1896), p. 1268; Ray to Ella Woodbridge, January 14, 1899, NAR, HR 55A-H.12.6; *The Independent*, January 15, 1903, pp. 162–63; *NYT*, December 1, 1935.

28. This paragraph is based on an examination of *Congressional Directories* for the period under study.

29. CKM 1898a, p. 5; HJC 1913, pp. 4–5.

30. SAR 1898, 83; *Halter v. Nebraska*, 205 *U.S.* 34, 41–42 (1907); SAR 1909–13, pp. 8, 45–46.

31. HJC 1927, p. 8; HJC 1928, p. 6.

32. Hatton to Rep. Chauncey Reed, June 23, 1941, NAR, 77A-D20.

33. Morris Sica, "The School Flag Movement: Origin and Influence," *Social Education*, 54 (October 1990), p. 381; *NYT*, May 21, 1898.

34. The *Nation*, December 6, 1900, pp. 439–40; *The Independent*, January 15, 1903, pp. 162–63; The *Public*, July 25, 1913, p. 697.

35. Woodrow Wilson, "Spurious Versus Real Patriotism in Education," *The School Review* (December 1899), pp. 603–04.

36. E. Benjamin Andrews, "Patriotism and the Public Schools," *The Arena*, 3 (December 1890), p. 71; *CW*, pp. 381, 383–84; Chauncey Colgrove, "Patriotism in our Public Schools," *American Magazine of Civics*, 9 (1896–97), pp. 124, 126.

37. Henry Foster, "The Decadence of Patriotism and What It Means," *The Arena*, 19 (1898), pp. 740–41, 747, 751.

38. Andrews, pp. 76–77; *The Nation*, August 2, 1906, p. 92; *The Public*, July 25, 1913, p. 698; *The Independent*, May 11, 1914, p. 237.

39. *The Independent*, January 15, 1903, p. 163.

40. S. S. Condo, *Our Flag and the Red Flag* (Marion, IN: S. S. Condo, 1915), pp. 9–10, 13, 15–16; *Mother Earth*, July 1916, p. 535, April 1917, pp. 35–36; *Blast*, July 1, 1916, p. 5; BW, p. 25; SG, pp. 156–57.

41. Sources for this paragraph and the next are primarily stories indexed in the *New York Times Index* (many of which are summarized in DP, pp. 160–76) and cases reported in legal references, such as *State v. Shumaker*, 175 *P.* 978

(1918); *State v. Schlueter*, 23 A. 2d 249 (1941); *State v. Peacock*, 25 A. 2d 491 (1942), and *Johnson v. State*, 163 S.W. 2d 153 (1942). The 1958 Illinois case is *People v. Von Rosen*, 147 N.E. 2d 327.

42. DAR 1916, p. 1138.

43. DAR 1916, p. 1138, 1150; *SAR-M*, July, 1931, p. 71.

44. *NYT*, July 22, 1900, April 11, 1917.

45. James Brown, *The Flag of the United States: Its Use in Commerce* (Washington: U.S. Department of Commerce, Trade Promotion Series No. 218, 1941), unpaginated preface; *NYT*, May 26, 1952. The Commerce Department pamphlet includes a complete text of all state flag desecration law then in force.

46. *CT*, December 6, 1959; *NYT*, May 26, 1960, January 14, 1963, March 28, 1964; *BG*, May 26, 1960; ALI, p. 416.

47. This paragraph is based on a survey of annual state attorneys general reports; for example, the material for Michigan is drawn from the *Biennial Report of the Attorney General of Michigan*, 1940–42, p. 171, and the Massachusetts information is based on *Opinions of the Attorney General of Massachusetts*, 1913–16, vol. 4, pp. 472–73.

48. *AM* 1904, p. 639; DAR 1916, pp. 1136, 1139; AFA 1909–13, p. 51; DAR 1918, pp. 84–85; Bernard Cigrand, *Laws and Customs Regulating the Use of the Flag of the United States* (Chicago: Marshall Field, 1917), p. 12; Nat Brandt, "To the Flag," American Heritage, 22 (June 1971), p. 74; SG, pp. 236–37; *NYT*, July 3, 1957, June 14, 1960.

49. *NYT*, April 10, 1917. For changes in the provisions of the state laws, see the sources cited in Chapter One, footnote 67.

50. *NYT*, April 10, 1917, May 1, 1917, March 28, 1918; DP, pp. 163–64.

51. *State v. Shumaker*, 175 P. 978, 979 (1918); *Johnson v. State*, 163 S.W. 2d 153, 154, 157 (1942).

52. *Ex Parte Starr*, 263 F. 145, 146–47 (1920).

53. *State v. Peacock*, 25 A. 2d 491, 493 (1942); *Street v. New York*, 394 U.S. 576 (1969).

54. *NYT*, June 29, 1914; *NYT*, April 4, 15, 21, 25, June 21, July 7, 1917; Paul Avrich, *Sacco and Vanzetti: The Anarchist Background* (Princeton: Princeton University Press, 1991), pp. 104–05.

55. *NYT*, November 1, 1925, March 15, 1931; *People v. Katzowitz*, 267 N.Y.S. 748 (1933); *NYT*, July 20, 1940, April 17, 1941, December 10, 1942, May 9, 1945; *State v. Schlueter*, 23 A. 2d 249 (1941).

56. *CT*, May 2, 1946; *NYT*, November 15, 28, 1946, March 23, 1947, June 10, 1948, January 30, 1951.

57. *NYT*, March 27, June 2, 3, 1916.

58. *NYT*, March 3–8, 10, 13–15, 18, 1917.

59. AFA 1909–13, pp. 47–48; DAR 1914, p. 1169; *NYT*, June 15, 1923; BW, p. 26.

60. HJC, 1918, pp. 5, 10; HJC, 1927, p. 3; *CR* (1927), pp. 5931–33.

61. HJC, 1927, pp. 13–16, 19; *CR* (1942), p. A3012.

62. Dale Featherling, *Mother Jones: The Miners' Angel* (Carbondale: Southern Illinois Univ. Press, 1974), pp. 118–20; George McGovern and Leonard Guttridge, *The Great Coalfield War* (Boston: Houghton-Mifflin, 1971), p. 173; David Goldberg, *A Tale of Three Cities: Labor Organization and Protest in*

Paterson, Passaic and Lawrence, 1916–1921 (New Brunswick: Rutgers Univ. Press 1990), p. 72; Harold Knight, *Working in Colorado* (Boulder: Univ. of Colorado, 1971), p. 107.

63. *CR:* (1890), p. 10697; (1904), p. 3176; (1908), pp. 6317, 6600; (1913) pp. 4157–58; (1914) p. 11882; (1918) pp. 3752–53; HJC (1918), p. 7.

64. *CR:* (1928), pp. 5000–03; (1930), pp. 3106–08; (1943) p. 5874; Adams to Rep. Frank Cornell, June 14, 1943, NAR, 78A-D17.

65. For general background on domestic tensions that impacted on the civil liberties climate during the 1907–45 period, see RJG.

66. *NYT,* September 29, 1922, September 16, 1925, August 17, 1930, October 21, 1930; Robert Quirk, *An Affair of Honor: Woodrow Wilson and the Occupation of Veracruz* (New York: Norton, 1967); Arthur Link, *Woodrow Wilson and the Progressive Era* (New York: Harper & Row, 1963), pp. 123–25.

67. H. C. Peterson and Gilbert Fite, *Opponents of War, 1917–18* (Seattle: Univ. of Washington Press, 1957), pp. 45–6, 84, 152–53; *CT:* April 3, 10, 1917; T.H. Watkins, *The Great Depression* (Boston: Little, Brown, 1993), pp. 157–58.

68. *NYT,* January 2, 1917; HJC 1918, pp. 8–9.

69. On red flag laws, see Robert Murray, *Red Scare* (New York: McGraw Hill, 1955), pp. 233–34; Zechariah Chafee, *Free Speech in the United States* (New York: Atheneum, 1941), pp. 159–63, 362–66; Julian Jaffe, *Crusade Against Radicalism: New York During the Red Scare* (Port Washington, NY: Kennikat, 1972), pp. 80–82; *NYT,* May 8, 1913; and especially Elmer Million, "Red Flags and the Flag," *Rocky Mountain Law Review,* 13 (1940–41), pp. 47–60.

70. Jaffe, p. 80; Chafee, p. 160; RP, p. 67.

71. See the sources cited in footnote 69, above.

72. *Minersville School District v. Gobitis,* 108 F. 2d 683 (1940). In general, on the flag saluting controversy, see David Manwaring, *Render Unto Caesar: The Flag Salute Controversy* (Chicago: Univ. of Chicago Press, 1962) and LS.

73. *Minersville School District v. Gobitis,* 310 U.S. 586, 595–96 (1940); RJG, p. 261.

74. Manwaring, pp. 166, 183; *McKee v. State,* 37 N.E. 2d 940 (1941); LS, pp. 11–16.

75. *Stromberg v. California,* 283 U.S. 359 (1931).

76. *West Virginia Board of Education v. Barnette,* 319 U.S. 624, 641–42 (1943).

77. *Gitlow v. New York,* 268 U.S. 652 (1925); *Schenck v. U.S.,* 249 U.S. 47 (1919); *Abrams v. U.S.,* 250 U.S. 616 (1919).

78. *Street v. New York,* 394 U.S. 576 (1969); *Johnson v. Texas,* 109 S. Ct. 2533, 2544 (1989); *U.S. v. Eichman,* 110 S. Ct. 2404 (1990); *Atlanta Constitution,* July 2, 1989.

Chapter 3

1. Data on flag desecration bills is derived from the annual indexes of bills published in the *CR.*

2. ALI, pp. 411, 415; *Handbook of the National Conference of Commissioners on Uniform State Laws and Proceedings of the Annual Conference, 1966*, pp. 176, 427; *NYT*, August 26, 1965; *DAR-R*, Senate Document No. 5, 91st Cong., 1st Sess., 1969, p. 61.

3. *CT*, March 9, 1966; *Terre Haute Tribune*, April 15, 1967; *CR* (1966), p. A1758.

4. *NYT*, April 1, 2, May 10, 1966; *New York Herald Tribune*, April 4, 1966; *Hinton v. State*, 154 *S.E.* 2d 246 (1967); *Anderson et al v. Georgia*, 390 *U.S.* 206 (1968).

5. *NYT*, April 12, December 2, 1966.

6. *NYT*, July 2, 1966; *People v. Street*, 229 *N.E.* 2d 187 (1967); *People v. Street*, 24 *N.Y.S.* 2d 848.

7. Material in this and the next paragraph is taken from Brief of Appellant, *Street v. New York*, in the Supreme Court of the United States, October Term, 1968, No. 5.

8. Material in this and the next paragraphs is taken from Brief for Appellees, *Street v. New York*, in the Supreme Court of the United States, October Term, 1968, No. 5.

9. Laura Kalman, *Abe Fortas* (New Haven: Yale Univ. Press, 1990), p. 285; *Street v. New York*, 394 *U.S.* 576, 593 (1969).

10. *Street v. New York*, 394 *U.S.* 576, 594 (1969); W. Wat Hopkins, *Mr. Justice Brennan and Freedom of Expression* (New York: Praeger, 1991), p. 110.

11. Information on behind-the-scenes development at the Court in connection with the *Street* case is based on HJC 1989a, p. 73; Bernard Schwartz, *Super Chief: Earl Warren and His Court* (New York: New York Univ. Press, 1983), pp. 595–96, 599, 601, 604–05, 733; Kalman, pp. 285–86, 616–17; and an examination of papers in the Library of Congress, Washington, D.C., deposited by the following former Supreme Court justices: Earl Warren, Boxes 325, 567, 585; William Brennan, Boxes 183, 416; Thurgood Marshall, Box 542; Hugo Black, Box 408; William Douglas, Box 1441.

12. *Street v. New York*, 394 *U.S.* 576, 594–95, 604–05 (1969).

13. *Street v. New York*, 394 *U.S.* 576, 609–10, 610–11, 616–17.

14. *NYT*, March 24, May 13, 24, 1967.

15. *NYT*, April 5, May 21, 1967; *CT*, April 5, 1967; *WP*, May 21, 1967; plus, for this and the following paragraphs, virtually daily coverage in *Terre Haute Tribune* and *Terre Haute Star*, April-May 1967; *CR* (1967), p. 10380; and the report in the March 1970 issue of the *AAUP Bulletin*, pp. 52–61.

16. For major accounts of the Radich affair upon which this and the next few paragraphs are largely based, see "A Test Case for Old Glory," *Life*, March 3, 1967, pp. 18–25; Laurie Adams, *Art on Trial* (New York: Walker & Co., 1976), pp. 140–68; *NYT*, May 21, October 29, 1967; Fred Graham, "The Supreme Court and the Flag," *AA* (March 1971), p. 27; Carl Baldwin, "Art and the Law: The Flag in Court Again," *AA* (May/June 1974), pp. 50–54.

17. *People v. Radich*, 279 *N.Y.S.*2d 680, 684, 685, 688 (1967).

18. *People v. Radich*, 294 *N.Y.S.*2d 285 (1968); *People v. Radich*, 308 *N.Y.S.* 2d 846, 849 (1970); *NYT*, March 1, 1970.

19. *People v. Radich*, 308 *N.Y.S.*2d 846, 856, 857 (1970).

20. *The Nation,* November 30, 1970, p. 573; *Commonweal,* December, 1970, p. 295; Lucy Lippard, "Flagged Down: The Judson Three and Friends," *AA* (May 1972), pp. 48–53. According to *Old Glory: The American Flag in Contemporary Art* (Cleveland: Cleveland Center for Contemporary Art, 1994), a catalog accompanying an extensive exhibit of flag art, much of the "desecrating" variety, the Judson Three ended up paying the fine as their convictions were never voided even though Radich eventually won his case after extensive appeals.

21. Baldwin, pp. 50, 54; Graham, p. 27; Adams, pp. 166, 168; *Radich v. New York,* 401 *U.S.* 531 (1971).

22. *U.S. ex rel. Radich v. Criminal Court of the City of New York,* 450 F. 2d 745, (1972); *U.S. ex rel. Radich v. Criminal Court of the City of New York,* 385 F Supp. 165, 178 (1974); *Spence v. Washington,* 418 *U.S.* 405 (1974).

23. *U.S. ex rel. Radich v. Criminal Court of the City of New York,* 385 F Supp. 165, 179–80, 183 (1974).

24. *Decatur (Illinois) Herald-Review,* April 2, 1989; *People v. Lindsay,* 282 *N.E.* 2d 431 (1972).

25. *CR1,* p. 106304.

26. *CR1,* pp. 7717, 7784, 17553.

27. *CR1,* pp. A1578, A2184, A2708, A3753, A4090, A42231, A4955, 13983; HJC 1967b, pp. 34, 217; *DAR Magazine,* June–July 1967, p. 563, October 1967, p. 725; *SAR-M,* June 1967, p. 20.

28. See the discussion in DP, pp. 159–60.

29. HJC 1967b, p. 118; *CR1* pp. 10008, 16446.

30. *CR1,* pp. 16455, 16458, 16476; HJCa 1967, p. 104.

31. *CR1,* pp. 991l, 1007, 10093; *NYT,* April 20, 1967.

32. *CR1,* p. 10320. See HJC 1967b; the texts of the bills are printed at pp. 1–27 and 346–49.

33. HJC 1967b, pp. 90–91, 277; HJC 1967a, pp. 5–7.

34. HJC 1967a, pp. 1, 4; *NYT,* June 6, 21, 1967; *WP,* June 6, 21, 1967.

35. *CR1,* pp. 16498–99; *Ann Arbor News,* June 21, 1967; *DN,* June 21, 1967.

36. *Life,* July 1967, p. 4; *Time,* June 30, 1967, p. 17; *NYT,* June 25, 1968, July 5, 1968; *CR* 1968, pp. 18358, 18558; SJC 1968.

37. 18 U.S.C. §700 (1988).

38. *CR1,* pp. 10647, 11727, 16444, 16478–79, 16481.

39. *CR1,* pp. A2484, 10007, 10647, 10849, 10898, 11696, 11727, 16444, 16448, 16454, 16464, 16475–76, 16481–82; HJC 1967b, pp. 63–64, 70–74, 190, 269.

40. *CR1,* pp. A2660, 15855, 16442, 16446–47, 16484–85; HJC 1967a, pp. 46, 84.

41. *CR1,* pp. 16446, 16460; HJC 1967b, pp. 37, 40.

42. HJC 1967b, pp. 44, 70–71, 133, 245, 257; *CR1,* pp. 11695, 12041, 12378, 16470; *CSM,* June 23, 1967.

43. *CR1,* pp. 16449–50, 16489–90.

44. HJC 1967b, pp. 45; *CR1,* pp. 16449, 16464, 16475; HJC1967b, p. 3.

45. HJC 1967b, pp. 55, 67–69, 253.

46. *CR1,* pp. 10849, 10898, 11695, 16447–48, 16455–56, 16462, 16486.

47. HJC 1967b, pp. 90–1; *CR1*, pp. A2728, 11923, 11977, 12042, 16473, 16480.

48. *CR1*, pp. 16444–45, 16455, 16484, 16487.

49. *CR1*, pp. 16451–52, 16462, 16464, 16471, 16483.

50. *Newsweek*, July 3, 1967, p. 29; *NYT*, June 7, 1967; *CR1*, pp. 16462, 16465; HJC 1967a, p. 16.

51. *CR1*, pp. 12306, 13729; HJC 1967b, pp. 17–21; *CR1*, pp. 16463, 16469.

52. *NYT*, June 15, 1967; *WP*, May 10, June 14, 1967; *Life*, July, 1967, p. 4; *The Nation*, June 19, 1967, July 17, 1967, p. 205; *Commonweal*, October 18, 1968, p. 77; *The Christian Century*, June 14, 1967, p. 772; HJC 1967b, pp. 154, 307; *CR1*, pp. 16465, 16467–68.

53. *CR1*, pp. 15652–53, 16472; *NYT*, June 14, 1971.

54. *CR1*, pp. 15652–53, 16452, 16454, 16474; HJC 1967a, pp. 62, 79.

55. *CR1*, pp. 16469, 16474–75, 16492.

56. *Commonweal*, October 16, 1968, p. 77; *The Christian Century*, June 14, 1967, p. 772; *The Nation*, June 29, 1970, p. 211.

Chapter 4

1. A compilation of flag desecration laws in effect in 1967 is published in HJC 1967b, pp. 324–46. Changes can be determined by examining updated lists of the penalties provided in state flag desecration laws published in "Flag Burning, Flag Waving and the Law," *Valparaiso University Law Review* 4 (1970), 362–7; Dennis Tushla, "Flag Desecration: The Unsettled Issue," *Notre Dame Lawyer* 46 (1970), 218–20; and JH, pp. 53–224. The Kent law is reported in *NYT*, June 4, 1970.

2. New York General Business Law §136 (Consolidated 1966).

3. *CSM*, March 15, 1973; *AA*, May 1972, p. 51; "Flag Laws Still Wave," *Civil Liberties*, September 1970, p. 1; *Civil Liberties*, May 1971, p. 5; "Note: Freedom of Speech and Symbolic Conduct: The Crime of Flag Desecration," *Arizona Law Review* 12 (1970), pp. 72–3; "Flag Desecration as Constitutionally Protected Symbolic Speech," *Iowa Law Review* 56 (1971), p. 618; Kenneth Hicks, "*Spence v. Washington; Smith v. Goguen*: Symbolic Speech and Flag Desecration," *Columbia Human Rights Law Review* 6 (1974–5), p. 544.

4. All cases turned up by a WESTLAW search of reported relevant federal and state prosecutions were surveyed, as were all other relevant reported cases that were referred to in these cases or other sources. While some reported cases may have escaped the attention of the author, it seems unlikely that they amount to more than a few at most.

5. DP, pp. 203, 218.

6. *Deeds v. State*, 474 S.W.2d 718 (1971); *State v. Farrell*, 223 N.W.2d, 270, 272, 273 (1974).

7. *State v. Saulino*, 277 N.E.2d 580, 583 (1971); *Delorme v. State*, 488 S.W. 2d 808, 813 (1973); *State v. Mitchell*, 288 N.E.2d 216, 220 (1972).

8. *Halter v. Nebraska*, 205 U.S. 34, 41 (1907); *State v. Waterman*, 190 N.W.2d 809, 811 (1971); *People v. Cowgill*, 78 Cal. Reptr. 853, 855 (1969); *Sutherland v. Dewulf*, 323 F. Supp. 740, 745 (1971).

9. *AA*, May 5, 1972, p. 51; *Quarterly Journal of Speech*, 57 (1971), p. 31.

10. Brief for Appellee, *Smith v. Goguen*, in the Supreme Court of the United States, October Term, 1973, No. 72–1254.

11. *State v. van Camp*, 281 A.2d 584 (1971); *Crosson v. Silver*, 319 F. Supp. 1084, 1086, 1087 (1970); *U.S. v. Crosson*, 462 F.2d 96 (1972); *Crosson v. U.S.* 409 U.S. 1064 (1972); *People v. Vaughan*, 514 P.2d. 1318, 1323, 1324 (1973).

12. *Goguen v. Smith*, 471 F.2d 88, 91, 95 (1972); *Smith v. Goguen*, 415 U.S. 566 (1974).

13. *State v. Kool*, 212 N.W.2d 518, 521 (1973); *People v. Keough*, 290 N.E.2d 819 (1972); *Korn v. Elkins*, 317 F. Supp. 136 (1970).

14. *State v. Saionz*, 261 N.E.2d 135 (1969); *State v. Claxton*, 501 P.2d 192 (1972); *Hoffman v. U.S.*, 445 F. 2d 226, 229 (1971); *NYT*, November 22, 1968; *Franz v. Commonwealth*, 186 S.E.2d 71, 72 (1972); *WP*, June 5, 1969.

15. *State v. Hershey*, 289 N.E.2d 190, 192 (1972); *State v. Kent*, No. 36,423, Hawaii Circuit Court, December 9, 1966; *State v. Liska*, 291 N.E.2d 498, 499 (1971); *State v. Nicola*, 182 N.W.2d, 870, 872 (1971); *Herrick v. Commonwealth*, 188 S.E.6d, 209, 210 (1972); *State v. Hodsdon*, 289 A.2d 635 (1972); *People v. Meyers*, 321 N.E.2d 142 (1974).

16. *Smith v. Goguen*, 415 U.S. 566, 581–82 (1974); *Commonwealth v. Young*, 325 A.2d 315 (1974); *Royal v. Superior Court of New Hampshire*, 531 F.2d 1084 (1976).

17. *Alford v. Sacramento Judicial District*, 102 Cal. Reptr. 667, 668 (1972); *Parker v. Morgan*, 322 F. Supp. 585, 586–87,588, 590 (1971).

18. *Long Island Moratorium Committee v. Cahn*, 437 F.2d 344, 348, 349 (1970); 418 U. S. 907 (1974).

19. *State v. Zimmelman*, 301 A.2d, 129, 135 (1973); *Miami v. Wolfenberger*, 265 S.E.2d 732, 733, 734 (1972).

20. *State v. Waterman*, 190 N.W.2d 809 (Iowa 1971); *People v. Cowgill*, 78 Cal. Rptr. 853 (1969); *State v. Mitchell*, 288 N.E.2d 216 (Ohio 1972); *State v. Saionz*, 261 N.E.2d 135 (Ohio 1969); *Franz v. Commonwealth*, 86 S.E.2d 71 (Va. 1972); *People v. Vaughan*, 514 P.2d 318 (Colo. 1973); *NYT*, February 21, August 1, 1971; *State v. Kasnett*, 283 N.E. 2d 636, 637, 639 (Ohio 1972); *State v. Kasnett*, 297 N.E. 2d 537, 538 (Ohio 1973).

21. *NYT*, October 16, 1969, March 18, 21, 1970; *WP*, March 18, 1970; Richard Frisbie, "What So Proudly We Hailed," *U.S. Catholic and Jubilee*, February 1971.

22. *NYT*, January 31, 1970; *Baisch v. State*, 351 N.Y.S.2d 517 (1974); *Chicago Today*, March 26, 1971; *State v. Hodsdon*, 289 A. 2d 635 (1972); *Commonwealth v. Lorenc*, 281 A. 2d 743 (1971); *Commonwealth v. Janoff*, 266 A.2d 657 (1970); *WSJ*, May 12, 1970.

23. *State v. Saulino*, 277 N.E. 2d 580 (Ohio 1971); *U.S. v. Radich*, 385 F Supp. 165 (1974); *Van Slyke v. State*, 489 S.W. 2d 590 (1973); *DMN*, July 25, August 8, 1970; *DTH*, August 11, September 11, 1970.

24. "Who Owns the Stars and Stripes?" *Time*, July 6, 1970, pp. 8–15; "New Glory?" *Newsweek*, June 15, 1970; "Decalomania over the American Flag," *Life*, 19 July 1989, 32–3; *NYT*, January 26, 1969, January 28, July 5, 19, 1970.

25. *NYT*, June 21, 1967; *NYT*, January 10, July 5, 1971; Fred Graham, "The Supreme Court and the Flag," *AA*, March 1971, p. 27; *The New Republic*, June 12, 1971, p. 19; *Time*, July 6, 1970, p. 15; *Commonweal*, October 18, 1968, pp. 76–77.

26. John Bannerman, "Official Symbols: Use and Abuse," *New Mexico Law Review* 1 (1971), pp. 363, 365 n. 63; *DMN*, August 8, 1970; "Exploiting the American Flag: Can the Law Distinguish Criminal from Patriot?" *Maryland Law Review* 30 (1970), pp. 347–48; *DTH*, June 30, July 3, 20, 1970; *NYT*, January 10, 1971; *Chicago Today*, June 13, 1971.

27. *Time*, July 6, November 2, 1970; *Washington Star*, October 18, 1970; *NYT*, June 4, 1970, January 13, 1972; *Smith v. Goguen*, 415 *U.S.* 566, 575 (1974).

28. *NYT*, March 28, 29, 1970; *VV*, June 11, 1970, p. 65.

29. *Newsweek*, June 30, 1969, June 15, 1970; *Time*, July 11, 1969, July 6, 1970; *NYT*, July 4, 1969; *CST*, July 5, 1970.

30. Scot Guenter, "The Hippies and the Hardhats: The Struggle for Semiotic Control of the Flag of the United States in the 1960s," *FB*, 130 (1989), p. 137; *CST*, July 5, 1970.

31. *NYT*, May 29, 1970; *New York Review of Books*, July 2, 1970, p. 3; *VV*, June 11, 1976, p. 1; *Current Events*, November 11, 1970, p. 2; *U.S. Catholic and Jubilee*, February 1971; *CST*, July 5, 1970.

32. *NYT*, July 11, 1968; *CDN*, January 15, 1971; *CST Sunday Midwest Magazine*, June 13, 1971; *Newsweek*, June 30, 1969.

33. *New York Review of Books*, July 2, 1970, p. 3; *Time*, July 6, 1970, pp. 14, 15; *CDN*, June 10, 1970; Abe Laufe, *The Wicked Stage: A History of Theater Censorship and Harassment in the United States* (New York: Frederick Ungar, 1978), p. 150; 334 *F. Supp.* 634 (1971); 459 *F.* 2d 282 (1972). A number of these incidents were first brought to my attention by Rosalind Moss, a Richmond, Virginia flag researcher, who recounts them along with others in her paper, "Tangled in the Stars and Covered with the Stripes: Symbolic Struggles over Flag Use and National Direction in the 1960s," presented to the November 1990 convention of the American Studies Association in New Orleans.

34. John Pullen, *Patriotism in America* (New York: American Heritage, 1971), pp. 12–13, 184–85; Guenter, "The Hippies and the Hardhats," pp. 136–37; *NYT*, May 16, 190; *National Observer*, June 1, 1970.

35. *National Observer*, July 13, 1970; *CST*, June 1, 1970; Pullen, p. 185; *The Nation*, June 7, 1971; *Chicago Today*, May 20, 1971; *CDN*, May 6, 1971.

36. *Time*, July 6, 1970; *Civil Liberties*, September, 1970, p. 1; *Renn v. State*, 495 *S.W.*2d 932 (1973).

37. *U.S. v. Crosson*, 462 *F.*2d 96, 101 (1972); *Joyce v. U.S.*, 454 *F.*2d 971, 974, 975, 976 (1971); *State v. Liska*, 268 *N.E.*2d 824, 826, 827 (1970); *State v. Mitchell*, 288 *N.E.*2d 216, 219, 228 (1972).

38. *LAT*, February 17, 1973; *NYT*, December 11, 1970, August 3, 1974.

39. *BG*, April 3, 8, November 18, 1970; *Pittsburgh Post-Gazette*, November 18, 1970; *NYT*, November 21, 1970.

40. *State v. Kasnett,* 297 N.E.2d 537 (1973); *The New Republic,* June 12, 1971, p. 19; *CST Sunday Midwest Magazine,* June 13, 1971, p. 16; *BG,* January 13, 1974; *Civil Liberties,* September, 1970, p. 1; *NYT,* July 5, 1971.

41. *Look,* July 14, 1970; *Commonweal,* March 27, 1970, p. 61; *NYT,* May 5, 1968, April 20, 1969, July 8, 1970.

42. *BG,* December 13, 1970; *DP,* p. 191; *NYT,* August 20, 1969, May 22, 1970; *WP,* May 25, 1970.

43. *Pittsburgh Catholic,* June 8, 15, 1973, March 29, 1974; *Pittsburgh Post-Gazette,* March 26, 1974; *Pittsburgh Press,* March 26, 1974.

44. *Deeds v. State,* 474 S.W.2d 718 (1971); *DTH,* May 22, 26, June 23, 24, 25, 1970; *DMN,* June 23, 24, 25, 26, 1970.

45. *Johnson v. State,* 706 S.W.2d 120 (1986); *Johnson v. State,* 755 S.W.2d 92 (1988); *Texas v. Johnson,* 109 S. Ct. 2533 (1989).

46. *Street v. New York,,* 394 *U.S.* 576, 604–05 (1969).

47. Ibid., 593; *Terminiello v. Chicago,* 337 *U.S.* 1, 4 (1949); *New York Times v. Sullivan,* 376 *U.S.* 254, 270 (1964); *FCC v. Pacifica,* 438 *U.S.* 726, 745 (1978); *Consolidated Edison Co. v. Public Service Commission,* 447 *U.S.* 530, 537, 541 (1980).

48. *Chaplinsky v. New Hampshire,* 315 *U.S.* 568, 572 (1942); *Brandenburg v. Ohio,* 395 *U.S.* 444, 447 (1969); *Hustler Magazine v. Falwell,* 485 *U.S.* 46, 55, 56 (1988).

49. *Stromberg v. California,* 283 *U.S.* 259 (1931); *W. Va. Board of Education v. Barnette,* 319 *U.S.* 624 (1943); *Thornhill v. Alabama,* 310 *U.S.* 88 (1940); *Cox v. Louisiana,* 379 *U.S.* 536 (1965); *Tinker v. Des Moines Indep. Community School Dist.,* 393 *U.S.* 503 (1969).

50. *Milkwagon Driver's Union v. Meadowmoor Dairies, Inc.,* 312 *U.S.* 275, 293 (1941); *Adderly v. Florida,* 385 *U.S.* 39, 50–51 (1966); *Cohen v. California,* 403 *U.S.* 15, 26 (1971).

51. *Tinker v. Des Moines Indep. Community School Dist.,* 393 *U.S.* 503, 509 (1969); *Schacht v. U.S.,* 398 *U.S.* 58 (1970); *Boos v. Barry,* 108 S. Ct. 1157 (1988).

52. *Tinker v. Des Moines Indep. Community School Dist.,* 393 *U.S.* 503 (1969); *Cox v. Louisiana,* 379 *U.S.* 536, 555 (1965); *U.S. v. O'Brien,* 391 *U.S.* 367, 376 (1968); *RJG,* p. 435.

53. Ibid., p. 377.

54. *Clark v. Community for Creative Non-Violence,* 468 *U.S.* 288 (1984); *Boos v. Barry,* 485 *U.S.* 312, 321; Randolph Collins, "The Constitutionality of Flag Burning," *American Criminal Law Review,* 28 (1991), p. 913.

55. *Smith v. Goguen,* 415 *U.S.* 566 (1974); *Spence v. Washington,* 418 *U.S.* 405 (1974).

56. *Boston Phoenix,* January 8, 1974; *NYT,* February 24, 1970; *BG,* February 25, 26, 1970.

57. *Commonwealth v. Goguen,* 279 N.E.2d 606; *Goguen v. Smith,* 343 F Supp. 161, 166–67 (1972); *BG,* September 9, 1973; *Boston Phoenix,* January 8, 1974; *NYT,* February 3, 1972.

58. *Goguen v. Smith,* 471 F.2d 88, 91, 95, 96 (1972).

59. Ibid., 99, 101, 102, 103.

60. *Smith v. Goguen,* 415 *U.S.* 566, 575, 583 (1974).

61. *ST,* May 11, July 10, 17, October 15, 31, 1970.

62. *State v. Spence,* 490 *P.*2d 1321, 1326 (1971); *State v. Spence,* 506 *P*2d 293, 302–05 (1973).

63. *Spence v. Washington,* 418 *U.S.* 405, 408–10, 420 (1974).

64. Ibid., 411–12, 414.

65. Ibid., 414; *Smith v. Goguen,* 415 *U.S.* 566, 574, 580–81 (1974).

66. Material on behind-the-scenes developments at the Supreme Court concerning the *Goguen* case are based on an examination of the files of the following former Supreme Court justices at the Library of Congress, Washington, D.C.: William Brennan, Boxes 317, 421; William Douglas, Box 1647; Thurgood Marshall, Box 126

67. Developments behind-the-scenes at the Supreme Court concerning the *Spence* case are based on an examination of the files of the following former Supreme Court justices at the Library of Congress, Washington, D.C.: William Douglas, Boxes 1619, 1651; Thurgood Marshall, Box 129.

68. *Smith v. Goguen,* 415 *U.S.* 566, 590–91 (1974); *Spence v. Washington,* 418 *U.S.* 405, 416 (1974).

69. *Smith v. Goguen,* 415 *U.S.* 566, 599, 602, 603; *Spence v. Washington,* 418 *U.S.* 405, 417, 421(1974).

70. *Radich v. New York,* 403 *U.S.* 531 (1971).

71. *Cowgill v. California,* 400 *U.S.* 956 (1970); *Joyce v. U.S.,* 405 *U.S.* 969 (1972); *California v. Sacramento Municipal Court,* 409 *U.S.* 1109 (1973); *Cahn v. Long Island Moratorium Committee,* 418 *U.S.* 906 (1974); *Van Slyke v. Texas,* 418 *U.S.* 907 (1974); *Royal v. Superior Court,* 429 *U.S.* 867 (1976); *Crosson v. U.S.,* 409 *U.S.* 1064 (1972); *Sutherland v. Illinois,* 418 *U.S.* 906 (1974); *Farrell v. Iowa,* 418 *U.S.* 907 (1974); *Farrell v. Iowa,* 421 *U.S.* 1007 (1975); *Sutherland v. Illinois,* 425 *U.S.* 947 (1976); *Bangert v. U.S.* 454 *U.S.* 860 (1981); *Kime v. U.S.,* 459 *U.S.* 949 (1982); *Bowles v. Georgia,* 465 *U.S.* 1112 (1984).

72. *Sutherland v. Illinois,* 418 *U.S.* 1007 (1975); *Farrell v. Iowa,* 418 *U.S.* 907 (1974); *People v. Sutherland,* 292 *N.E.*2d 746, 749; *State v. Farrell,* 209 *N.W.*2d 103, 107 (1973).

73. *People v. Sutherland,* 329 *N.E.*2d 820 (1975); *State v. Farrell,* 223 *N.W.*2d 270, 271, 273; *Farrell v. Iowa,* 421 *U.S.* 1007 (1975); *Sutherland v. Illinois,* 425 *U.S.* 947 (1976).

74. *U.S. ex rel. Radich v. Criminal Court of the City of New York,* 385 *F Supp.* 165, 171, 177, 180 (1974).

75. Thomas Tedford, *Freedom of Speech in the United States* (New York: Random House, 1985), p. 295; *NYN,* March 30, 1989; ALI, pp. 419–20.

76. For a collection of the texts of state flag desecration laws in effect in 1981, see JH, pp. 53–220.

77. *The Docket* (Newsletter of the Massachusetts Civil Liberties Union), August 1974; *NYT,* August 7, 1974.

78. *DTH,* July 7, 1970; Texas Penal Code Ann. §42.09 (Vernon, 1974).

79. *Street v. New York,* 394 *U.S.* 576, 592 (1969); *Texas Bar Journal,* March 1975, p. 245.

80. ALI, pp. 416–17, 420.

Chapter 5

1. For general information on the RCP, see A. Belden Field, *Trotskyism and Maoism: Theory and Practice in France and the United States* (New York: Praeger, 1988), pp. 205–29, 276–83; Harvey Klehr, *Far Left of Center: The American Radical Left Today* (New Brunswick, NJ.: Transaction, 1988), pp. 92–96; George Vickers, "A Guide to the Sectarian Left," *The Nation*, May 17, 1980, p. 596; *LAT*, August 19, 1979. The court cases referred to (including, in some cases, various reported stages on the same cases) are, aside from the *Johnson* case that is fully discussed and cited below: *Monroe v. State*, 295 *S.E.2d* 512 (1982); *Monroe v. State Court of Fulton County*, 571 *F Supp.* 1023, (1983); *Monroe v. State Court of Fulton Country*, 739 *F.2d* 568 (1984); *Ohio v. Blumberg*, Ohio Court of Appeals, Eleventh District, Portage County, Case No. 1035, July 22, 1981 (unpublished, DAP); *U.S. v. Kime*, Cr-80-95-G, U.S. District Court for the Middle District of N. Carolina, June 12, 1981 (unpublished, DAP); *U.S. v. Kime*, No. 81–5160 (L), U.S. Court of Appeals for the Fourth Circuit, January 28, 1982 (unpublished, DAP); *U.S. v. Kime*, 459 *U.S.* 949 (1982); *Bowles v. State*, *S.E.2d* 250 (1983); *Bowles v. Georgia* 465 *U.S.* 1112 (1984); *Bowles v. Jones*, 758 *F.2d* 1479 (1985).

2. *U.S. v. Kime*, 459 *U.S.* 949 (1982).

3. Ibid., 951 (1982).

4. *Monroe v. State Court of Fulton County*, 739 *F.2d* 568, 572, 574 (1984).

5. Ibid., 575.

6. The legal history of the *Johnson* case can be traced in GLJ (DAP); *Johnson v. State*, 706 *S.W.* 2d 120 (1986); *Johnson v. State*, 755 *S.W.* 2d 92 (1988); and *Texas v. Johnson*, 491 *U.S.* 397 (1989).

7. Information in this and surrounding paragraphs is primarily based on GLJ, the unpublished transcript of Johnson's December 1984 trial in Dallas (DAP); for the quoted material, see pp. 771–72, 774.

8. *Johnson v. State*, 706 *S.W.2d* 120, 123–24 (1986); *Spence v. Washington*, 418 *U.S.* 405 (1974); *Deeds v. State*, 474 *S.W.2d* 718 (1971).

9. This and the following paragraph are drawn from *Johnson v. State*, 755 *S.W.2d* 92, 93, 94–98 (1988); *Boos v. Barry*, 485 *U.S.* 312 (1988).

10. See, for example, *NYT*, *LAT* and *WP*, all for October 18, 1988.

11. A comprehensive chronology of the 1988 Pledge of Allegiance controversy is contained in Whitney Smith, "The American Flag in the 1988 Presidential Campaign," *FB*, 128 (1988), pp. 176–95. See also *The New Republic*, July 4, 1988, p. 4; *Time*, September 5, 1988, p. 15; and John Concannon, "The Pledge of Allegiance and the First Amendment," *Suffolk University Law Review*, 23 (1989), pp. 1019–1047; *W. Va. Bd. of Educ. v. Barnette*, 319 U.S. 624 (1943).

12. *WP*, October 13, 1988; *LAT*, September 21, 1988; *NYT*, June 26, 1989; *Time*, October 3, 1988, p. 16.

13. *NYT*, June 26, 1989; *WP*, June 24, 28, 1989.

14. Among the more useful general accounts of the February–March 1989 SAIC Scott Tyler "flag on the floor" controversy, see Steven Dubin, *Arresting Art: Impolitic Art and Uncivil Actions* (New York: Routledge, 1992), pp. 102–24; Elizabeth Hess, "Capture the Flag: Is Dread Scott's Flag-Piece Art, Treason

or Both," *VV*, April 4, 1989, pp. 25–31; Jean Fulton and Benjamin Seaman, "The Flag Fracas," *New Art Examiner*, May 1989, pp. 30–32; *NYT*, June 11, July 3, 1989; Sylvia Hochfield, "Flag Furor," *Art News*, Summer 1989, pp. 43–7; and *LAT*, March 13, 1989.

15. *CT*, March 13, 15, 1989.

16. *NYT*, March 17, 1989; *Charlotte Observer*, March 17, 1989; *CR2*, pp. S2793–94; *LAT*, March 13, 1989; *WP*, March 19, 1989; *CST*, March 20, 1989.

17. This and the following paragraphs are all drawn from the text of the Supreme Court ruling in *Texas v. Johnson*, 491 *U.S.* 397 (1989). Other cases cited in the text are *Monroe v. State Court of Fulton County*, 739 *F.*2d 568 (1984); *U.S. v. O'Brien*, 391 *U.S.* 367, 376 (1968); *Chaplinsky v. New Hampshire*, 315 *U.S.* 568 (1942); *Brandenburg v. Ohio*, 395 *U.S.* 444 (1969); *FCC v. Pacifica Foundation*, 438 *U.S.* 726, 745 (1978); *Spence v. Washington*, 418 *U.S.* 405, (1974); *Boos v. Barry*, 485 *U.S.* 312 (1988); *Street v. New York*, 394 *U.S.* 576 (1969); *Schacht v. U.S.*, 398 *U.S.* 58 (1970).

18. *NYN*, July 2, 1989; *Newsweek*, July 3, 1989; *Texas v. Johnson*, 491 *U.S.* 397, 418–19 (1989).

19. See *Congressional Quarterly*, July 1, 1989; *CR2*, pp. S7189, S7458, S8105–06; H3239, H3380–H3438.

20. *NYT*, July 4, 1989; *U.S. News & World Report*, October 30, 1989.

21. *WT*, June 23, 1989; *WP*, June 23, 28, 1989; *Indianapolis Star*, June 23, 1989; *LAT*, June 23, 1989.

22. *Time*, July 3, 1989; *Columbia (SC) State*, June 23, 1989; *NYP*, June 23, 1989; *NYDN*, June 23, 1989.

23. Brief for Petitioner, *Texas v. Johnson*, in the Supreme Court of the United States, No. 88–155, October Term, 1988; *Halter v. Nebraska*, 205 *U.S.* 34 (1907).

24. *Texas v. Johnson*, 491 *U.S.* 397, 421 (Justice Rehnquist dissenting), 436 (Justice Stevens dissenting) (1989).

25. HJC 1989a, pp. 228, 231.

26. *Lexington Herald-Leader*, June 30, 1989; *LAT*, July 14, 1989.

27. *Salt Lake Tribune*, July 2, 1989; *WP*, June 30, 1989; *NYT*, July 2, 1989; *Philadelphia Inquirer*, July 2, 1989.

28. *Jet*, July 17, 1989; *NYDN*, August 8, 1989; *New Jersey Record*, July 12, 1989.

29. *WP*, July 23, October 15, 1989.

30. *Texas v. Johnson*, 491 *U.S.* 397, 410–11, 414, 415, 417, 418.

31. SJC 1989b, pp. 4–5; HJC 1989b, p. 9.

32. SJC 1989b, pp. 4–9.

33. *Smith v. Goguen*, 415 *U.S.* 566, 591 (Justice Blackmun dissenting) (1974).

34. HJC 1989a, p. 202.

35. SJC 1989b, p. 26; HJC 1989b, p. 22.

36. *LAT*, June 29, 1989; *WP*, July 1, August 5, 1989.

37. *CR2*, S12655, S13647, H5562, H6997.

38. Flag Protection Act of 1989, Public Law No. 101–131, 103 Stat. 777 (amending 18 United States Code § 700).

39. HJC 1989b, p. 22; SJC 1989a, p. 20.

40. *U.S. v. Haggerty,* 731 *F Supp.* 425 (1990); *U.S. v. Eichman,* 731 *F Supp.* 1123 (1990).

41. Brief for the United States, in the Supreme Court of the United States, *U.S. v. Eichman,* Nos. 89–1433 and 89–1434, October Term, 1989.

42. Official Transcript, Proceedings before the U.S. Supreme Court, *U.S. v. Eichman,* Nos. 89–1433 and 89–1434, May 14, 1990.

43. Ibid.; Brief for Appellees, in the Supreme Court of the United States, *U.S. v. Eichman,* Nos. 89–1433 and 89–1434, October Term, 1989.

44. *U.S. v. Eichman,* 496 *U.S.* 310 (1990).

45. *U.S. v. Eichman,* 496 *U.S.* 310, 319 (Justice Stevens dissenting).

46. *WP,* June 13, 19, 1990; *SLPD* June 12, 1990; *Wall Street Journal,* June 12, 1990; *USA Today,* June 13, 1990;

47. *Cleveland Plain Dealer,* June 20, 1990; *CR3,* p. H4087, S8736.

48. *CSM,* June 25, 1990; *NYT,* October 13, 1992; *State v. Jimenez,* 838 *S.W.*2d. 455 (1992). Robert Justin Goldstein, "This Flag is Not for Burning: Snuffing Out Symbolic Speech," *The Nation,* July 18, 1994, pp. 84–86.

49. *CSM,* June 13, 1990; *National Journal,* June 23, 1990.

50. *WP,* June 12, 1990; *WSJ,* June 12, 1990.

51. SJC Hearings, 1989a; *SLPD,* June 12, 1990; *CR3,* p. H4079.

52. *CR3,* pp. H4065, S8642; SJC 1990, p. 30.

53. *BG,* July 2, 1989; *NYN,* July 2, 1989; *NYT,* July 1, 1990; *LAT,* July 8, 1990.

54. *WP,* June 24, 1989.

55. *NYT,* August 1, 1989; ST, October 14, 1989.

56. *W. Virginia Bd. of Educ. v. Barnette,* 319 *U.S.* 624, 641 (1943), 385 *F.Supp.* 165, 184 (1974).

Appendix

The Text of Three Key Documents in the American Flag DesecrationControversy

Document 1: The model flag desecration law recommended by the American Flag Association and used as the basis for most state flag desecration laws that were passed during the 1897–1932 period (Source: Circular of Information, The American Flag Association, 1900).

Form of Legislative Act recommended by the Executive Committee of the American Flag Association, to be used to obtain legislation to protect the flag from desecration. ...

Section I. Any person who in any manner, for exhibition or display shall place or cause to be placed, any words or marks or inscriptions or picture or design or device or symbol or token or notice or drawing or advertisement of any nature whatever upon any flag, standard, color or ensign of the United States, or shall expose or shall cause to be exposed to public view any such flag, standard, color or ensign of the United States upon which shall be printed, painted or otherwise placed or which shall be attached, appended, affixed or annexed any words, or figures, or numbers or marks, or inscriptions or picture or design or device or symbol or token or notice or drawing or any advertisement of any nature or kind whatever, or who shall expose to public view or shall manufacture or sell or expose for sale or have in possession for sale or for use any article or thing or substance being an article of merchandise or a receptacle of merchandise upon which shall have been printed, painted or otherwise placed, a representation of any such flag, standard, color or ensign of the United States, to advertise or call attention to or to decorate or to ornament or to mark or to distinguish the article or thing on which so placed, or shall publicly mutilate, trample upon or publicly deface, or defy, or defile, or cast contempt, either by words or act, upon any such flag, standard, color or ensign of the United States shall be guilty of a misdemeanor.

Section 2. The words flag, standard, color or ensign of the United States as used in this act shall include any flag, any standard, any color or any ensign or any representation of a flag, standard, color or ensign or a picture of a flag, standard, color or ensign made of any substance whatever or represented on any substance whatever, and of any size whatever evidently purporting to be either of said flag, standard, color or ensign of the United States or a picture or a representation of either thereof, upon which shall be shown the colors, the stars and the stripes in any number in either thereof or by which the person seeing the same without deliberation may believe the same to represent the flag or the colors or the standard or the ensign or the United States of America. ...

Document 2: The 1968 Federal Flag Desecration Law (18 U.S.C. § 700[a-c] [1988]).

Be it enacted by the Senate and House of Representatives of the United States of America in Congress assembled, that chapter 33 of title 18, United States Code, is amended by inserting immediately preceding section 701 thereof, a new section as follows:

"§ 700. Desecration of the flag of the United States; penalties

"(a) whoever knowingly casts contempt upon any flag of the Unites States by publicly mutilating, defacing, defiling, burning, or trampling upon it shall be fined not more than $1,000 or imprisoned for not more than one year, or both.

"(b) The term 'flag of the United States' as used in this section shall include any flag, standard, colors, ensign, or any picture representation of either or of any part or parts of either, made of any substance or represented on any substance, of any size evidently purporting to be either of said flag, standard, colors, or ensign of the United States of America, or a picture or a representation of either, upon which shall be shown the colors, the stars and the stripes, in any number of either thereof, or of any part or parts of either, by which the average person seeing the same without deliberation may believe the same to represent the flag, standard, colors, or ensign of the United States of America.

"(c) Nothing in this section shall be construed as indicating an intent on the part of Congress to deprive any State, territory, possession, or the Commonwealth of Puerto Rico of jurisdiction over any offense over which it would have jurisdiction in the absence of this section."

Document 3: The Federal Flag Protection Act of 1989, Public Law No. 101–131, 103 Stat. 777 (amending 18 U.S.C. § 700 [Document 2]).

Be it enacted by the Senate and House of Representatives of the United States of America in Congress assembled,

SECTION 1. SHORT TITLE

This Act may be cited as the "Flag Protection Act of 1989".

SECTION 2. CRIMINAL PENALTIES WITH RESPECT TO THE PHYSICAL INTEGRITY OF THE UNITED STATES FLAG

(a) IN GENERAL—Subsection (a) of section 700 of title 18, United States Code, is amended to read as follows:

"(a)(1) Whoever knowingly mutilates, defaces, physically defiles, burns, maintains on the floor or ground, or tramples upon any flag of the United States shall be fined under this title or imprisoned for not more than one year, or both.

"(2)This subsection does not prohibit any conduct consisting of the disposal of a flag when it has become worn or soiled."

(b) DEFINITION—Section 700(b) of title 18, United States Code, is amended to read as follows:

"(b) As used in this section, the term 'flag of the United States' means any flag of the United States, or any part thereof, made of any substance, of any size, in a form that is commonly displayed."

SECTION 3. EXPEDITED REVIEW OF CONSTITUTIONAL ISSUES

Section 700 of title 18, United States Code, is amended by adding at the end the following:

"(d)(1) An appeal may be taken directly to the Supreme Court of the United States from any interlocutory or final judgment, decree, or order issued by a United States district court ruling upon the constitutionality of subsection (a).

"(2) The Supreme Court shall, if it has not previously ruled on the question, accept jurisdiction over the appeal and advance on the docket and expedite to the greatest extent possible."

About the Book and Author

THIS BOOK IS THE FIRST comprehensive history of the American flag desecration controversy, from the late nineteenth century to the present. Early efforts to "protect" the flag from mainstream political and commercial use were later transformed into attacks against political dissidents who were characterized as "un-American". Goldstein argues that the recurrent controversy over flag desecration reflects societal insecurities, especially deep fears that the nation is "coming apart", and demonstrates a widespread misunderstanding of the *substance* of political freedom that the flag merely symbolizes.

Robert Justin Goldstein is professor of political science at Oakland University, Rochester, Michigan. His specialty is the history of civil liberties in modern democratic societies. He has published widely in both scholarly and popular outlets on topics concerning civil liberties developments in the United States and Europe since 1800. His books include *Political Repression in Modern America: From 1870 to the Present* (1978), *Political Censorship of the Arts and the Press in Nineteenth-Century Europe* (1989) and *Censorship of Political Caricature in Nineteenth-Century France* (1989).

Index

Note: Individual Supreme Court decisions are listed under heading "Supreme Court." Other legal rulings and individual flag desecration incidents are listed by the state in which they occurred under the heading, "Flag desecration, incidents of and prosecutions (by state)."